Shojo Beat

Story & Art by
MITSUBA TAKANASHI

CONTENTS

STORY THUS FAR

Nobara Sumiyoshi is a first-year student in high school who lives for her one passion, volleyball. She's the successor to "Seiryu," the high-class ryotei restaurant her family runs, but she enrolled in Crimson Field High School expressly to play volleyball.

Nobara begins living and working in Crimson Dorm, the dorm for the boys' volleyball recruits. There she meets Yushin and falls in love, only to be rejected. In the midst of this the girls' team gets a new coach, Coach Shima. The goal of her strict training regimen is to get the girls to the Spring Tournament! Nobara leaves her teammates behind to seek out intensive training with the Eagles, a team led by Shima's younger brother Ryo. There Nobara improves her technique and mental readiness.

Nobara's absence makes Yushin realize how important she is to him, and he declares his feelings to her!! The two promise each other to become a couple only after they've both made it to the Spring Tournament.

Returning to Crimson High, Nobara overcomes a clash with Kanako and the team becomes whole again. The first step on the path to the Spring Tournament is the Newcomers Tournament. On day one of the Newcomers Tournament, the girls pull off overwhelming victories and advance to the next day. But then…!!

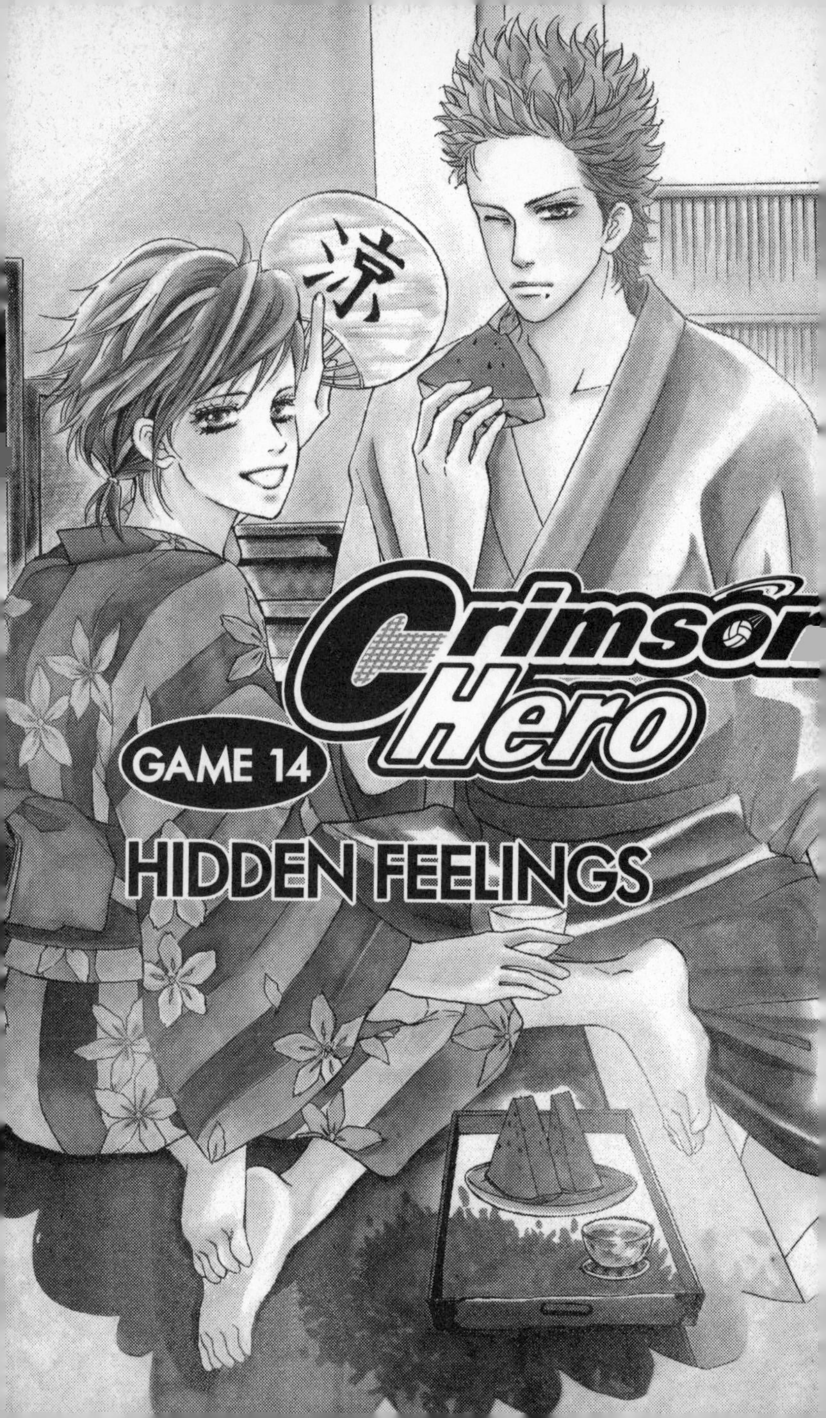
涼
Crimson Hero
GAME 14
HIDDEN FEELINGS

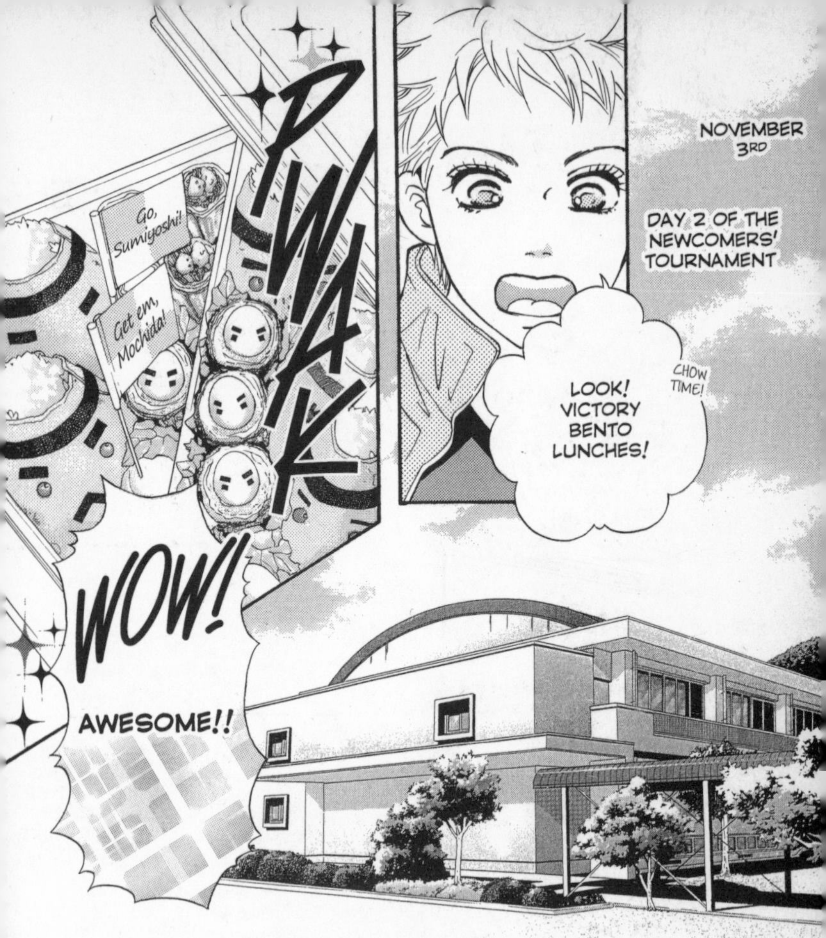
NOVEMBER 3RD
DAY 2 OF THE NEWCOMERS' TOURNAMENT
LOOK! VICTORY BENTO LUNCHES!
CHOW TIME!
PWAK
Go, Sumiyoshi!
Get em, Mochida!
WOW!!
AWESOME!!

THE MAKING OF Crimson Hero

HI AGAIN. IT'S BEEN A WHILE. HERE AT LONG LAST IS *CRIMSON HERO* VOLUME 10. VOLUME 10...! IN HONOR OF THIS, I DREW A CLOSE-UP OF NOBARA FOR THE COVER. LIKE IT? I STILL PLAN TO DO A CLOSE-UP OF YOU-KNOW-WHO WITH YOU-KNOW-WHO. I THINK IT'S ABOUT TIME TO GO FULL-OUT WITH THE LOVE STORY. IT WON'T BE A WILD N' CRAZY ROMANCE 'CUZ CRIMSON HERO IS A COMING-OF-AGE MANGA, BUT I'M HOPING TO CRAFT A LOVE STORY THAT'S JUST RIGHT FOR THIS MANGA. THE CHARACTERS ARE GROWING UP AND MATURING. I'M ENJOYING MYSELF AS THE ARTIST, BUT IT'S BEEN SO LONG SINCE I STARTED WORKING ON THIS TITLE THAT I BET YOU READERS HAVE GROWN AND MATURED QUITE A BIT TOO. I HAVE THIS IDEA THAT *CRIMSON HERO* REACHES AN OLDER AUDIENCE. PEOPLE WRITE THAT HOUSEWIVES READ IT AND KIDS READ IT WITH THEIR MOMS. AND COLLEGE STUDENTS READ IT. AND ONCE IN A WHILE SOMEONE WILL SAY HER BOYFRIEND READS IT. I'M JUST THRILLED THAT IT'S BEING READ BY A DIVERSE GROUP OF FANS. I'LL KEEP PITCHING AS HARD AND AS FAST AS I CAN UNTIL THE VERY END. OH, THIS VOLUME ALSO CONTAINS A BONUS CHAPTER CALLED "CRIMSON CAPSULE STORY." IT FIRST APPEARED IN *DELUXE MARGARET*. (EVEN THOUGH IT'S A BONUS STORY, IT'S KIND OF CONNECTED. SORRY.) I WANTED TO DO SOME SCENES THAT I HAVEN'T MANAGED TO WORK INTO THE MAIN STORY. AND NOW WITHOUT FURTHER ADO, I PRESENT TO YOU...VOLUME 10!

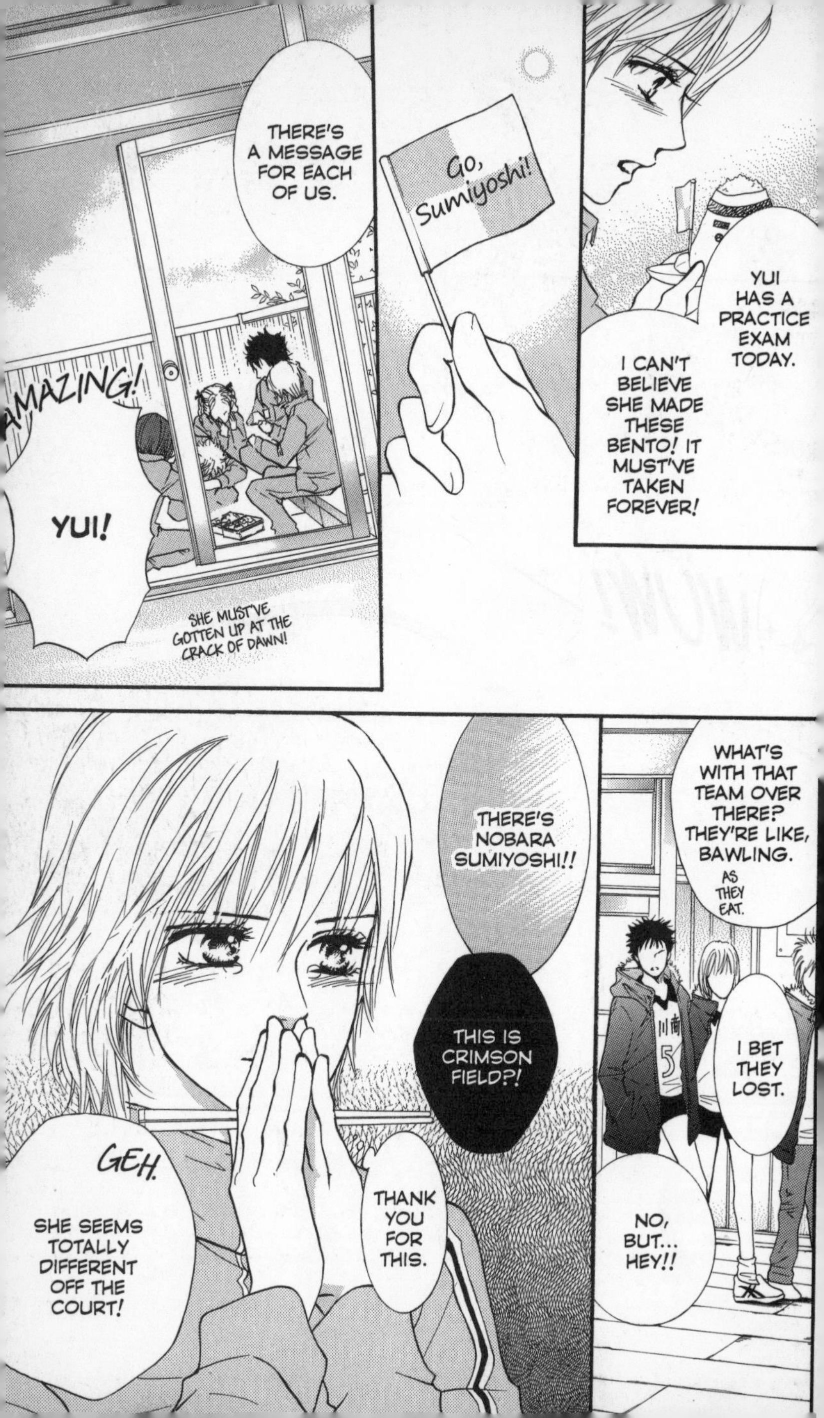
YUI HAS A PRACTICE EXAM TODAY.
I CAN'T BELIEVE SHE MADE THESE BENTO! IT MUST'VE TAKEN FOREVER!
Go, Sumiyoshi!
THERE'S A MESSAGE FOR EACH OF US.
AMAZING!
YUI!
SHE MUST'VE GOTTEN UP AT THE CRACK OF DAWN!
WHAT'S WITH THAT TEAM OVER THERE? THEY'RE LIKE, BAWLING.
AS THEY EAT.
I BET THEY LOST.
NO, BUT... HEY!!
THERE'S NOBARA SUMIYOSHI!!
THIS IS CRIMSON FIELD?!
THANK YOU FOR THIS.
GEH.
SHE SEEMS TOTALLY DIFFERENT OFF THE COURT!

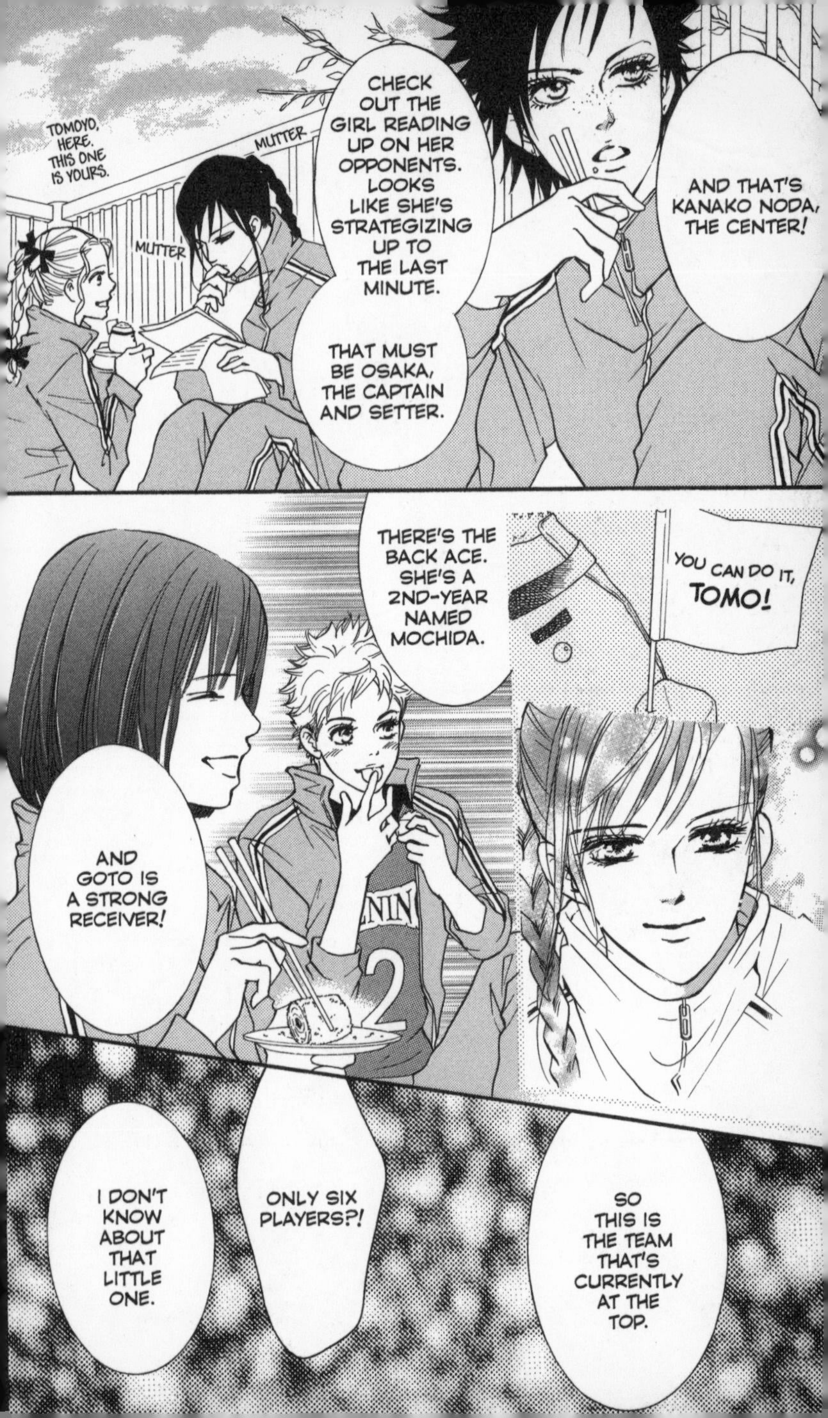
AND THAT'S KANAKO NODA, THE CENTER!
CHECK OUT THE GIRL READING UP ON HER OPPONENTS. LOOKS LIKE SHE'S STRATEGIZING UP TO THE LAST MINUTE.
THAT MUST BE OSAKA, THE CAPTAIN AND SETTER.
MUTTER
MUTTER
TOMOYO, HERE. THIS ONE IS YOURS.
YOU CAN DO IT, TOMO!
THERE'S THE BACK ACE. SHE'S A 2ND-YEAR NAMED MOCHIDA.
AND GOTO IS A STRONG RECEIVER!
2
SO THIS IS THE TEAM THAT'S CURRENTLY AT THE TOP.
ONLY SIX PLAYERS?!
I DON'T KNOW ABOUT THAT LITTLE ONE.

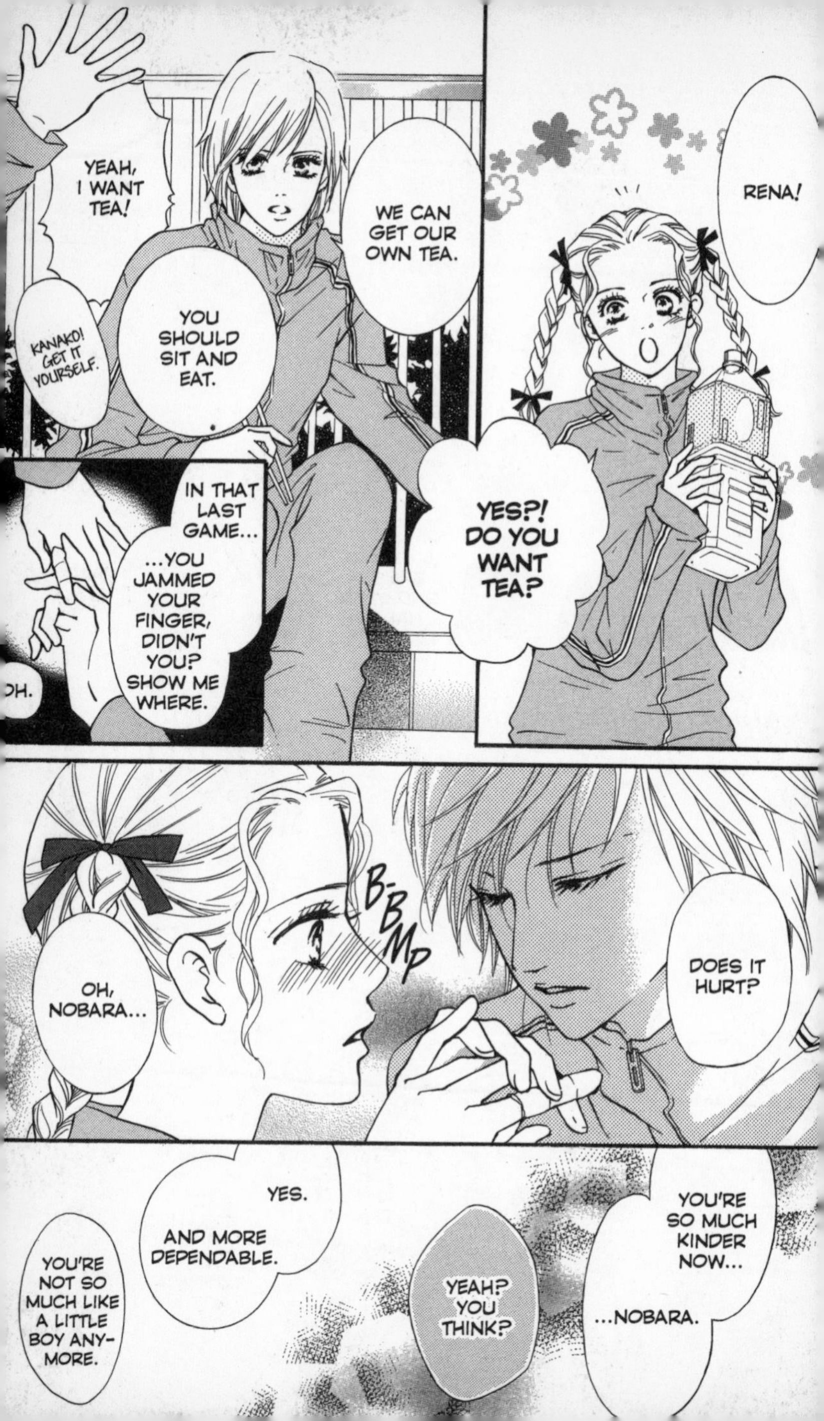
RENA!
YES?! DO YOU WANT TEA?
WE CAN GET OUR OWN TEA.
YEAH, I WANT TEA!
YOU SHOULD SIT AND EAT.
KANAKO! GET IT YOURSELF.
IN THAT LAST GAME...
...YOU JAMMED YOUR FINGER, DIDN'T YOU? SHOW ME WHERE.
OH.
DOES IT HURT?
B-BMP
OH, NOBARA...
YOU'RE SO MUCH KINDER NOW...
...NOBARA.
YEAH? YOU THINK?
YES.
AND MORE DEPENDABLE.
YOU'RE NOT SO MUCH LIKE A LITTLE BOY ANY-MORE.

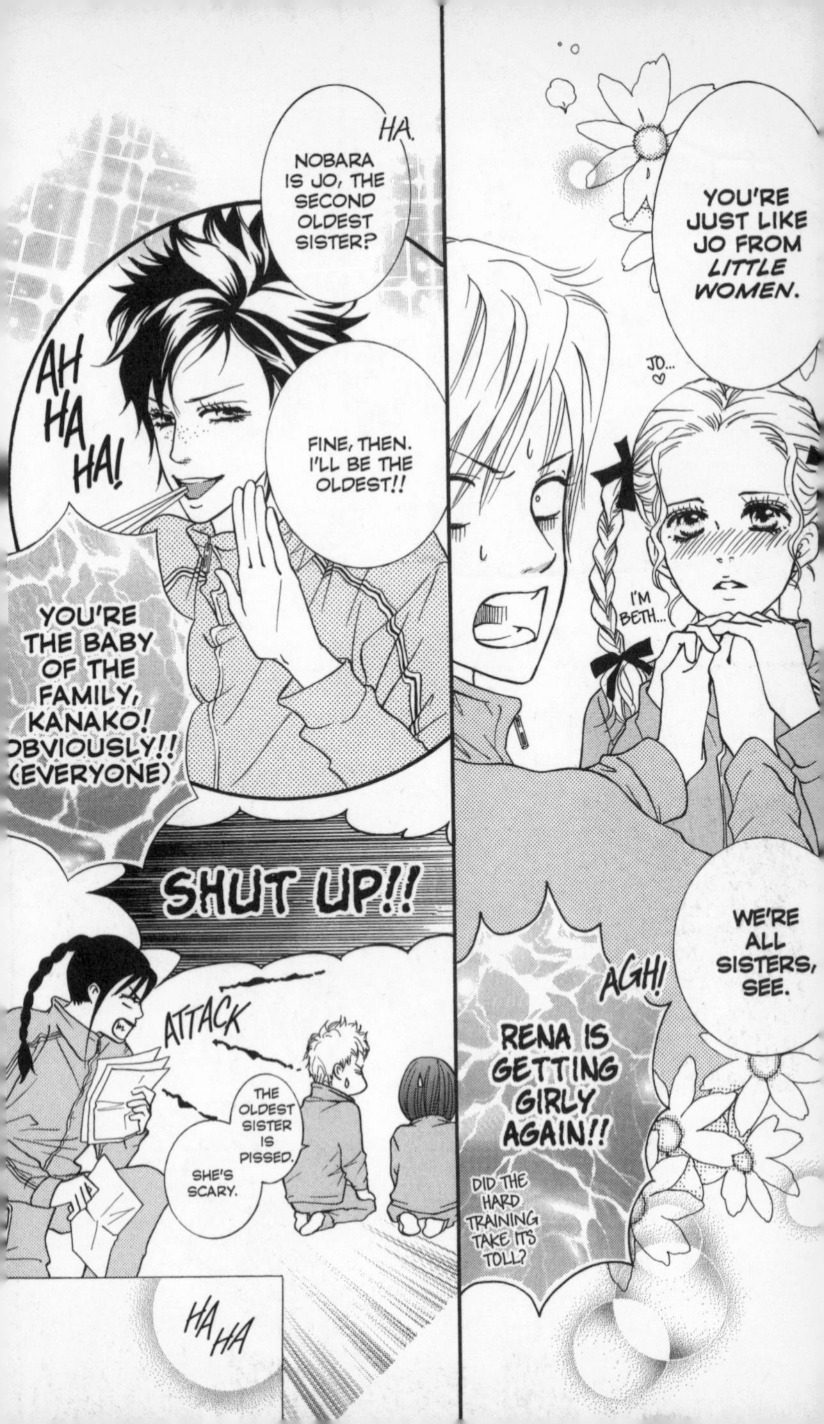
YOU'RE JUST LIKE JO FROM *LITTLE WOMEN*.
JO...
I'M BETH...
WE'RE ALL SISTERS, SEE.
AGH!
RENA IS GETTING GIRLY AGAIN!!
DID THE HARD TRAINING TAKE ITS TOLL?
HA.
NOBARA IS JO, THE SECOND OLDEST SISTER?
FINE, THEN. I'LL BE THE OLDEST!!
AH HA HA HA!
YOU'RE THE BABY OF THE FAMILY, KANAKO! OBVIOUSLY!! (EVERYONE)
SHUT UP!!
ATTACK
THE OLDEST SISTER IS PISSED.
SHE'S SCARY.
HA HA

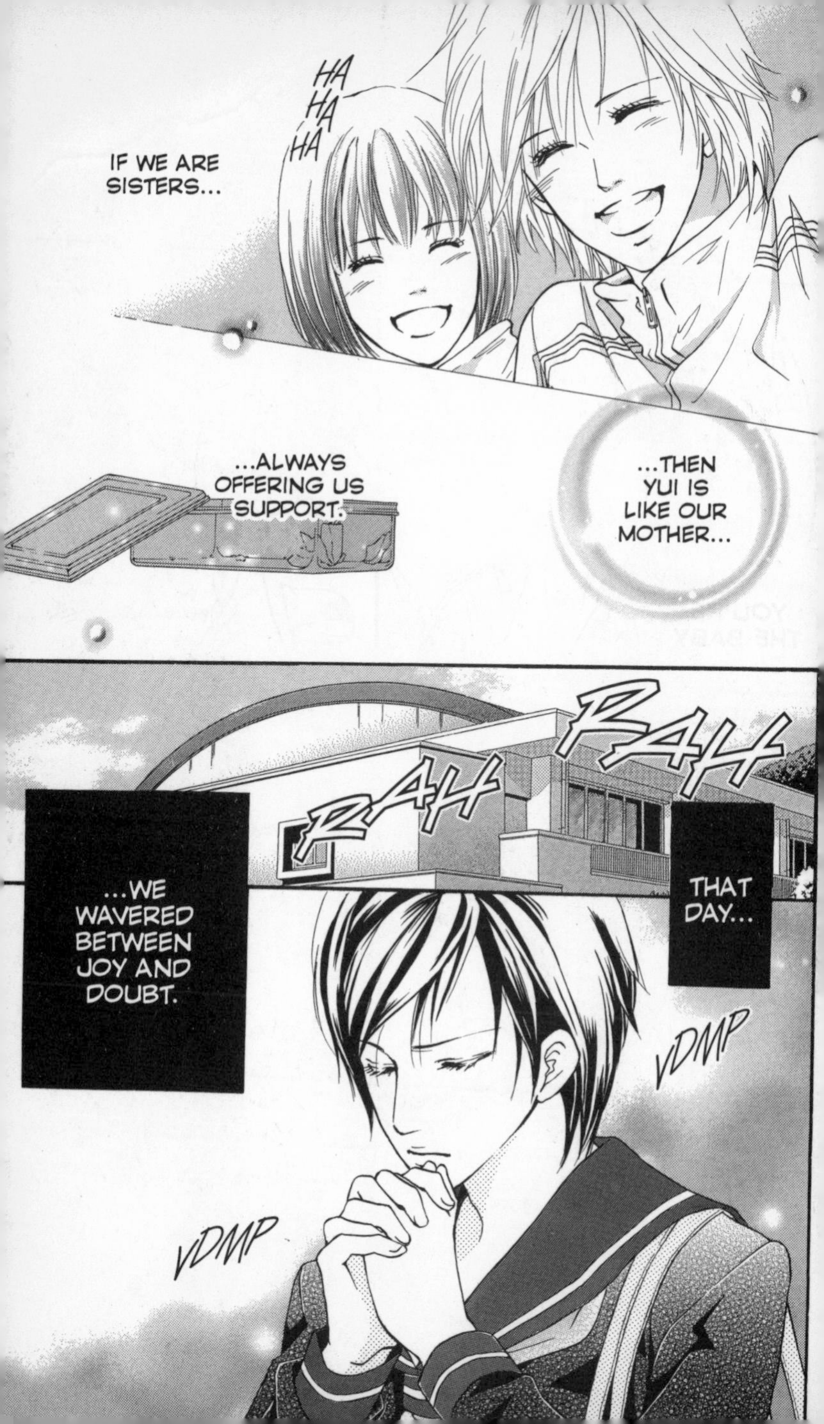
HA HA HA
IF WE ARE SISTERS...
...THEN YUI IS LIKE OUR MOTHER...
...ALWAYS OFFERING US SUPPORT.
RAH RAH
THAT DAY...
...WE WAVERED BETWEEN JOY AND DOUBT.
VDMP
VDMP

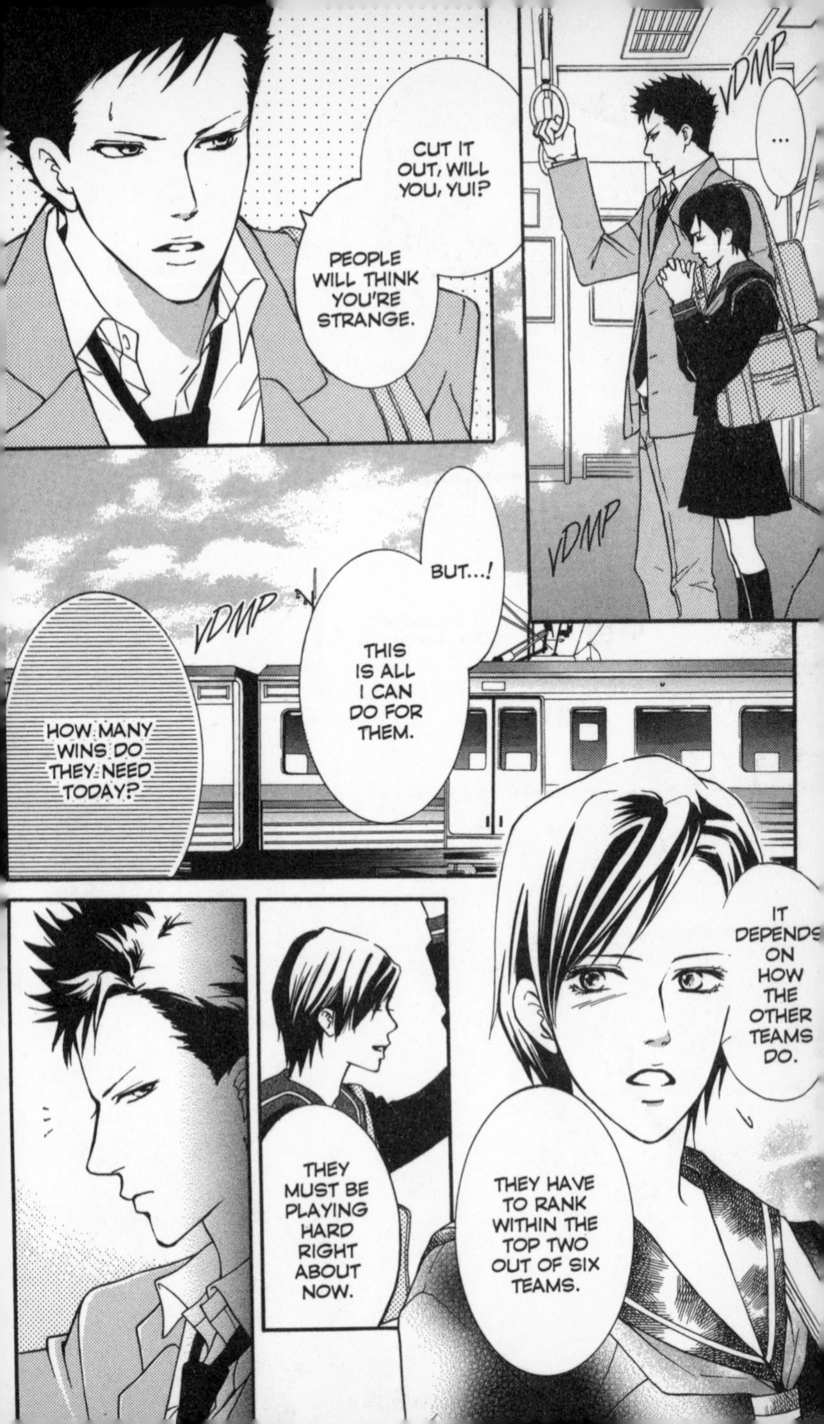
VDMP
...
VDMP
CUT IT OUT, WILL YOU, YUI?
PEOPLE WILL THINK YOU'RE STRANGE.
BUT...!
THIS IS ALL I CAN DO FOR THEM.
VDMP
HOW MANY WINS DO THEY NEED TODAY?
IT DEPENDS ON HOW THE OTHER TEAMS DO.
THEY HAVE TO RANK WITHIN THE TOP TWO OUT OF SIX TEAMS.
THEY MUST BE PLAYING HARD RIGHT ABOUT NOW.

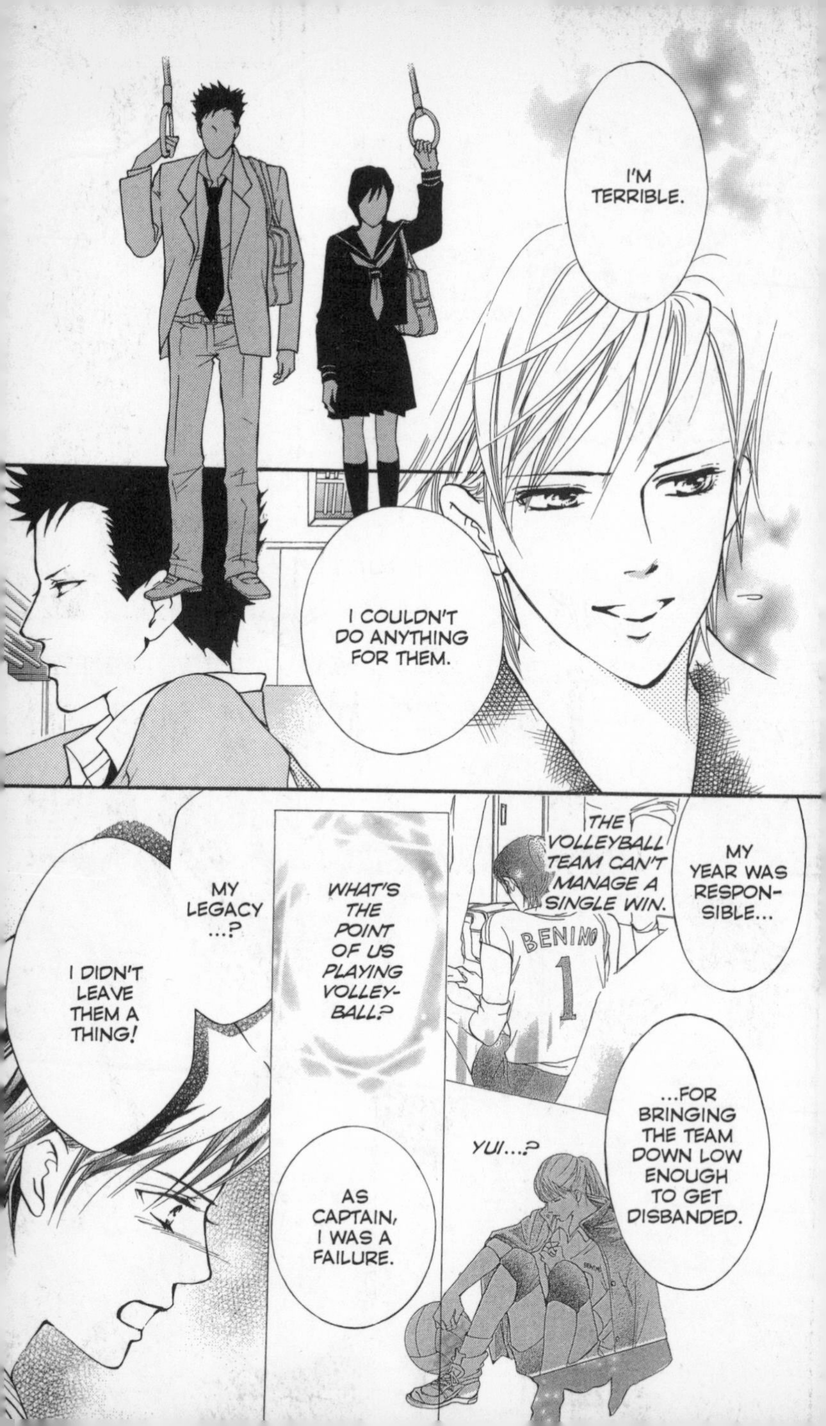
I'M TERRIBLE.
I COULDN'T DO ANYTHING FOR THEM.
MY YEAR WAS RESPONSIBLE...
THE VOLLEYBALL TEAM CAN'T MANAGE A SINGLE WIN.
...FOR BRINGING THE TEAM DOWN LOW ENOUGH TO GET DISBANDED.
YUI...?
BENINO
1
WHAT'S THE POINT OF US PLAYING VOLLEYBALL?
AS CAPTAIN, I WAS A FAILURE.
MY LEGACY ...?
I DIDN'T LEAVE THEM A THING!

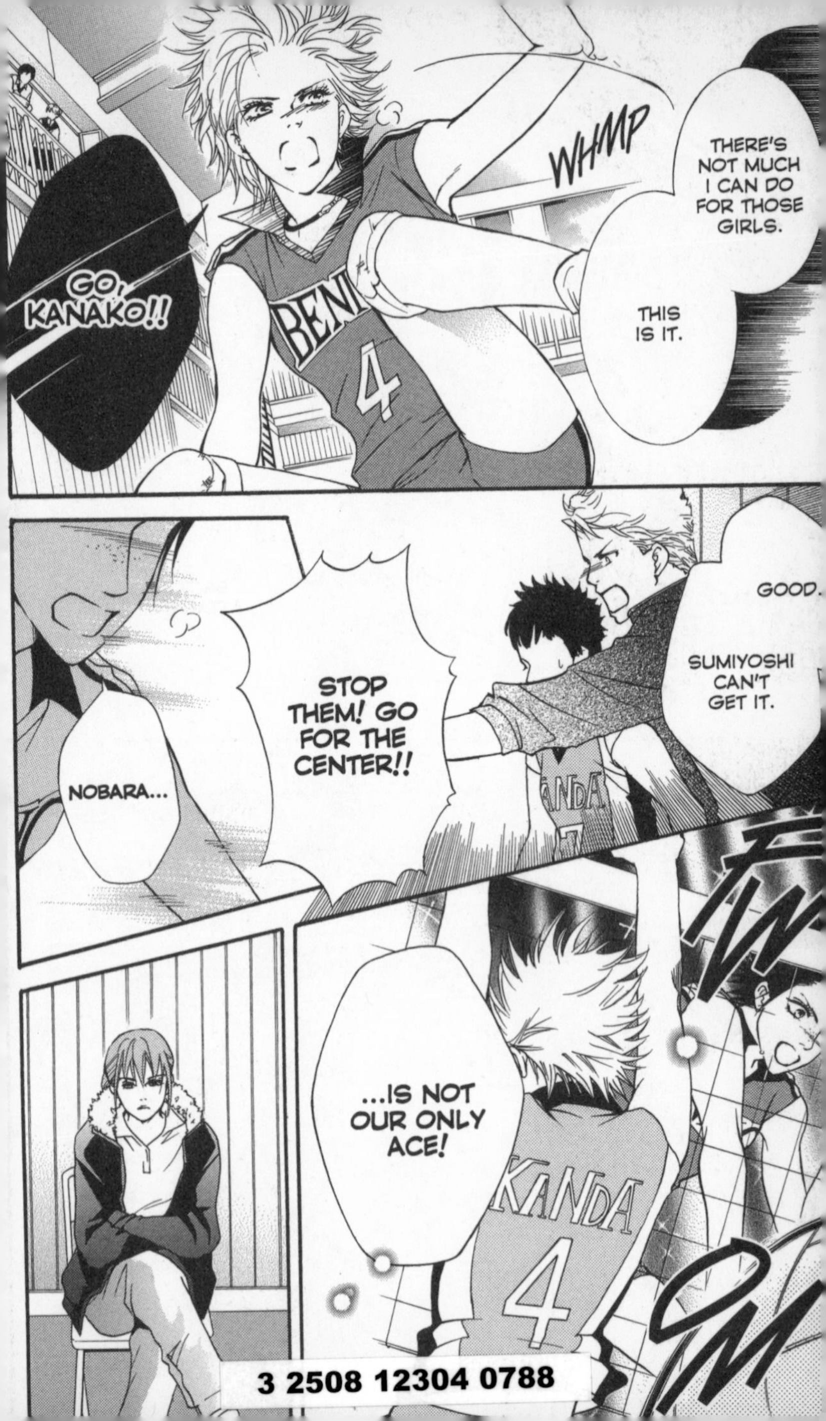
THERE'S NOT MUCH I CAN DO FOR THOSE GIRLS.
THIS IS IT.
WHMP
GO, KANAKO!!
GOOD.
SUMIYOSHI CAN'T GET IT.
STOP THEM! GO FOR THE CENTER!!
NOBARA...
...IS NOT OUR ONLY ACE!

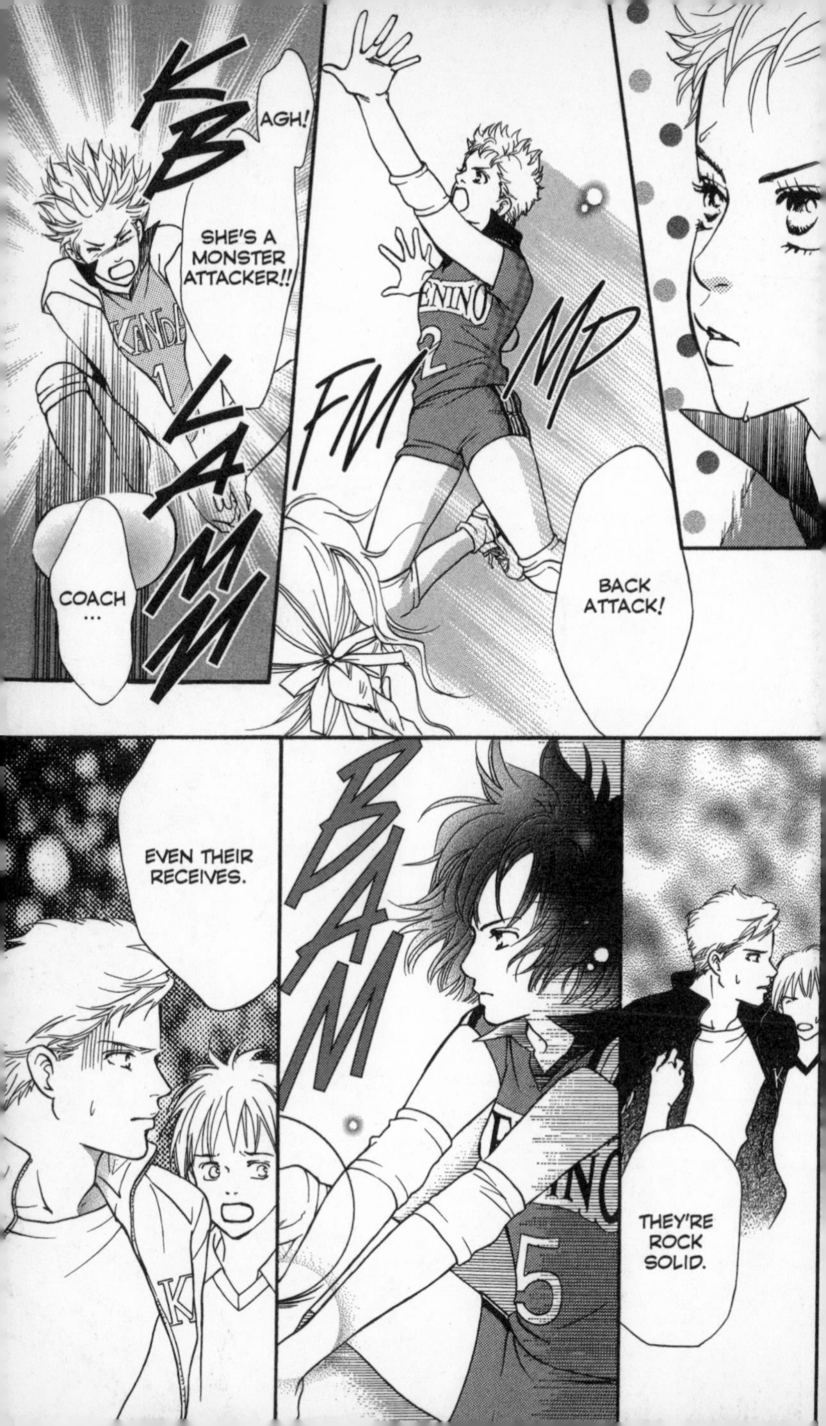
BACK ATTACK!
FMMP
AGH!
KBLAMMM
SHE'S A MONSTER ATTACKER!!
COACH ...
THEY'RE ROCK SOLID.
BAM
EVEN THEIR RECEIVES.

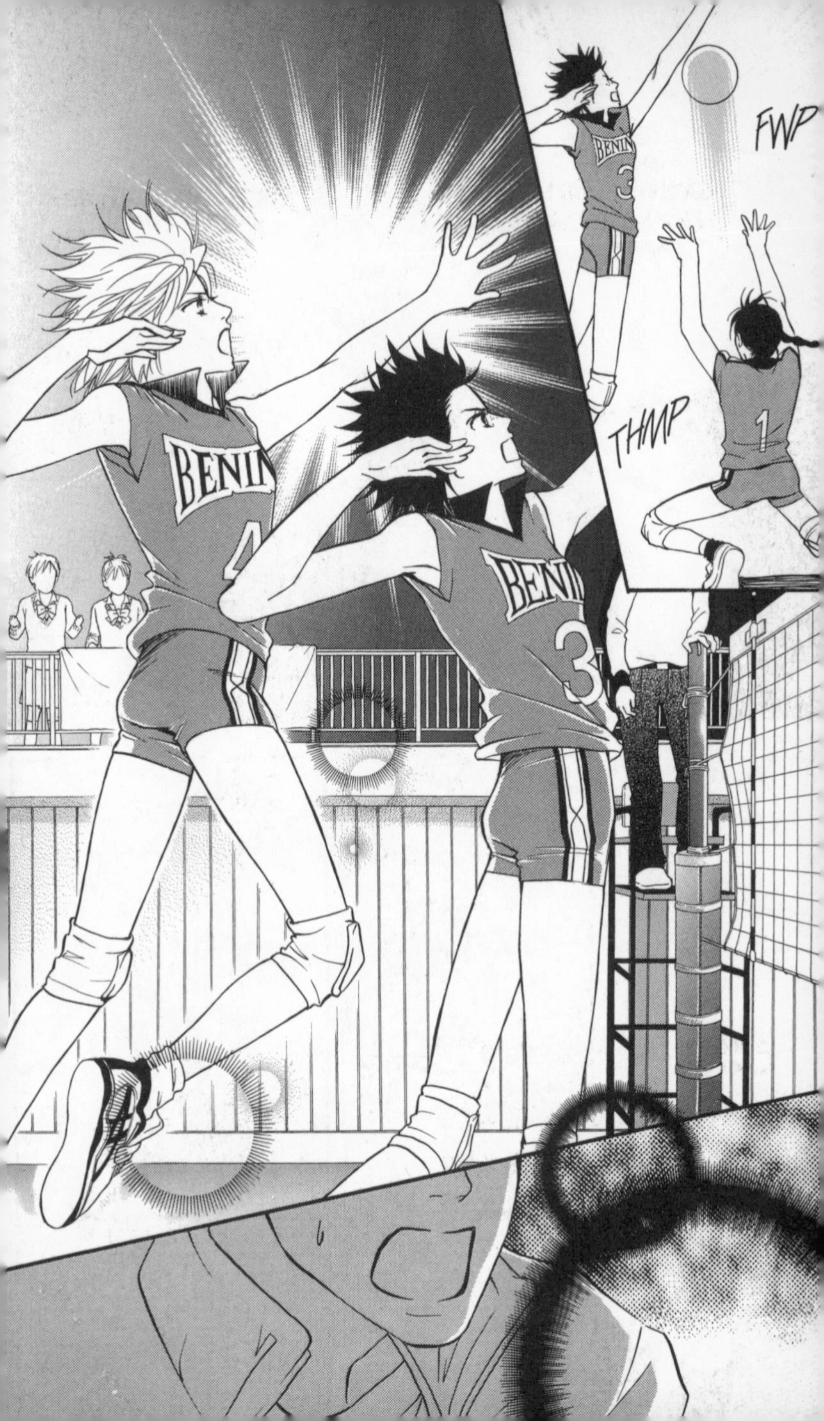
FWP
THMP

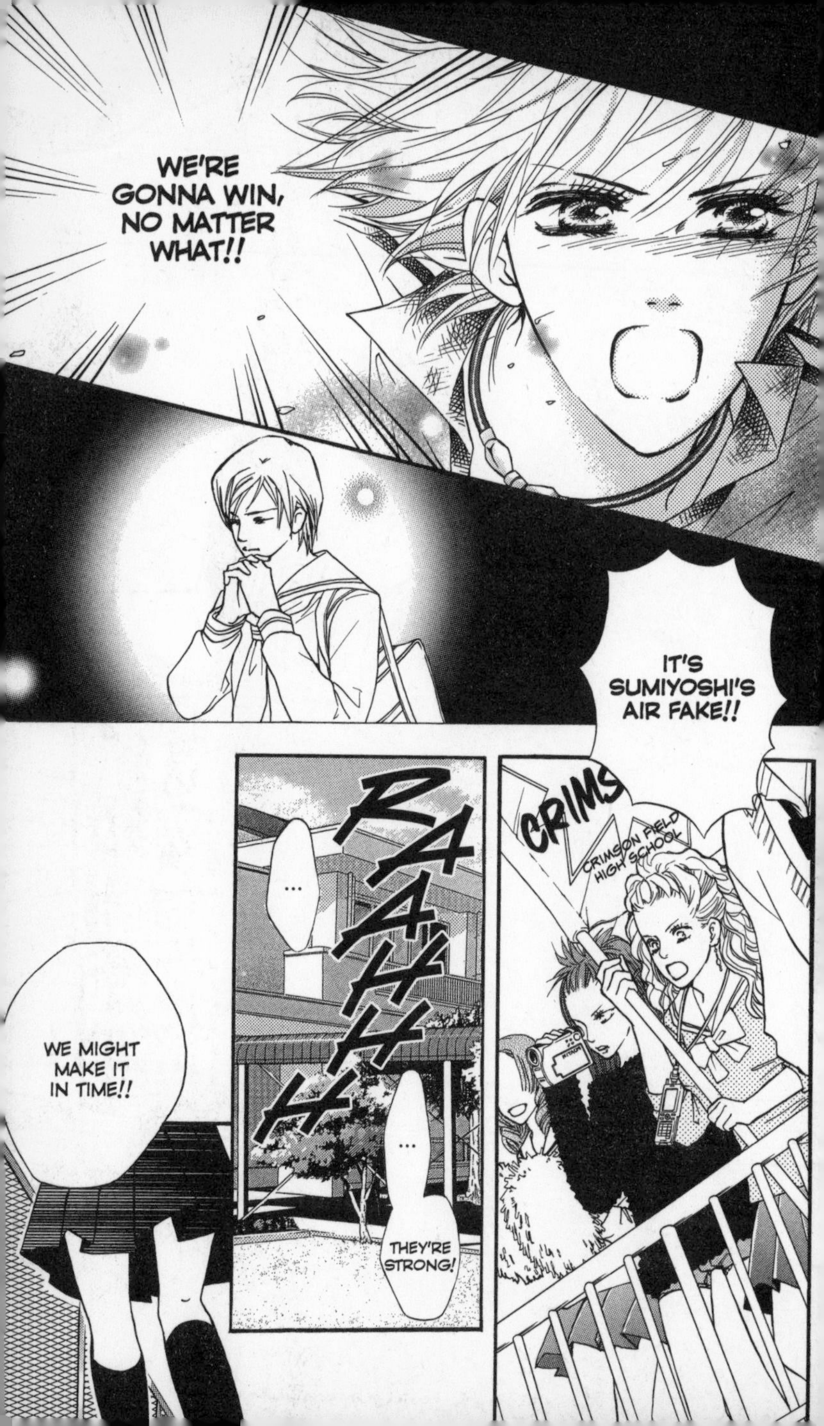
WE'RE GONNA WIN, NO MATTER WHAT!!
IT'S SUMIYOSHI'S AIR FAKE!!
CRIMS
CRIMSON FIELD HIGH SCHOOL
RAHHHH
...
...
THEY'RE STRONG!
WE MIGHT MAKE IT IN TIME!!

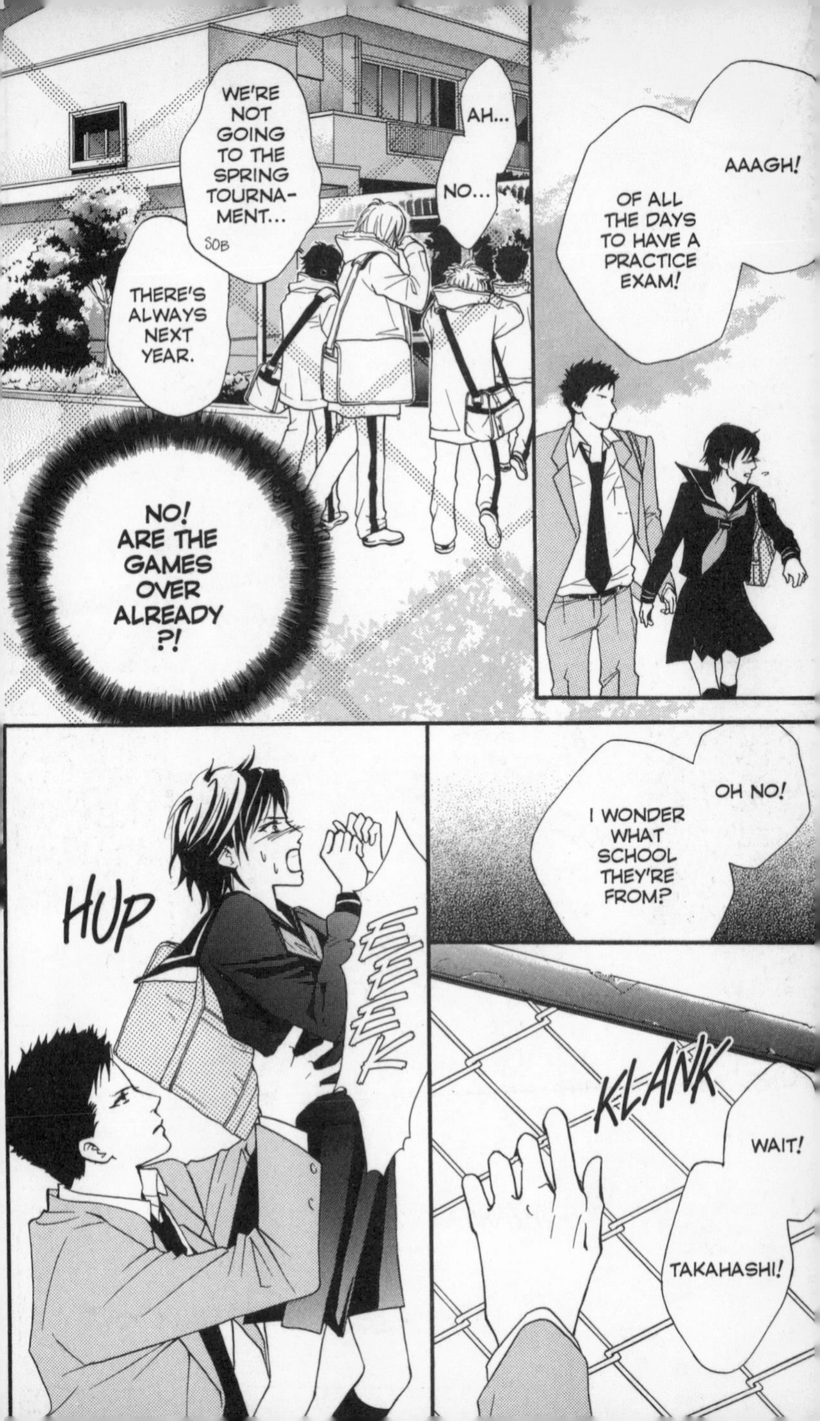
AAAGH!
OF ALL THE DAYS TO HAVE A PRACTICE EXAM!
AH...
NO...
WE'RE NOT GOING TO THE SPRING TOURNA-MENT...
SOB
THERE'S ALWAYS NEXT YEAR.
NO! ARE THE GAMES OVER ALREADY?!
OH NO!
I WONDER WHAT SCHOOL THEY'RE FROM?
KLANK
WAIT!
TAKAHASHI!
EEEEK
HUP

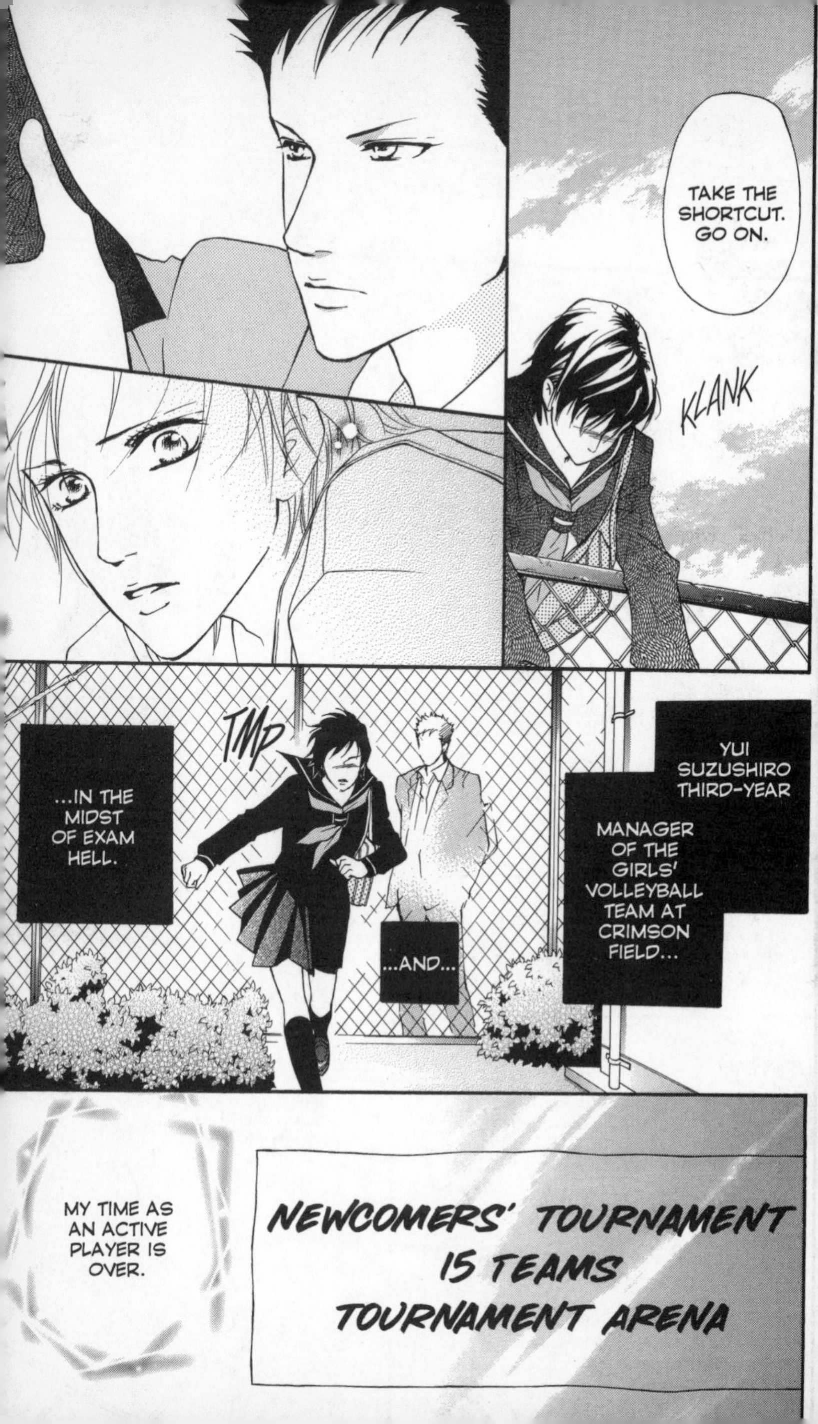
TAKE THE SHORTCUT. GO ON.
KLANK
YUI SUZUSHIRO THIRD-YEAR
MANAGER OF THE GIRLS' VOLLEYBALL TEAM AT CRIMSON FIELD...
...AND...
TMP
...IN THE MIDST OF EXAM HELL.
NEWCOMERS' TOURNAMENT
15 TEAMS
TOURNAMENT ARENA
MY TIME AS AN ACTIVE PLAYER IS OVER.

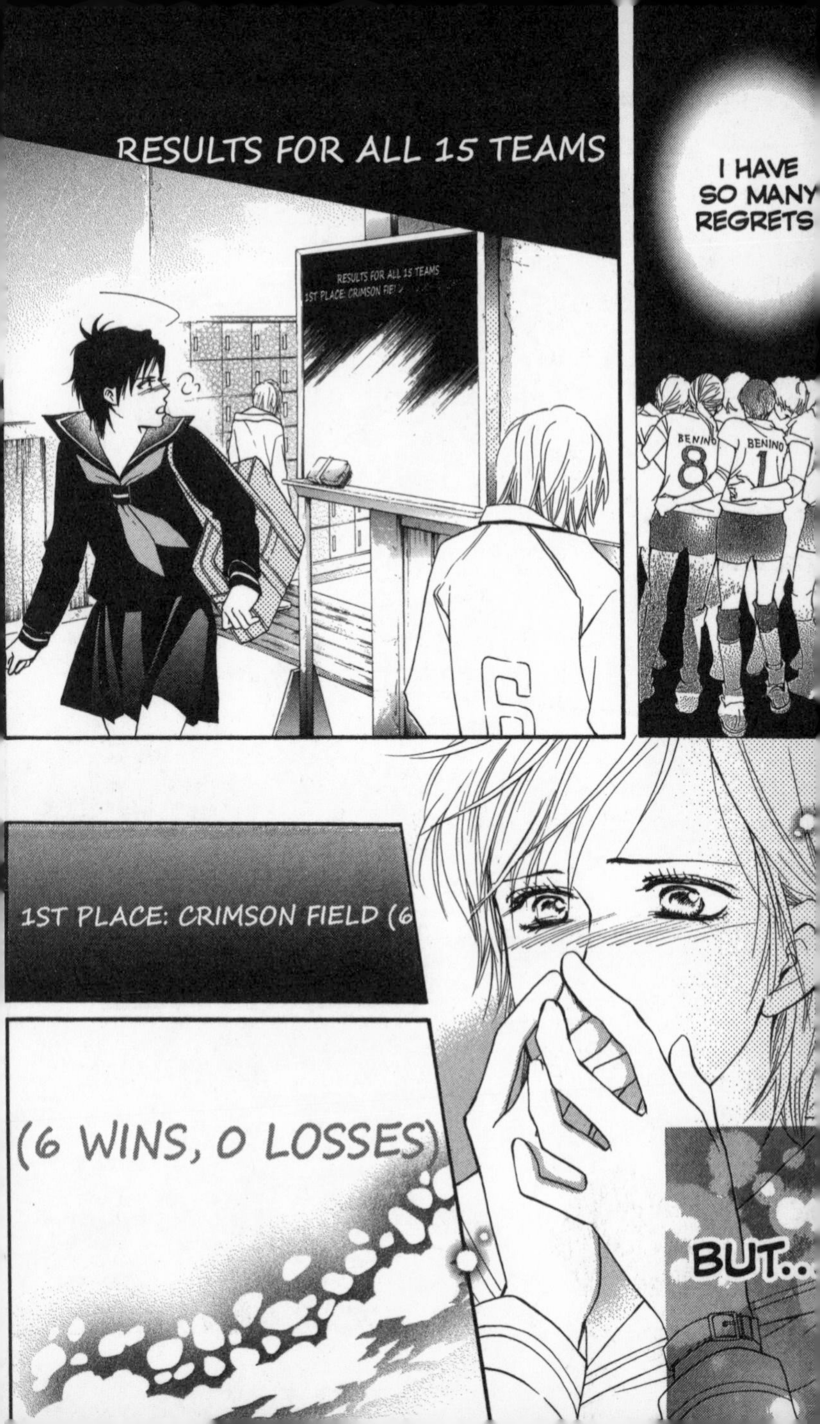
I HAVE SO MANY REGRETS
BENINO 8
BENINO 1
RESULTS FOR ALL 15 TEAMS
RESULTS FOR ALL 15 TEAMS
1ST PLACE: CRIMSON FIE!
6
1ST PLACE: CRIMSON FIELD (6
(6 WINS, 0 LOSSES)
BUT...

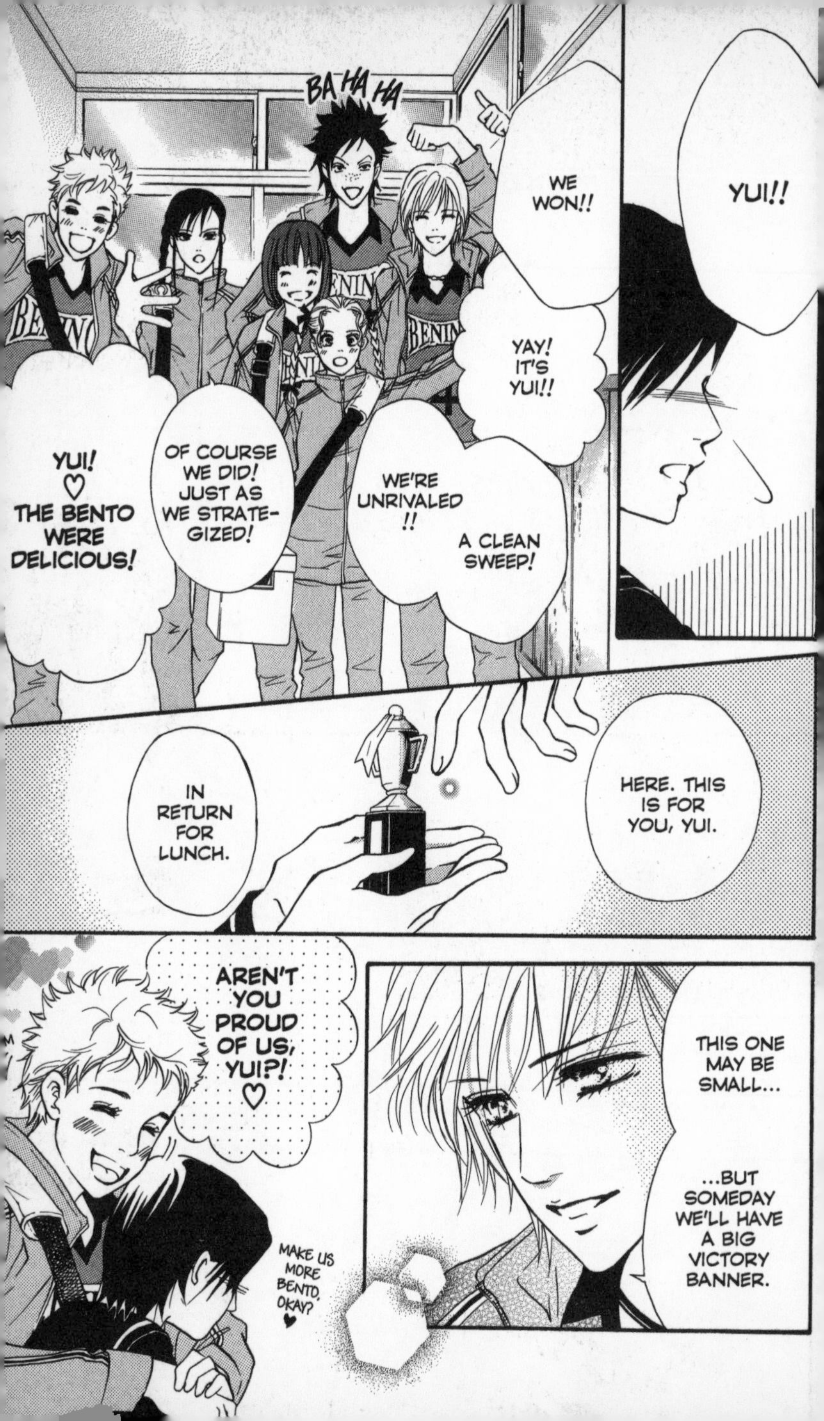
YUI!!
BA HA HA
WE WON!!
YAY! IT'S YUI!!
WE'RE UNRIVALED!!
A CLEAN SWEEP!
OF COURSE WE DID! JUST AS WE STRATE-GIZED!
YUI! ♡ THE BENTO WERE DELICIOUS!
HERE. THIS IS FOR YOU, YUI.
IN RETURN FOR LUNCH.
THIS ONE MAY BE SMALL...
...BUT SOMEDAY WE'LL HAVE A BIG VICTORY BANNER.
AREN'T YOU PROUD OF US, YUI?! ♡
MAKE US MORE BENTO, OKAY? ♥

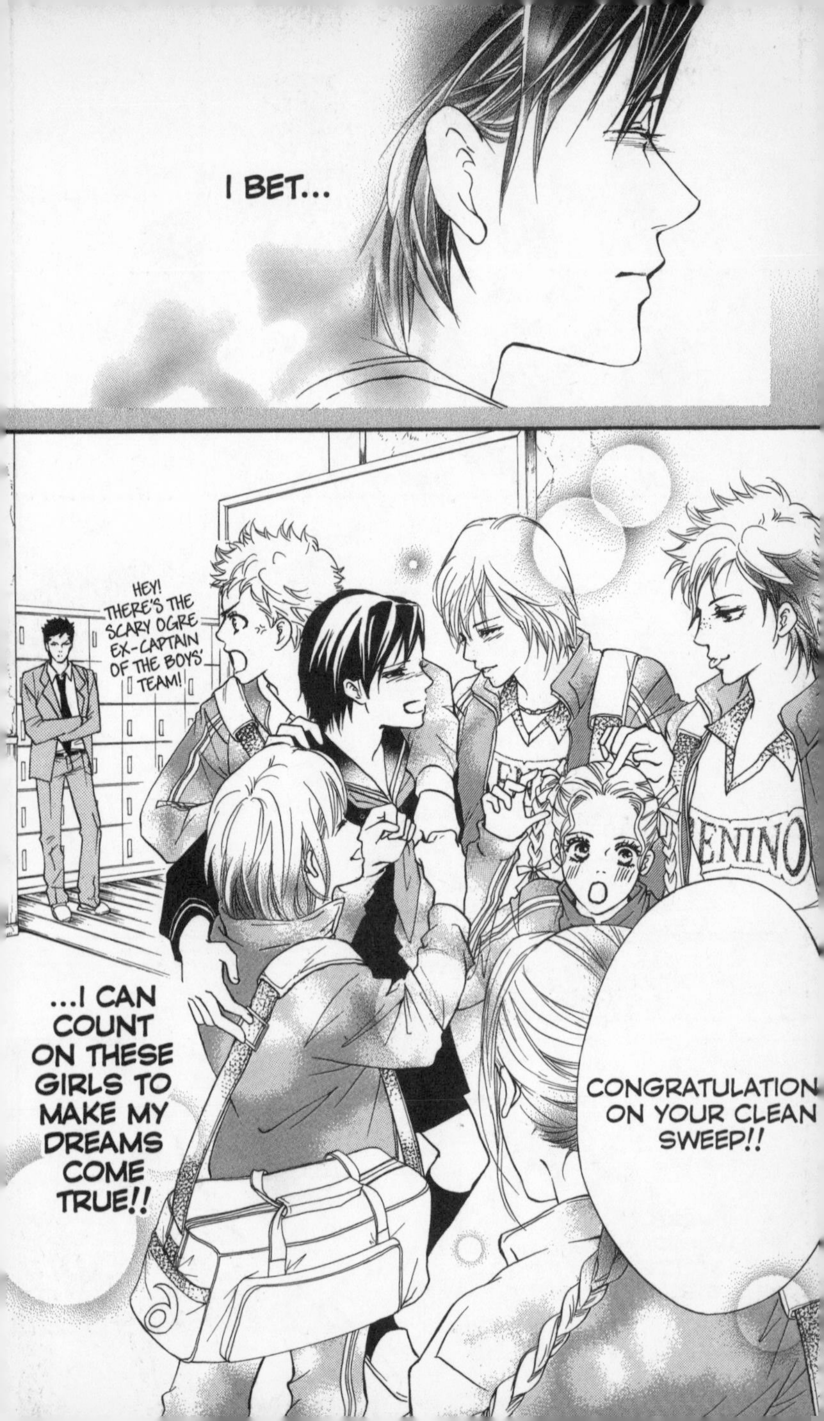
I BET...
...I CAN COUNT ON THESE GIRLS TO MAKE MY DREAMS COME TRUE!!
CONGRATULATION ON YOUR CLEAN SWEEP!!
HEY! THERE'S THE SCARY OGRE EX-CAPTAIN OF THE BOYS' TEAM!
ENINO

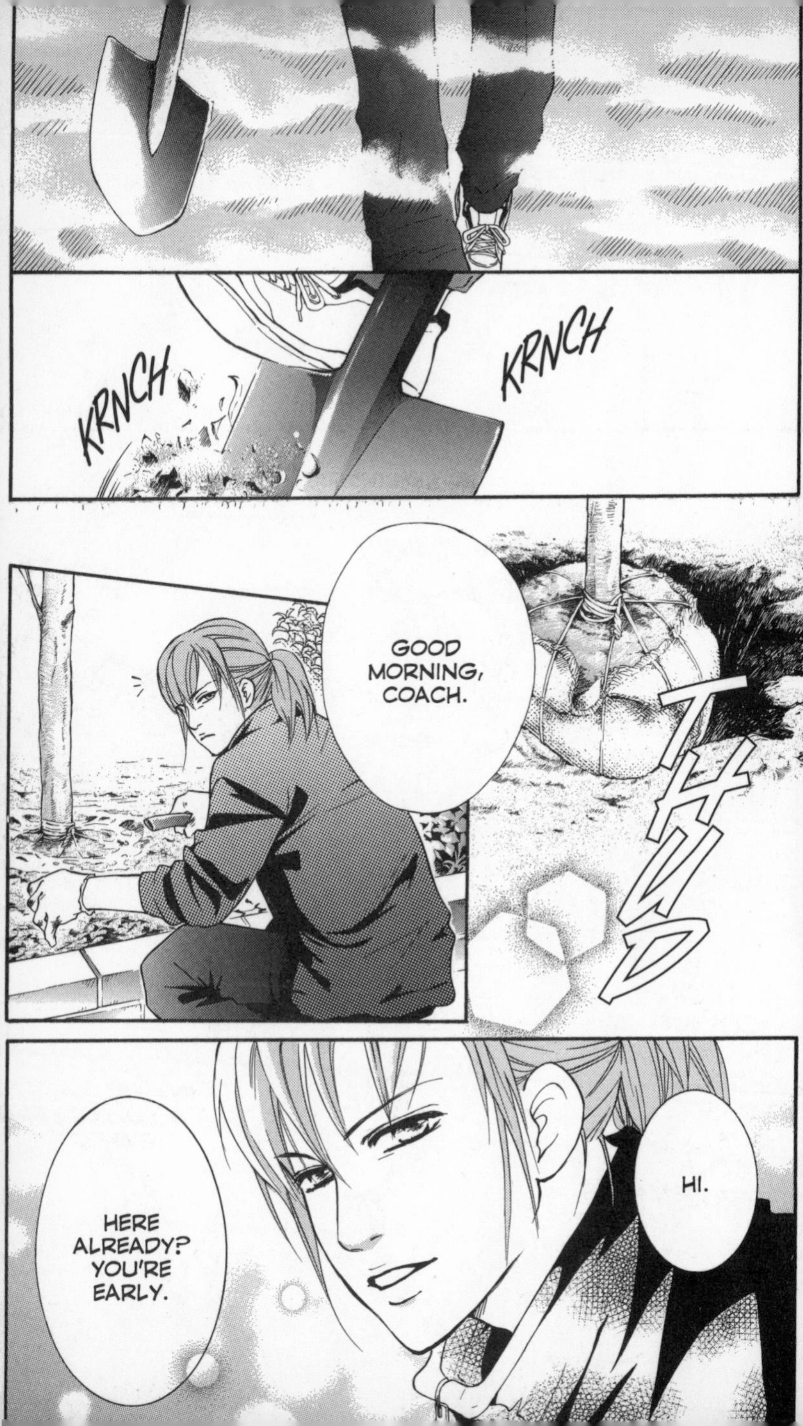
KRNCH
KRNCH
THUD
GOOD MORNING, COACH.
HI.
HERE ALREADY? YOU'RE EARLY.

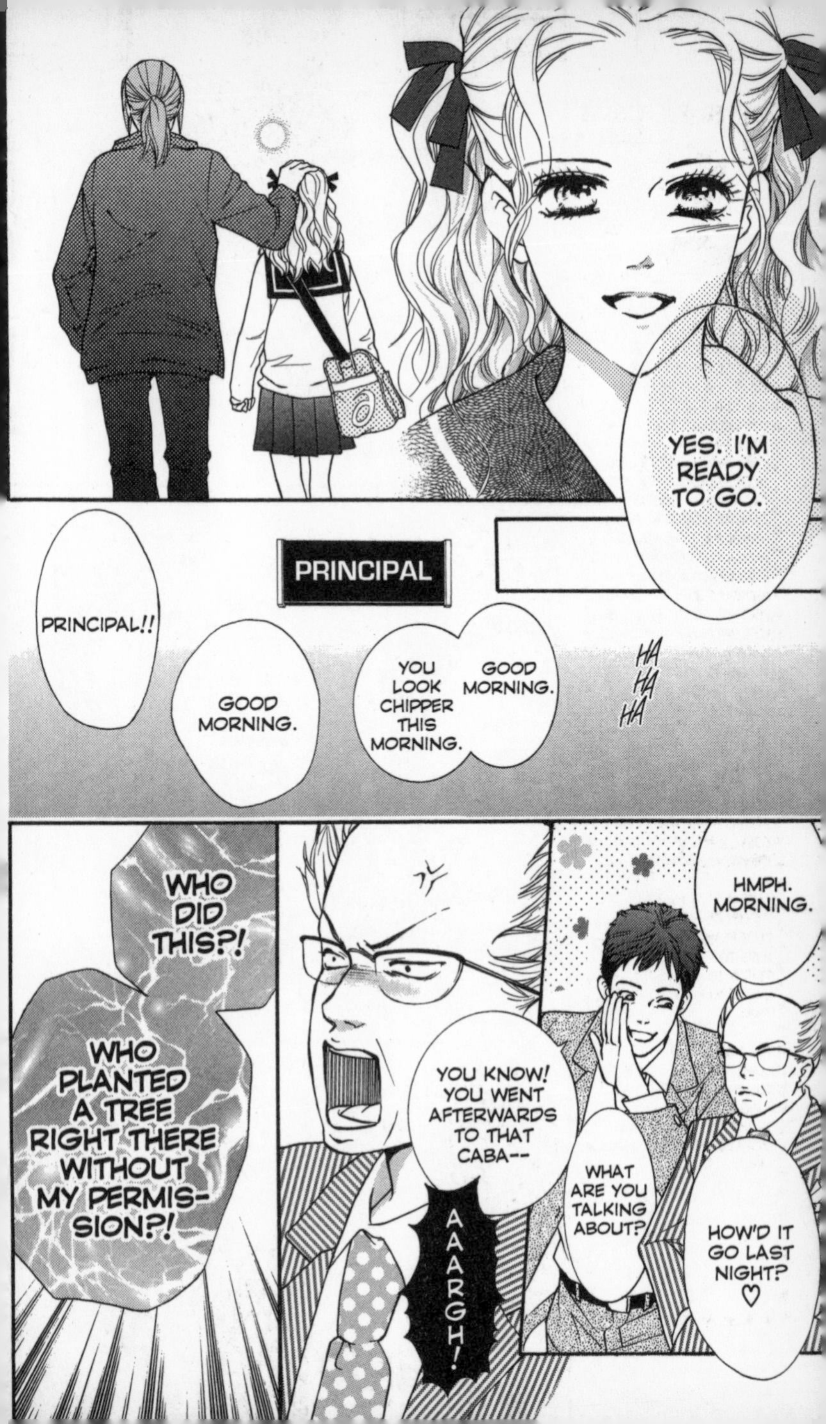
YES. I'M READY TO GO.
HA HA HA
GOOD MORNING.
YOU LOOK CHIPPER THIS MORNING.
PRINCIPAL
GOOD MORNING.
PRINCIPAL!!
HMPH. MORNING.
HOW'D IT GO LAST NIGHT? ♡
WHAT ARE YOU TALKING ABOUT?
YOU KNOW! YOU WENT AFTERWARDS TO THAT CABA--
AAAARGH!
WHO DID THIS?!
WHO PLANTED A TREE RIGHT THERE WITHOUT MY PERMIS-SION?!

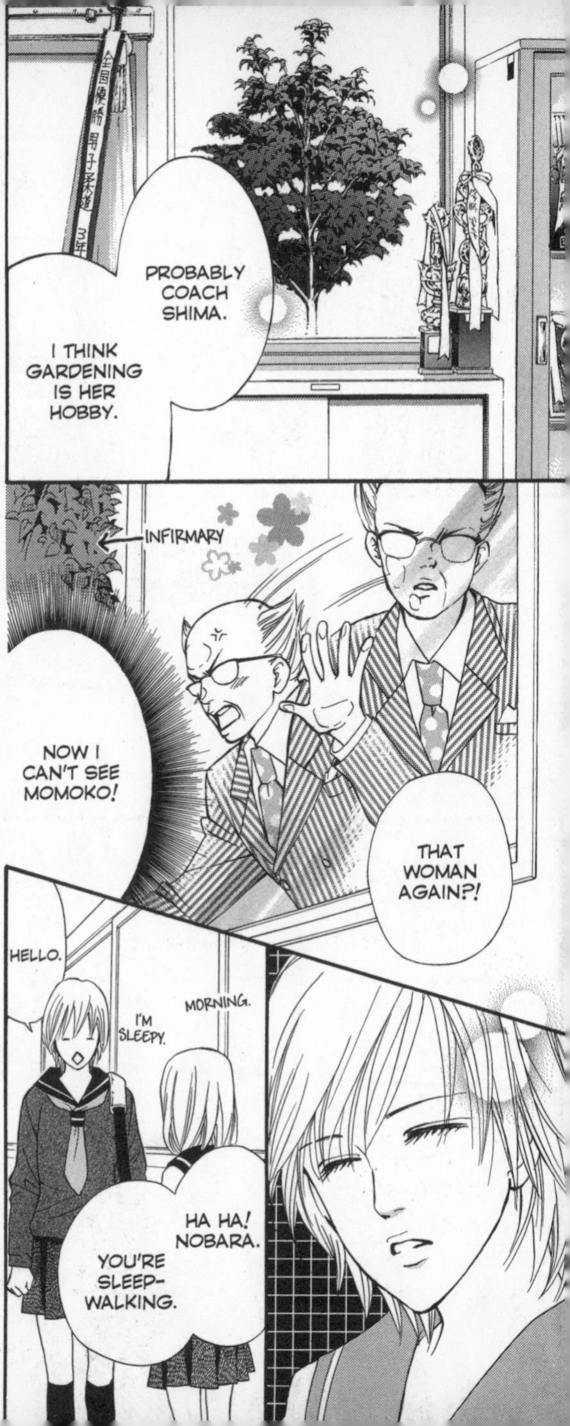
PROBABLY COACH SHIMA.
I THINK GARDENING IS HER HOBBY.
INFIRMARY
NOW I CAN'T SEE MOMOKO!
THAT WOMAN AGAIN?!
MORNING.
I'M SLEEPY.
HELLO.
HA HA! NOBARA.
YOU'RE SLEEP-WALKING.

MITSUBA CLUB

VoL. 1

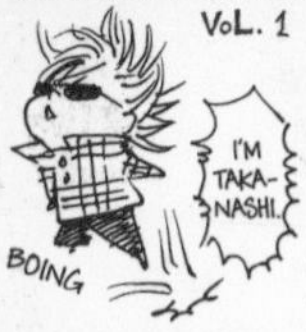
I'M TAKA-NASHI.
BOING

I TRIED FLYING. FOR NO REASON. IT'S SPRING. THERE WASN'T MUCH WINTER. IT DIDN'T EVEN SNOW IN TOKYO, DID IT? THE OTHER DAY, ABOUT A WEEK AGO, I WAS INVITED TO GO HIKING. I WENT AND ENDED UP MOUNTAIN CLIMBING. WE WERE CLIMBING FOR ABOUT TWO TO THREE HOURS. EXACTLY WHAT PART OF THAT WAS HIKING? THE FOLKS AROUND US HAD TREK POLES FOR MOUNTAIN CLIMBING!! AND THOSE COOL, FRESH-FACED PEOPLE? THEY'D TAKEN THE LIFT UP!! OH WELL. AT LEAST I GOT A WORKOUT. THE PLACE WE WENT WAS MT. TAKAO. WHILE I WAS THERE, I GOT A YAKUBARAI DONE TO DRIVE OFF ANY EVIL SPIRITS. THERE WERE ABOUT EIGHT MONKS CHANTING AT HIGH SPEED. WAS IT A ZEN TEMPLE? I WASN'T SURE. BUDDHIST ALTARS ARE SO COOL...!! ALL SHINY GOLD. *FANCY DANCE!* WAY COOL...!!!

LAST YEAR I HAD A RUN OF TROUBLES AND NOW I'M JUST PLAIN POOPED, SO I HOPE THIS YEAR IS MORE PEACEFUL. I HOPE THE EVIL SPIRITS WERE ALL CHASED AWAY.

IT'S ALMOST SPRING TOURNAMENT TIME. I WONDER IF I'LL BE ABLE TO GO THIS YEAR. I MIGHT HAVE TO WATCH ON TV, BUT BY THE TIME THIS BOOK COMES OUT, IT'LL BE OVER.

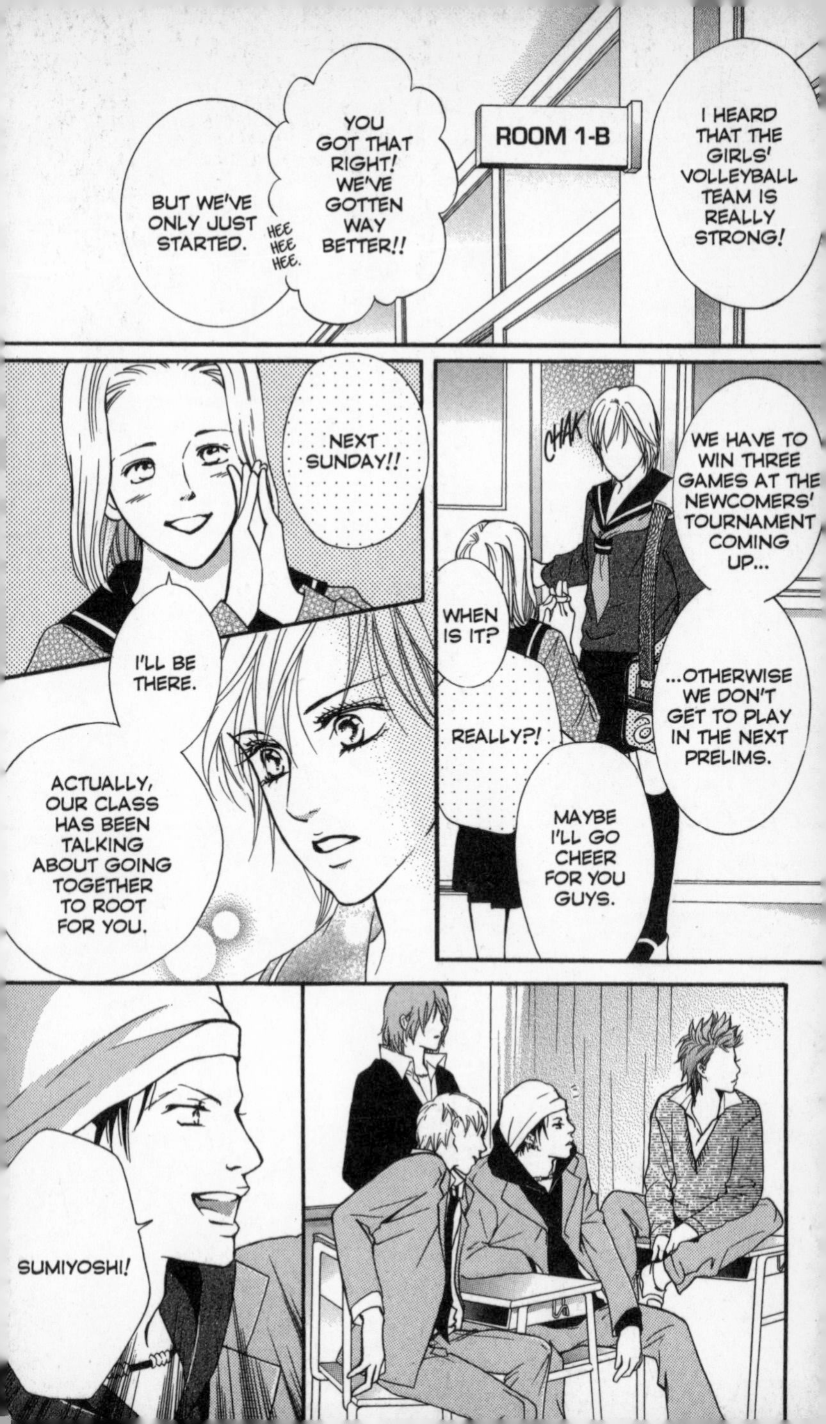
ROOM 1-B
I HEARD THAT THE GIRLS' VOLLEYBALL TEAM IS REALLY STRONG!
YOU GOT THAT RIGHT! WE'VE GOTTEN WAY BETTER!!
HEE HEE HEE.
BUT WE'VE ONLY JUST STARTED.
CHAK
WE HAVE TO WIN THREE GAMES AT THE NEWCOMERS' TOURNAMENT COMING UP...
WHEN IS IT?
...OTHERWISE WE DON'T GET TO PLAY IN THE NEXT PRELIMS.
REALLY?!
MAYBE I'LL GO CHEER FOR YOU GUYS.
NEXT SUNDAY!!
I'LL BE THERE.
ACTUALLY, OUR CLASS HAS BEEN TALKING ABOUT GOING TOGETHER TO ROOT FOR YOU.
SUMIYOSHI!

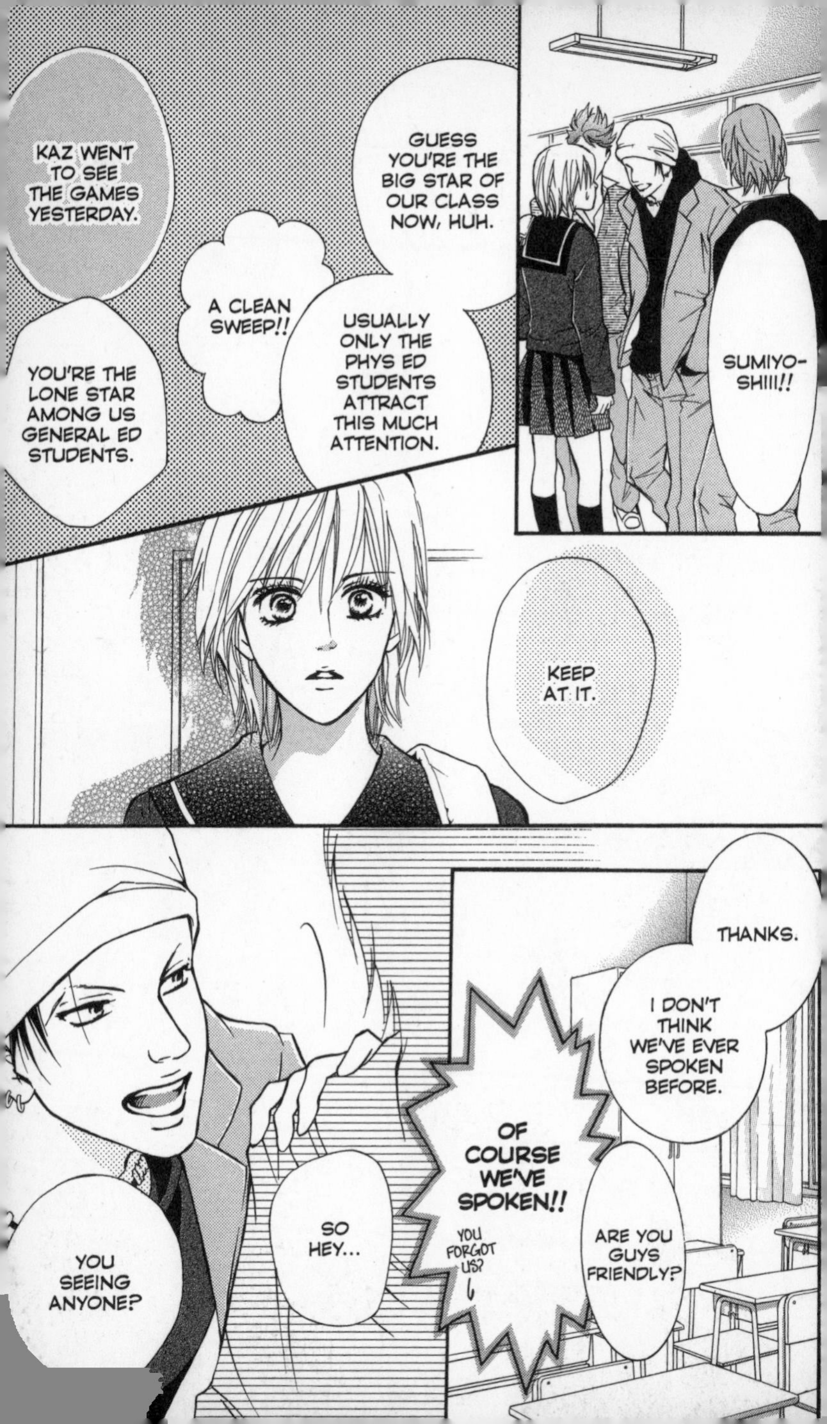
SUMIYO-SHIII!!
GUESS YOU'RE THE BIG STAR OF OUR CLASS NOW, HUH.
KAZ WENT TO SEE THE GAMES YESTERDAY.
USUALLY ONLY THE PHYS ED STUDENTS ATTRACT THIS MUCH ATTENTION.
A CLEAN SWEEP!!
YOU'RE THE LONE STAR AMONG US GENERAL ED STUDENTS.
KEEP AT IT.
THANKS.
I DON'T THINK WE'VE EVER SPOKEN BEFORE.
ARE YOU GUYS FRIENDLY?
OF COURSE WE'VE SPOKEN!!
YOU FORGOT US?
SO HEY...
YOU SEEING ANYONE?

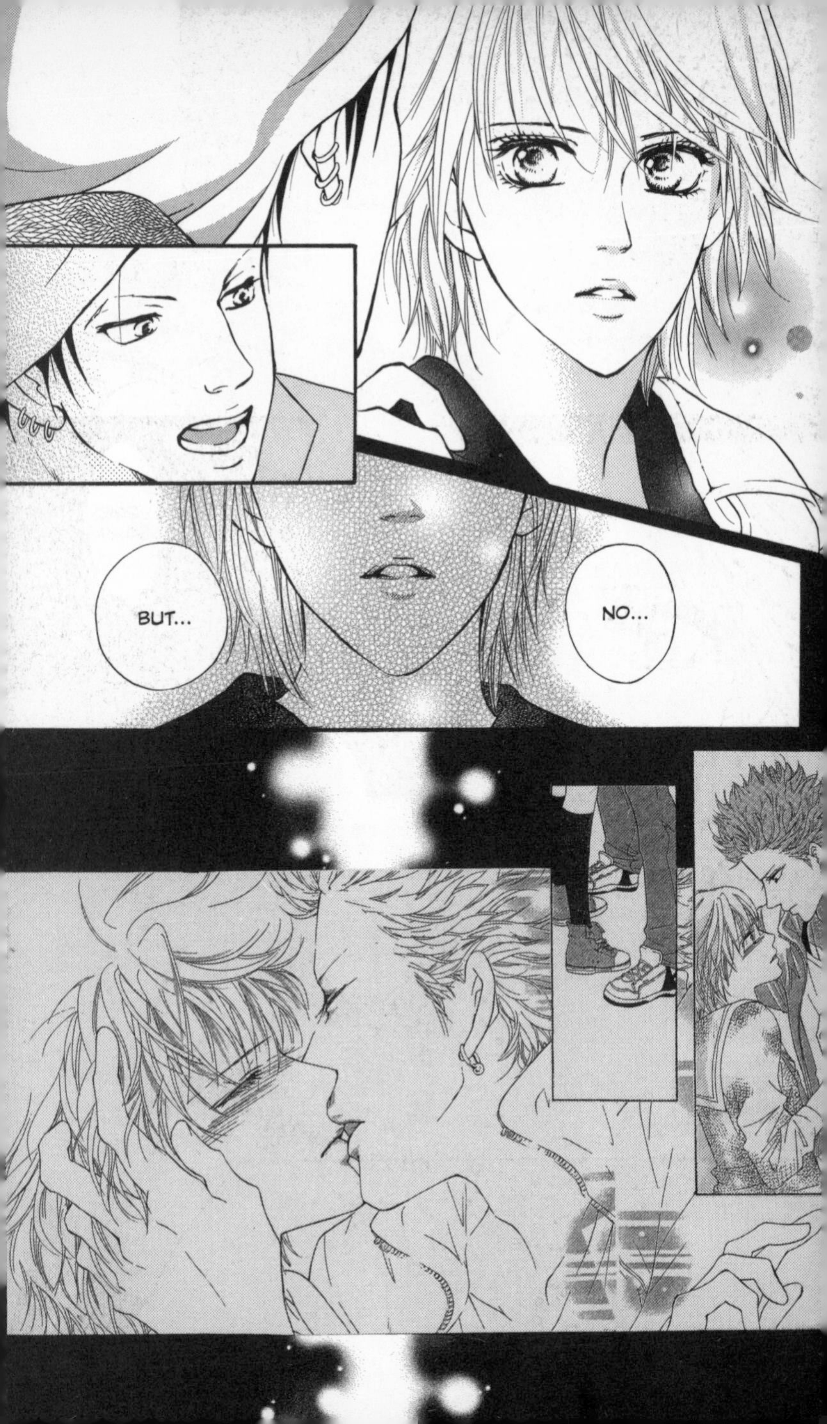
NO...
BUT...

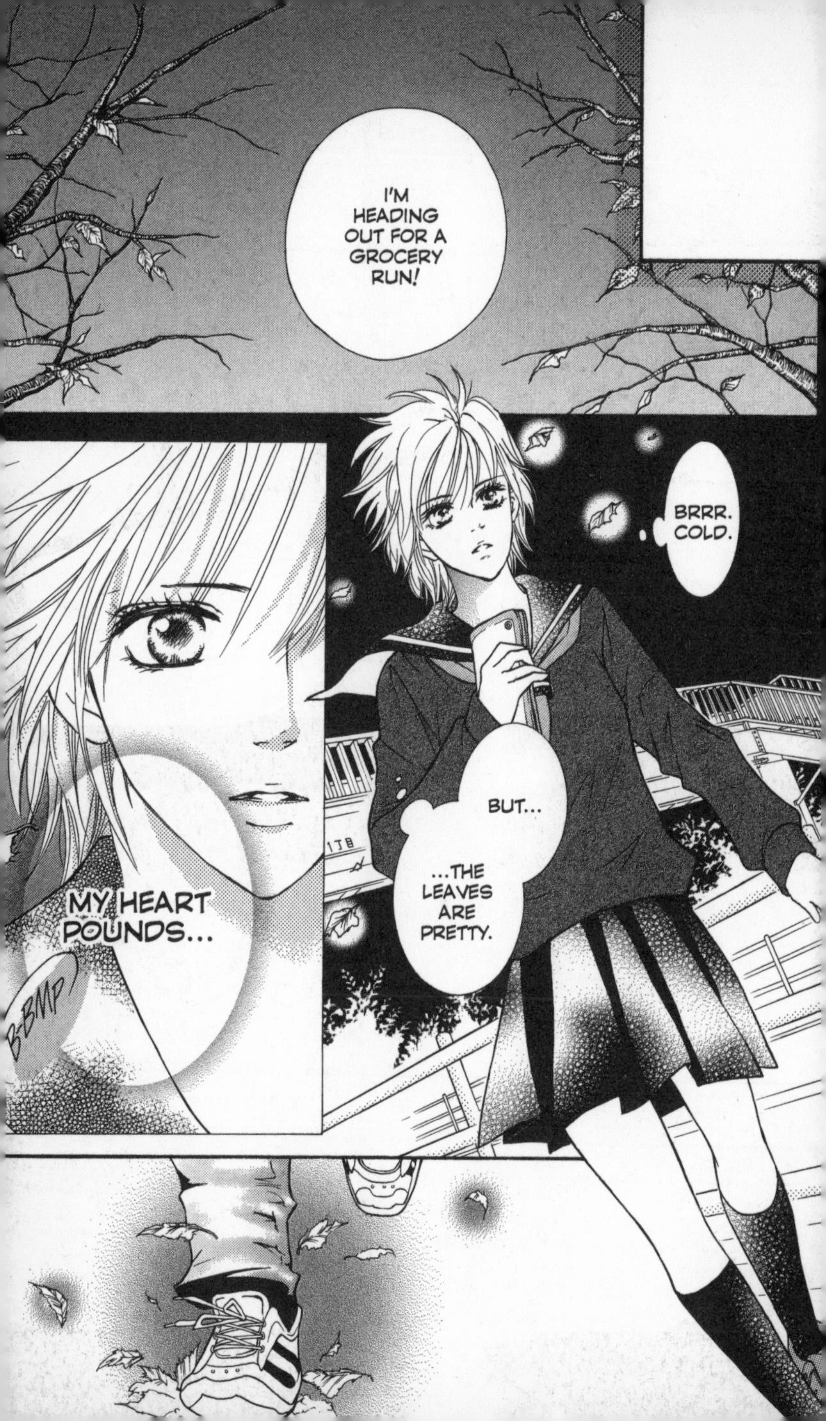
I'M HEADING OUT FOR A GROCERY RUN!
BRRR. COLD.
BUT...
...THE LEAVES ARE PRETTY.
MY HEART POUNDS...
B-BMP

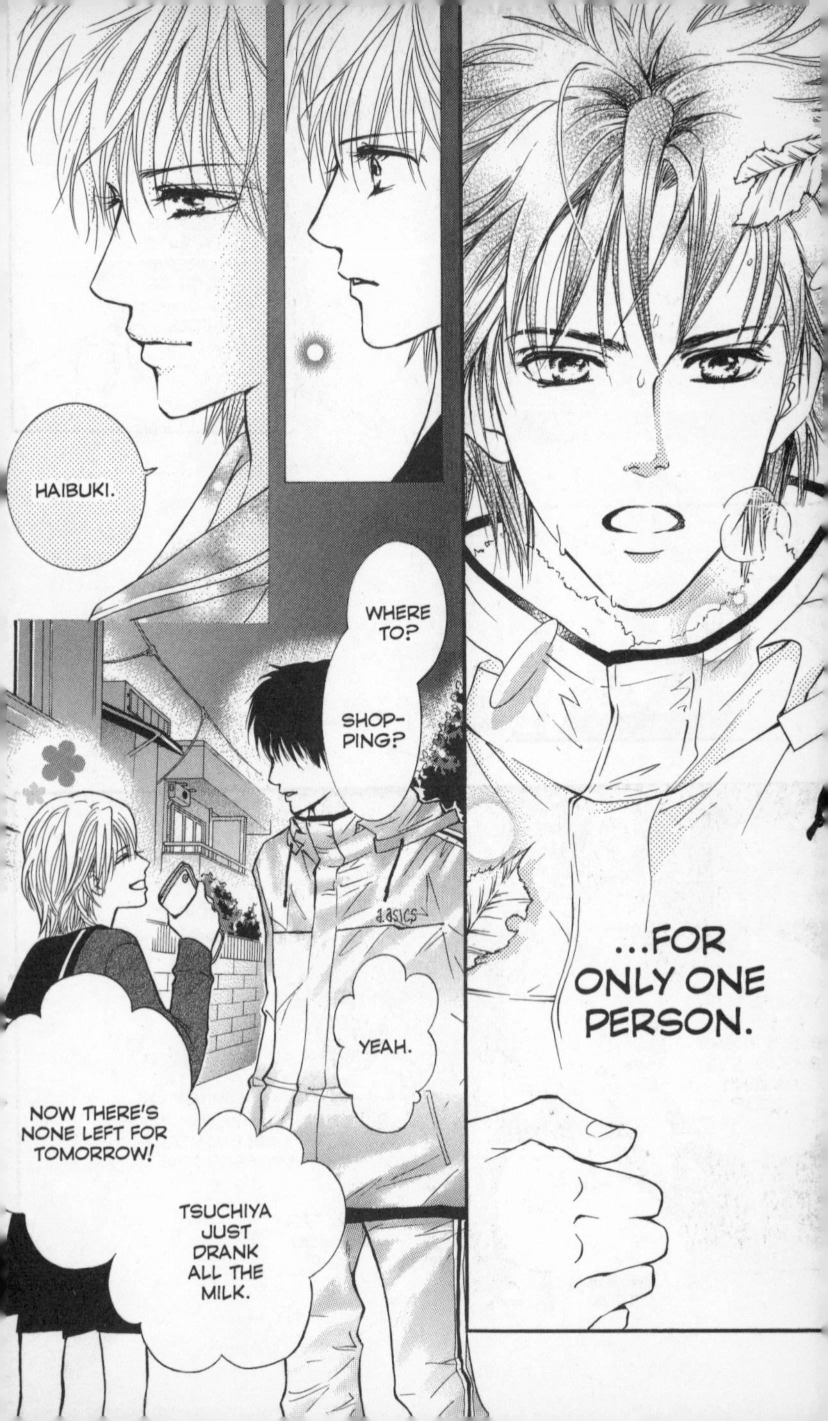
...FOR ONLY ONE PERSON.
HAIBUKI.
WHERE TO?
SHOP-PING?
YEAH.
TSUCHIYA JUST DRANK ALL THE MILK.
NOW THERE'S NONE LEFT FOR TOMORROW!

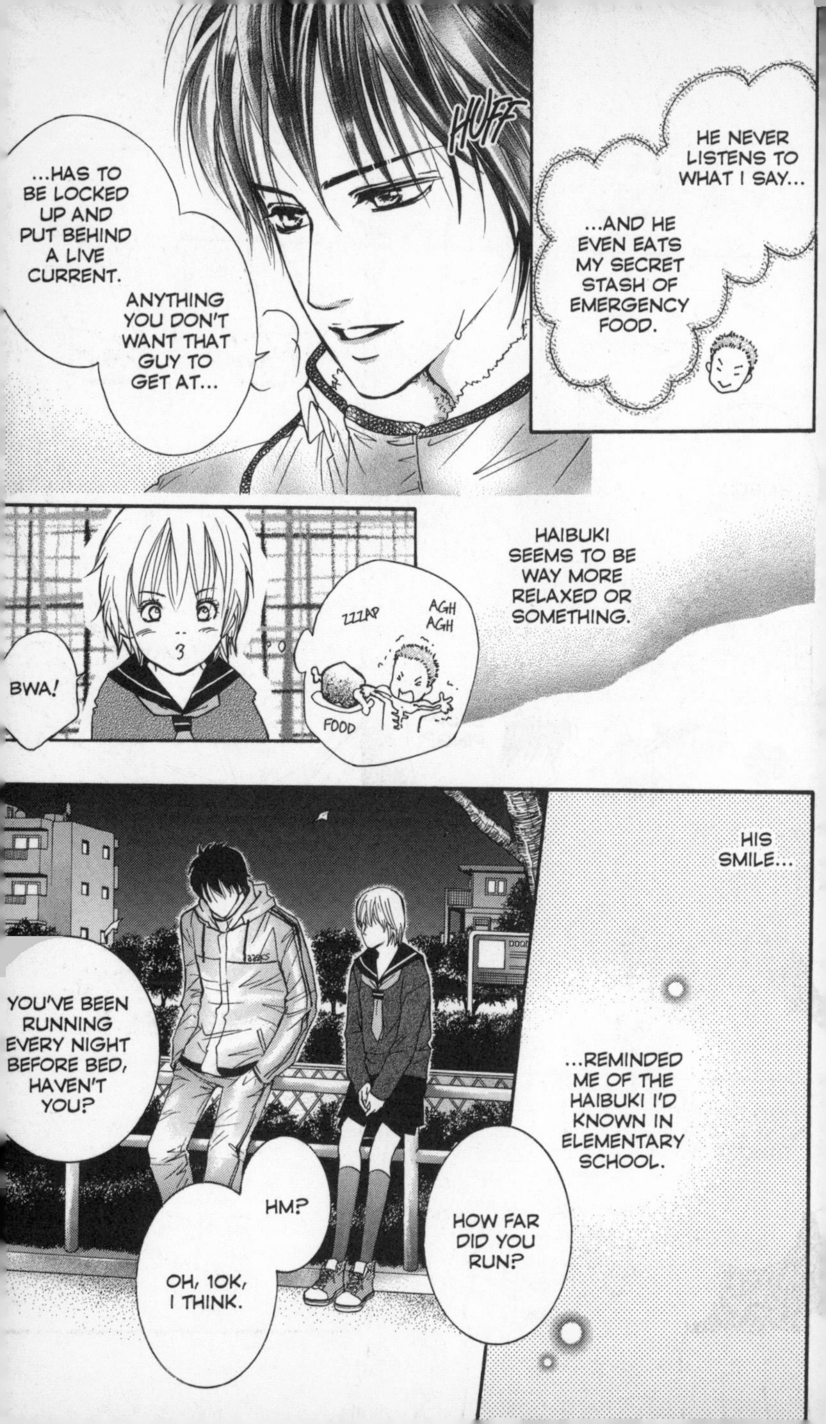
HE NEVER LISTENS TO WHAT I SAY...
...AND HE EVEN EATS MY SECRET STASH OF EMERGENCY FOOD.
HUFF
ANYTHING YOU DON'T WANT THAT GUY TO GET AT...
...HAS TO BE LOCKED UP AND PUT BEHIND A LIVE CURRENT.
HAIBUKI SEEMS TO BE WAY MORE RELAXED OR SOMETHING.
AGH AGH
ZZZAP
FOOD
BWA!
HIS SMILE...
...REMINDED ME OF THE HAIBUKI I'D KNOWN IN ELEMENTARY SCHOOL.
YOU'VE BEEN RUNNING EVERY NIGHT BEFORE BED, HAVEN'T YOU?
HM?
HOW FAR DID YOU RUN?
OH, 10K, I THINK.

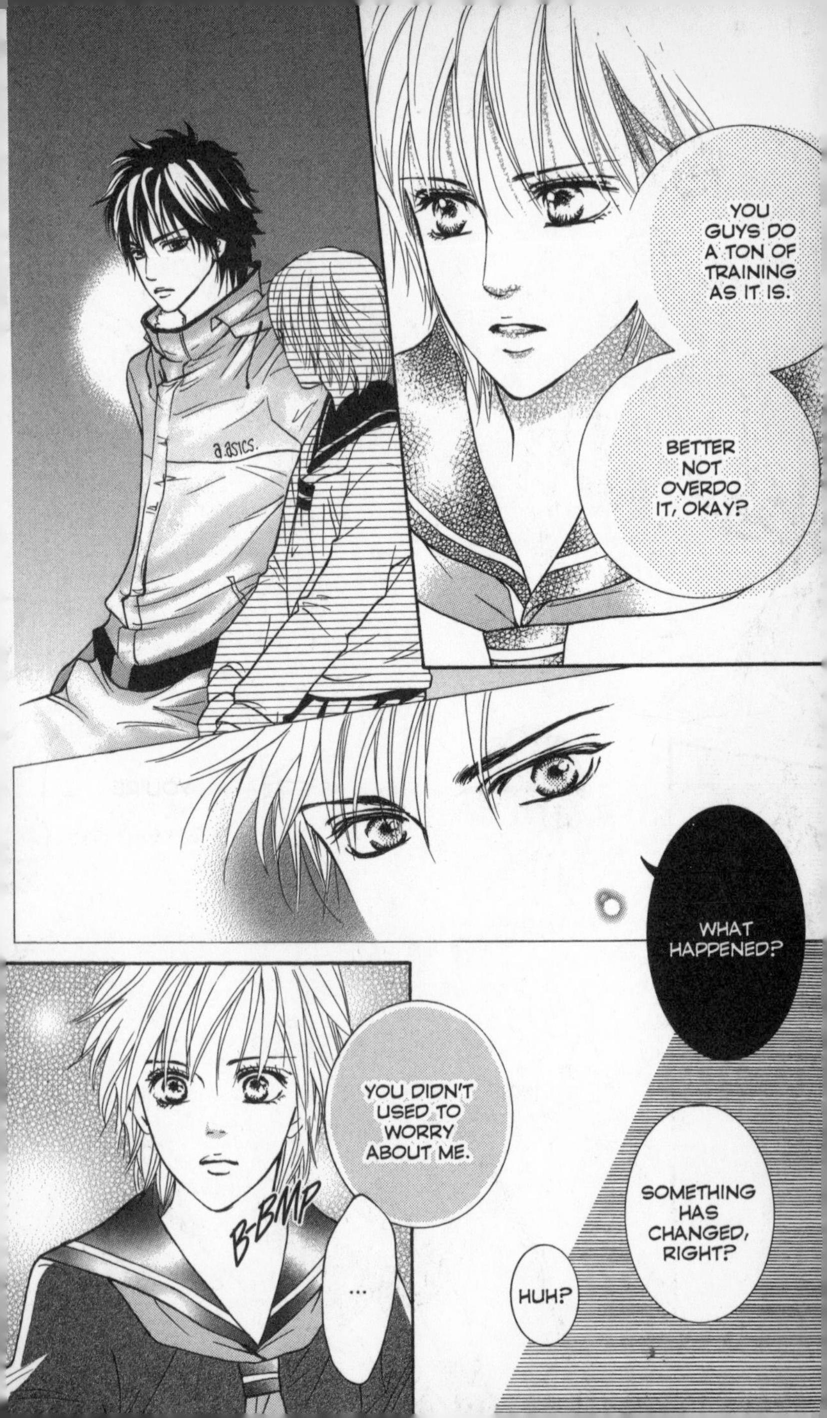
a.asics.
YOU GUYS DO A TON OF TRAINING AS IT IS.
BETTER NOT OVERDO IT, OKAY?
WHAT HAPPENED?
YOU DIDN'T USED TO WORRY ABOUT ME.
SOMETHING HAS CHANGED, RIGHT?
HUH?
B-BMP
...

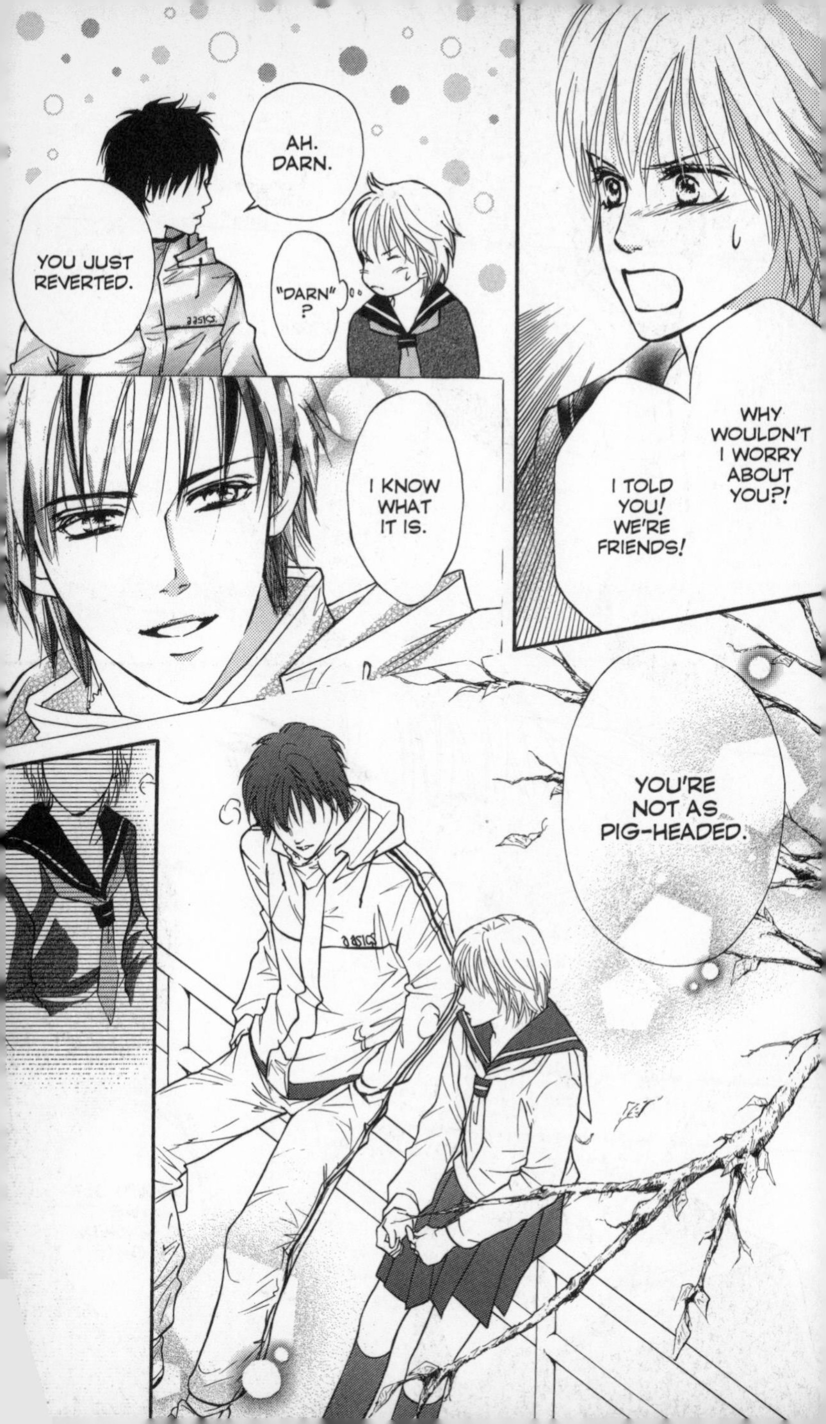
WHY WOULDN'T I WORRY ABOUT YOU?!
I TOLD YOU! WE'RE FRIENDS!
AH. DARN.
"DARN"?
YOU JUST REVERTED.
I KNOW WHAT IT IS.
YOU'RE NOT AS PIG-HEADED.

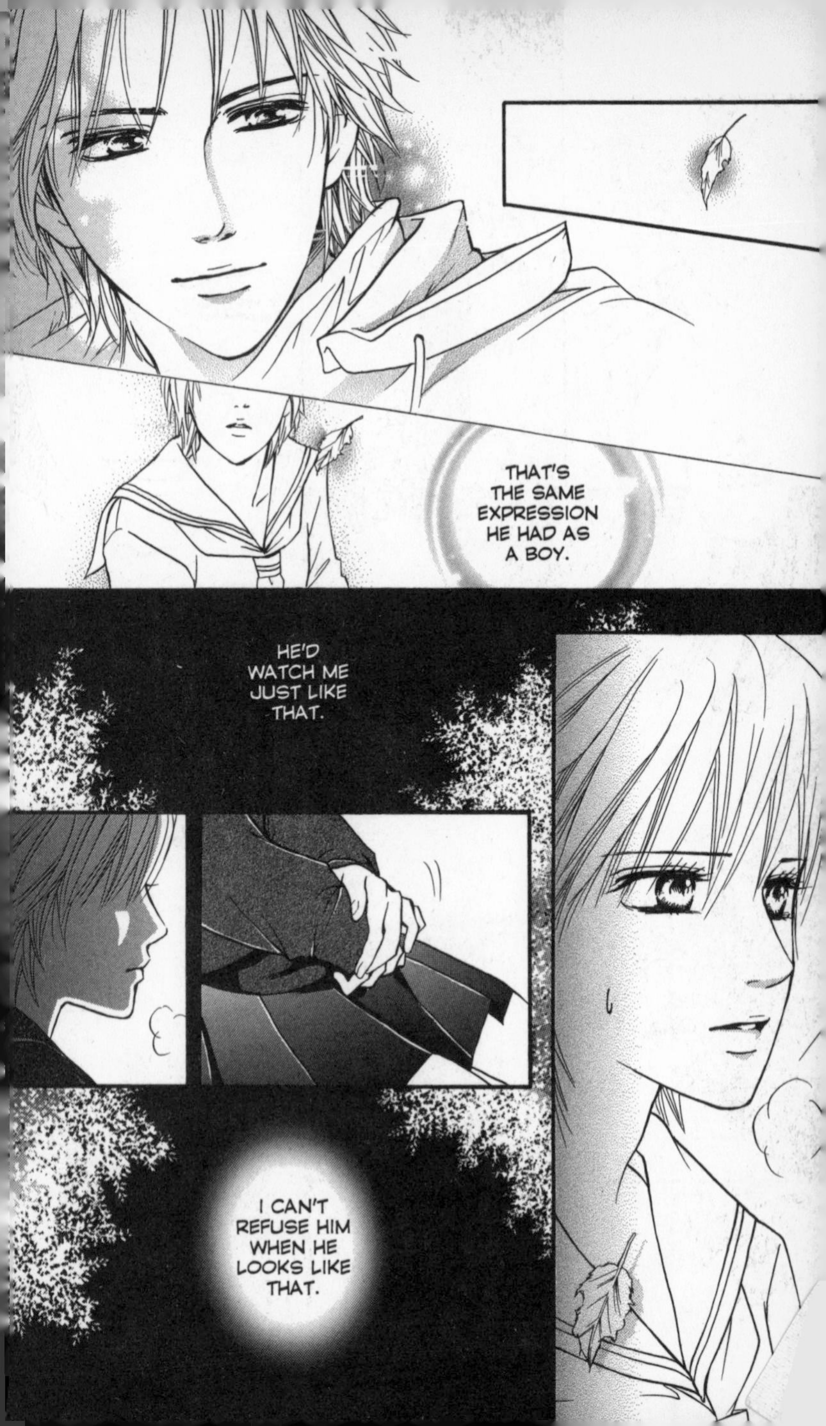
THAT'S THE SAME EXPRESSION HE HAD AS A BOY.
HE'D WATCH ME JUST LIKE THAT.
I CAN'T REFUSE HIM WHEN HE LOOKS LIKE THAT.

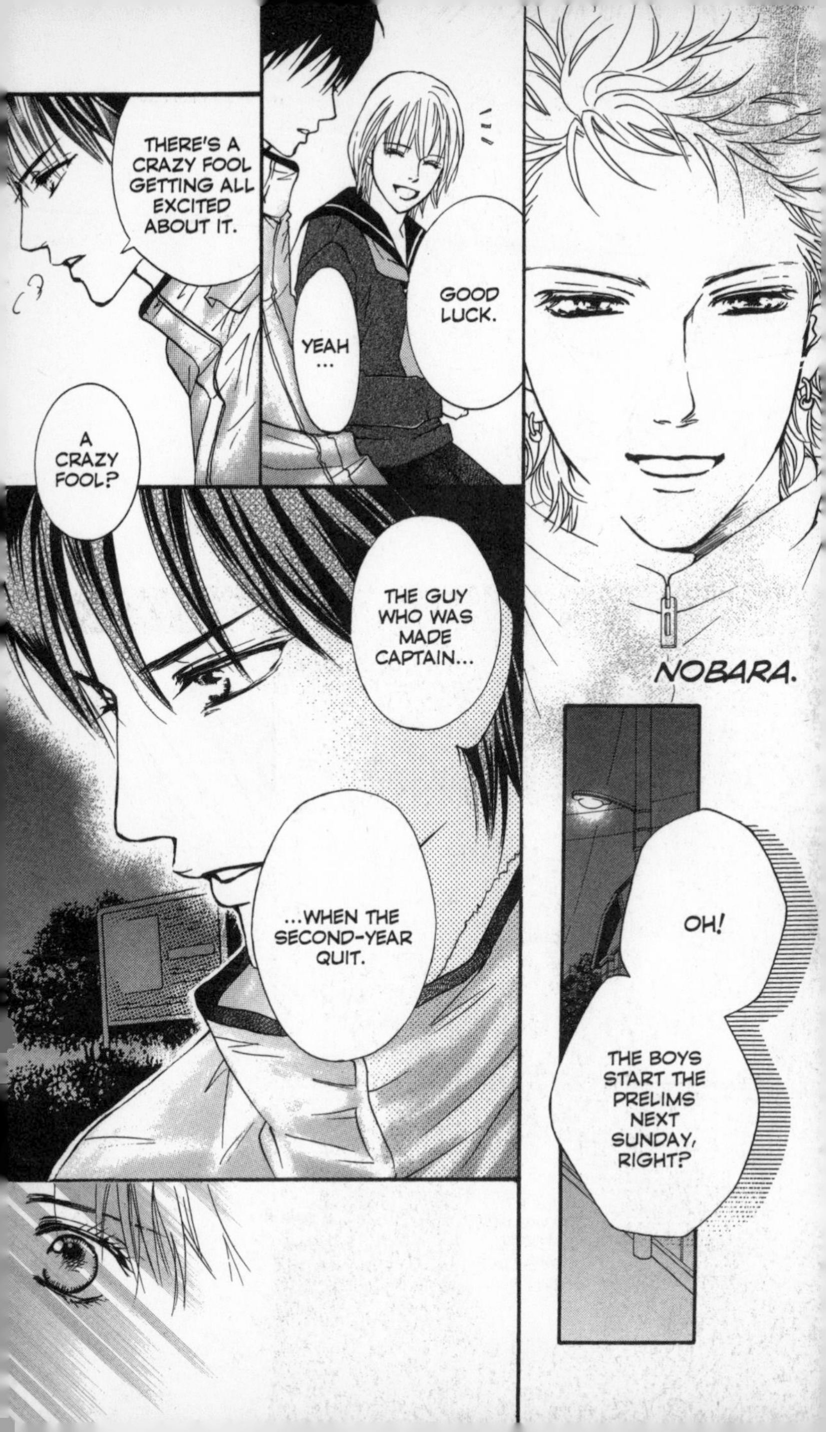
NOBARA.
OH!
THE BOYS START THE PRELIMS NEXT SUNDAY, RIGHT?
GOOD LUCK.
YEAH...
THERE'S A CRAZY FOOL GETTING ALL EXCITED ABOUT IT.
A CRAZY FOOL?
THE GUY WHO WAS MADE CAPTAIN...
...WHEN THE SECOND-YEAR QUIT.

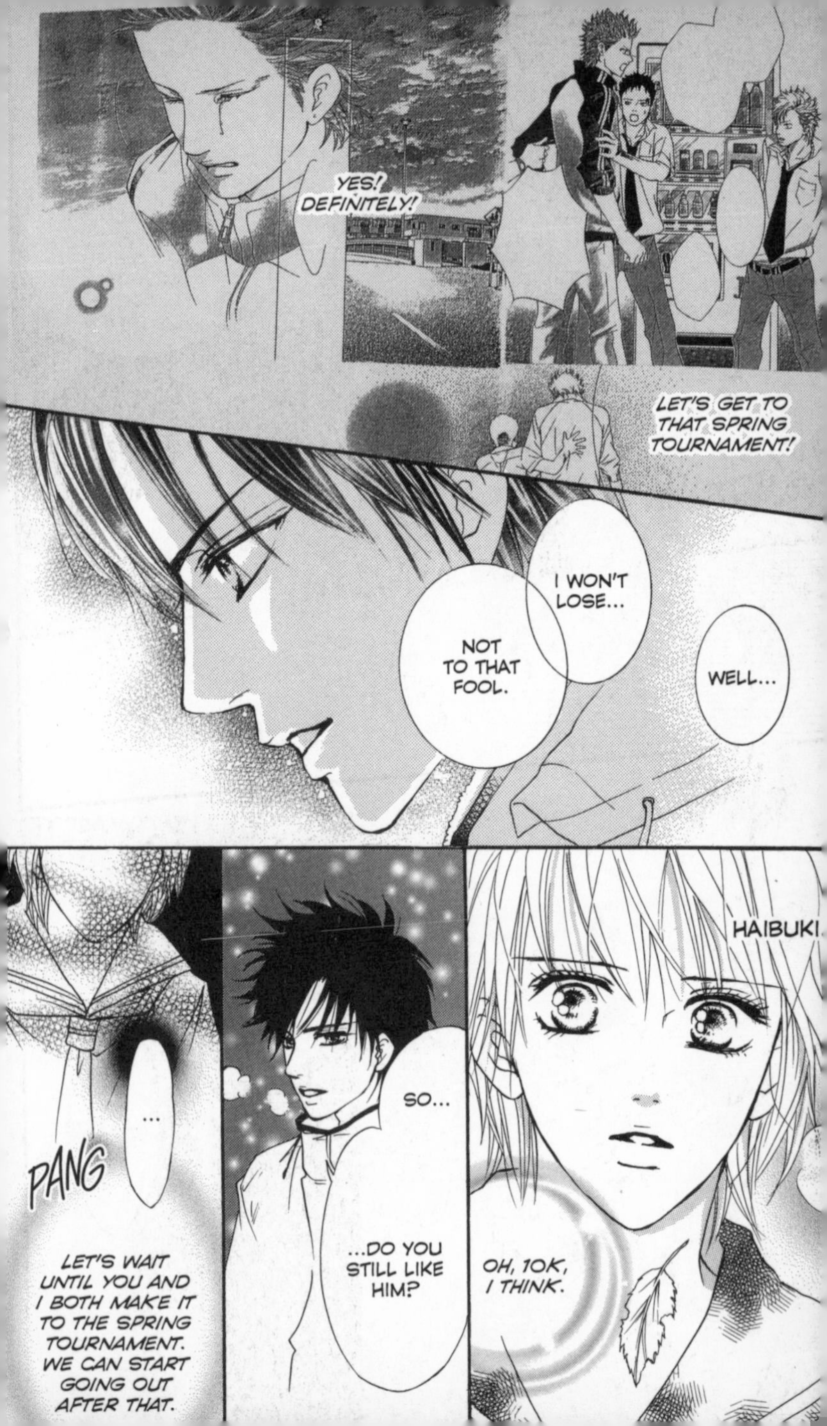
YES! DEFINITELY!
LET'S GET TO THAT SPRING TOURNAMENT!
WELL...
I WON'T LOSE...
NOT TO THAT FOOL.
HAIBUKI.
OH, 10K, I THINK.
SO...
...DO YOU STILL LIKE HIM?
...
PANG
LET'S WAIT UNTIL YOU AND I BOTH MAKE IT TO THE SPRING TOURNAMENT. WE CAN START GOING OUT AFTER THAT.

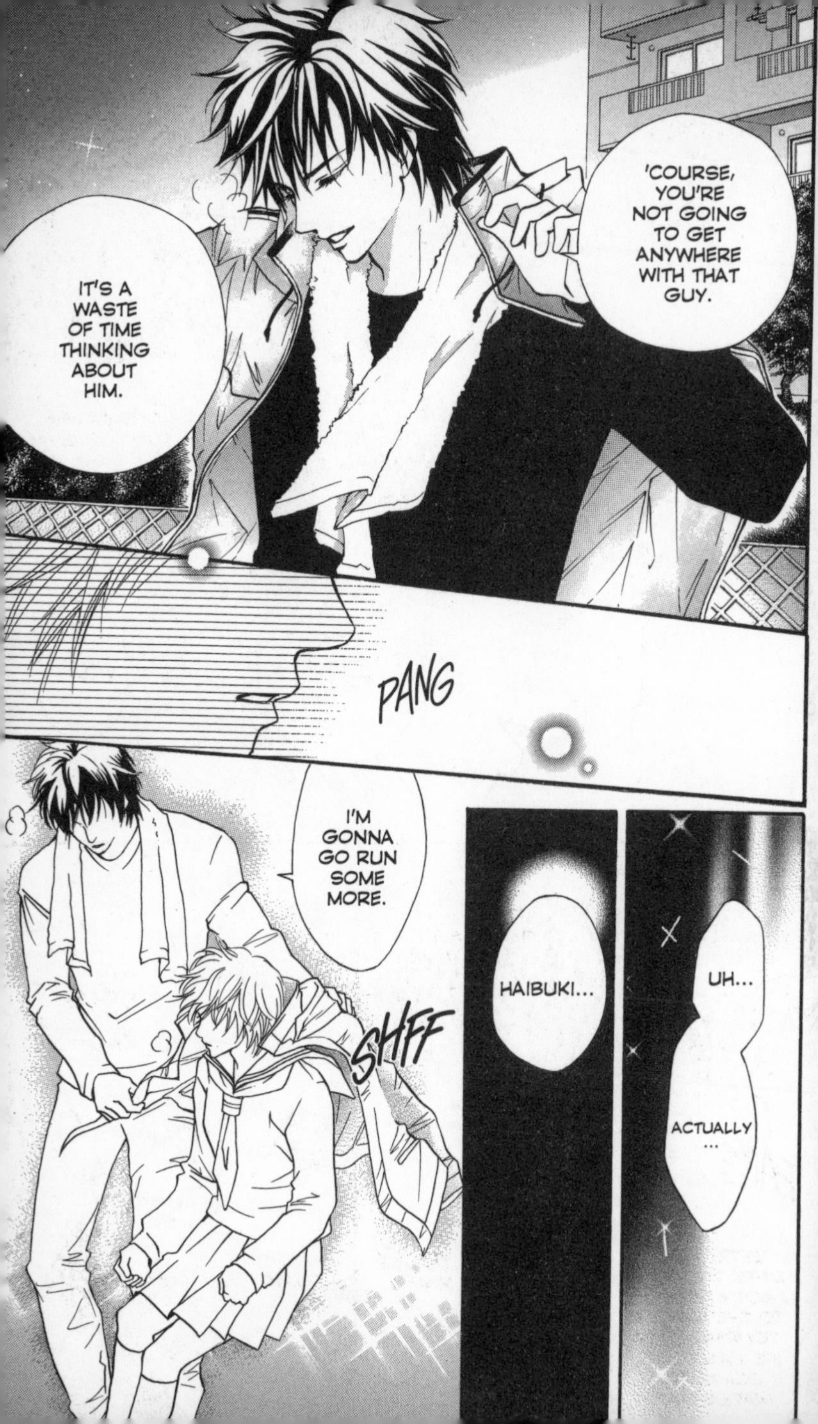
'COURSE, YOU'RE NOT GOING TO GET ANYWHERE WITH THAT GUY.
IT'S A WASTE OF TIME THINKING ABOUT HIM.
PANG
UH...
ACTUALLY ...
HAIBUKI...
I'M GONNA GO RUN SOME MORE.
SHFF

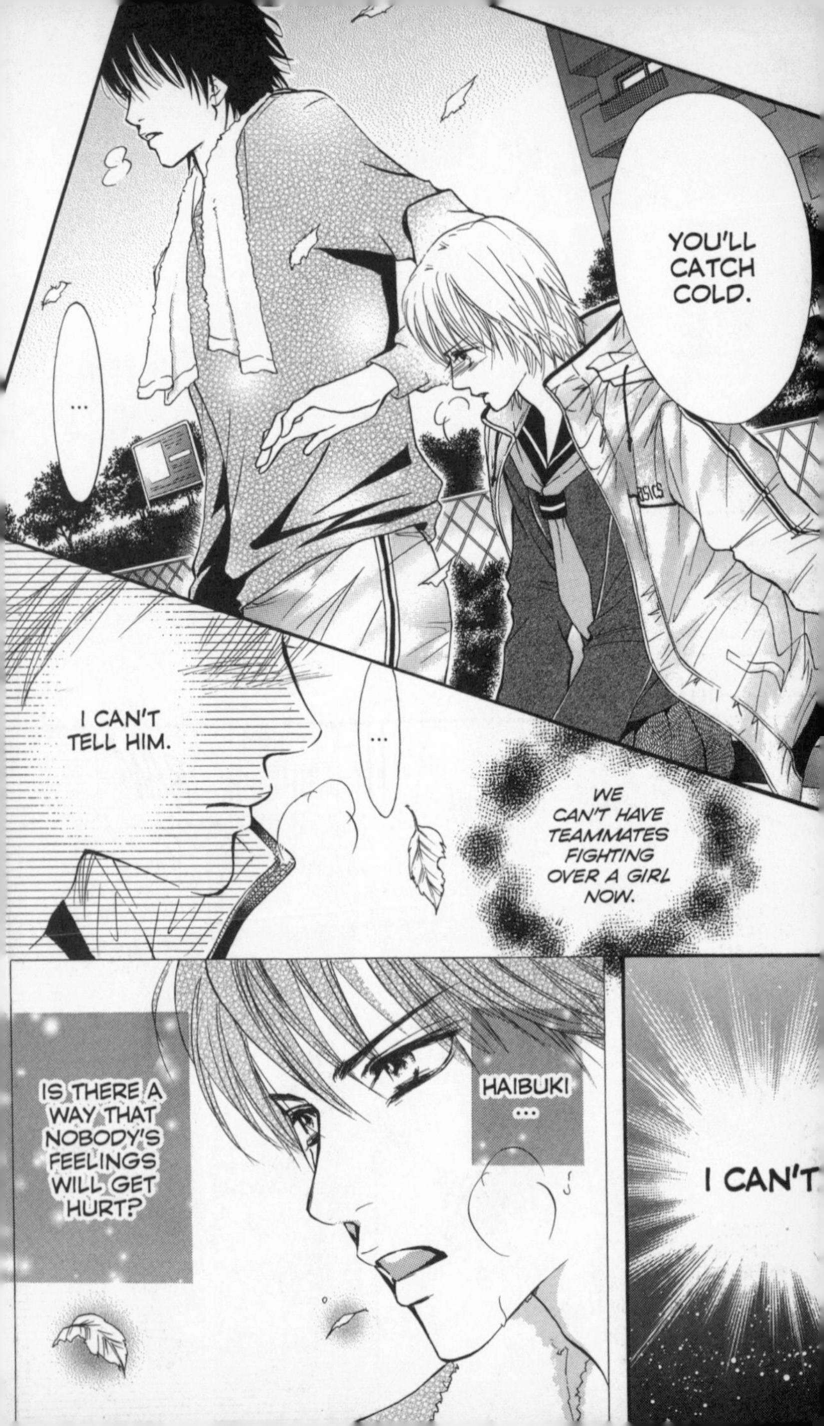
YOU'LL CATCH COLD.
...
WE CAN'T HAVE TEAMMATES FIGHTING OVER A GIRL NOW.
...
I CAN'T TELL HIM.
I CAN'T
HAIBUKI ...
IS THERE A WAY THAT NOBODY'S FEELINGS WILL GET HURT?

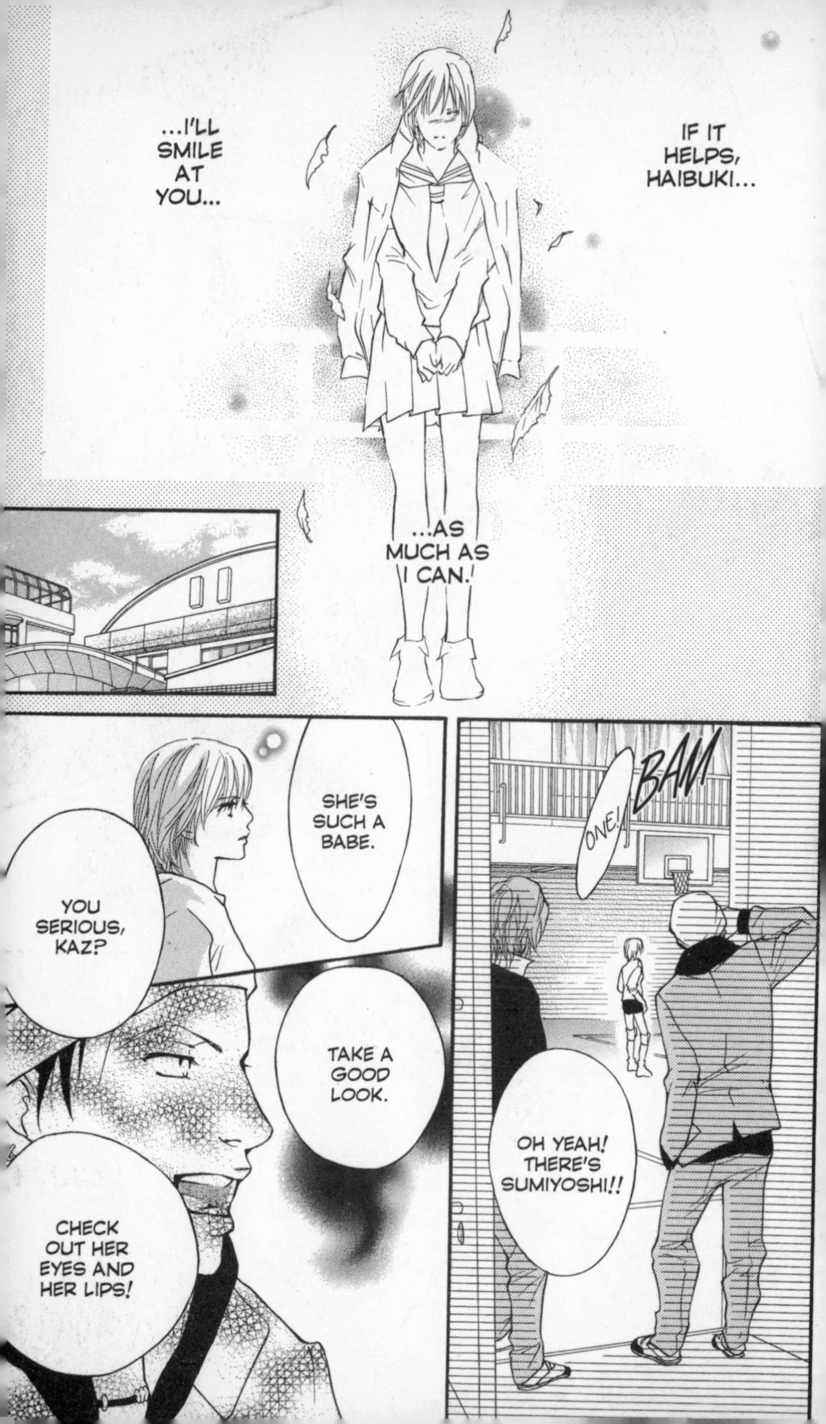
IF IT HELPS, HAIBUKI...
...I'LL SMILE AT YOU...
...AS MUCH AS I CAN.
ONE!
BAM
OH YEAH! THERE'S SUMIYOSHI!!
SHE'S SUCH A BABE.
YOU SERIOUS, KAZ?
TAKE A GOOD LOOK.
CHECK OUT HER EYES AND HER LIPS!

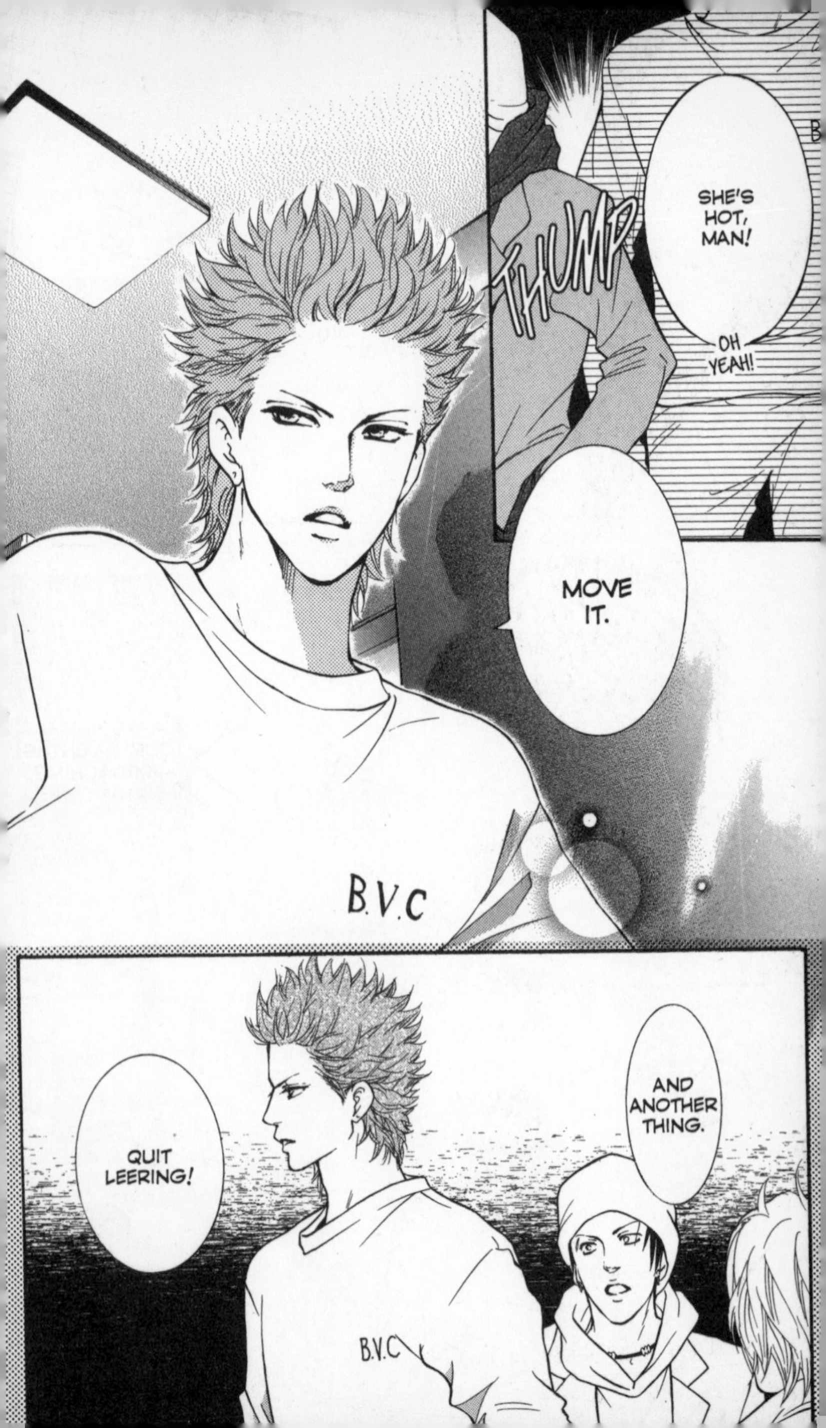
SHE'S HOT, MAN!
OH YEAH!
THUMP
MOVE IT.
B.V.C
AND ANOTHER THING.
QUIT LEERING!
B.V.C

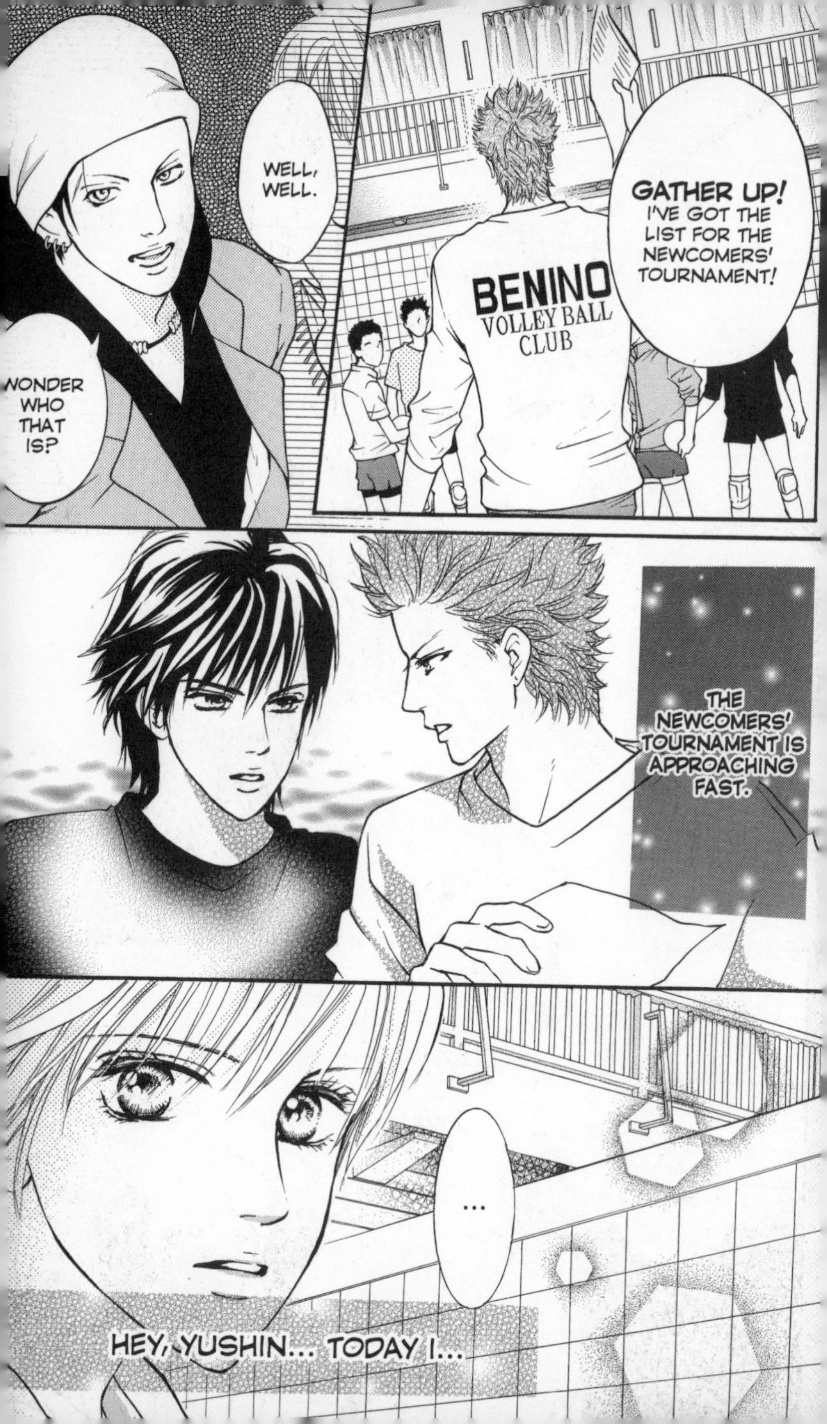
GATHER UP! I'VE GOT THE LIST FOR THE NEWCOMERS' TOURNAMENT!
BENINO VOLLEY BALL CLUB
WELL, WELL.
WONDER WHO THAT IS?
THE NEWCOMERS' TOURNAMENT IS APPROACHING FAST.
...
HEY, YUSHIN... TODAY I...

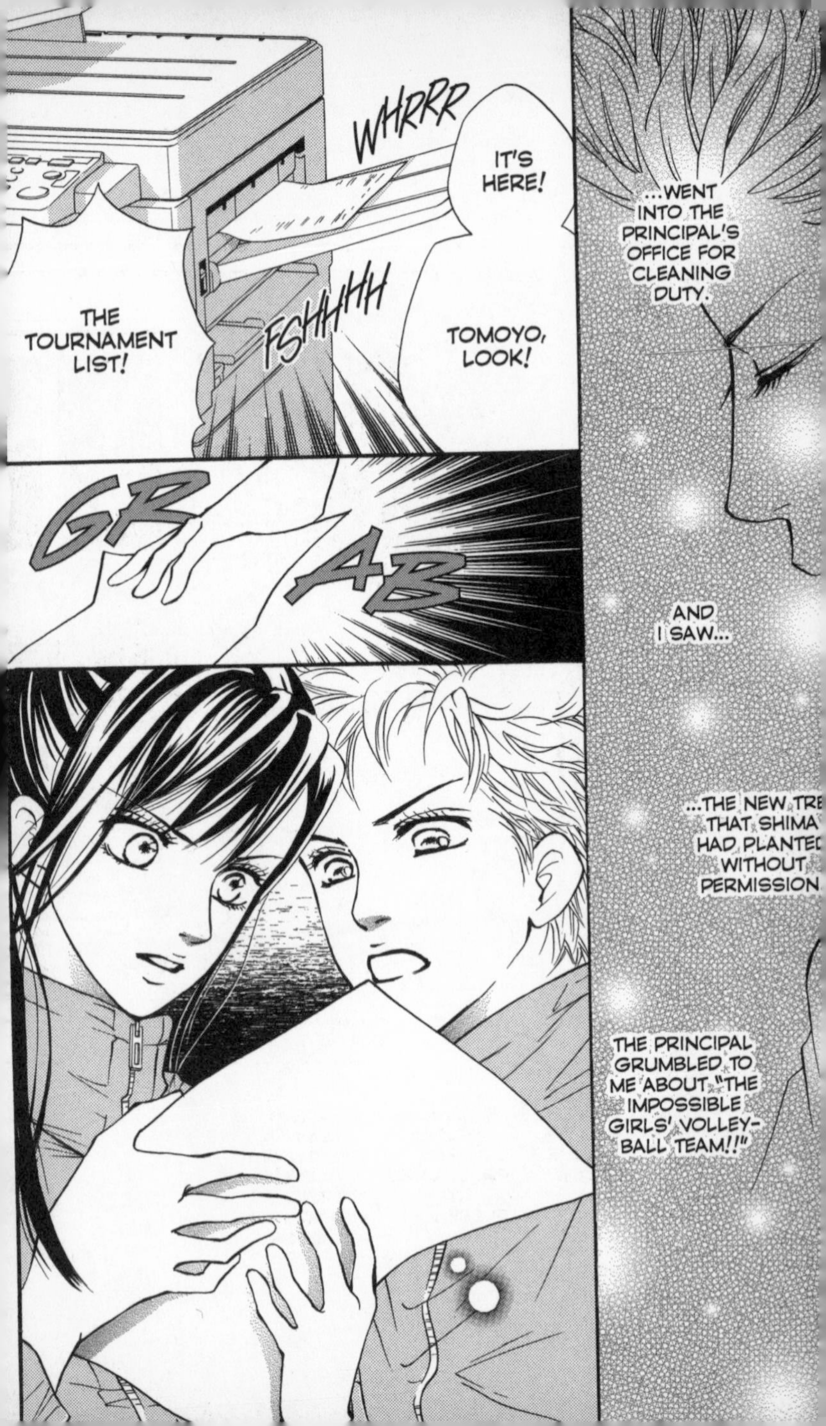
...WENT INTO THE PRINCIPAL'S OFFICE FOR CLEANING DUTY.
AND I SAW...
...THE NEW TRE THAT SHIMA HAD PLANTED WITHOUT PERMISSION.
THE PRINCIPAL GRUMBLED TO ME ABOUT "THE IMPOSSIBLE GIRLS' VOLLEY-BALL TEAM!!"
WHRRR
IT'S HERE!
TOMOYO, LOOK!
FSHHHH
THE TOURNAMENT LIST!
GRAB

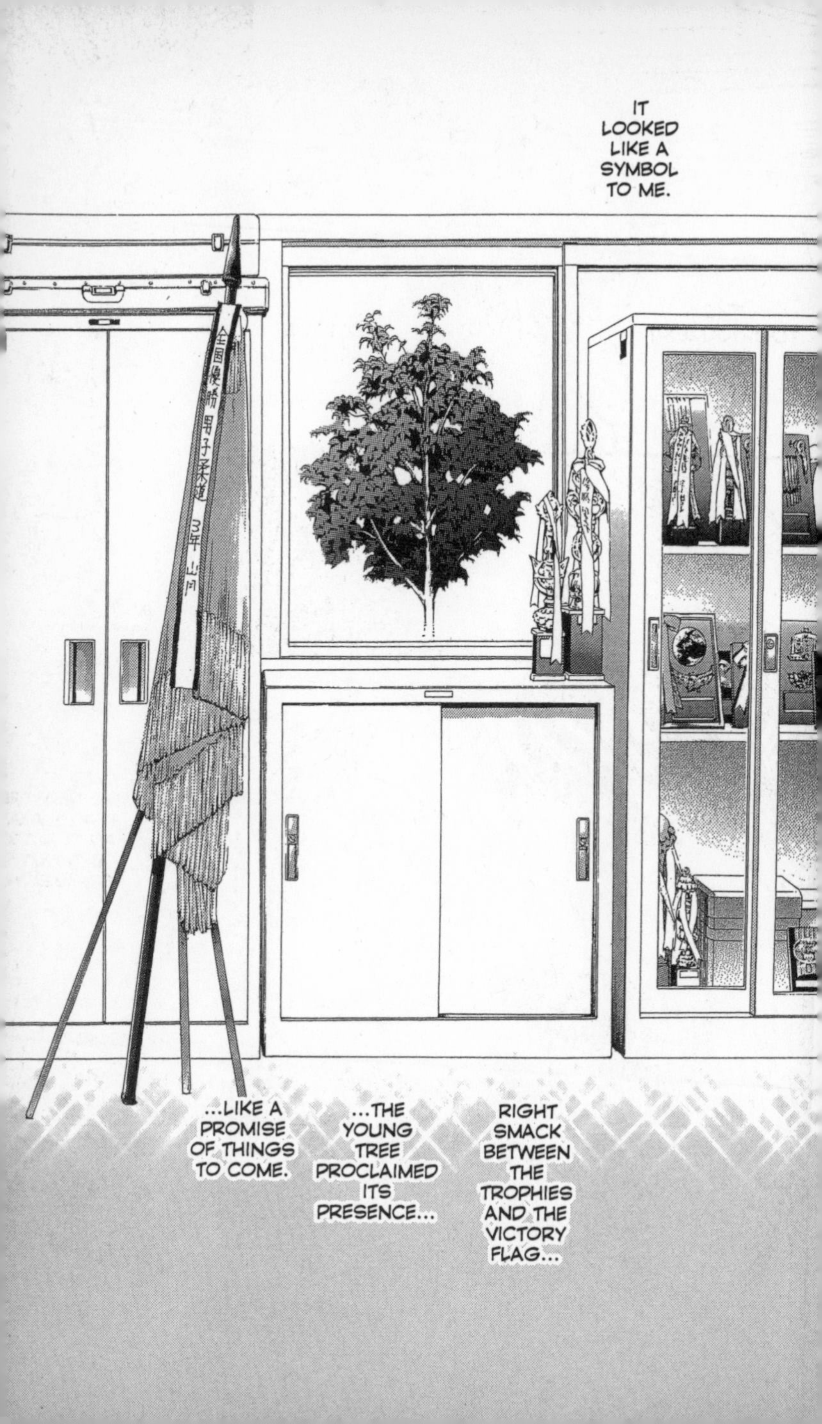
IT LOOKED LIKE A SYMBOL TO ME.
RIGHT SMACK BETWEEN THE TROPHIES AND THE VICTORY FLAG...
...THE YOUNG TREE PROCLAIMED ITS PRESENCE...
...LIKE A PROMISE OF THINGS TO COME.

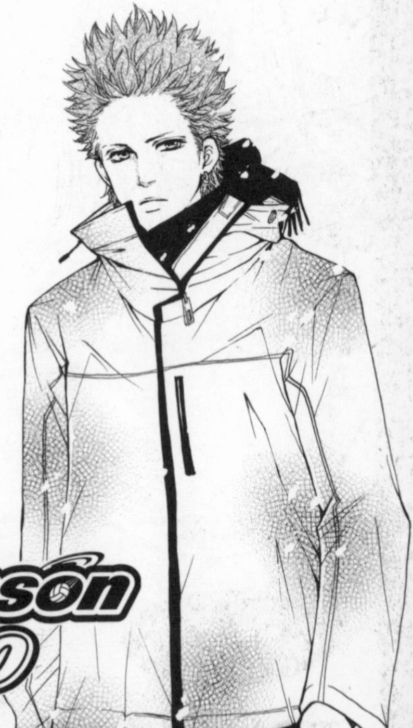

Crimson Hero

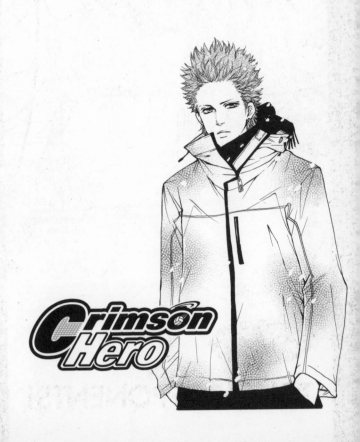

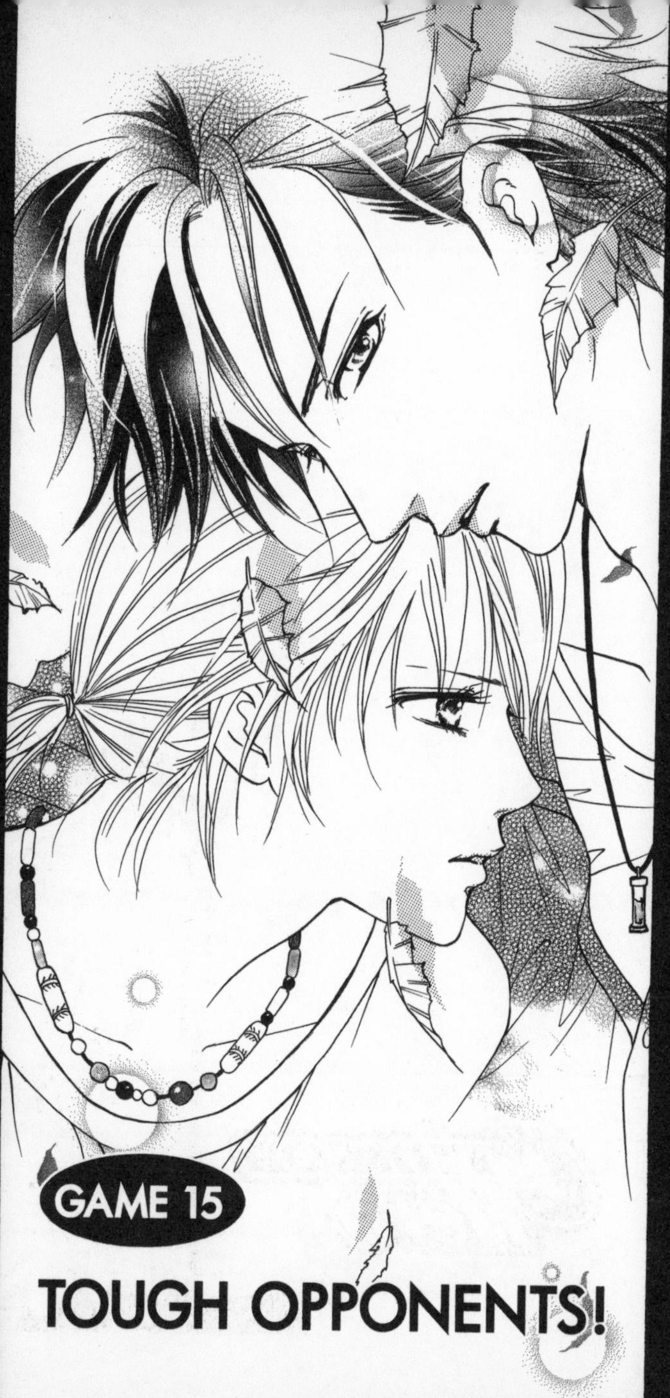
GAME 15
TOUGH OPPONENTS!

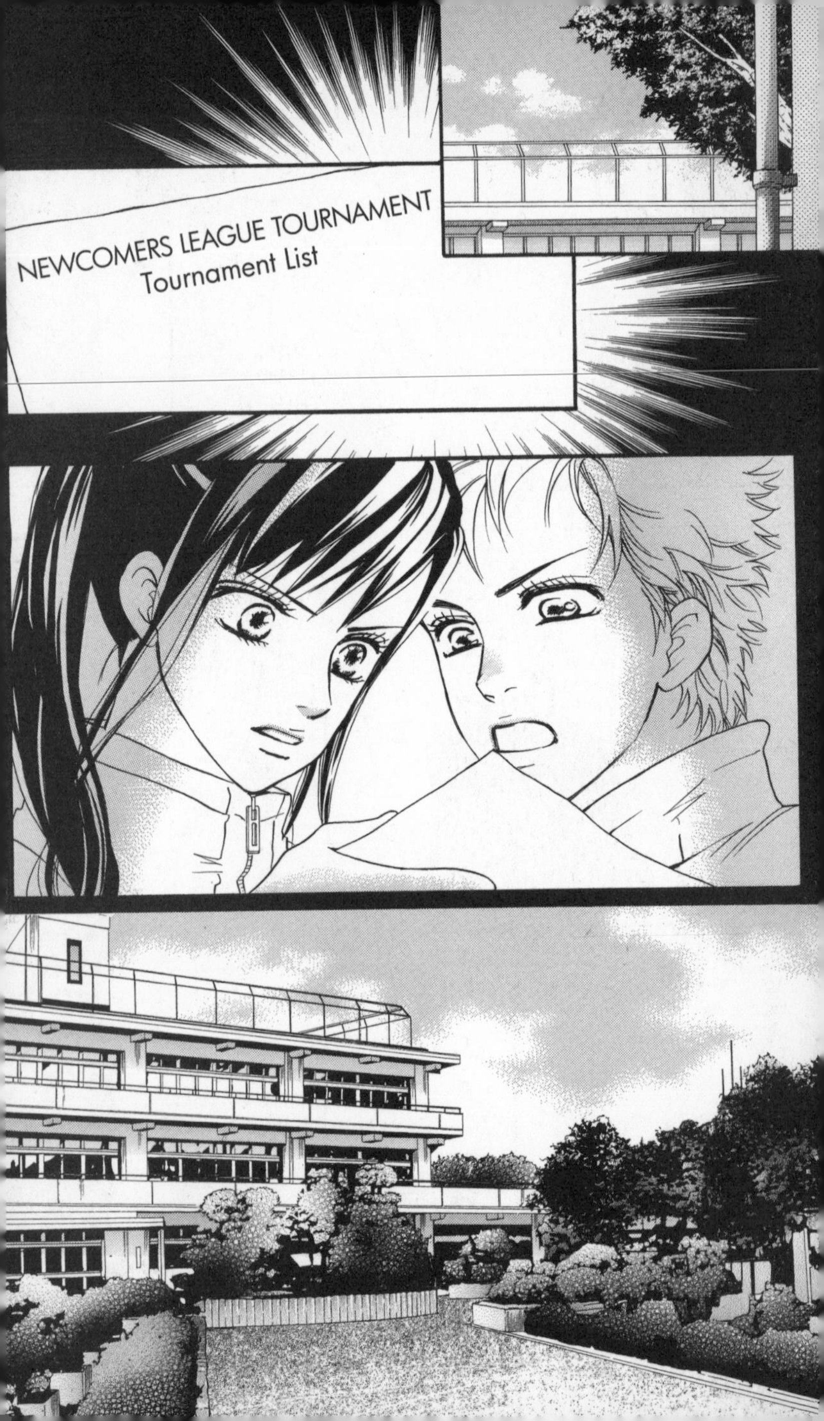
NEWCOMERS LEAGUE TOURNAMENT
Tournament List

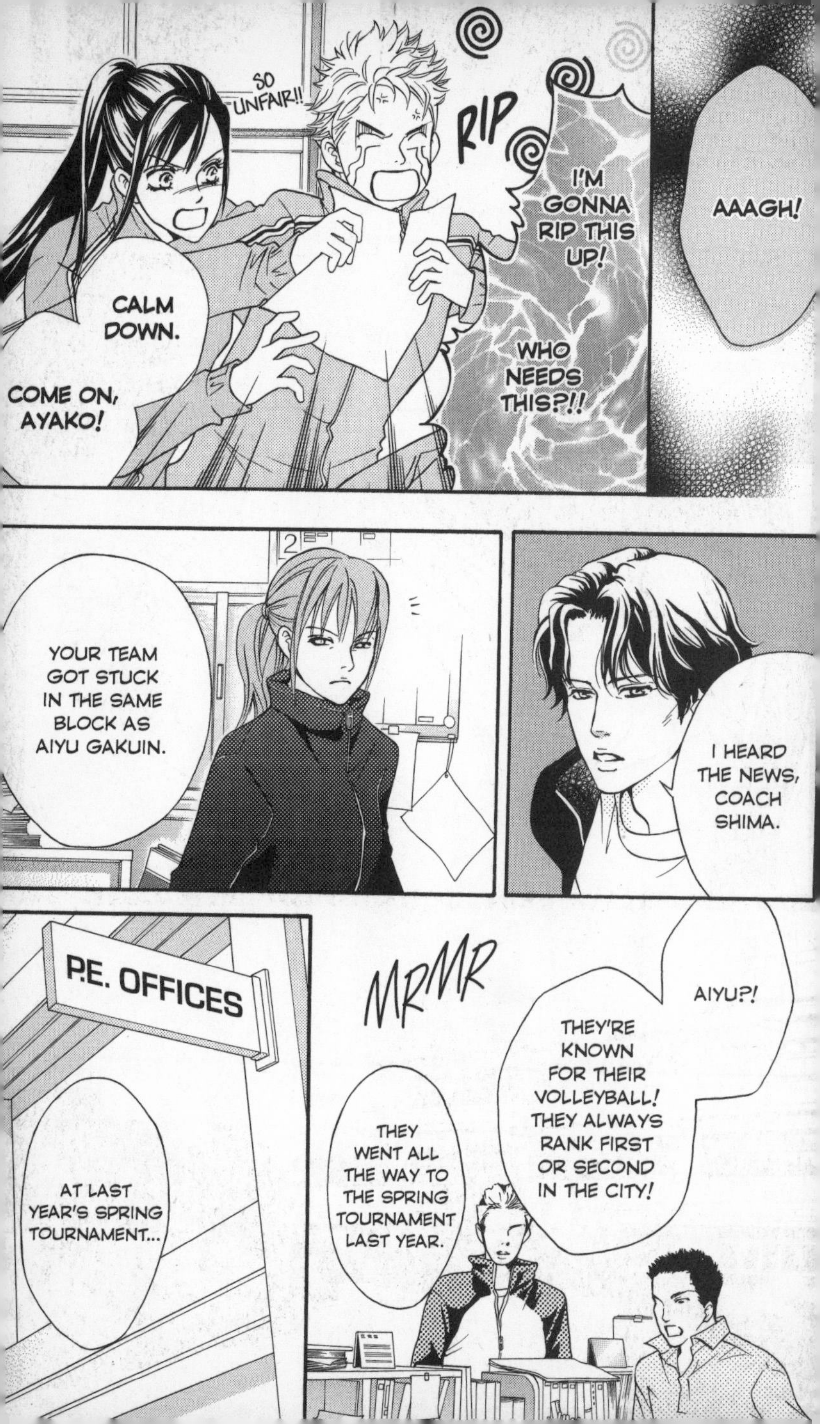
AAAGH!
RIP
I'M GONNA RIP THIS UP!
WHO NEEDS THIS?!!
SO UNFAIR!!
CALM DOWN.
COME ON, AYAKO!
I HEARD THE NEWS, COACH SHIMA.
YOUR TEAM GOT STUCK IN THE SAME BLOCK AS AIYU GAKUIN.
AIYU?!
THEY'RE KNOWN FOR THEIR VOLLEYBALL! THEY ALWAYS RANK FIRST OR SECOND IN THE CITY!
MRMR
THEY WENT ALL THE WAY TO THE SPRING TOURNAMENT LAST YEAR.
P.E. OFFICES
AT LAST YEAR'S SPRING TOURNAMENT...

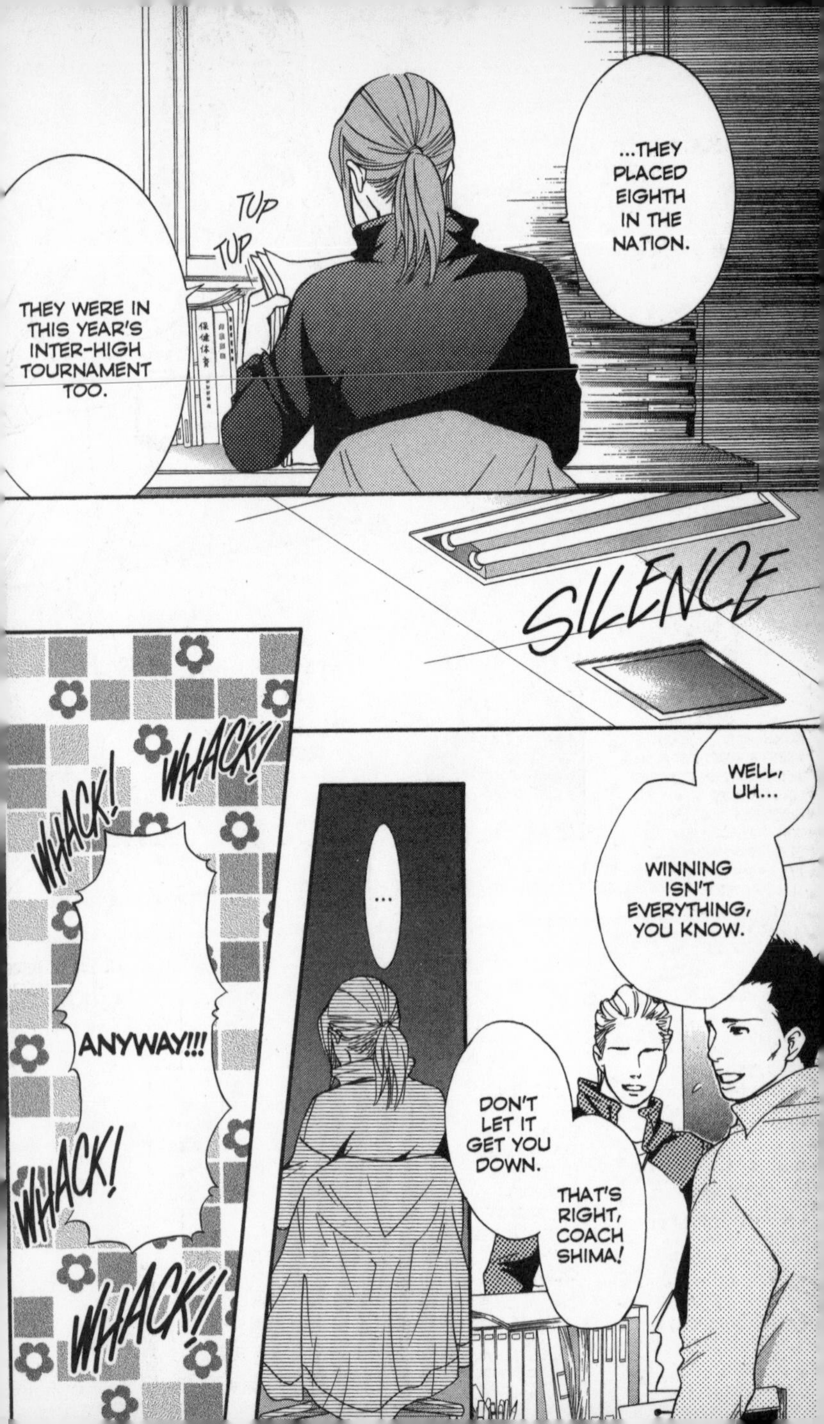
...THEY PLACED EIGHTH IN THE NATION.
TUP
TUP
THEY WERE IN THIS YEAR'S INTER-HIGH TOURNAMENT TOO.
SILENCE
WELL, UH...
WINNING ISN'T EVERYTHING, YOU KNOW.
DON'T LET IT GET YOU DOWN.
THAT'S RIGHT, COACH SHIMA!
...
WHACK!
WHACK!
ANYWAY!!!
WHACK!
WHACK!

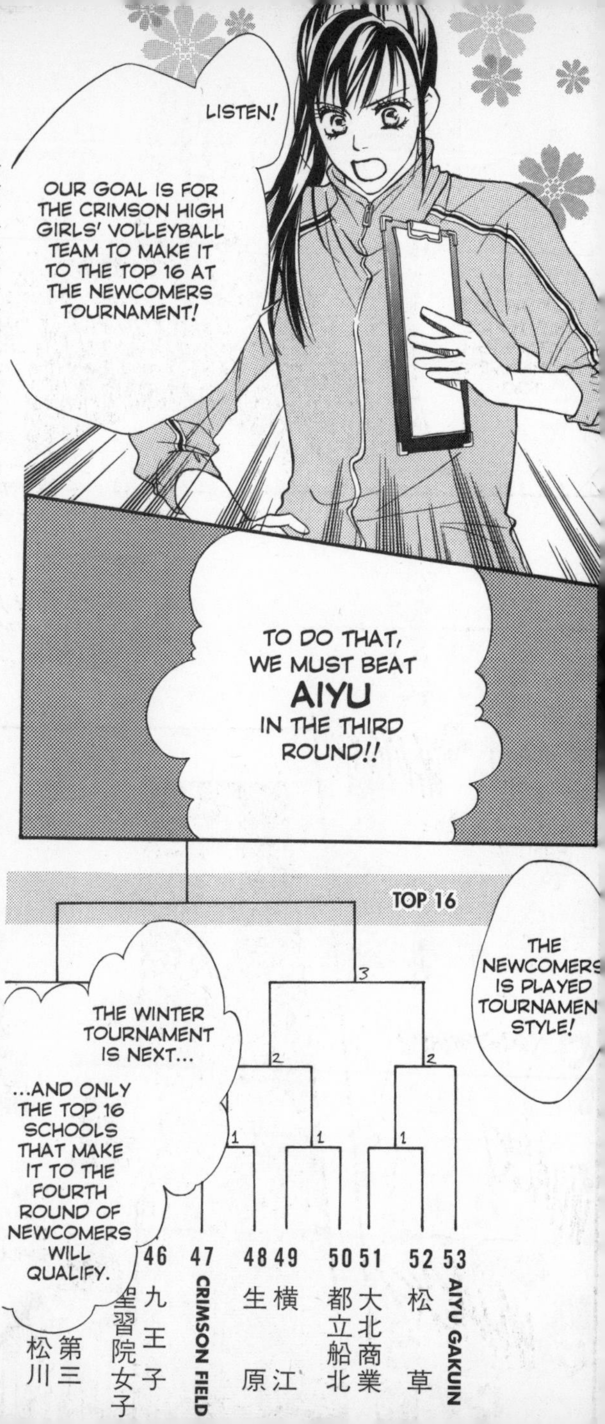
LISTEN!
OUR GOAL IS FOR THE CRIMSON HIGH GIRLS' VOLLEYBALL TEAM TO MAKE IT TO THE TOP 16 AT THE NEWCOMERS TOURNAMENT!
TO DO THAT, WE MUST BEAT AIYU IN THE THIRD ROUND!!
THE NEWCOMERS IS PLAYED TOURNAMEN STYLE!
TOP 16
THE WINTER TOURNAMENT IS NEXT...
...AND ONLY THE TOP 16 SCHOOLS THAT MAKE IT TO THE FOURTH ROUND OF NEWCOMERS WILL QUALIFY.
3
2
2
1
1
1
46
47
48
49
50
51
52
53
第三
松川
九王子
星習院女子
CRIMSON FIELD
生原
横江
都立船北
大北商業
松草
AIYU GAKUIN

MITSUBA CLUB

VoL. 2

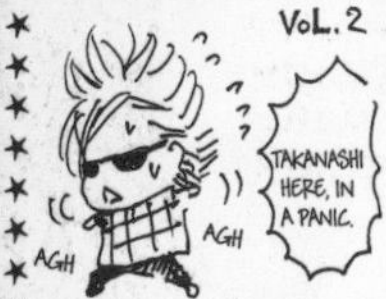
TAKANASHI HERE, IN A PANIC.
AGH
AGH

IN VOLUME 9 TAKANASHI MIXED UP ANNIE AND EMMA IN THE YELLOW MONKEY BAND. THAT'S RIGHT. IT WAS EMMA. APOLOGIES TO ALL FANS. MY BAD. WHEN WILL THEY RESUME PLAYING AGAIN? STILL NOT YET? I'M WAITING.

I PICKED UP A CAT IN NOVEMBER. SHE WAS ALL RAGGED AND SCRAWNY BUT IS TOTALLY HEALTHY NOW.

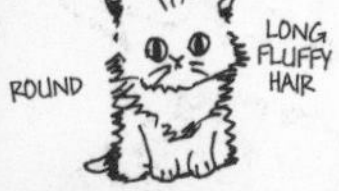
ROUND
LONG FLUFFY HAIR

I ALREADY HAVE A WHITE CAT NAMED CHIRO SO I WAS REALLY WORRIED ABOUT WHETHER THEY'D GET ALONG. WELL, I WOULDN'T SAY THEY LOVE EACH OTHER, BUT AT LEAST THEY'VE GOTTEN USED TO EACH OTHER. I CAN BREATHE A SIGH OF RELIEF. RECENTLY I'VE TAKEN TO CALLING CHIRO "BIG BROTHER," BUT WHEN BIG BROTHER SIDLES BY SHARO-TAN, HE PUNCHES HER.

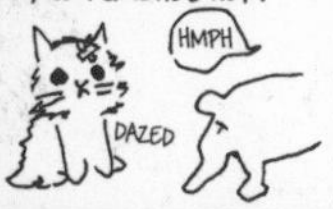
HMPH
DAZED

SHARO JUST LOOKS BLANK. MAYBE SHE'S NOT SENSITIVE TO THE PUNCHES. SHE'S VERY CUTE.

AT MY WORKPLACE, IF A CAT FALLS ASLEEP IN A CUTE POSITION, THEN AN IMPROMPTU PHOTO SHOOT STARTS.

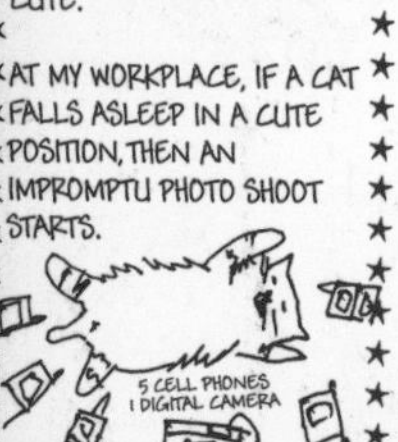
5 CELL PHONES
1 DIGITAL CAMERA

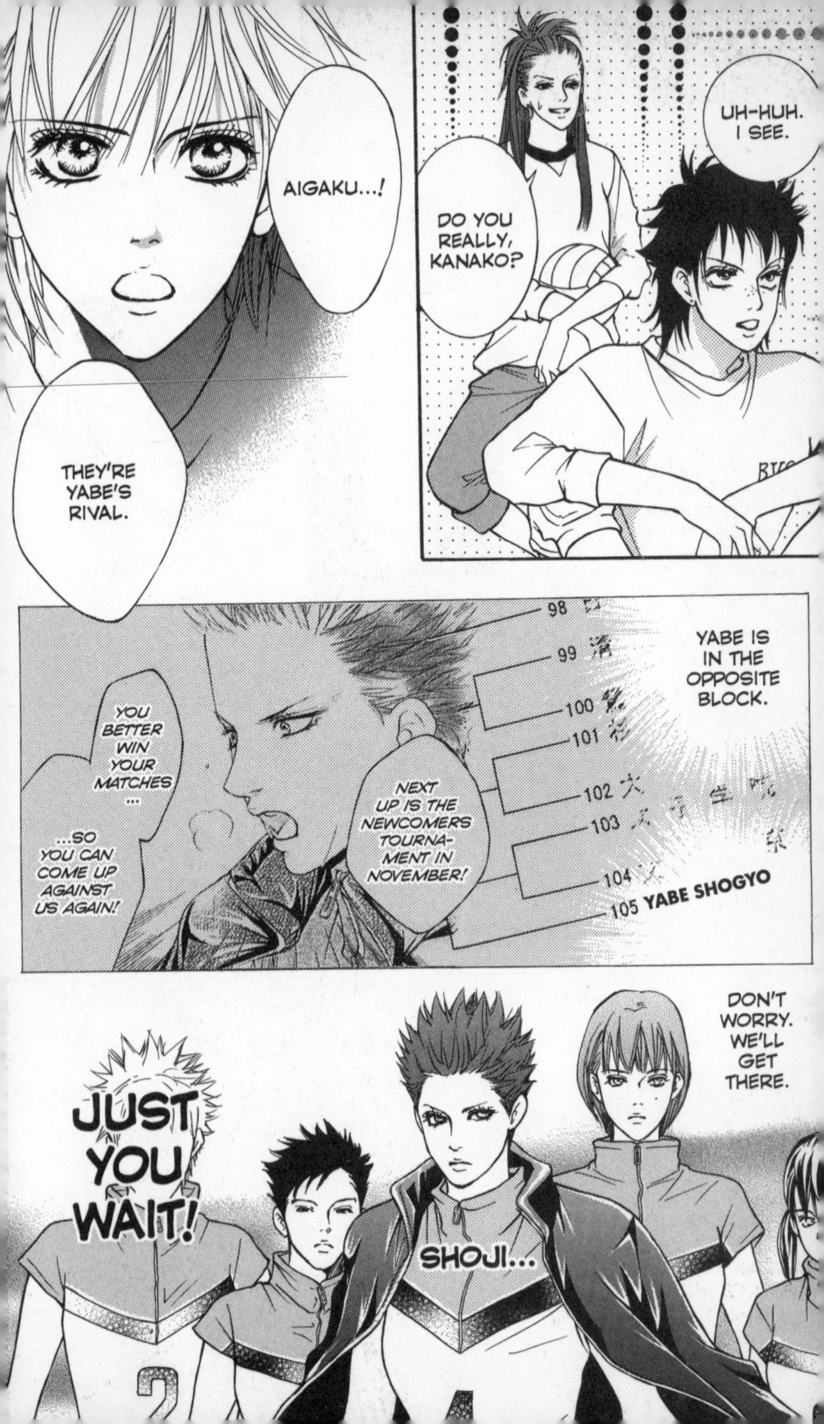
UH-HUH. I SEE.
DO YOU REALLY, KANAKO?
AIGAKU...!
THEY'RE YABE'S RIVAL.
YABE IS IN THE OPPOSITE BLOCK.
98
99
100
101
102
103
104
105 YABE SHOGYO
NEXT UP IS THE NEWCOMERS TOURNAMENT IN NOVEMBER!
YOU BETTER WIN YOUR MATCHES...
...SO YOU CAN COME UP AGAINST US AGAIN!
DON'T WORRY. WE'LL GET THERE.
SHOJI...
JUST YOU WAIT!

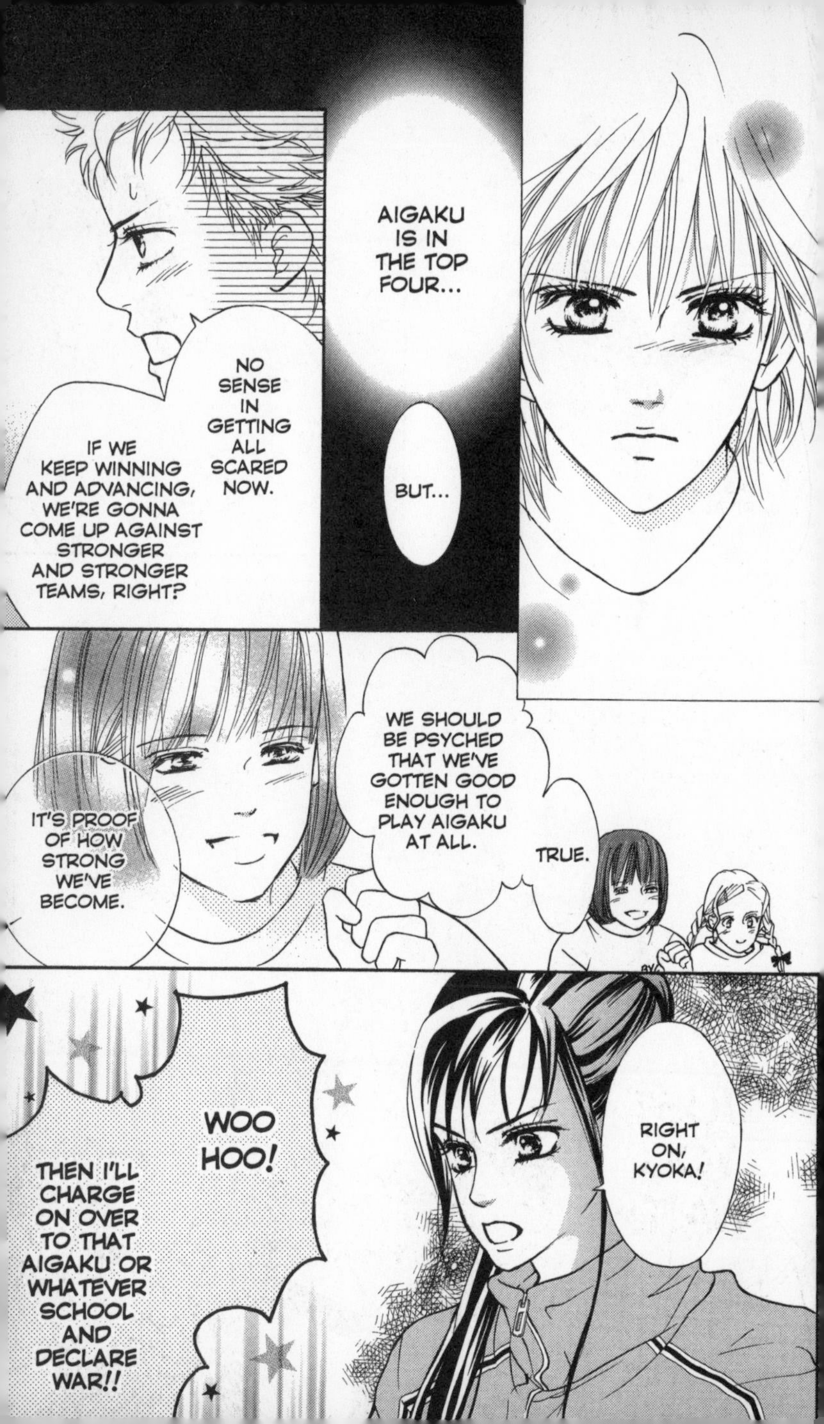
AIGAKU IS IN THE TOP FOUR...
BUT...
NO SENSE IN GETTING ALL SCARED NOW.
IF WE KEEP WINNING AND ADVANCING, WE'RE GONNA COME UP AGAINST STRONGER AND STRONGER TEAMS, RIGHT?
WE SHOULD BE PSYCHED THAT WE'VE GOTTEN GOOD ENOUGH TO PLAY AIGAKU AT ALL.
IT'S PROOF OF HOW STRONG WE'VE BECOME.
TRUE.
RIGHT ON, KYOKA!
WOO HOO!
THEN I'LL CHARGE ON OVER TO THAT AIGAKU OR WHATEVER SCHOOL AND DECLARE WAR!!

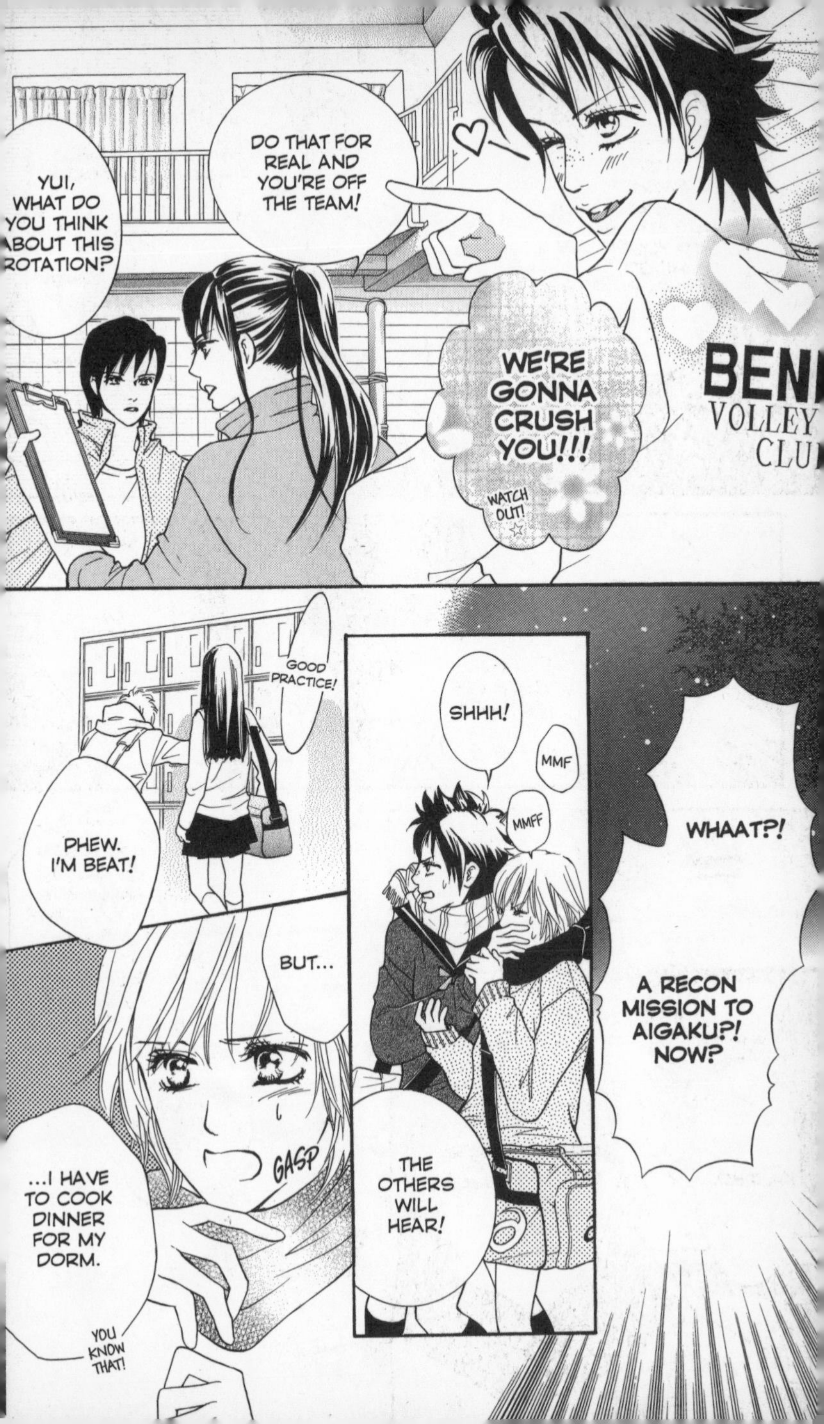
WE'RE GONNA CRUSH YOU!!!
WATCH OUT! ☆
BEN
VOLLEY
CLU
DO THAT FOR REAL AND YOU'RE OFF THE TEAM!
YUI, WHAT DO YOU THINK ABOUT THIS ROTATION?
WHAAT?!
A RECON MISSION TO AIGAKU?! NOW?
SHHH!
MMF
MMFF
THE OTHERS WILL HEAR!
GOOD PRACTICE!
PHEW. I'M BEAT!
BUT...
GASP
...I HAVE TO COOK DINNER FOR MY DORM.
YOU KNOW THAT!

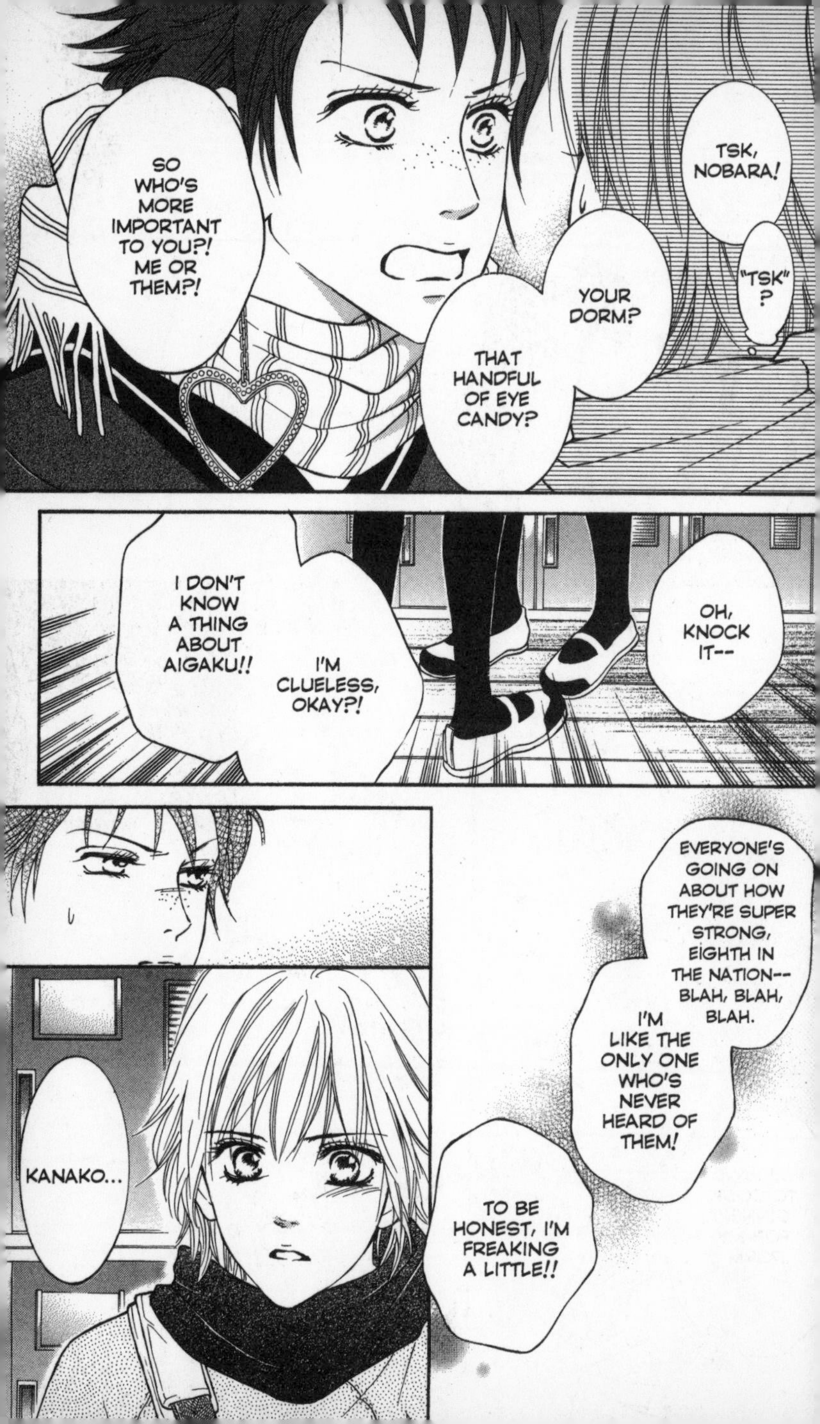
TSK, NOBARA!
"TSK"?
YOUR DORM?
THAT HANDFUL OF EYE CANDY?
SO WHO'S MORE IMPORTANT TO YOU?! ME OR THEM?!
OH, KNOCK IT--
I DON'T KNOW A THING ABOUT AIGAKU!! I'M CLUELESS, OKAY?!
EVERYONE'S GOING ON ABOUT HOW THEY'RE SUPER STRONG, EIGHTH IN THE NATION-- BLAH, BLAH, BLAH.
I'M LIKE THE ONLY ONE WHO'S NEVER HEARD OF THEM!
TO BE HONEST, I'M FREAKING A LITTLE!!
KANAKO...

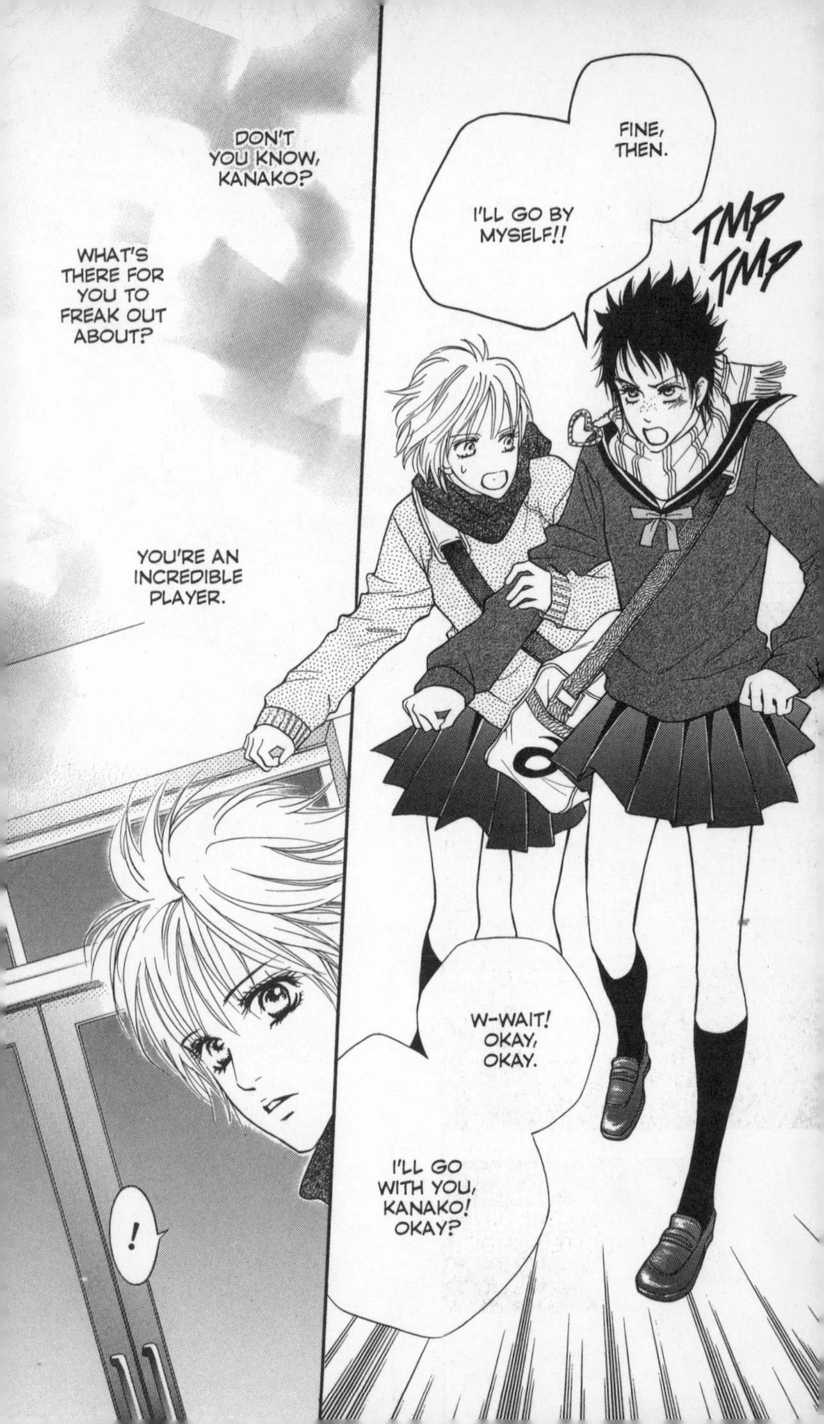
FINE, THEN.
I'LL GO BY MYSELF!!
TMP TMP
W-WAIT! OKAY, OKAY.
I'LL GO WITH YOU, KANAKO! OKAY?
DON'T YOU KNOW, KANAKO?
WHAT'S THERE FOR YOU TO FREAK OUT ABOUT?
YOU'RE AN INCREDIBLE PLAYER.
!

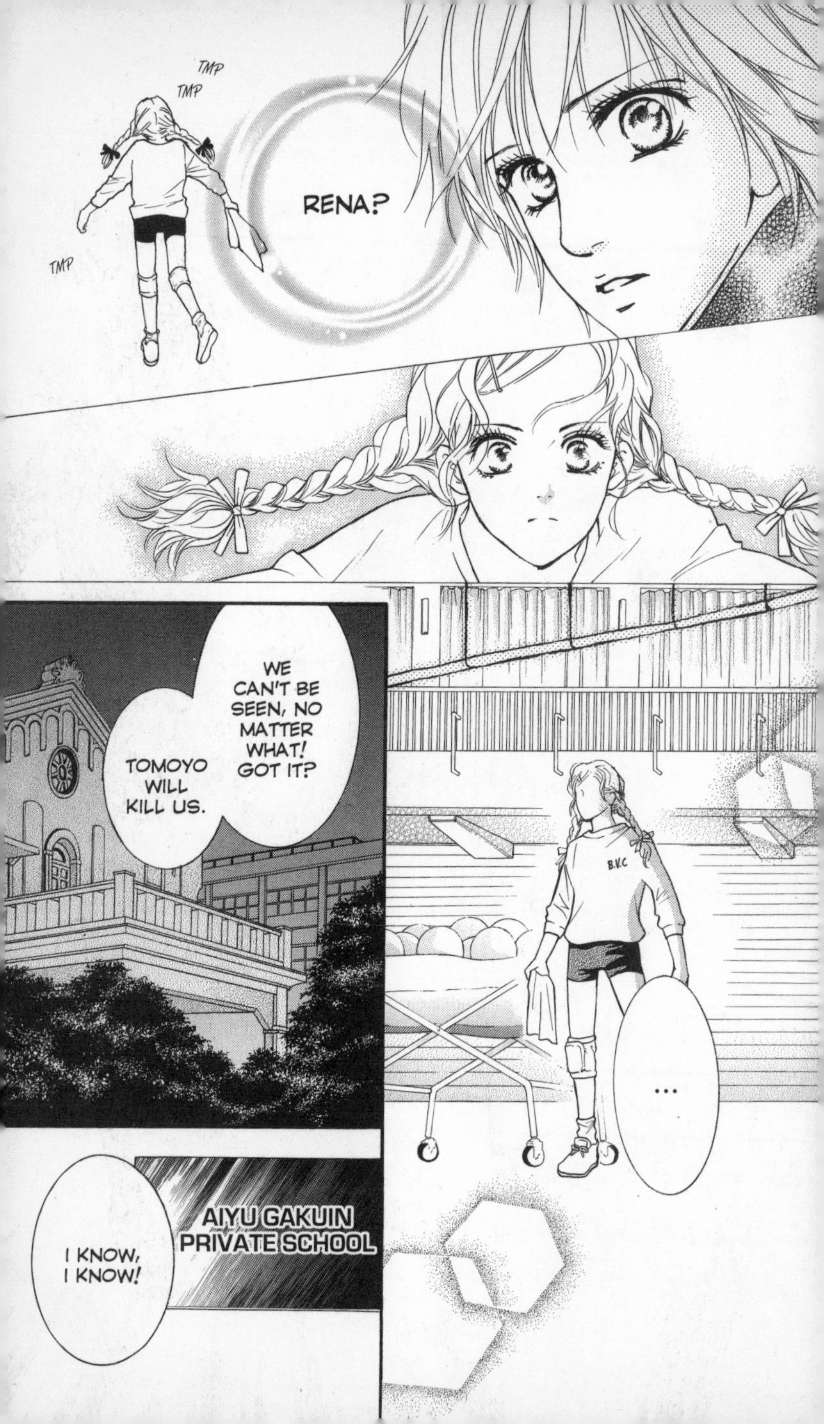
RENA?
TMP
TMP
TMP
B.V.C
...
WE CAN'T BE SEEN, NO MATTER WHAT! GOT IT?
TOMOYO WILL KILL US.
AIYU GAKUIN PRIVATE SCHOOL
I KNOW, I KNOW!

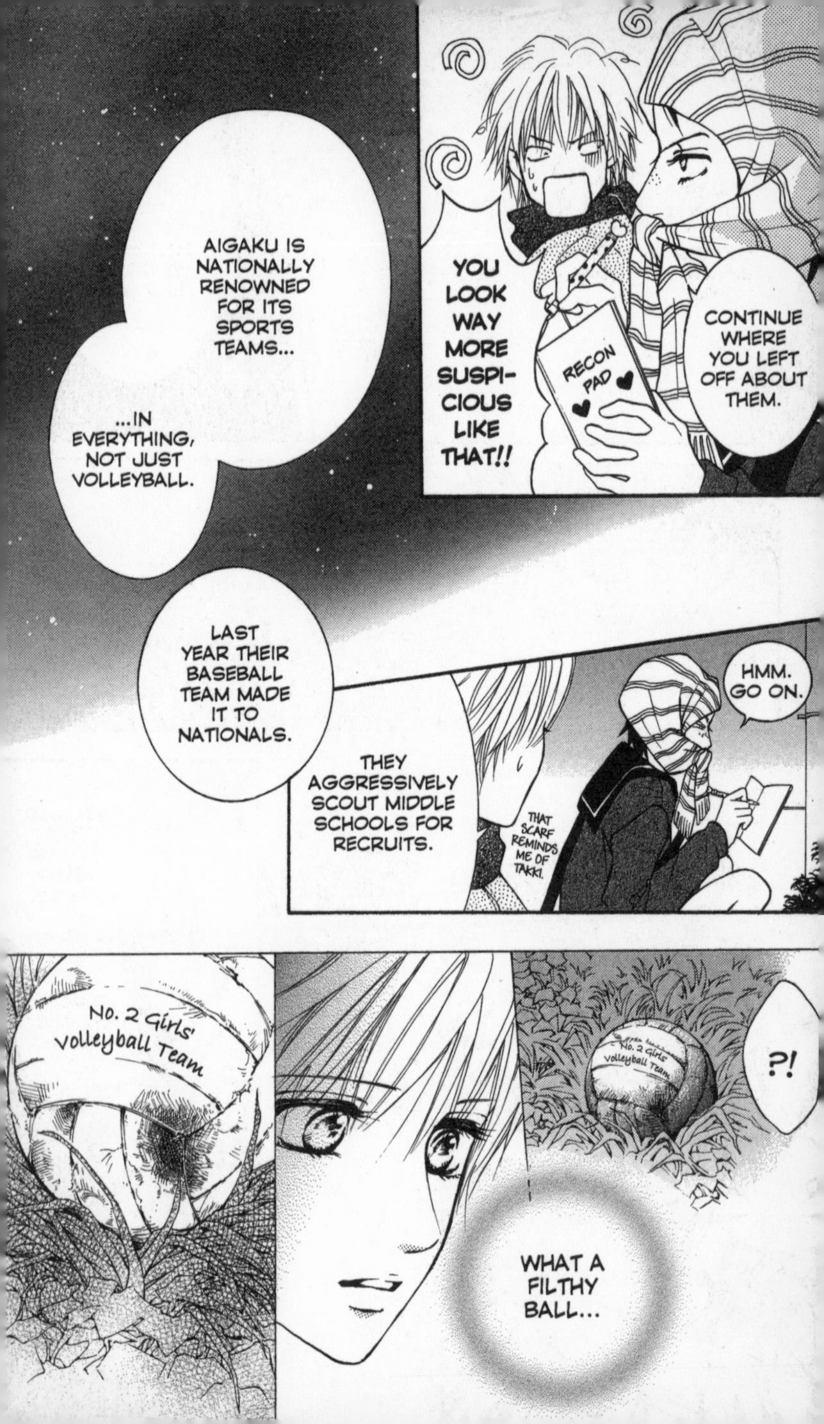
CONTINUE WHERE YOU LEFT OFF ABOUT THEM.
RECON PAD
YOU LOOK WAY MORE SUSPICIOUS LIKE THAT!!
AIGAKU IS NATIONALLY RENOWNED FOR ITS SPORTS TEAMS...
...IN EVERYTHING, NOT JUST VOLLEYBALL.
HMM. GO ON.
LAST YEAR THEIR BASEBALL TEAM MADE IT TO NATIONALS.
THEY AGGRESSIVELY SCOUT MIDDLE SCHOOLS FOR RECRUITS.
THAT SCARF REMINDS ME OF TAKKI.
No. 2 Girls volleyball Team
?!
WHAT A FILTHY BALL...
No. 2 Girls' volleyball Team

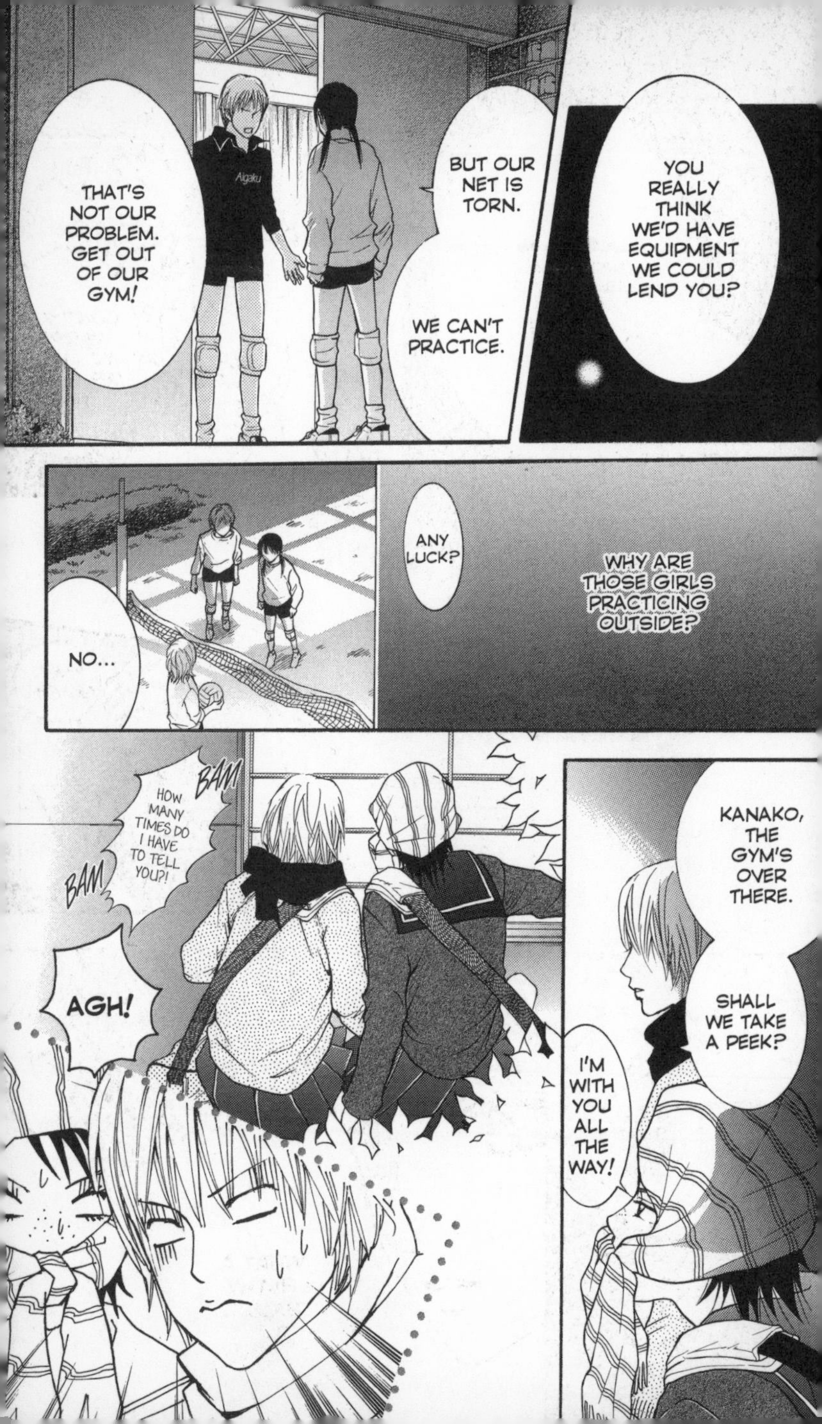
YOU REALLY THINK WE'D HAVE EQUIPMENT WE COULD LEND YOU?
BUT OUR NET IS TORN.
WE CAN'T PRACTICE.
THAT'S NOT OUR PROBLEM. GET OUT OF OUR GYM!
WHY ARE THOSE GIRLS PRACTICING OUTSIDE?
ANY LUCK?
NO...
KANAKO, THE GYM'S OVER THERE.
SHALL WE TAKE A PEEK?
I'M WITH YOU ALL THE WAY!
BAM
HOW MANY TIMES DO I HAVE TO TELL YOU?!
BAM
AGH!

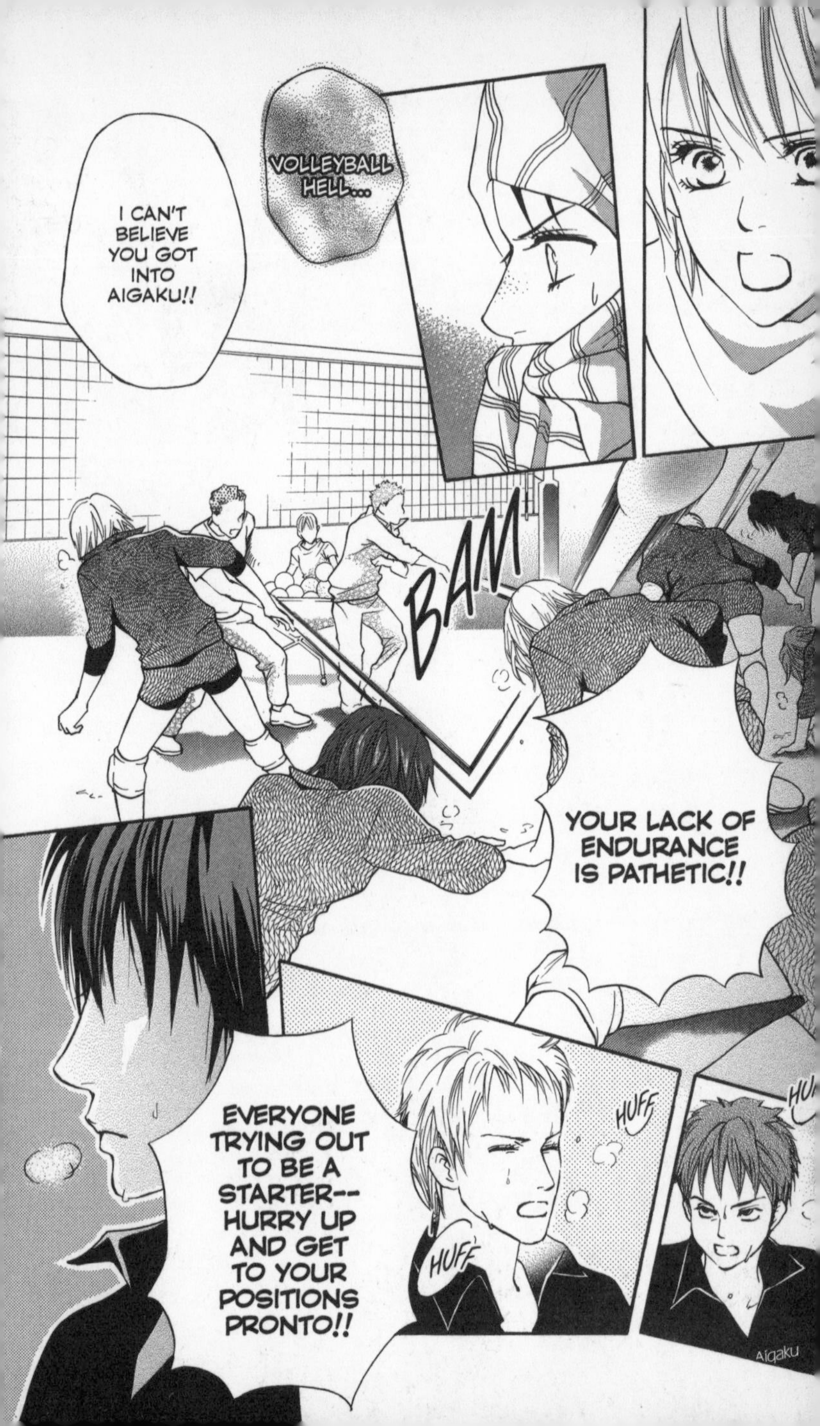
VOLLEYBALL HELL...
I CAN'T BELIEVE YOU GOT INTO AIGAKU!!
BAM
YOUR LACK OF ENDURANCE IS PATHETIC!!
HUFF
HUFF
EVERYONE TRYING OUT TO BE A STARTER-- HURRY UP AND GET TO YOUR POSITIONS PRONTO!!
Aigaku

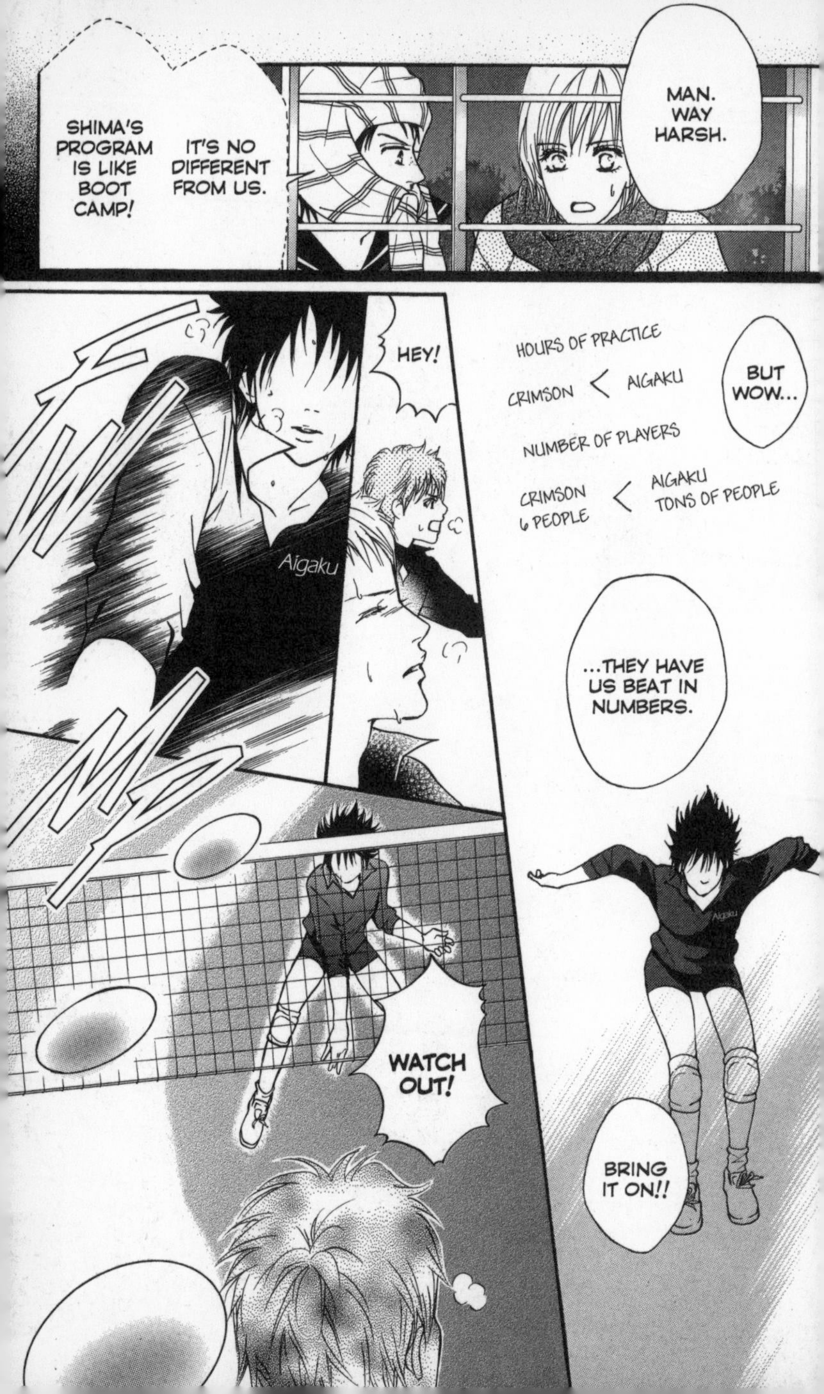

MAN. WAY HARSH.
IT'S NO DIFFERENT FROM US.
SHIMA'S PROGRAM IS LIKE BOOT CAMP!
BUT WOW...
HOURS OF PRACTICE
CRIMSON < AIGAKU
NUMBER OF PLAYERS
CRIMSON 6 PEOPLE < AIGAKU TONS OF PEOPLE
...THEY HAVE US BEAT IN NUMBERS.
BRING IT ON!!
Aigaku
HEY!
Aigaku
WATCH OUT!

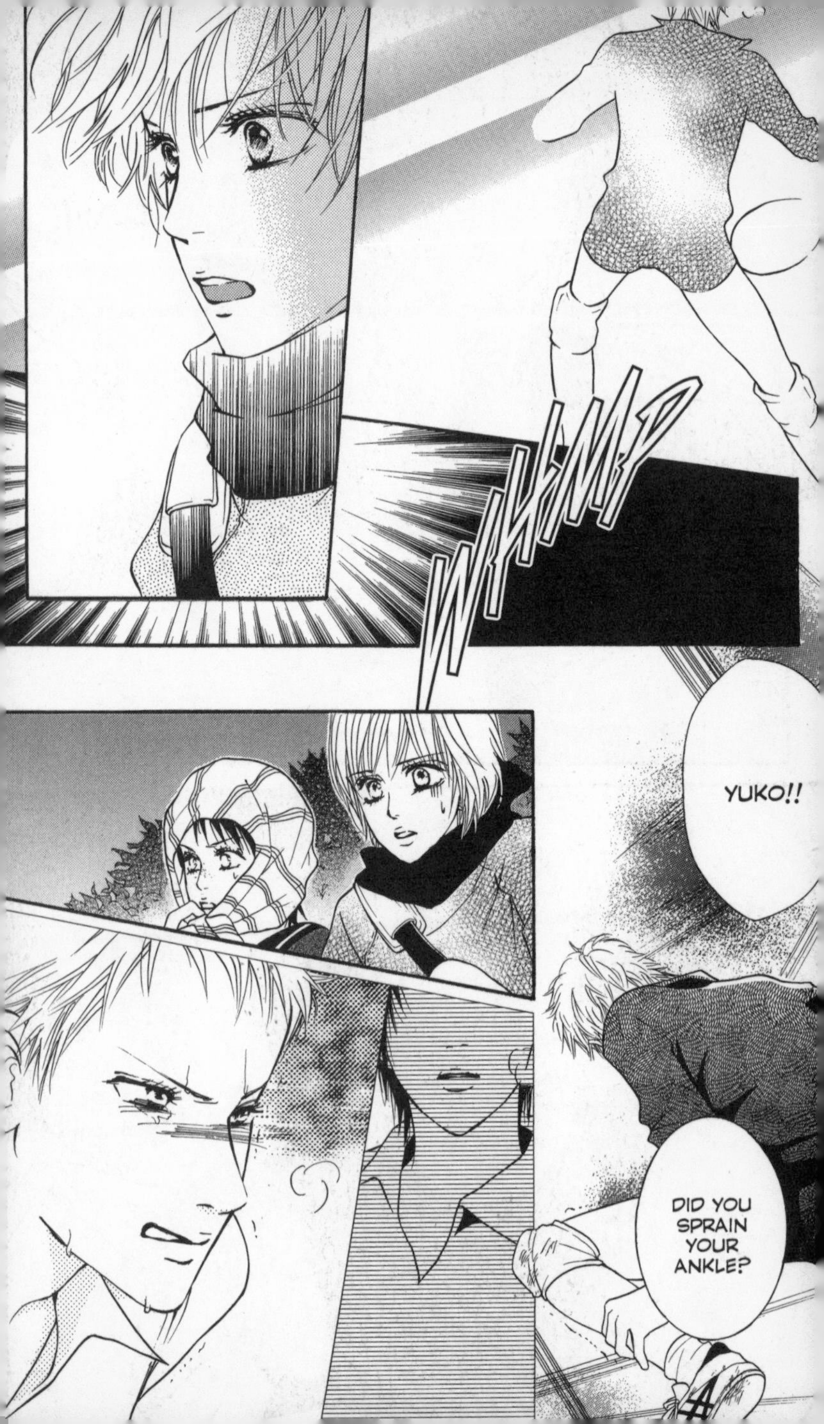
YUKO!!
DID YOU SPRAIN YOUR ANKLE?

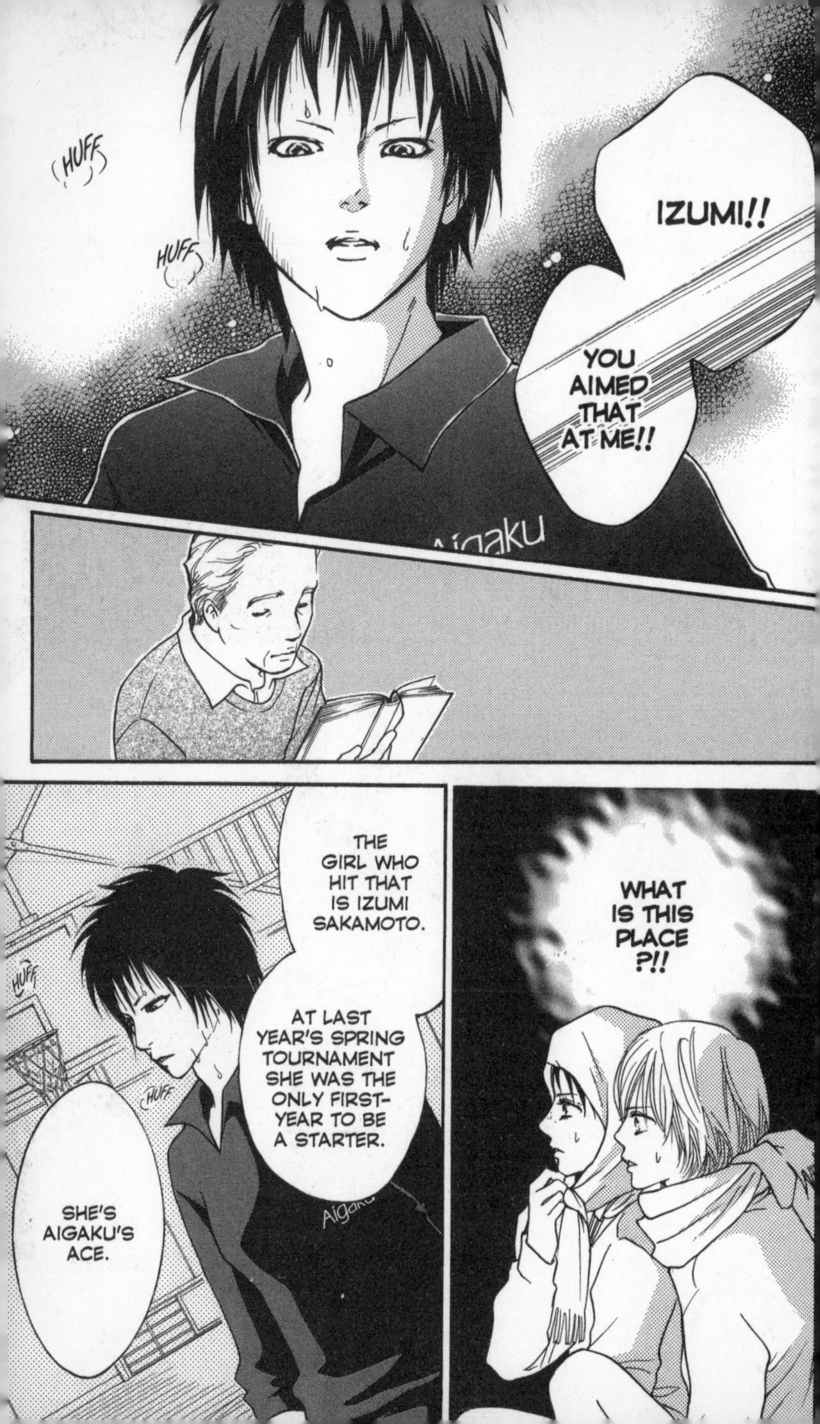
IZUMI!!
YOU AIMED THAT AT ME!!
HUFF
HUFF
Aigaku
WHAT IS THIS PLACE ?!!
THE GIRL WHO HIT THAT IS IZUMI SAKAMOTO.
AT LAST YEAR'S SPRING TOURNAMENT SHE WAS THE ONLY FIRST-YEAR TO BE A STARTER.
HUFF
HUFF
SHE'S AIGAKU'S ACE.

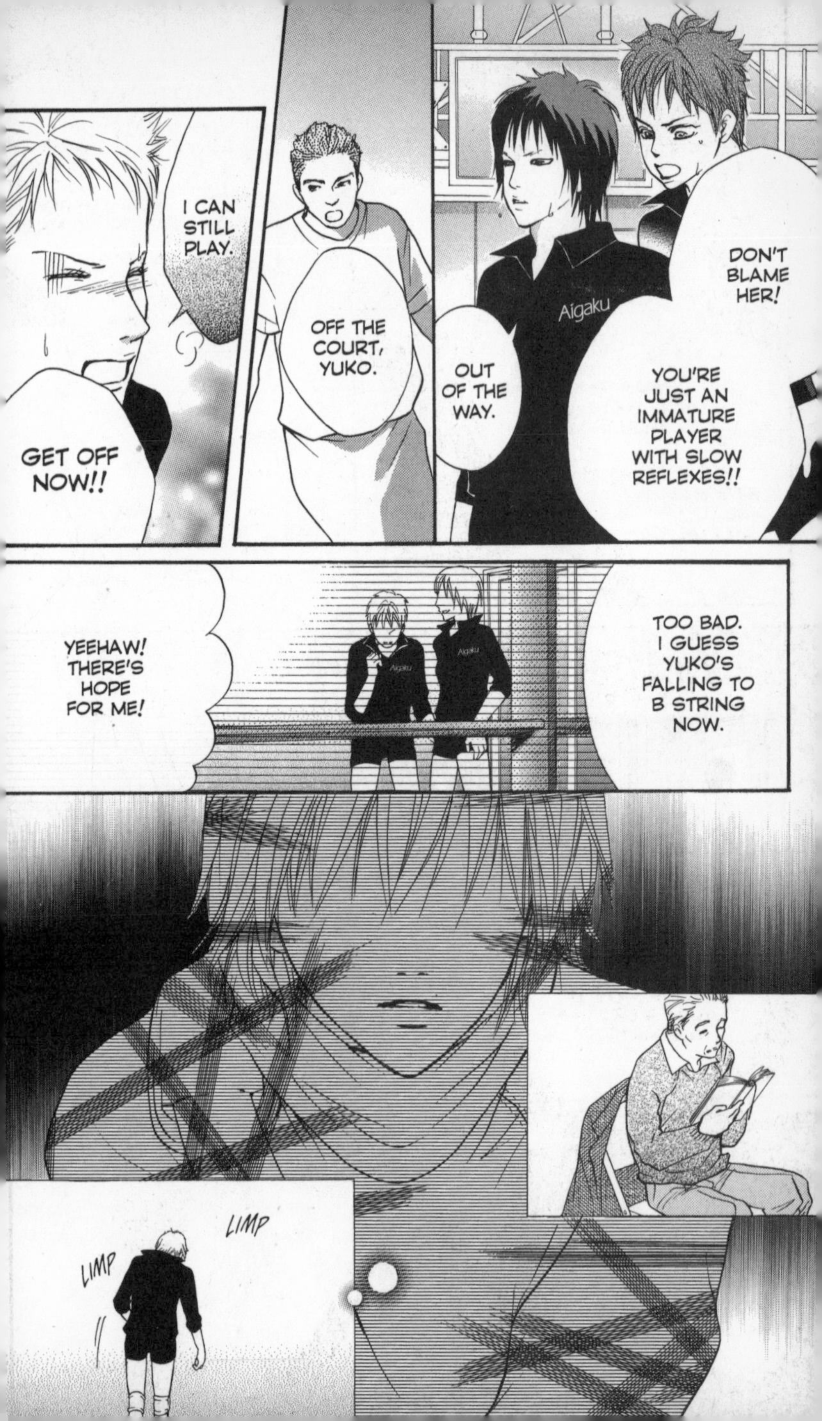
DON'T BLAME HER!
YOU'RE JUST AN IMMATURE PLAYER WITH SLOW REFLEXES!!
OUT OF THE WAY.
OFF THE COURT, YUKO.
I CAN STILL PLAY.
GET OFF NOW!!
TOO BAD. I GUESS YUKO'S FALLING TO B STRING NOW.
YEEHAW! THERE'S HOPE FOR ME!
LIMP
LIMP

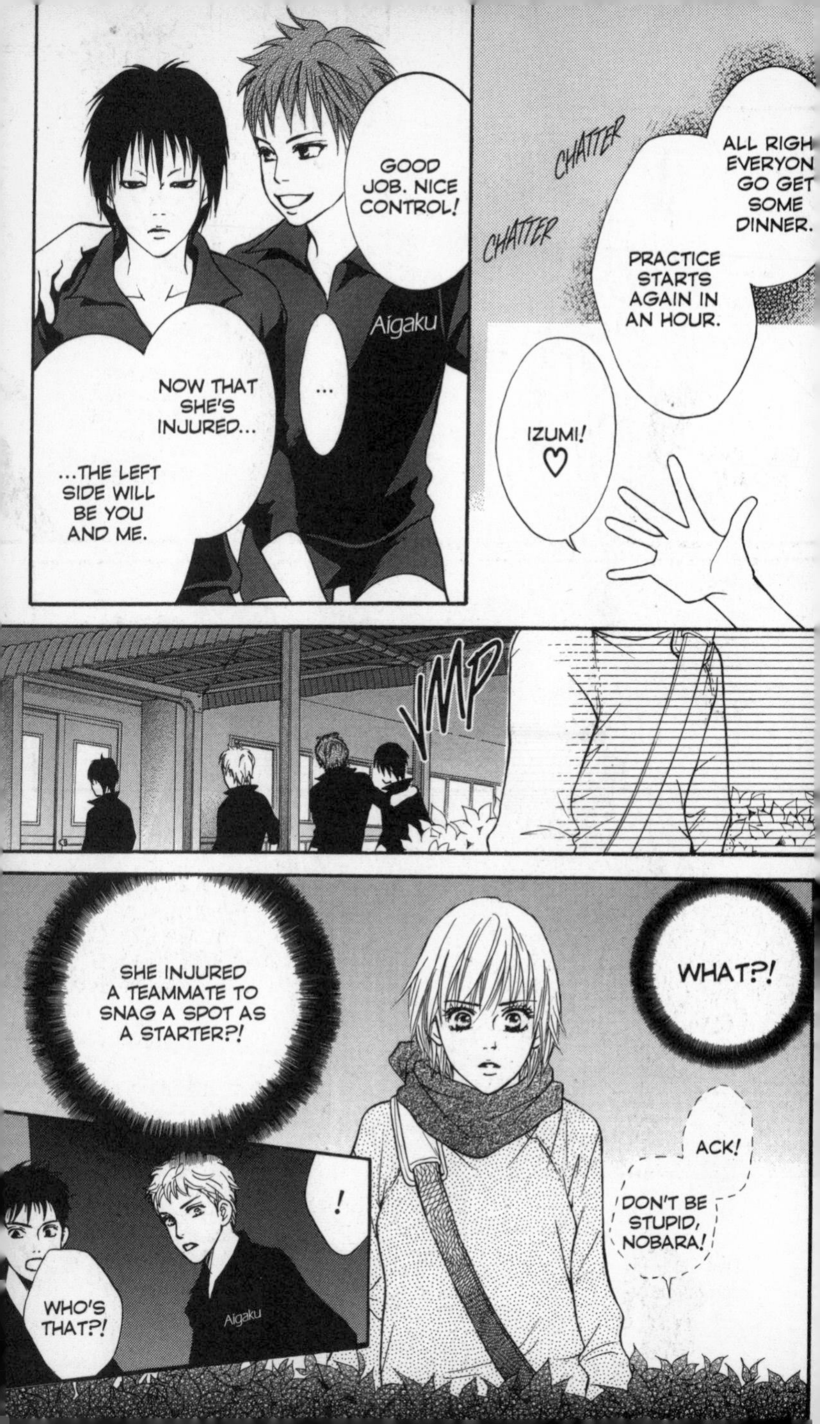
ALL RIGH EVERYON GO GET SOME DINNER.
PRACTICE STARTS AGAIN IN AN HOUR.
CHATTER
CHATTER
IZUMI! ♡
GOOD JOB. NICE CONTROL!
Aigaku
...
NOW THAT SHE'S INJURED...
...THE LEFT SIDE WILL BE YOU AND ME.
VMP
WHAT?!
SHE INJURED A TEAMMATE TO SNAG A SPOT AS A STARTER?!
ACK!
DON'T BE STUPID, NOBARA!
!
WHO'S THAT?!
Aigaku

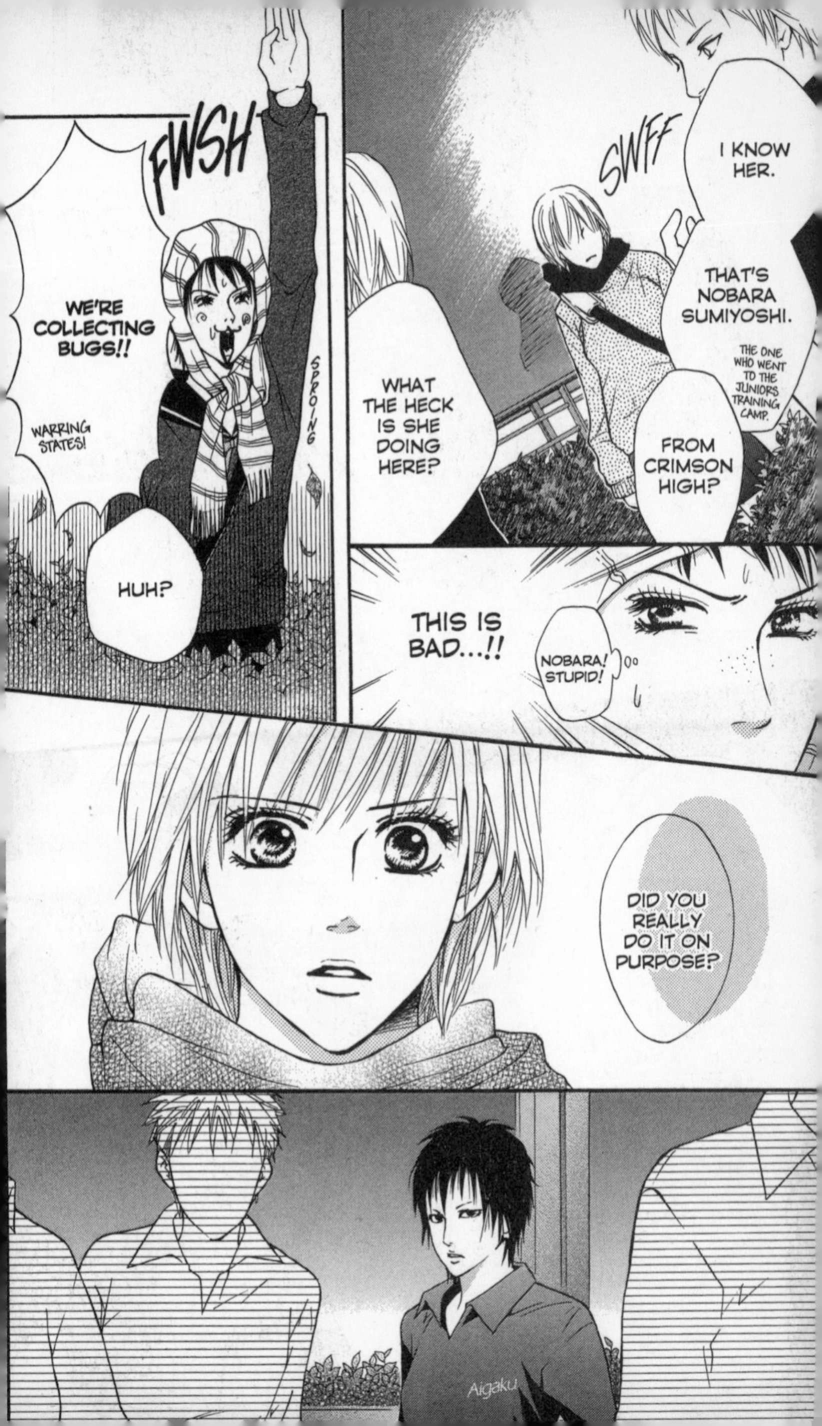
SWFF
I KNOW HER.
THAT'S NOBARA SUMIYOSHI.
THE ONE WHO WENT TO THE JUNIORS TRAINING CAMP.
FROM CRIMSON HIGH?
WHAT THE HECK IS SHE DOING HERE?
NOBARA! STUPID!
THIS IS BAD...!!
FWSH
WE'RE COLLECTING BUGS!!
WARRING STATES!
SPROING
HUH?
DID YOU REALLY DO IT ON PURPOSE?
Aigaku

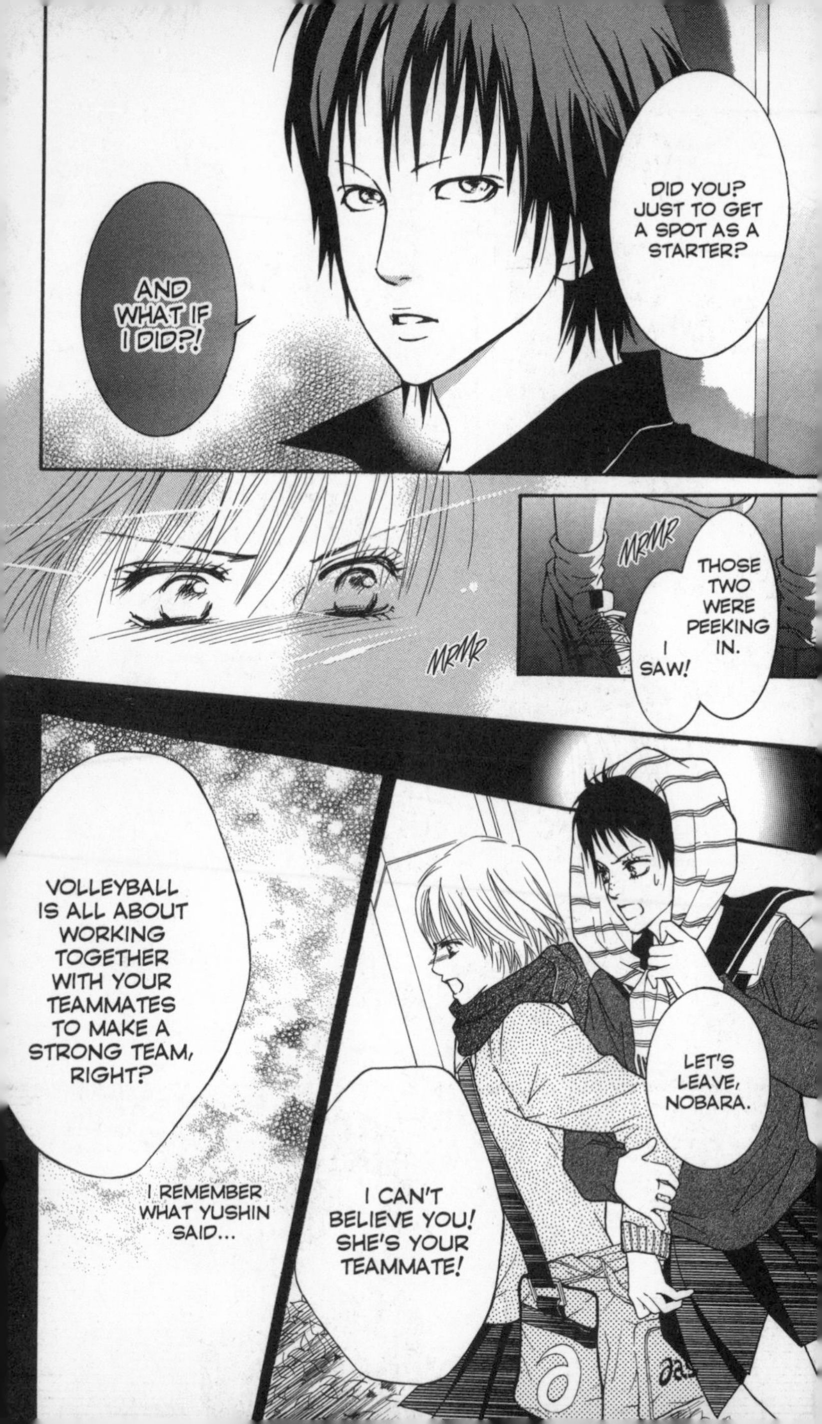
DID YOU? JUST TO GET A SPOT AS A STARTER?
AND WHAT IF I DID?!
MRMR
THOSE TWO WERE PEEKING IN. I SAW!
MRMR
LET'S LEAVE, NOBARA.
I CAN'T BELIEVE YOU! SHE'S YOUR TEAMMATE!
VOLLEYBALL IS ALL ABOUT WORKING TOGETHER WITH YOUR TEAMMATES TO MAKE A STRONG TEAM, RIGHT?
I REMEMBER WHAT YUSHIN SAID...

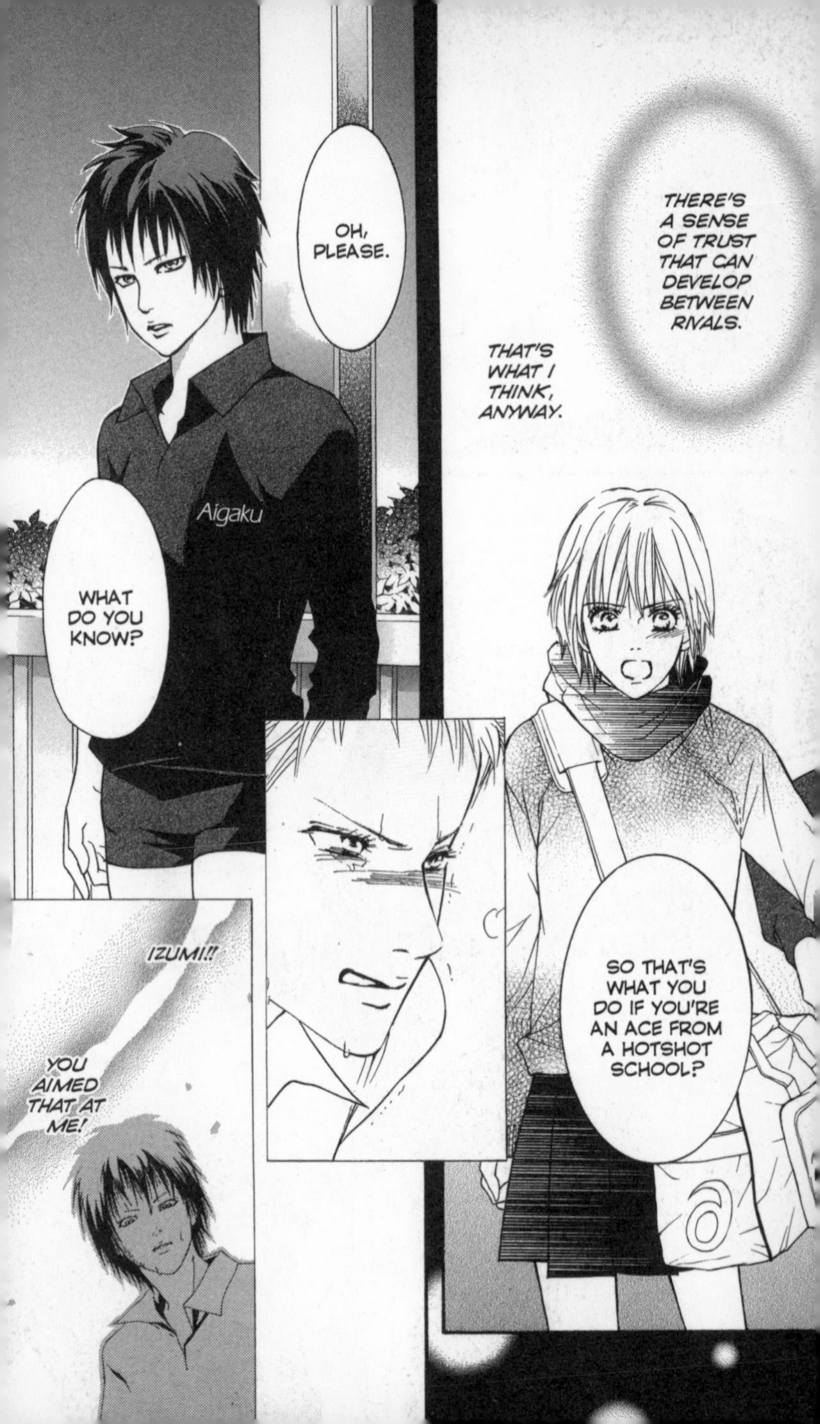
THERE'S A SENSE OF TRUST THAT CAN DEVELOP BETWEEN RIVALS.
THAT'S WHAT I THINK, ANYWAY.
SO THAT'S WHAT YOU DO IF YOU'RE AN ACE FROM A HOTSHOT SCHOOL?
OH, PLEASE.
Aigaku
WHAT DO YOU KNOW?
IZUMI!!
YOU AIMED THAT AT ME!

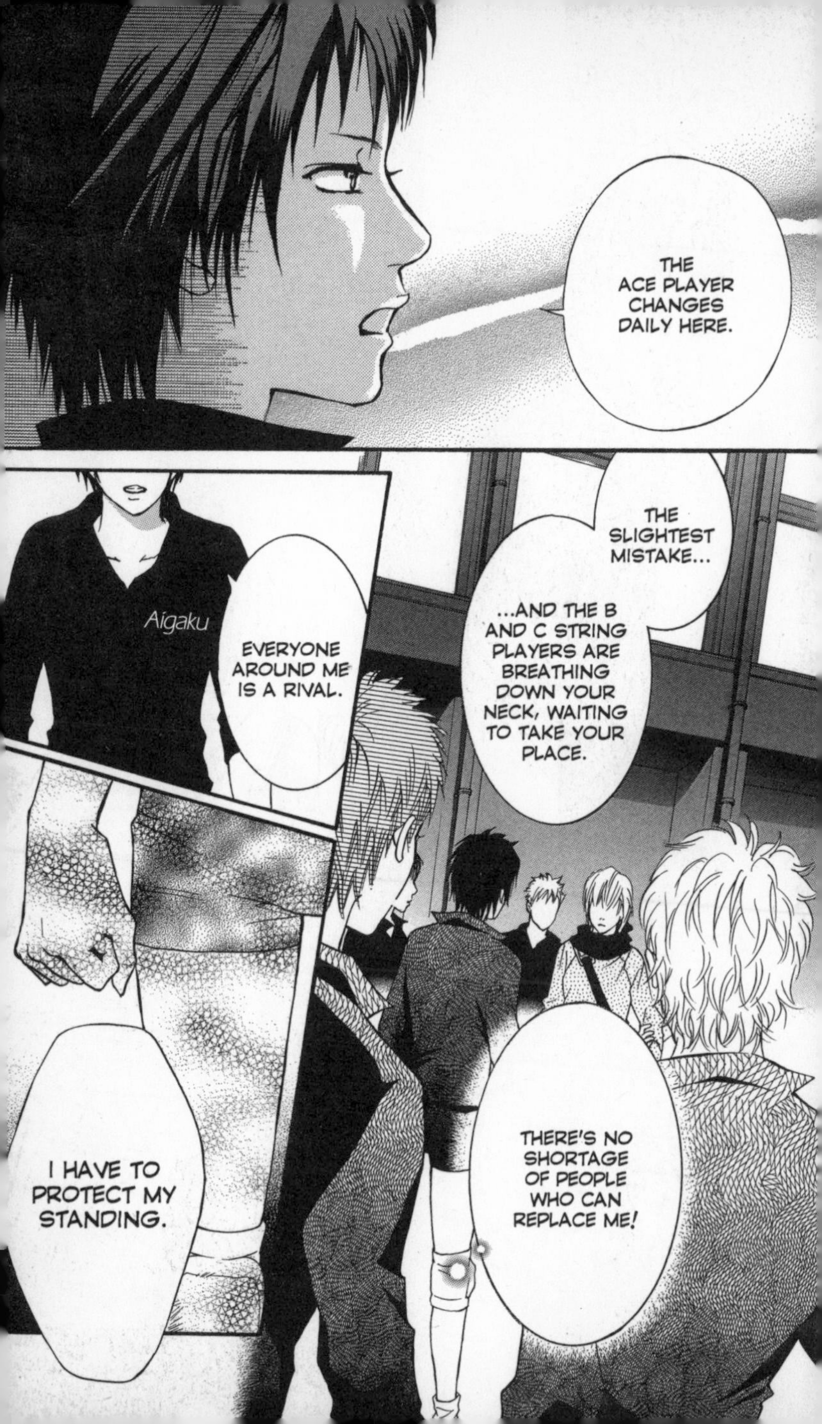
THE ACE PLAYER CHANGES DAILY HERE.
THE SLIGHTEST MISTAKE...
...AND THE B AND C STRING PLAYERS ARE BREATHING DOWN YOUR NECK, WAITING TO TAKE YOUR PLACE.
THERE'S NO SHORTAGE OF PEOPLE WHO CAN REPLACE ME!
Aigaku
EVERYONE AROUND ME IS A RIVAL.
I HAVE TO PROTECT MY STANDING.

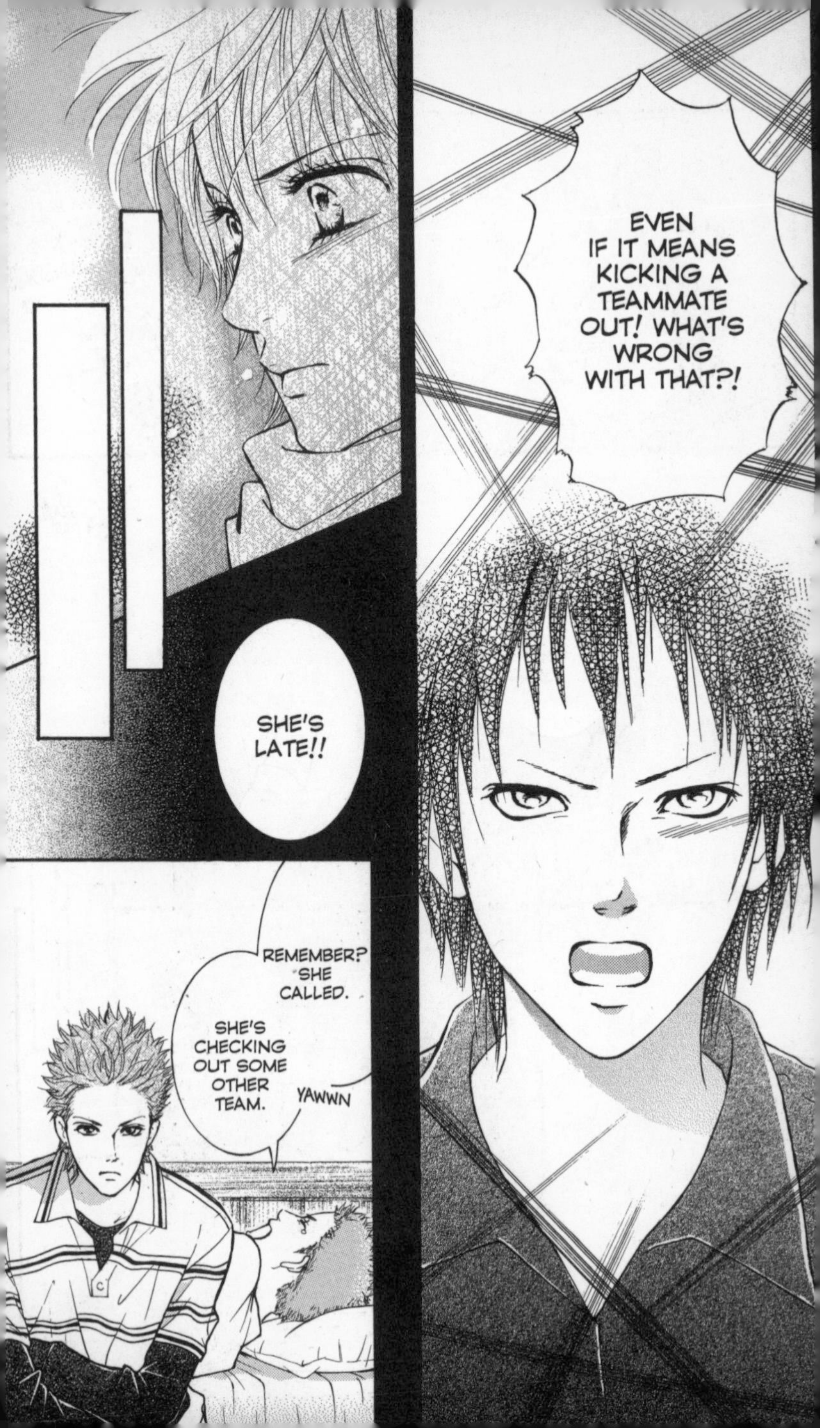
EVEN IF IT MEANS KICKING A TEAMMATE OUT! WHAT'S WRONG WITH THAT?!
SHE'S LATE!!
REMEMBER? SHE CALLED.
SHE'S CHECKING OUT SOME OTHER TEAM.
YAWWN

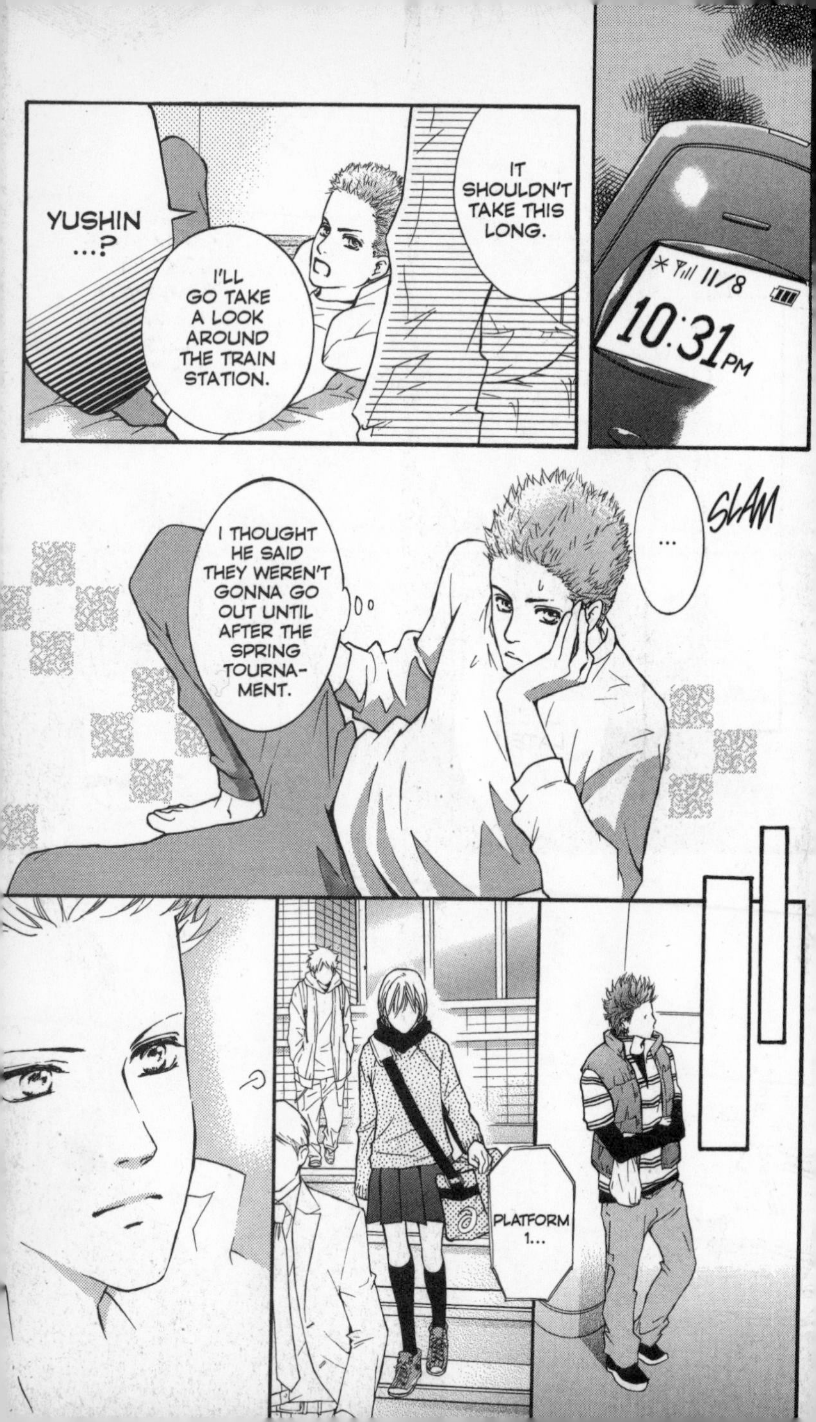
11/8
10:31PM
IT SHOULDN'T TAKE THIS LONG.
YUSHIN ...?
I'LL GO TAKE A LOOK AROUND THE TRAIN STATION.
SLAM
...
I THOUGHT HE SAID THEY WEREN'T GONNA GO OUT UNTIL AFTER THE SPRING TOURNA-MENT.
PLATFORM 1...

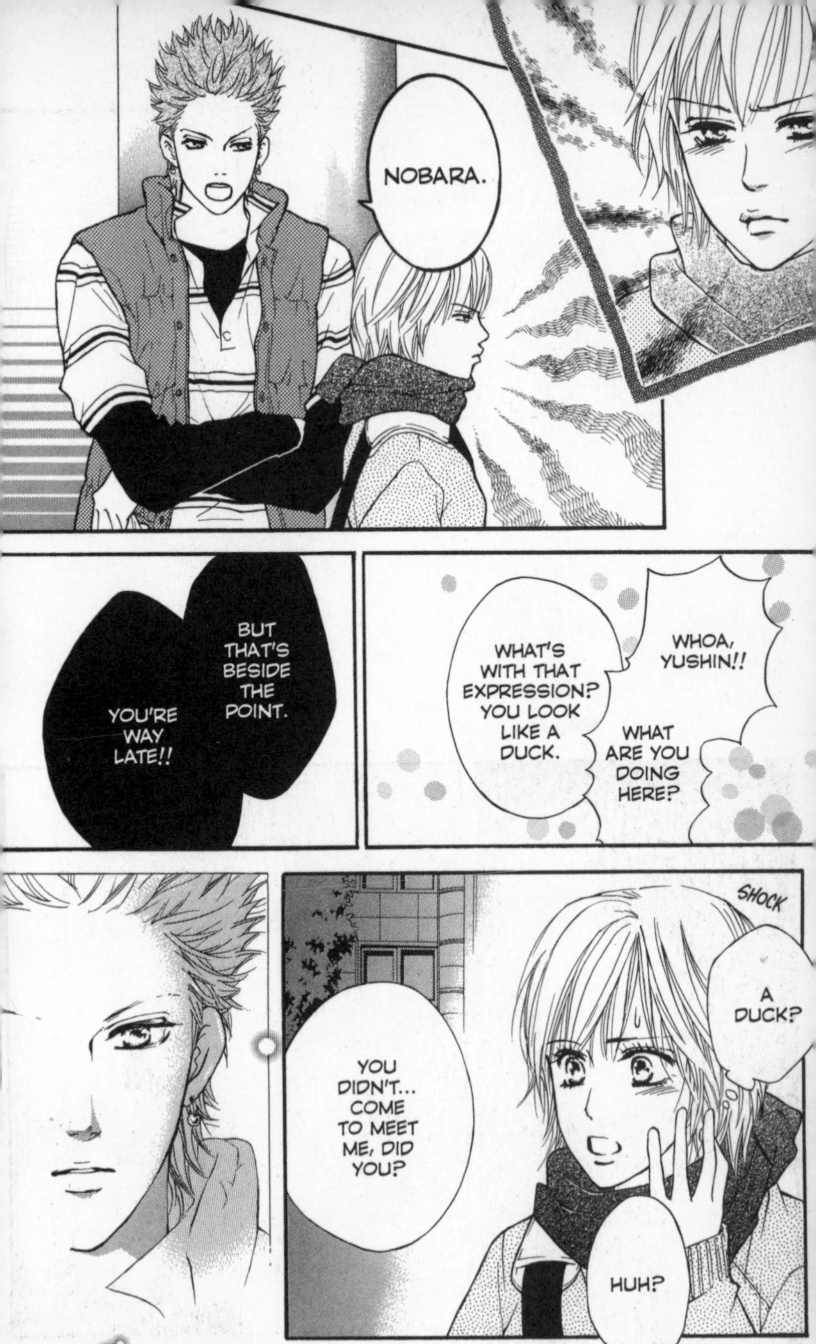
NOBARA.
WHOA, YUSHIN!!
WHAT ARE YOU DOING HERE?
WHAT'S WITH THAT EXPRESSION? YOU LOOK LIKE A DUCK.
BUT THAT'S BESIDE THE POINT.
YOU'RE WAY LATE!!
SHOCK
A DUCK?
YOU DIDN'T... COME TO MEET ME, DID YOU?
HUH?

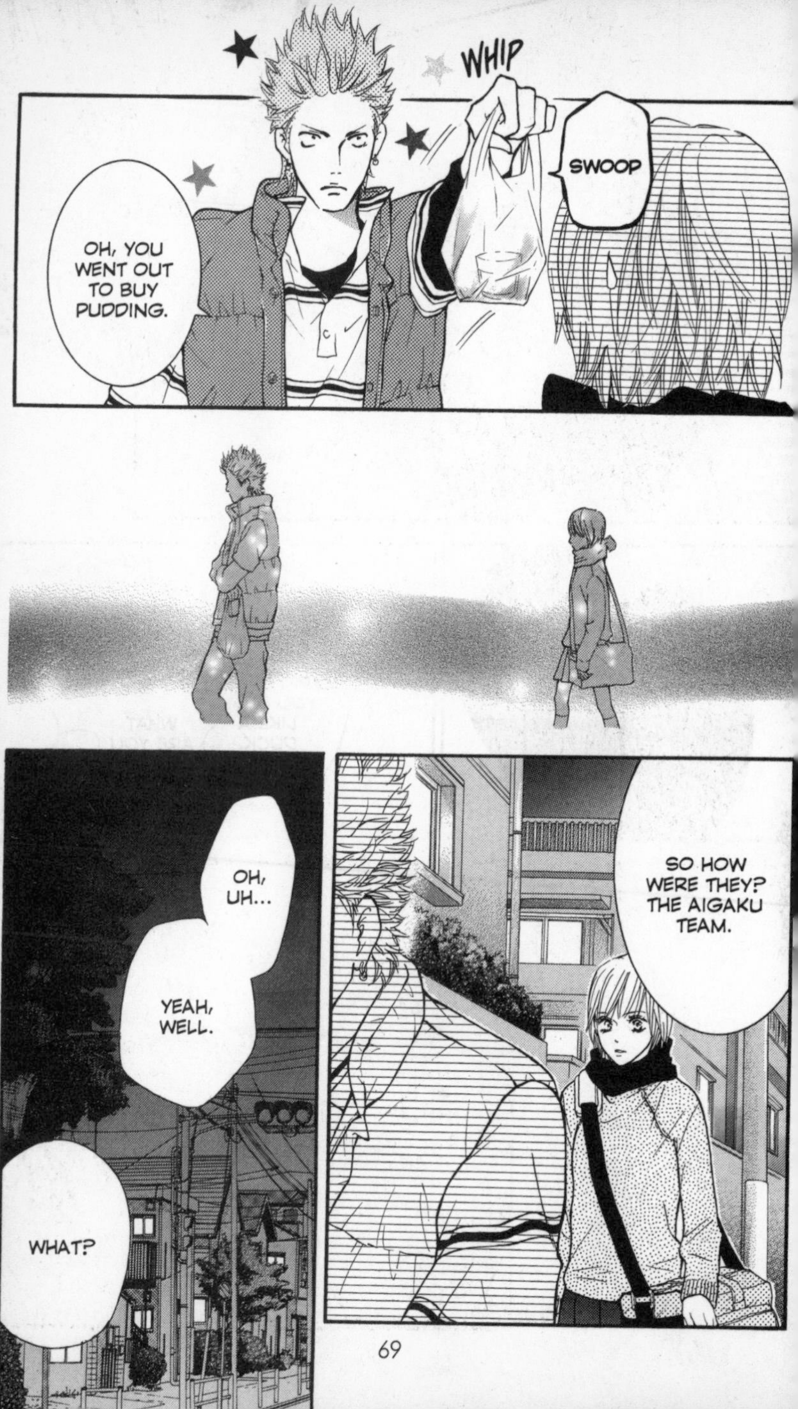
WHIP
SWOOP
OH, YOU WENT OUT TO BUY PUDDING.
SO HOW WERE THEY? THE AIGAKU TEAM.
OH, UH...
YEAH, WELL.
WHAT?

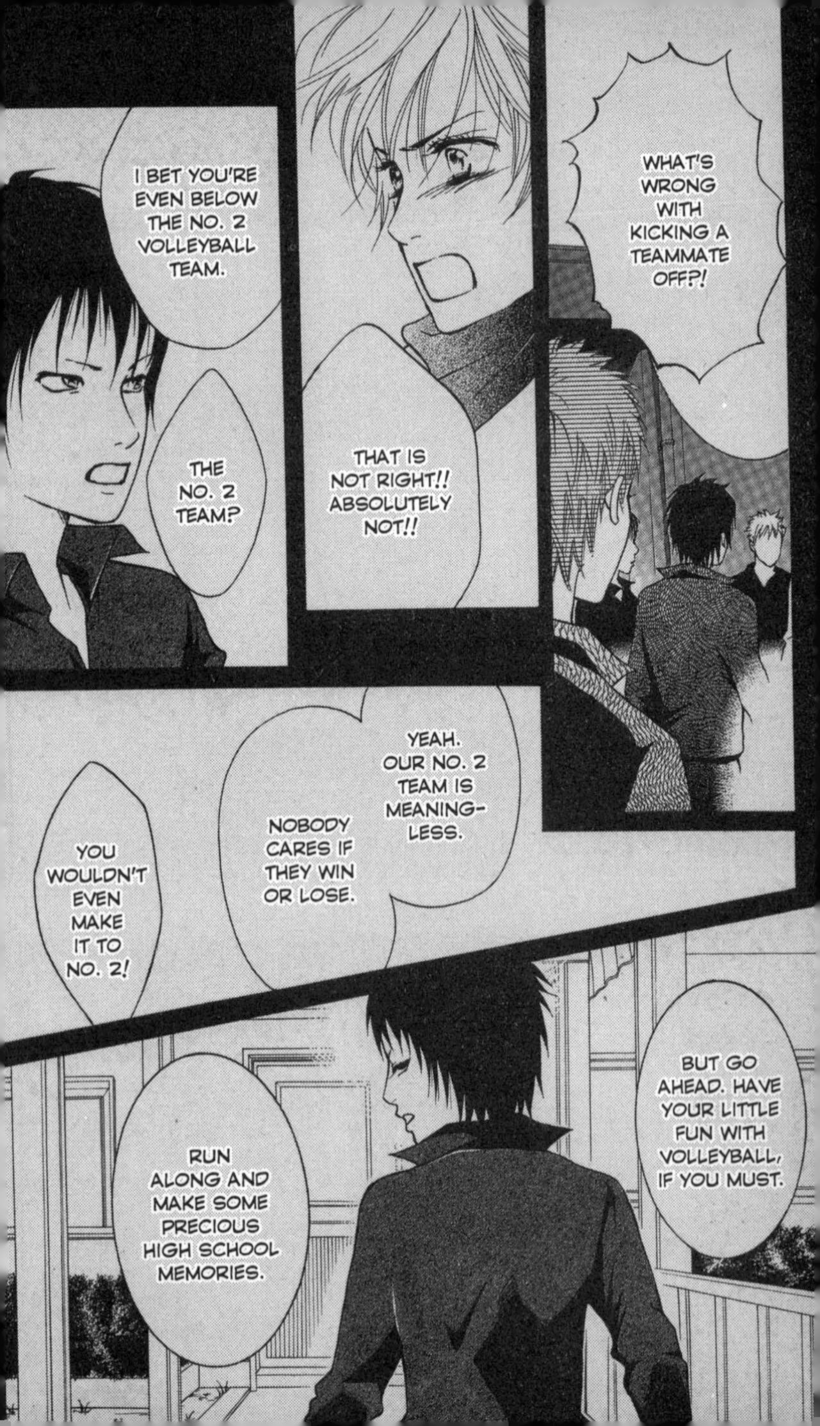
WHAT'S WRONG WITH KICKING A TEAMMATE OFF?!
THAT IS NOT RIGHT!! ABSOLUTELY NOT!!
I BET YOU'RE EVEN BELOW THE NO. 2 VOLLEYBALL TEAM.
THE NO. 2 TEAM?
YEAH. OUR NO. 2 TEAM IS MEANING-LESS.
NOBODY CARES IF THEY WIN OR LOSE.
YOU WOULDN'T EVEN MAKE IT TO NO. 2!
BUT GO AHEAD. HAVE YOUR LITTLE FUN WITH VOLLEYBALL, IF YOU MUST.
RUN ALONG AND MAKE SOME PRECIOUS HIGH SCHOOL MEMORIES.

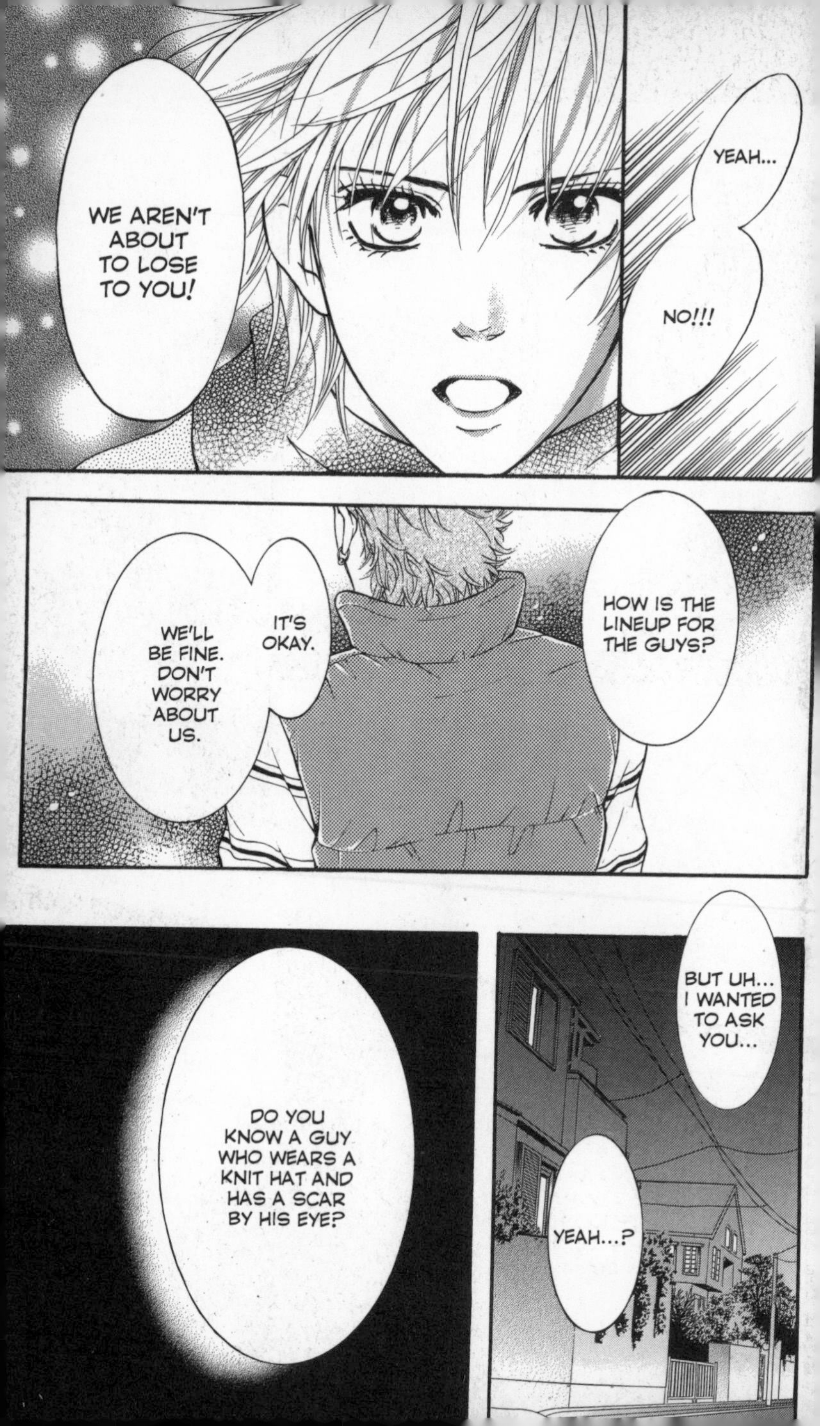
YEAH...
NO!!!
WE AREN'T ABOUT TO LOSE TO YOU!
HOW IS THE LINEUP FOR THE GUYS?
IT'S OKAY.
WE'LL BE FINE. DON'T WORRY ABOUT US.
BUT UH... I WANTED TO ASK YOU...
YEAH...?
DO YOU KNOW A GUY WHO WEARS A KNIT HAT AND HAS A SCAR BY HIS EYE?

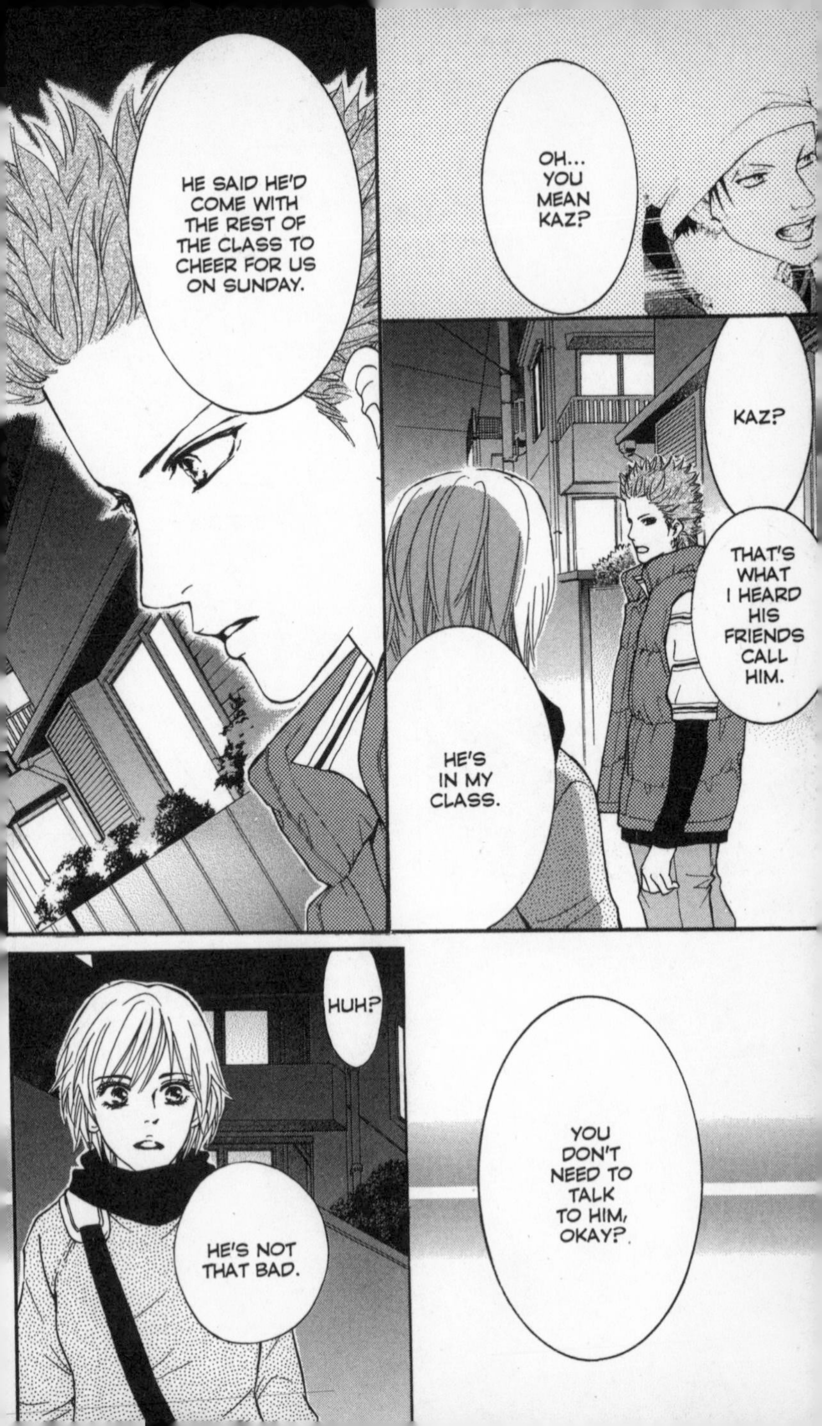
OH... YOU MEAN KAZ?
KAZ?
THAT'S WHAT I HEARD HIS FRIENDS CALL HIM.
HE'S IN MY CLASS.
HE SAID HE'D COME WITH THE REST OF THE CLASS TO CHEER FOR US ON SUNDAY.
YOU DON'T NEED TO TALK TO HIM, OKAY?
HUH?
HE'S NOT THAT BAD.

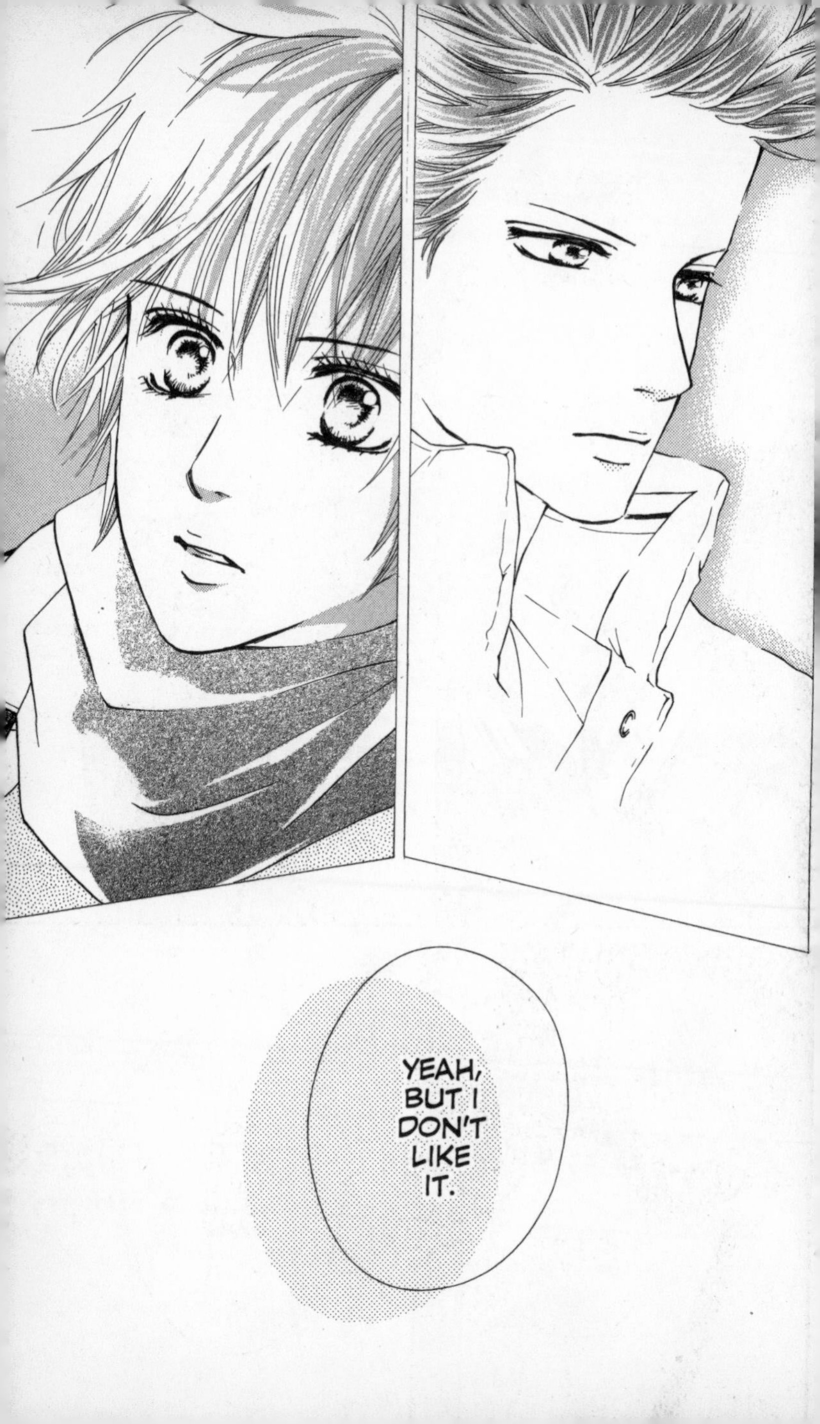
YEAH, BUT I DON'T LIKE IT.

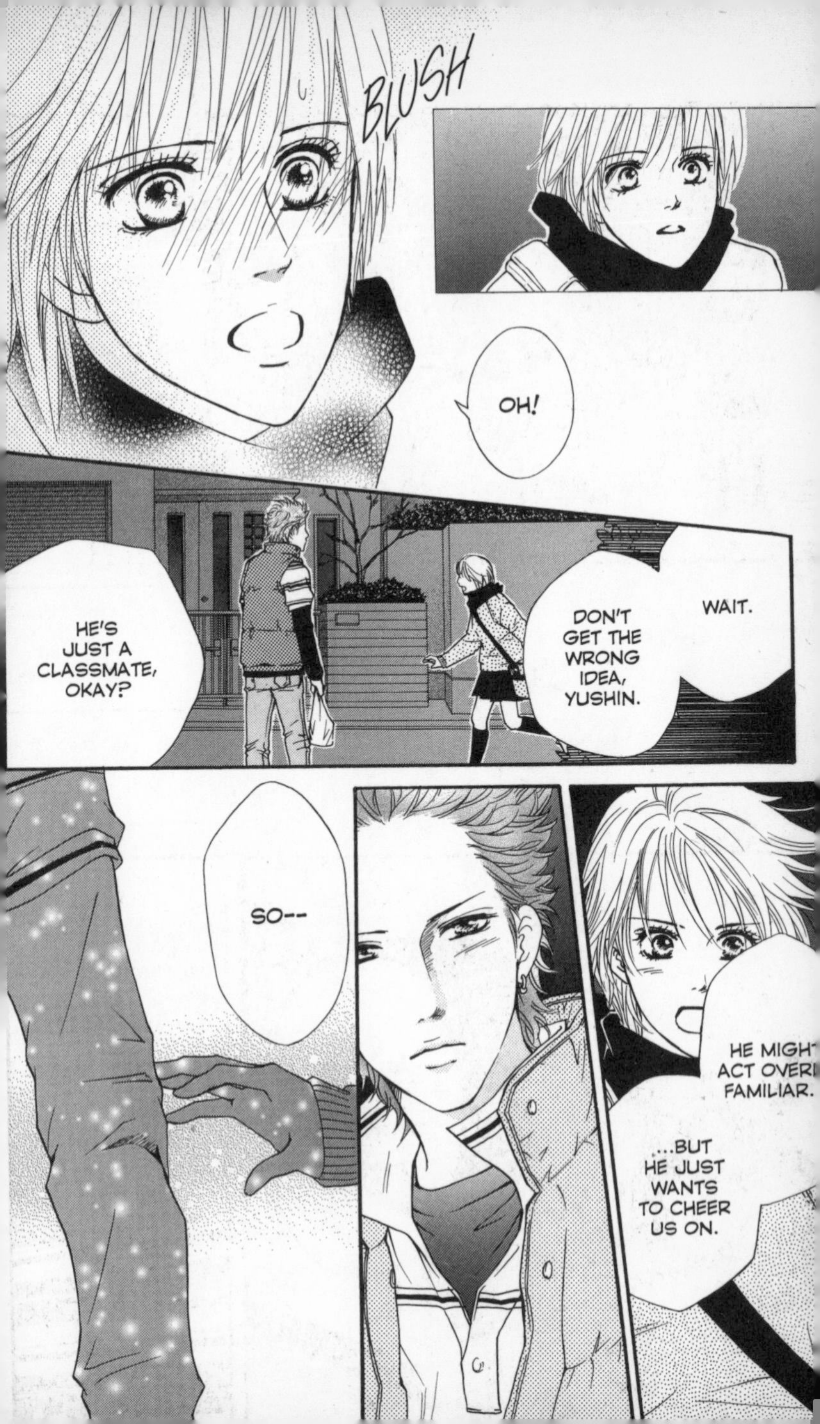
BLUSH
OH!
WAIT.
DON'T GET THE WRONG IDEA, YUSHIN.
HE'S JUST A CLASSMATE, OKAY?
HE MIGHT ACT OVERL FAMILIAR.
...BUT HE JUST WANTS TO CHEER US ON.
SO--

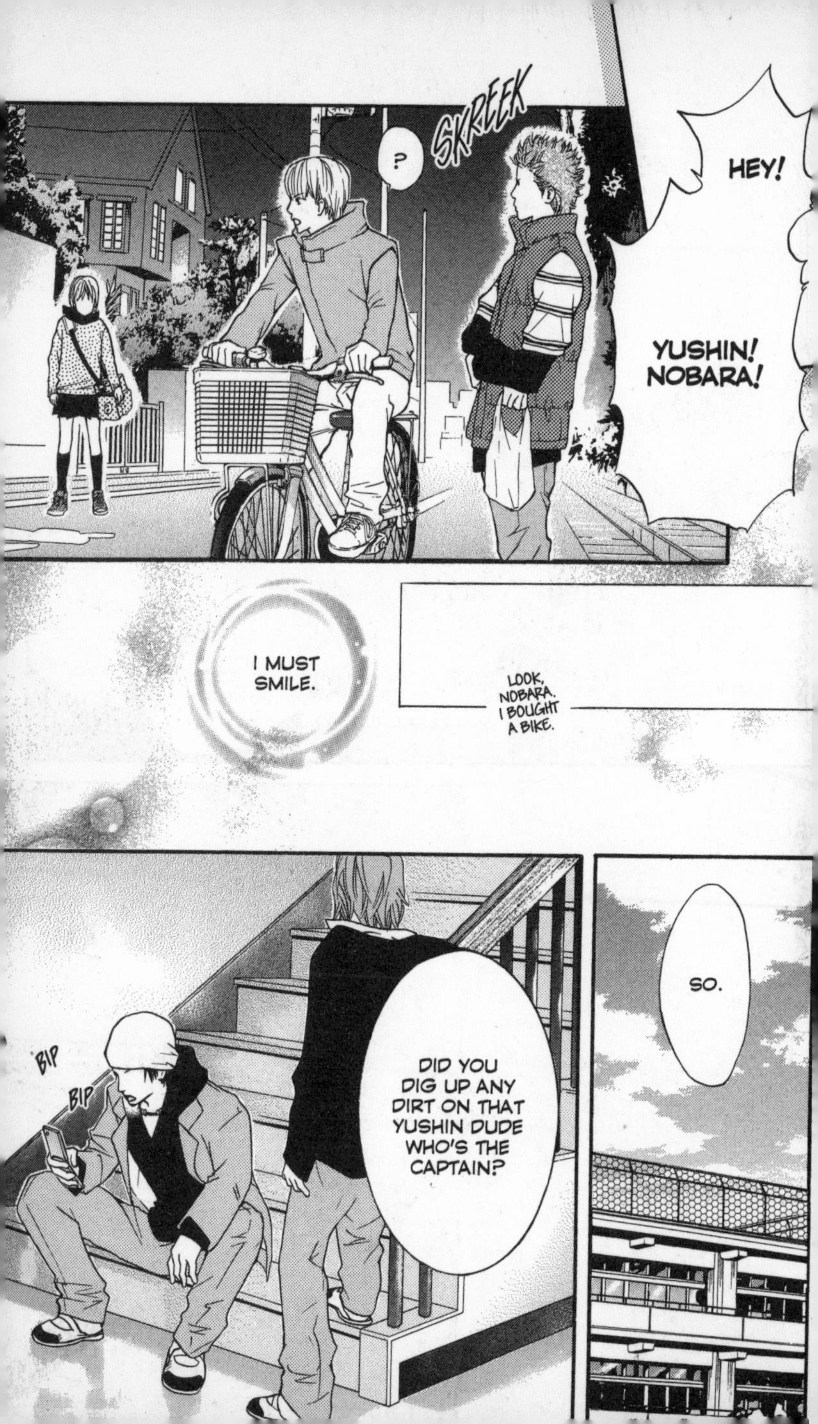
HEY!
YUSHIN! NOBARA!
SKREEK
?
LOOK, NOBARA. I BOUGHT A BIKE.
I MUST SMILE.
SO.
DID YOU DIG UP ANY DIRT ON THAT YUSHIN DUDE WHO'S THE CAPTAIN?
BIP
BIP

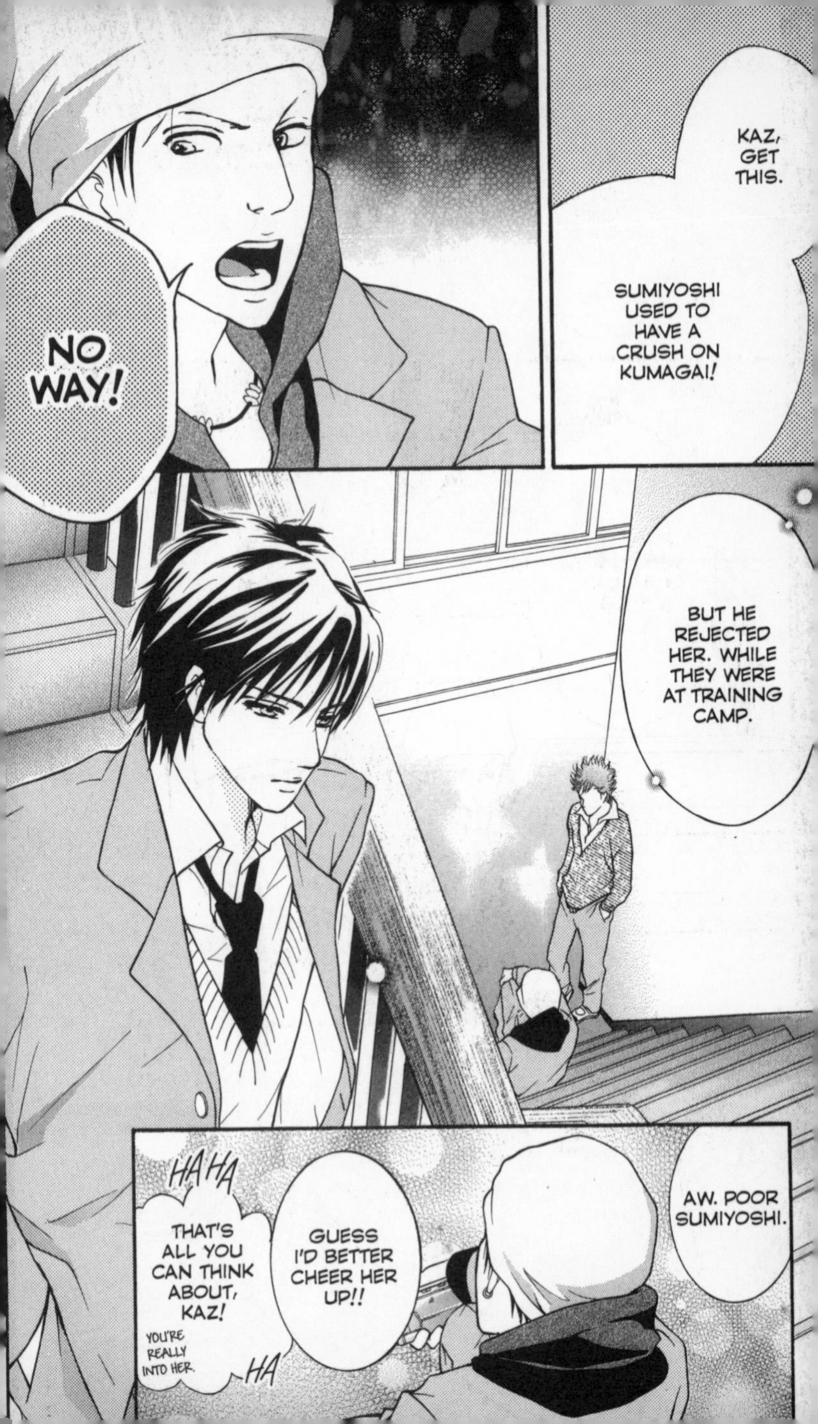
KAZ, GET THIS.
SUMIYOSHI USED TO HAVE A CRUSH ON KUMAGAI!
NO WAY!
BUT HE REJECTED HER. WHILE THEY WERE AT TRAINING CAMP.
AW. POOR SUMIYOSHI.
GUESS I'D BETTER CHEER HER UP!!
HAHA
THAT'S ALL YOU CAN THINK ABOUT, KAZ!
YOU'RE REALLY INTO HER.
HA

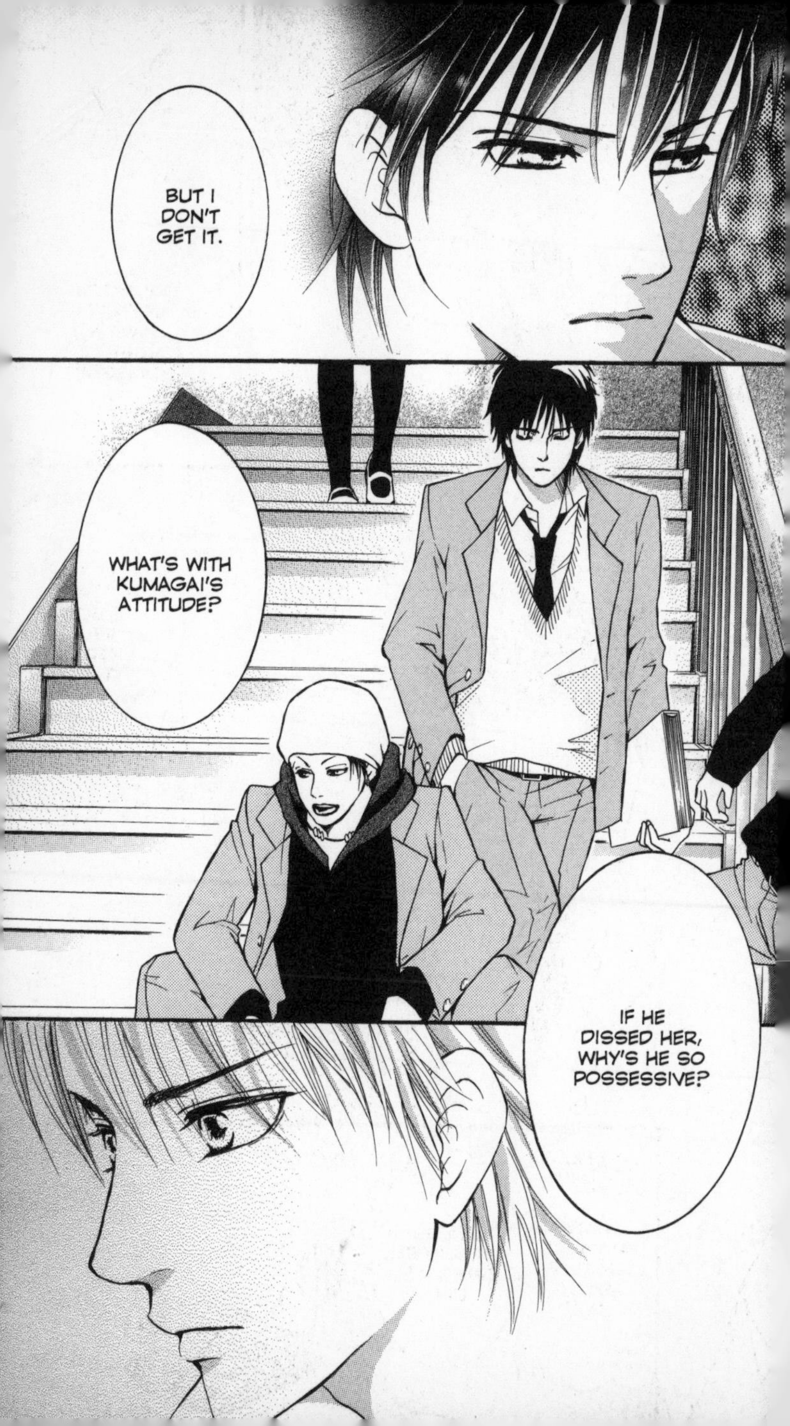
BUT I DON'T GET IT.
WHAT'S WITH KUMAGAI'S ATTITUDE?
IF HE DISSED HER, WHY'S HE SO POSSESSIVE?

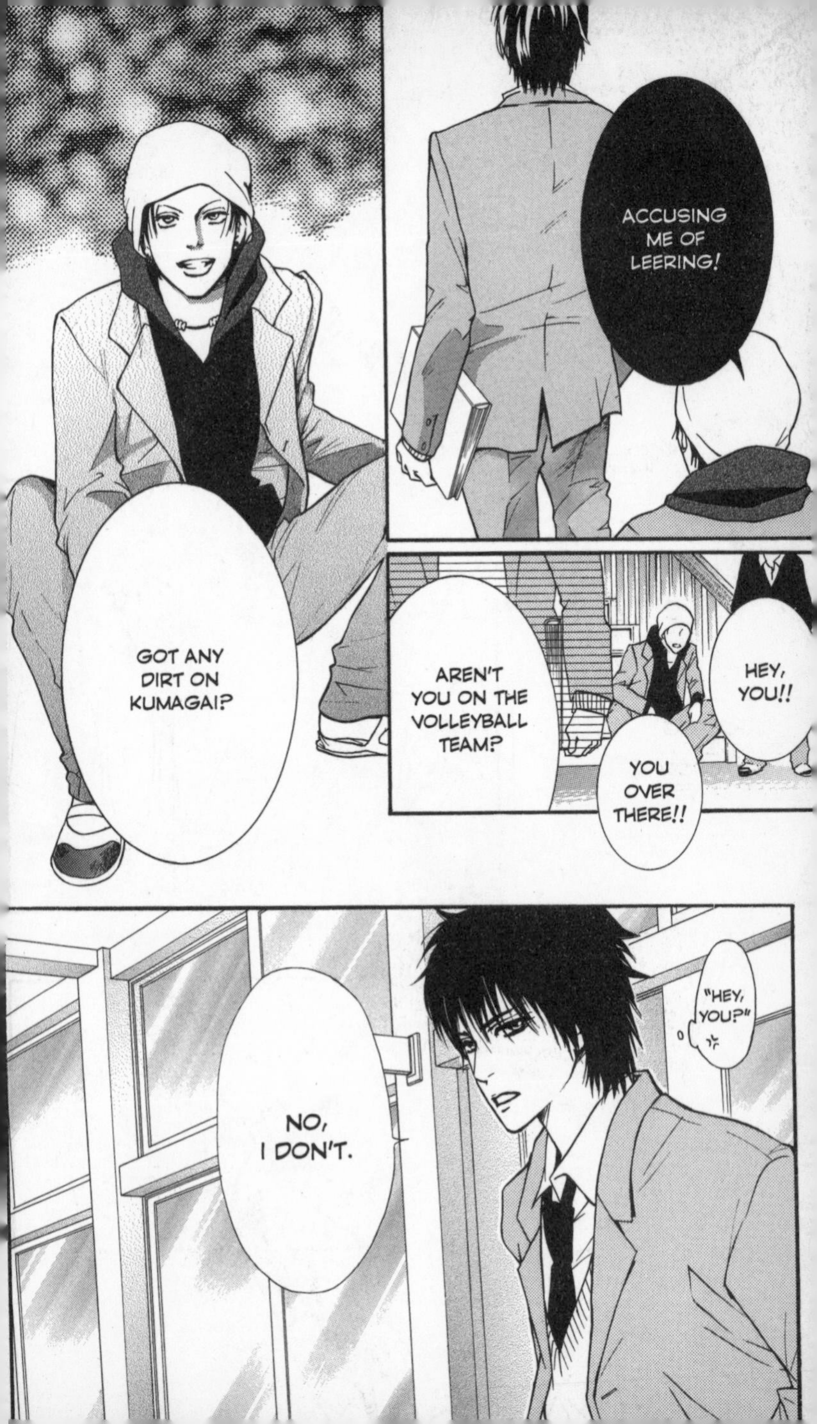
ACCUSING ME OF LEERING!
HEY, YOU!!
YOU OVER THERE!!
AREN'T YOU ON THE VOLLEYBALL TEAM?
GOT ANY DIRT ON KUMAGAI?
"HEY, YOU?"
NO, I DON'T.

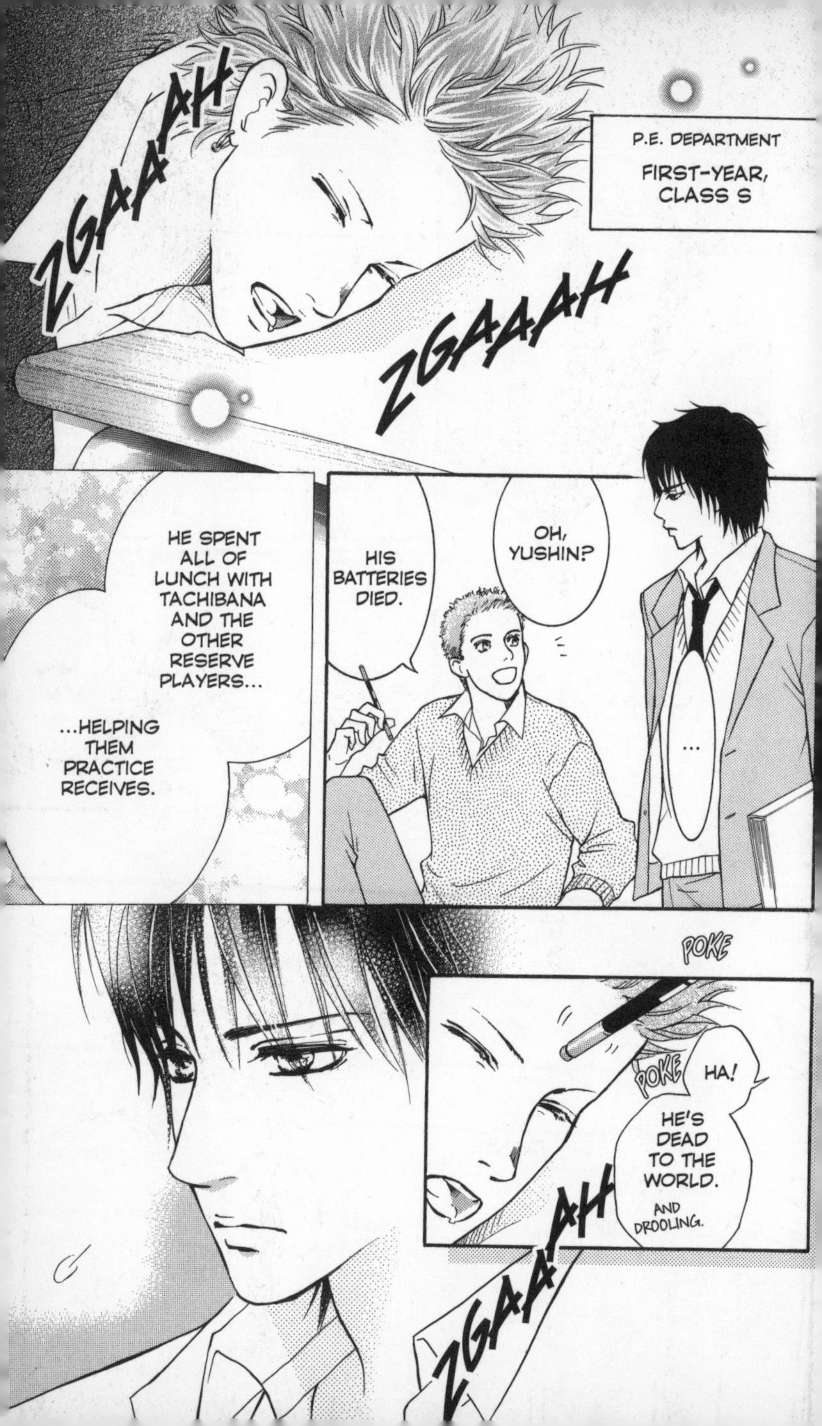
P.E. DEPARTMENT
FIRST-YEAR, CLASS S
ZGAAAH
ZGAAAH
OH, YUSHIN?
...
HIS BATTERIES DIED.
HE SPENT ALL OF LUNCH WITH TACHIBANA AND THE OTHER RESERVE PLAYERS...
...HELPING THEM PRACTICE RECEIVES.
POKE
POKE
HA!
HE'S DEAD TO THE WORLD.
AND DROOLING.
ZGAAAH

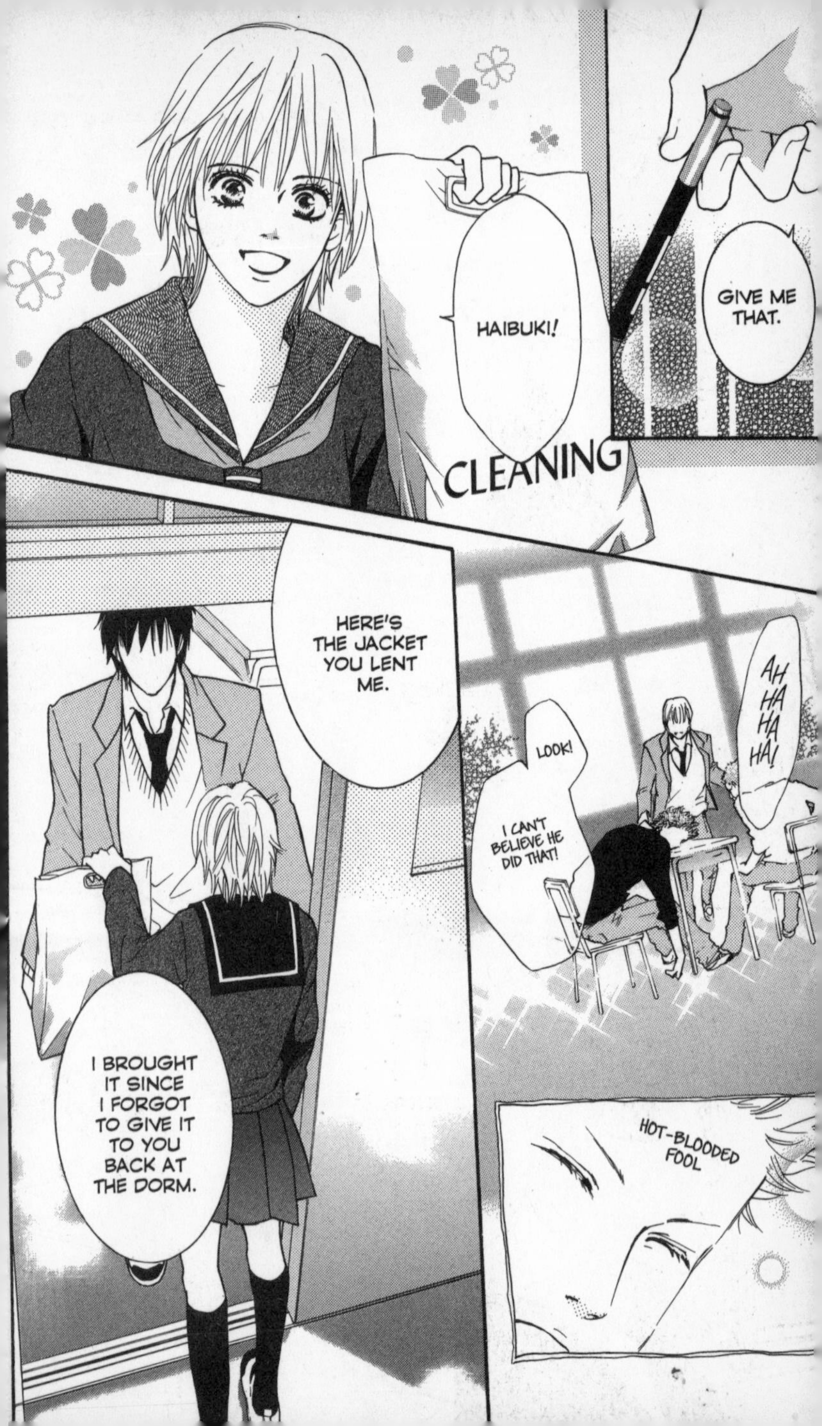
GIVE ME THAT.
HAIBUKI!
CLEANING
AH HA HA HA!
LOOK!
I CAN'T BELIEVE HE DID THAT!
HOT-BLOODED FOOL
HERE'S THE JACKET YOU LENT ME.
I BROUGHT IT SINCE I FORGOT TO GIVE IT TO YOU BACK AT THE DORM.

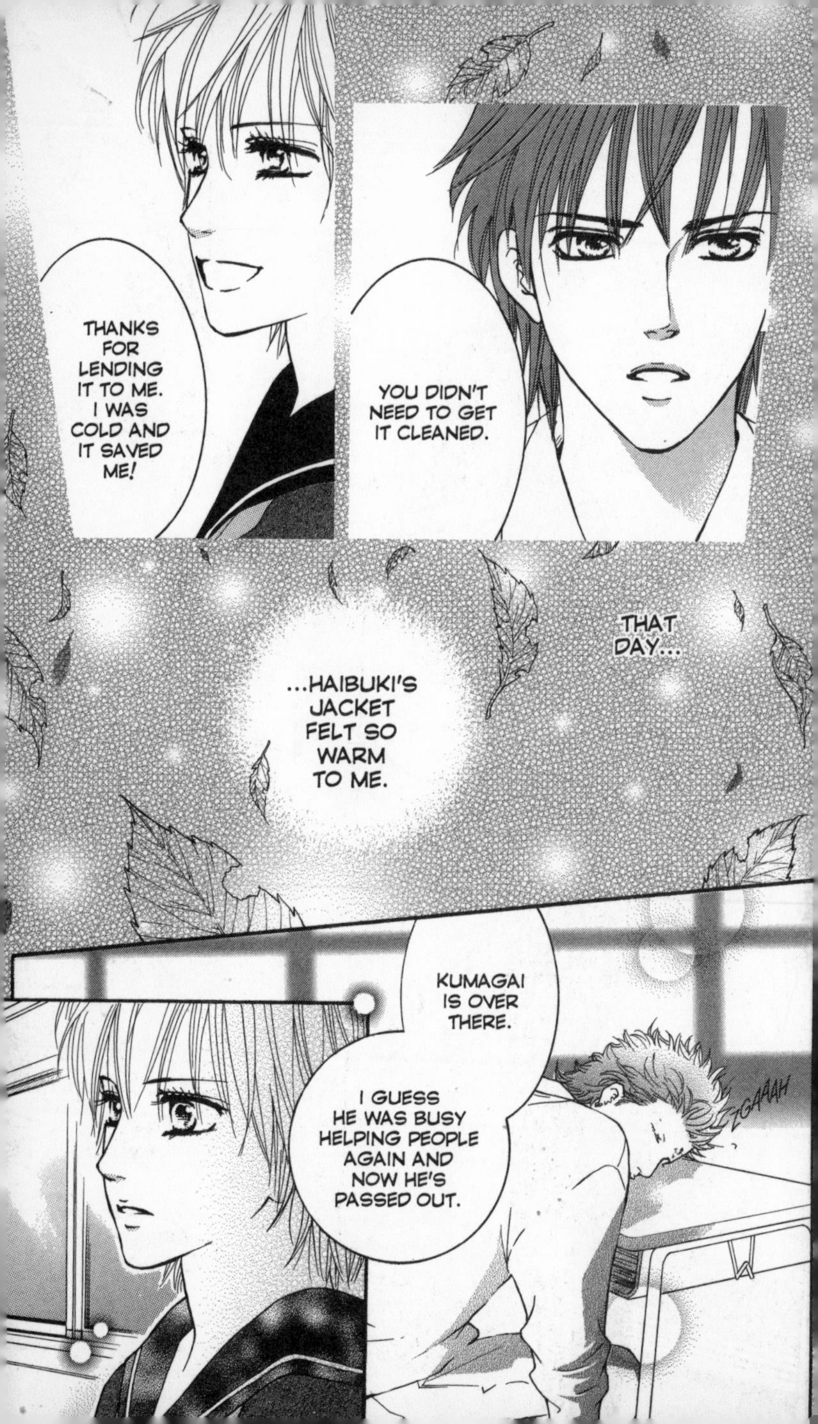
YOU DIDN'T NEED TO GET IT CLEANED.
THANKS FOR LENDING IT TO ME. I WAS COLD AND IT SAVED ME!
THAT DAY...
...HAIBUKI'S JACKET FELT SO WARM TO ME.
KUMAGAI IS OVER THERE.
I GUESS HE WAS BUSY HELPING PEOPLE AGAIN AND NOW HE'S PASSED OUT.
ZGAAAH

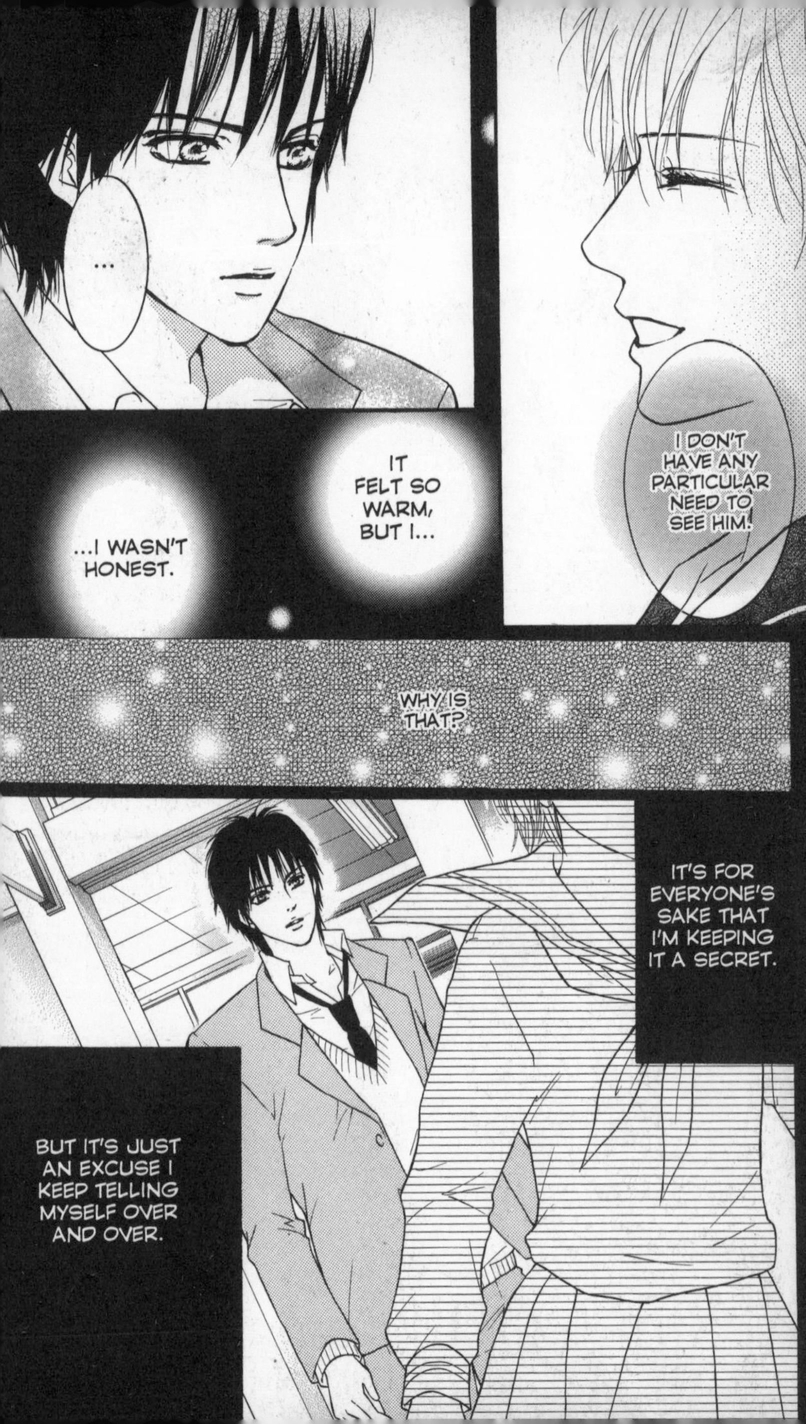
I DON'T HAVE ANY PARTICULAR NEED TO SEE HIM!
...
IT FELT SO WARM, BUT I...
...I WASN'T HONEST.
WHY IS THAT?
IT'S FOR EVERYONE'S SAKE THAT I'M KEEPING IT A SECRET.
BUT IT'S JUST AN EXCUSE I KEEP TELLING MYSELF OVER AND OVER.

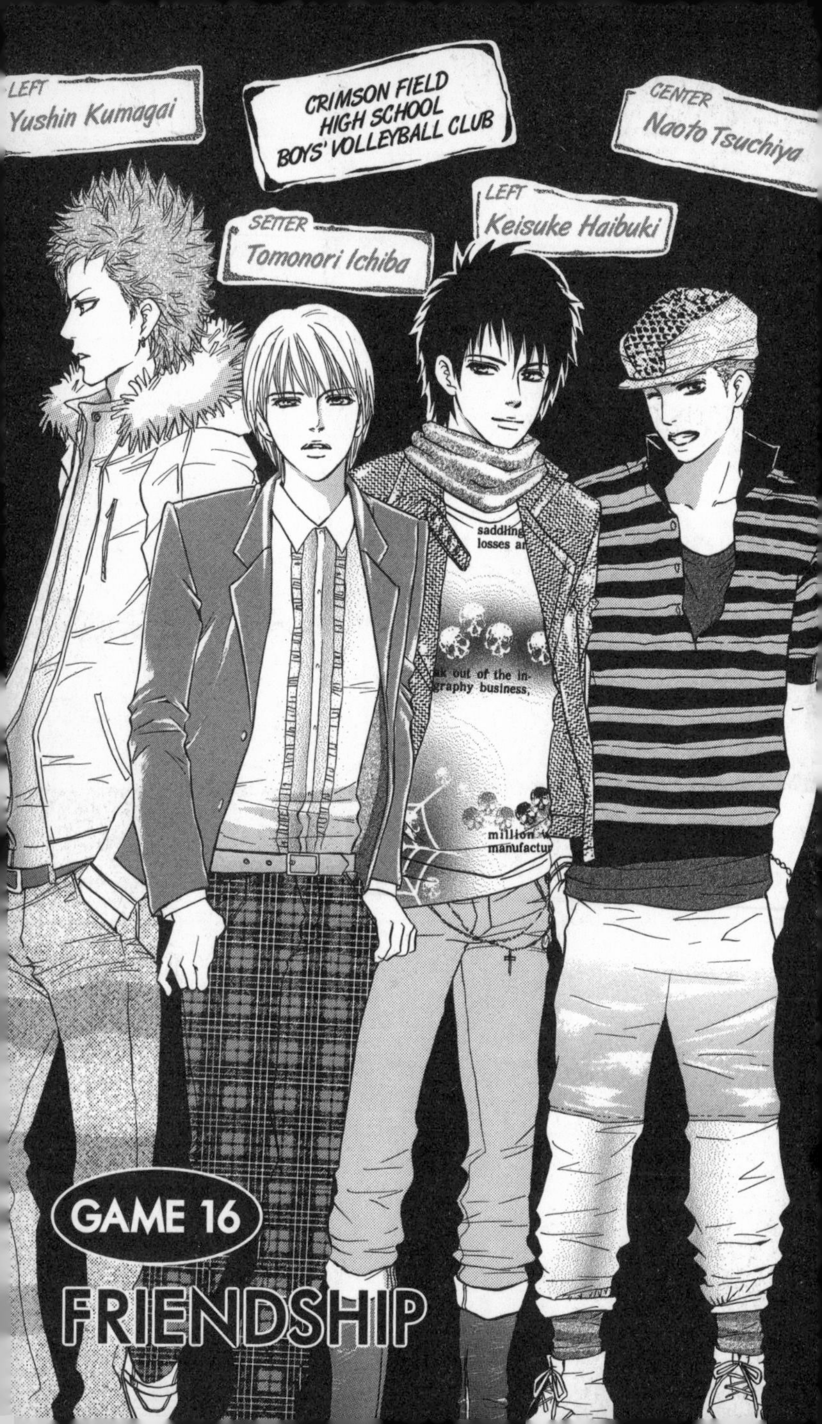
CENTER
Naoto Tsuchiya
CRIMSON FIELD HIGH SCHOOL BOYS' VOLLEYBALL CLUB
LEFT
Yushin Kumagai
LEFT
Keisuke Haibuki
SETTER
Tomonori Ichiba
GAME 16
FRIENDSHIP

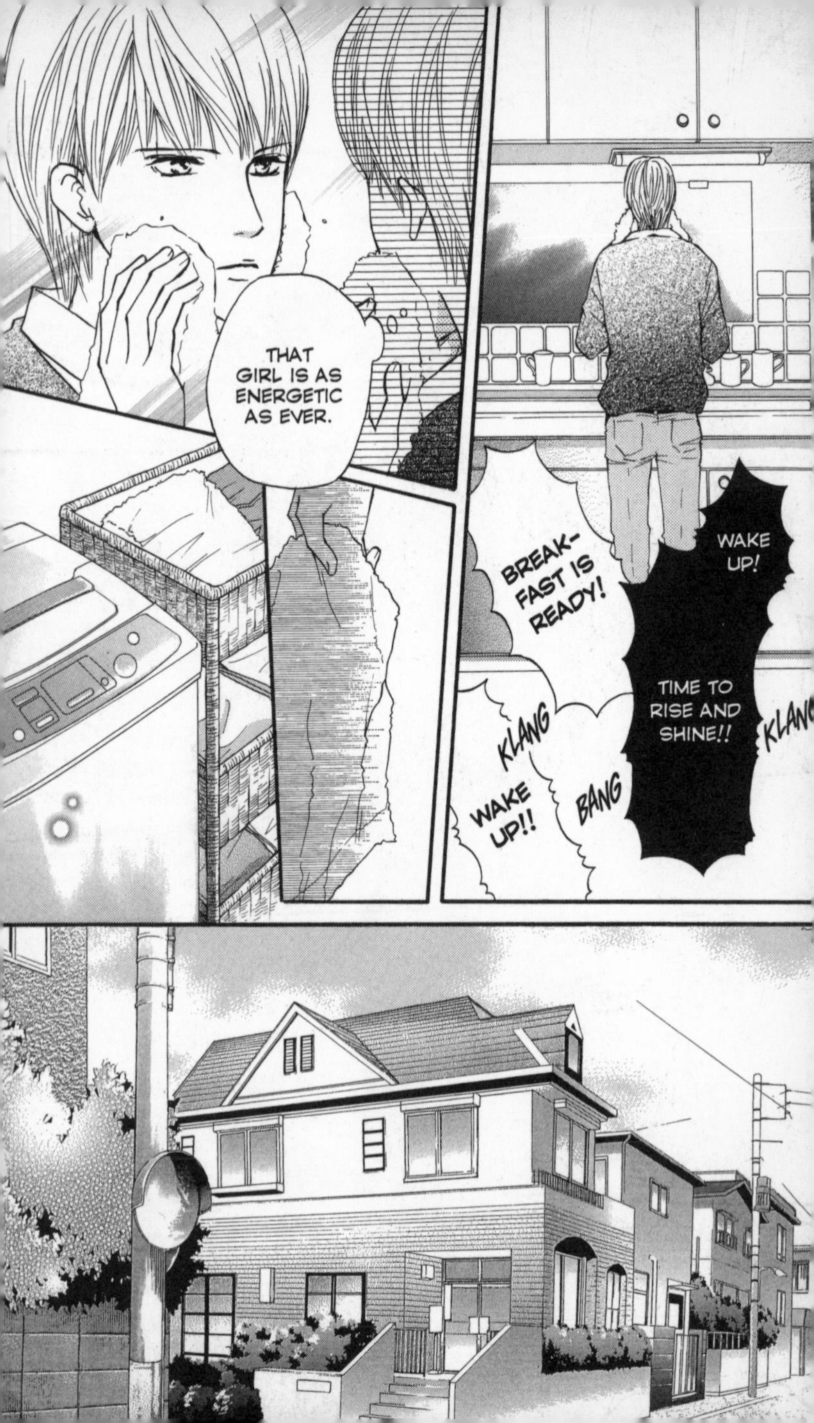
WAKE UP!
BREAK-FAST IS READY!
TIME TO RISE AND SHINE!!
KLANG
BANG
WAKE UP!!
THAT GIRL IS AS ENERGETIC AS EVER.

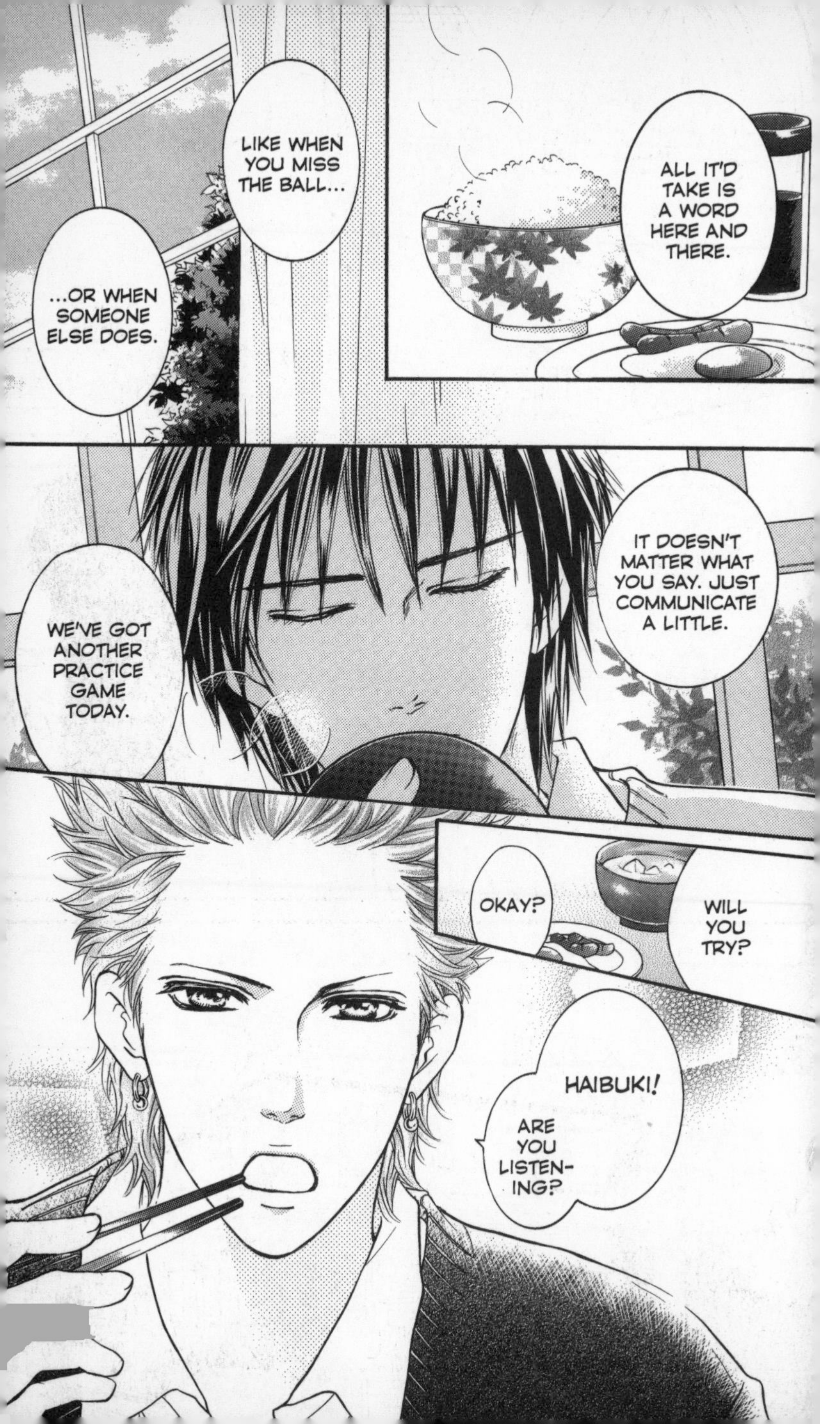
ALL IT'D TAKE IS A WORD HERE AND THERE.
LIKE WHEN YOU MISS THE BALL...
...OR WHEN SOMEONE ELSE DOES.
IT DOESN'T MATTER WHAT YOU SAY. JUST COMMUNICATE A LITTLE.
WE'VE GOT ANOTHER PRACTICE GAME TODAY.
WILL YOU TRY?
OKAY?
HAIBUKI!
ARE YOU LISTEN-ING?

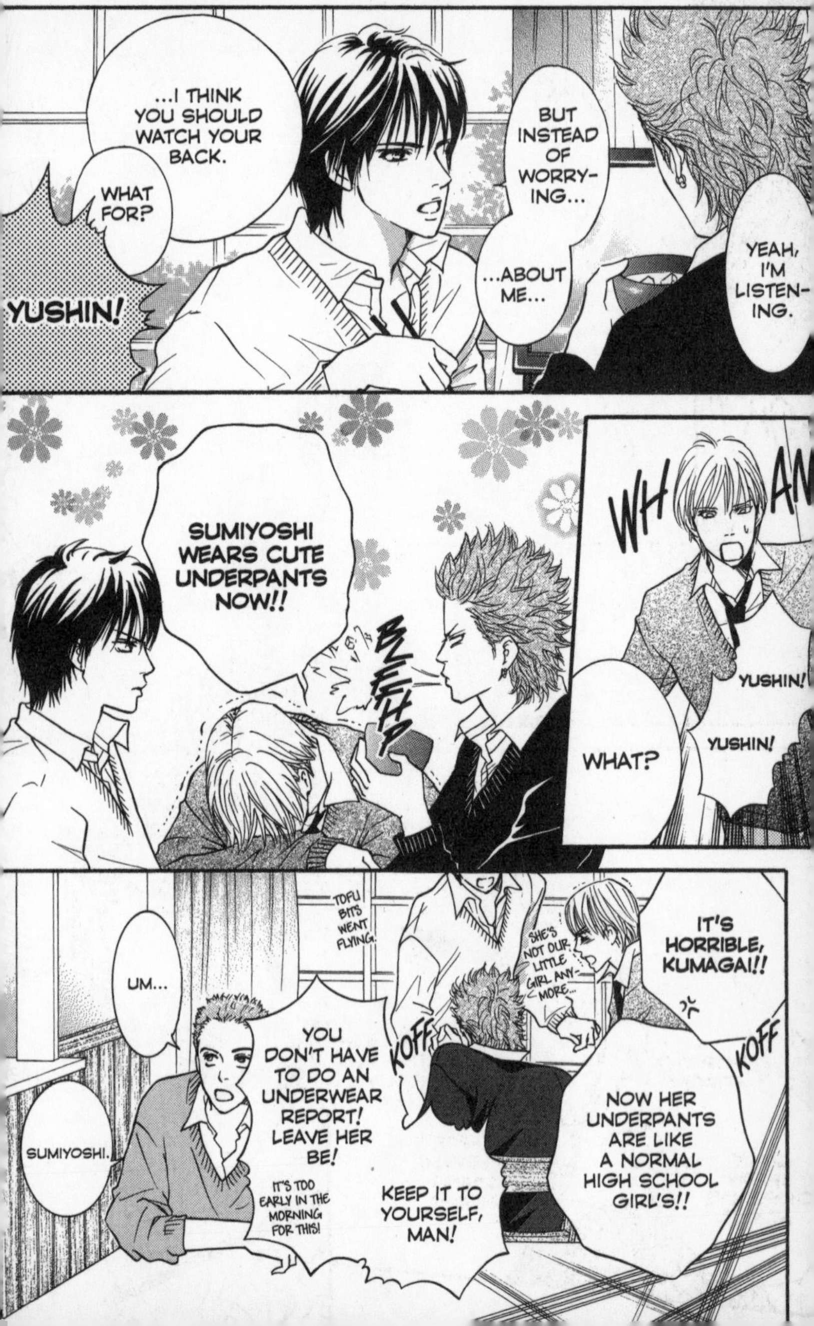
YEAH, I'M LISTEN-ING.
BUT INSTEAD OF WORRY-ING...
...ABOUT ME...
...I THINK YOU SHOULD WATCH YOUR BACK.
WHAT FOR?
YUSHIN!
WH
AM
YUSHIN!
YUSHIN!
WHAT?
SUMIYOSHI WEARS CUTE UNDERPANTS NOW!!
IT'S HORRIBLE, KUMAGAI!!
SHE'S NOT OUR LITTLE GIRL ANY-MORE...
KOFF
NOW HER UNDERPANTS ARE LIKE A NORMAL HIGH SCHOOL GIRL'S!!
TOFU BITS WENT FLYING.
KOFF
KEEP IT TO YOURSELF, MAN!
YOU DON'T HAVE TO DO AN UNDERWEAR REPORT! LEAVE HER BE!
IT'S TOO EARLY IN THE MORNING FOR THIS!
UM...
SUMIYOSHI.

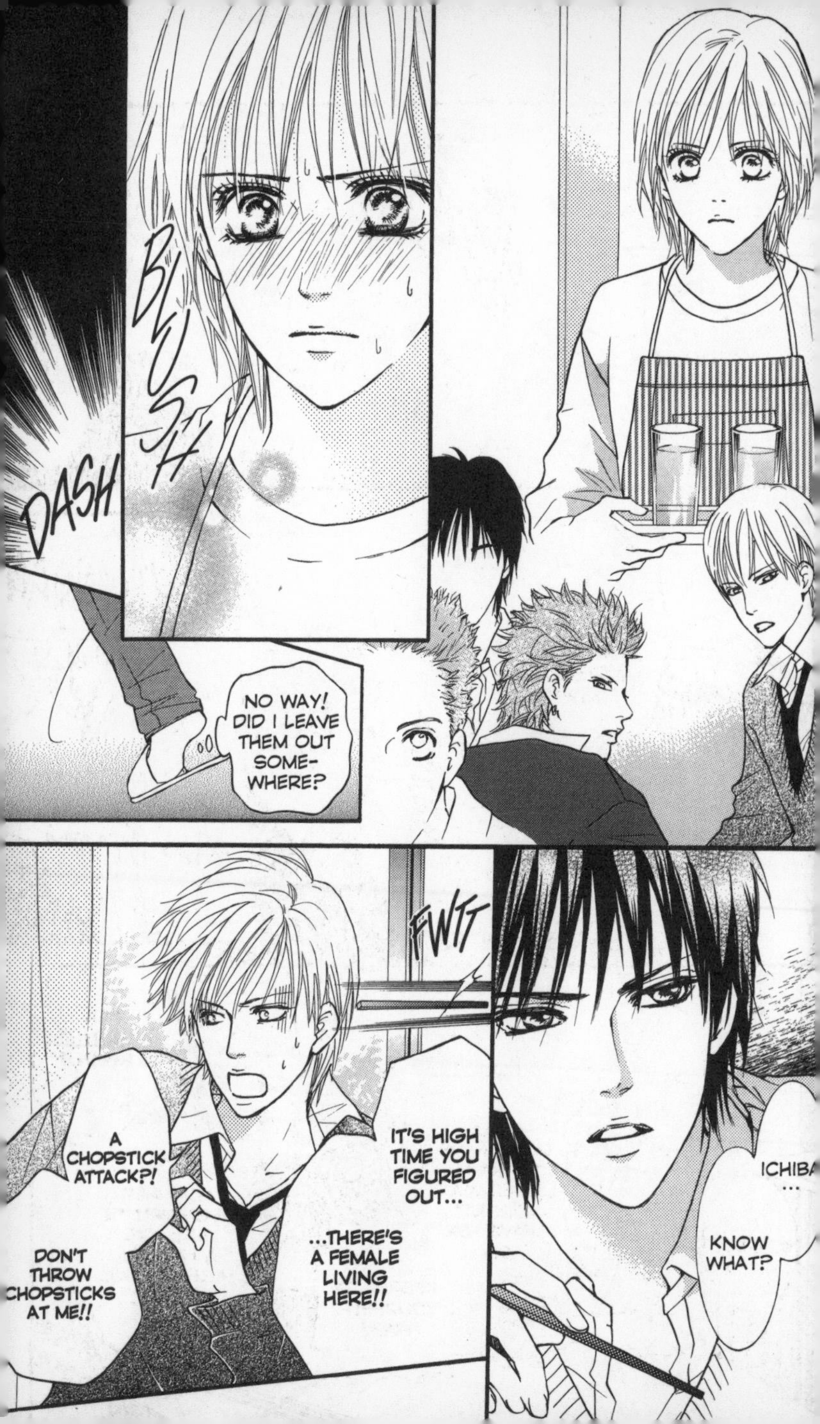
NO WAY! DID I LEAVE THEM OUT SOME-WHERE?
DASH
BLUSH
ICHIBA ...
KNOW WHAT?
IT'S HIGH TIME YOU FIGURED OUT...
...THERE'S A FEMALE LIVING HERE!!
FWTT
A CHOPSTICK ATTACK?!
DON'T THROW CHOPSTICKS AT ME!!

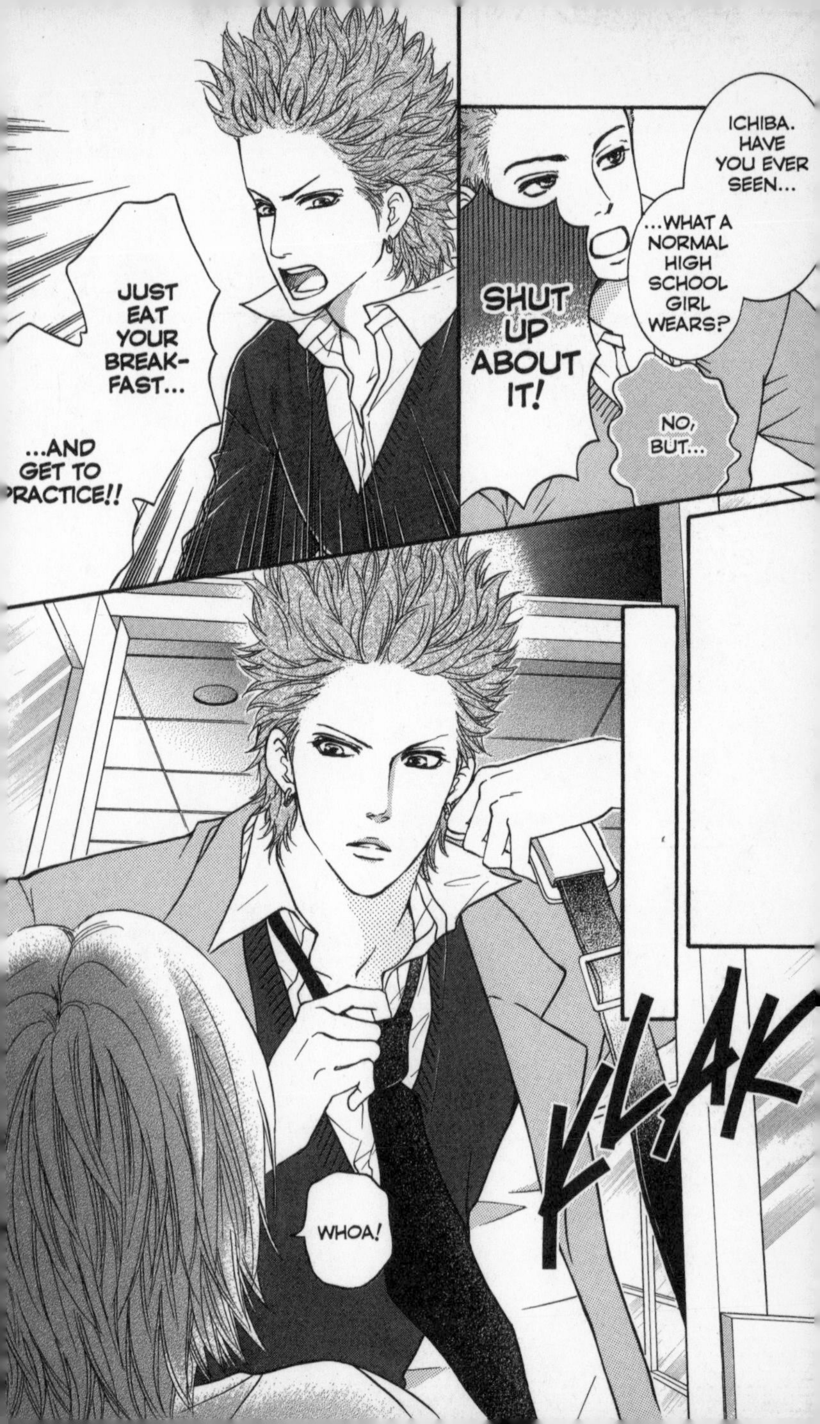
ICHIBA. HAVE YOU EVER SEEN...
...WHAT A NORMAL HIGH SCHOOL GIRL WEARS?
NO, BUT...
SHUT UP ABOUT IT!
JUST EAT YOUR BREAK-FAST...
...AND GET TO PRACTICE!!
KLAK
WHOA!

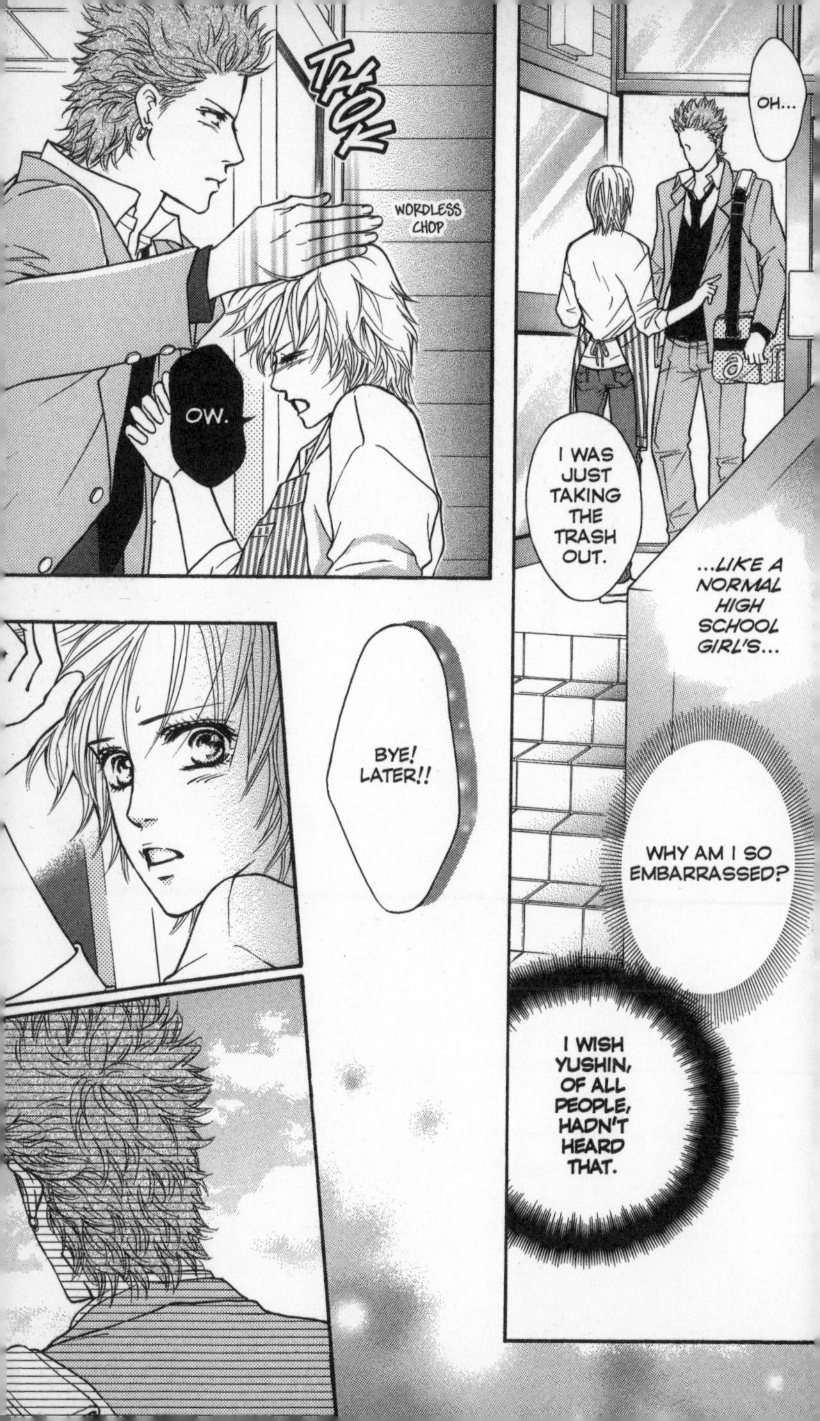
OH...
I WAS JUST TAKING THE TRASH OUT.
THOK
WORDLESS CHOP
OW.
...LIKE A NORMAL HIGH SCHOOL GIRL'S...
WHY AM I SO EMBARRASSED?
I WISH YUSHIN, OF ALL PEOPLE, HADN'T HEARD THAT.
BYE! LATER!!

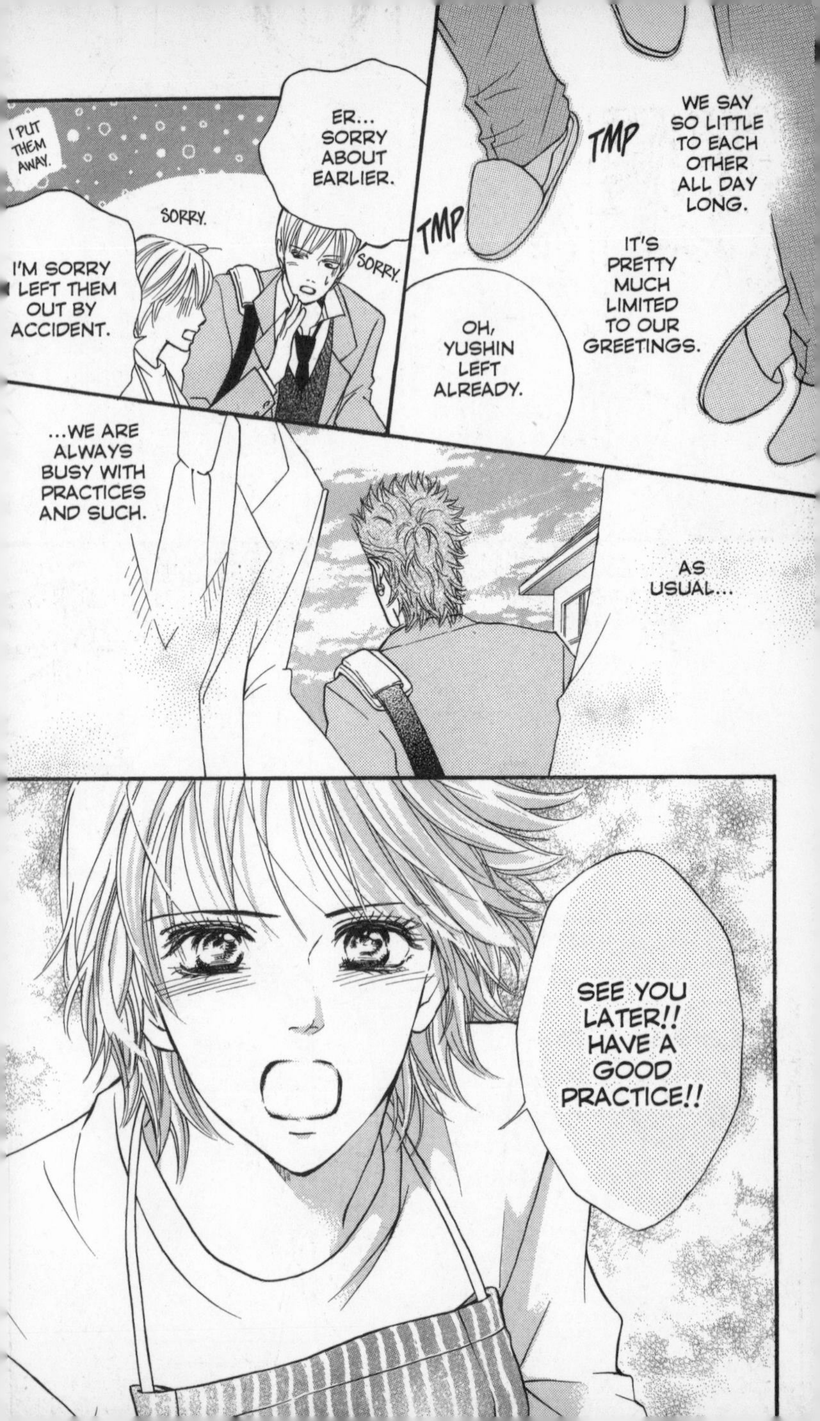
WE SAY SO LITTLE TO EACH OTHER ALL DAY LONG.
TMP
TMP
IT'S PRETTY MUCH LIMITED TO OUR GREETINGS.
OH, YUSHIN LEFT ALREADY.
ER... SORRY ABOUT EARLIER.
SORRY.
SORRY.
I PUT THEM AWAY.
I'M SORRY I LEFT THEM OUT BY ACCIDENT.
AS USUAL...
...WE ARE ALWAYS BUSY WITH PRACTICES AND SUCH.
SEE YOU LATER!! HAVE A GOOD PRACTICE!!

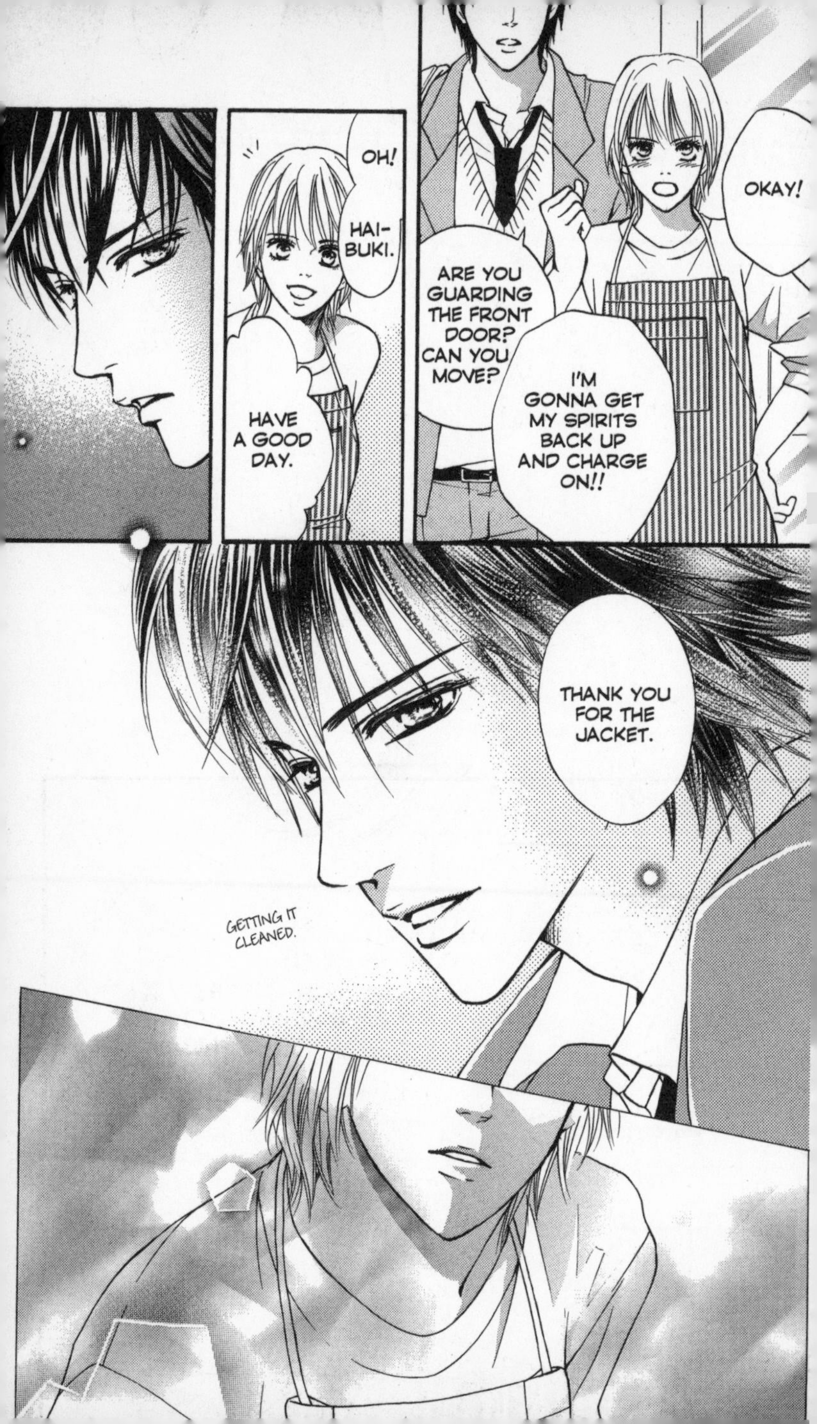
OKAY!
ARE YOU GUARDING THE FRONT DOOR? CAN YOU MOVE?
I'M GONNA GET MY SPIRITS BACK UP AND CHARGE ON!!
OH!
HAI-BUKI.
HAVE A GOOD DAY.
THANK YOU FOR THE JACKET.
GETTING IT CLEANED.

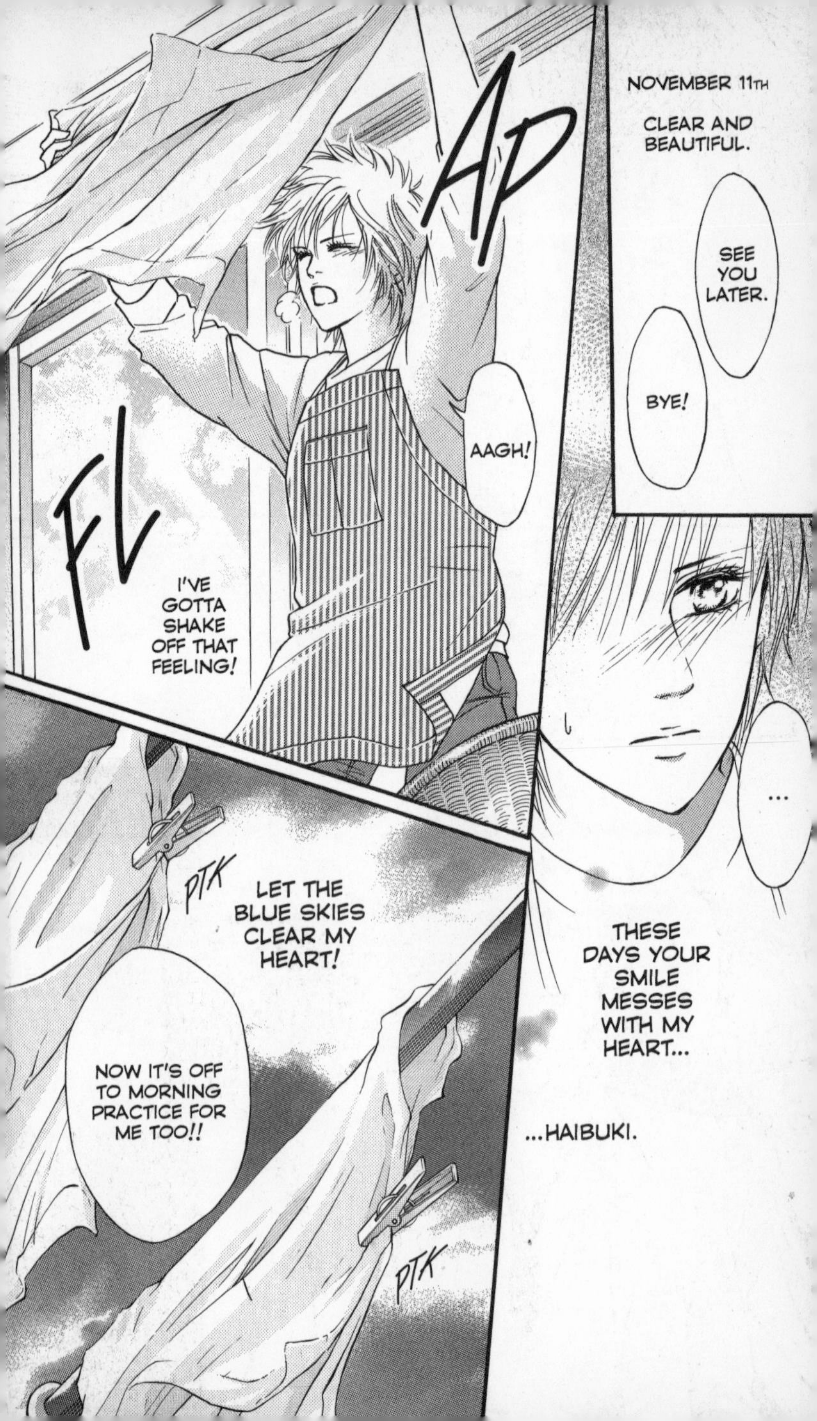
NOVEMBER 11TH
CLEAR AND BEAUTIFUL.
SEE YOU LATER.
BYE!
AP
AAGH!
I'VE GOTTA SHAKE OFF THAT FEELING!
FL
...
THESE DAYS YOUR SMILE MESSES WITH MY HEART...
...HAIBUKI.
PTK
LET THE BLUE SKIES CLEAR MY HEART!
NOW IT'S OFF TO MORNING PRACTICE FOR ME TOO!!
PTK

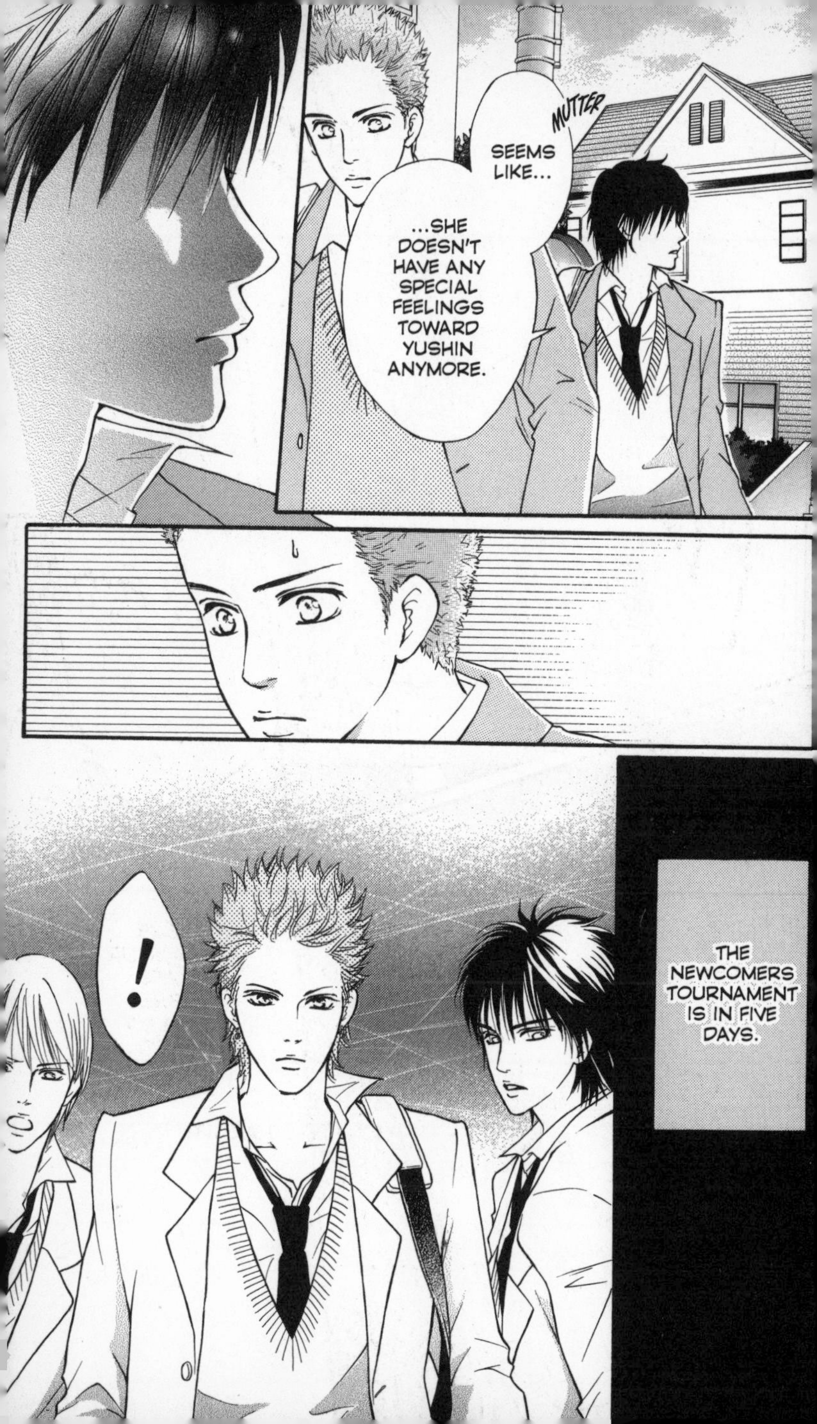
MUTTER
SEEMS LIKE...
...SHE DOESN'T HAVE ANY SPECIAL FEELINGS TOWARD YUSHIN ANYMORE.
THE NEWCOMERS TOURNAMENT IS IN FIVE DAYS.
!

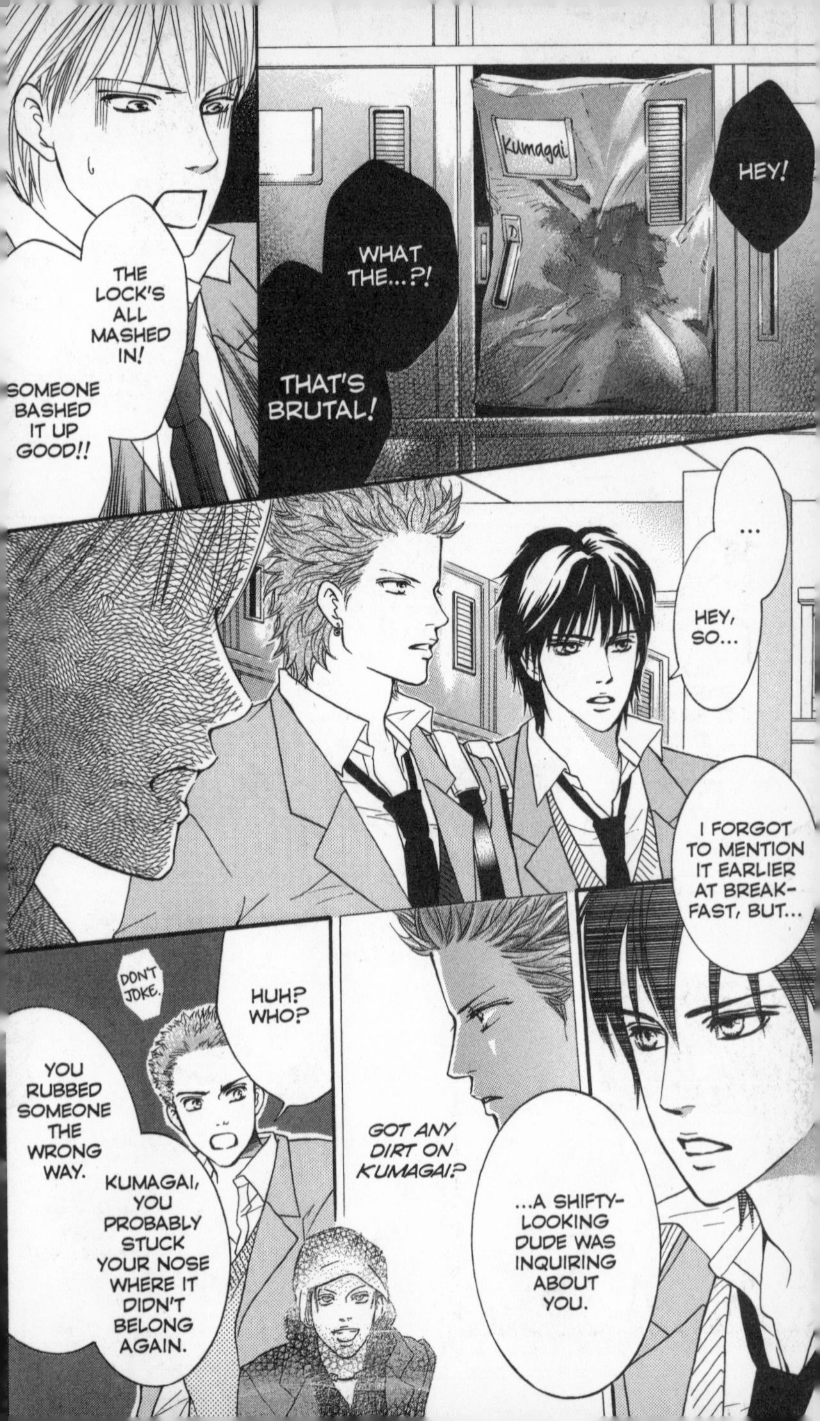
Kumagai
HEY!
WHAT THE...?!
THAT'S BRUTAL!
THE LOCK'S ALL MASHED IN!
SOMEONE BASHED IT UP GOOD!!
...
HEY, SO...
I FORGOT TO MENTION IT EARLIER AT BREAKFAST, BUT...
...A SHIFTY-LOOKING DUDE WAS INQUIRING ABOUT YOU.
GOT ANY DIRT ON KUMAGAI?
HUH? WHO?
DON'T JOKE.
YOU RUBBED SOMEONE THE WRONG WAY.
KUMAGAI, YOU PROBABLY STUCK YOUR NOSE WHERE IT DIDN'T BELONG AGAIN.

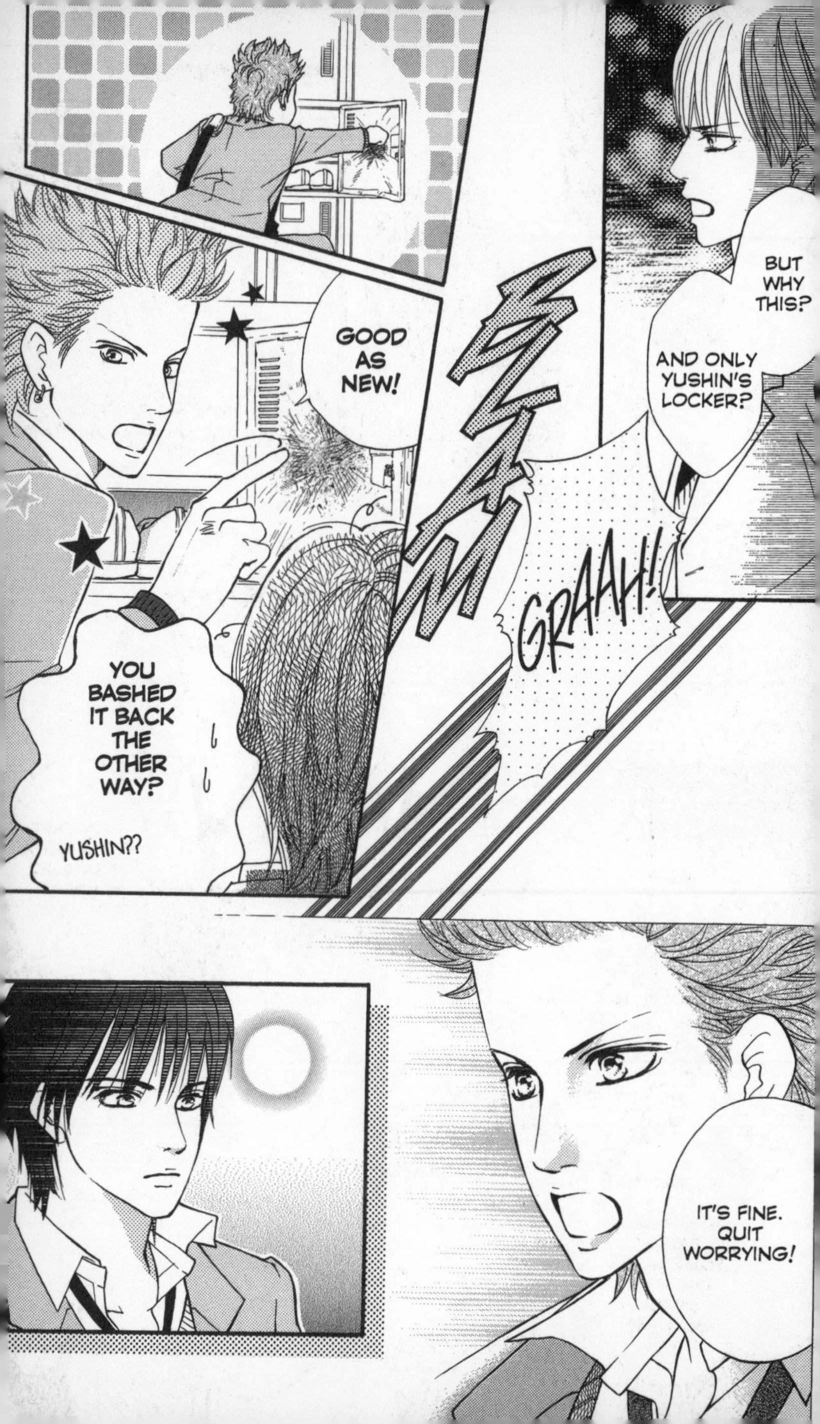
BUT WHY THIS?
AND ONLY YUSHIN'S LOCKER?
SLAM
GRAAH!
GOOD AS NEW!
YOU BASHED IT BACK THE OTHER WAY?
YUSHIN??
IT'S FINE. QUIT WORRYING!

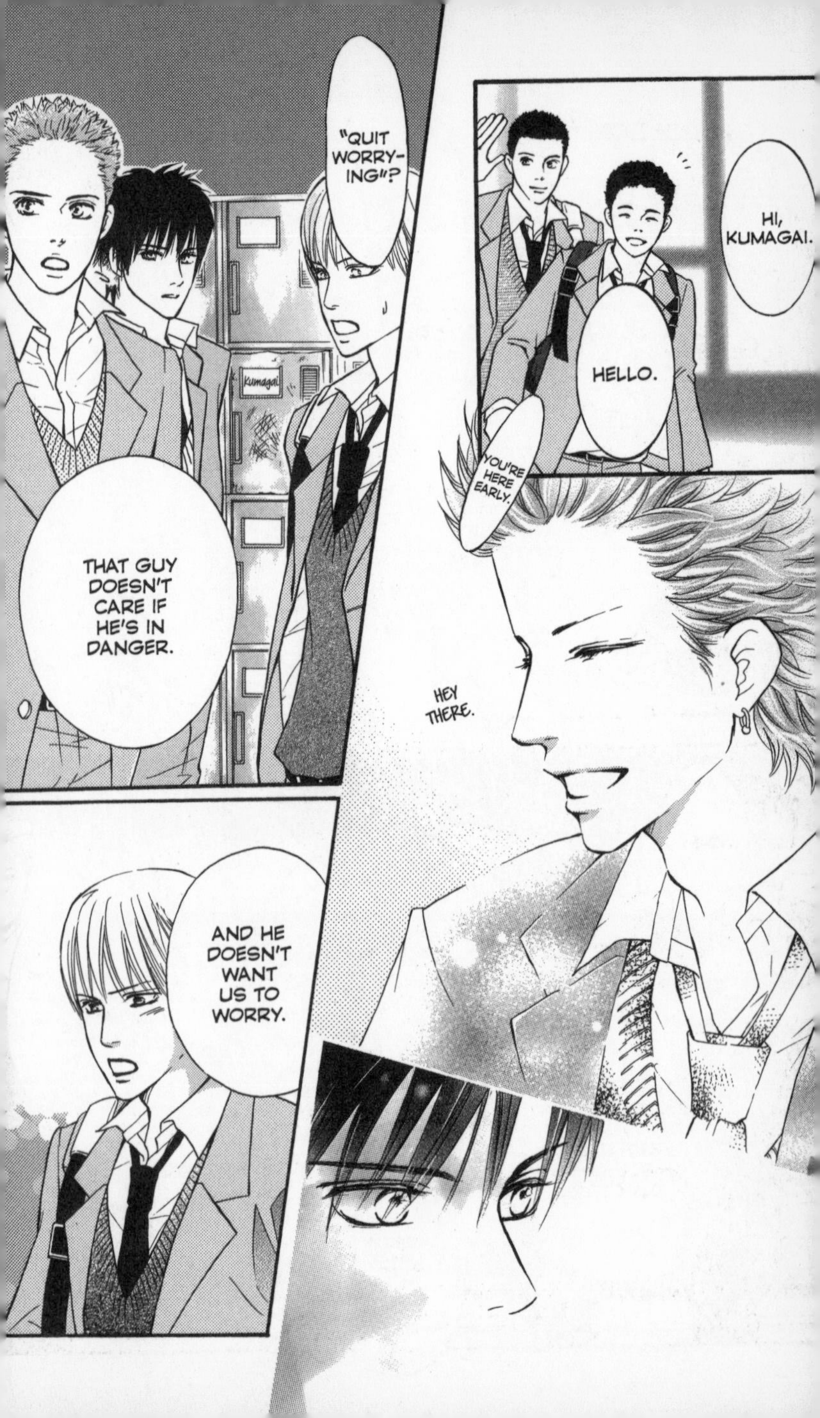
HI, KUMAGAI.
HELLO.
YOU'RE HERE EARLY.
HEY THERE.
"QUIT WORRYING"?
kumagai
THAT GUY DOESN'T CARE IF HE'S IN DANGER.
AND HE DOESN'T WANT US TO WORRY.

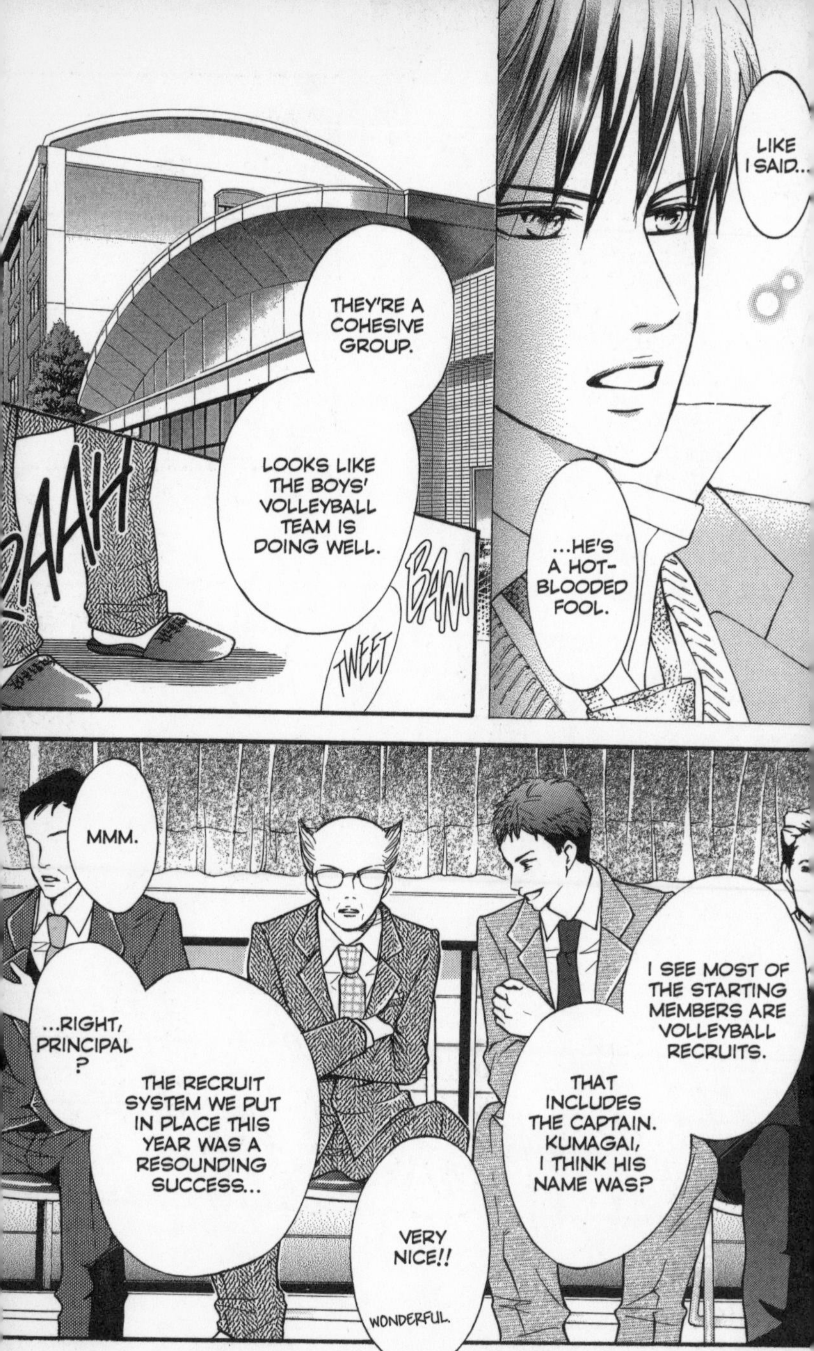
LIKE I SAID...
...HE'S A HOT-BLOODED FOOL.
THEY'RE A COHESIVE GROUP.
LOOKS LIKE THE BOYS' VOLLEYBALL TEAM IS DOING WELL.
BAM
TWEET
DAAH
I SEE MOST OF THE STARTING MEMBERS ARE VOLLEYBALL RECRUITS.
THAT INCLUDES THE CAPTAIN. KUMAGAI, I THINK HIS NAME WAS?
VERY NICE!!
WONDERFUL.
THE RECRUIT SYSTEM WE PUT IN PLACE THIS YEAR WAS A RESOUNDING SUCCESS...
...RIGHT, PRINCIPAL?
MMM.

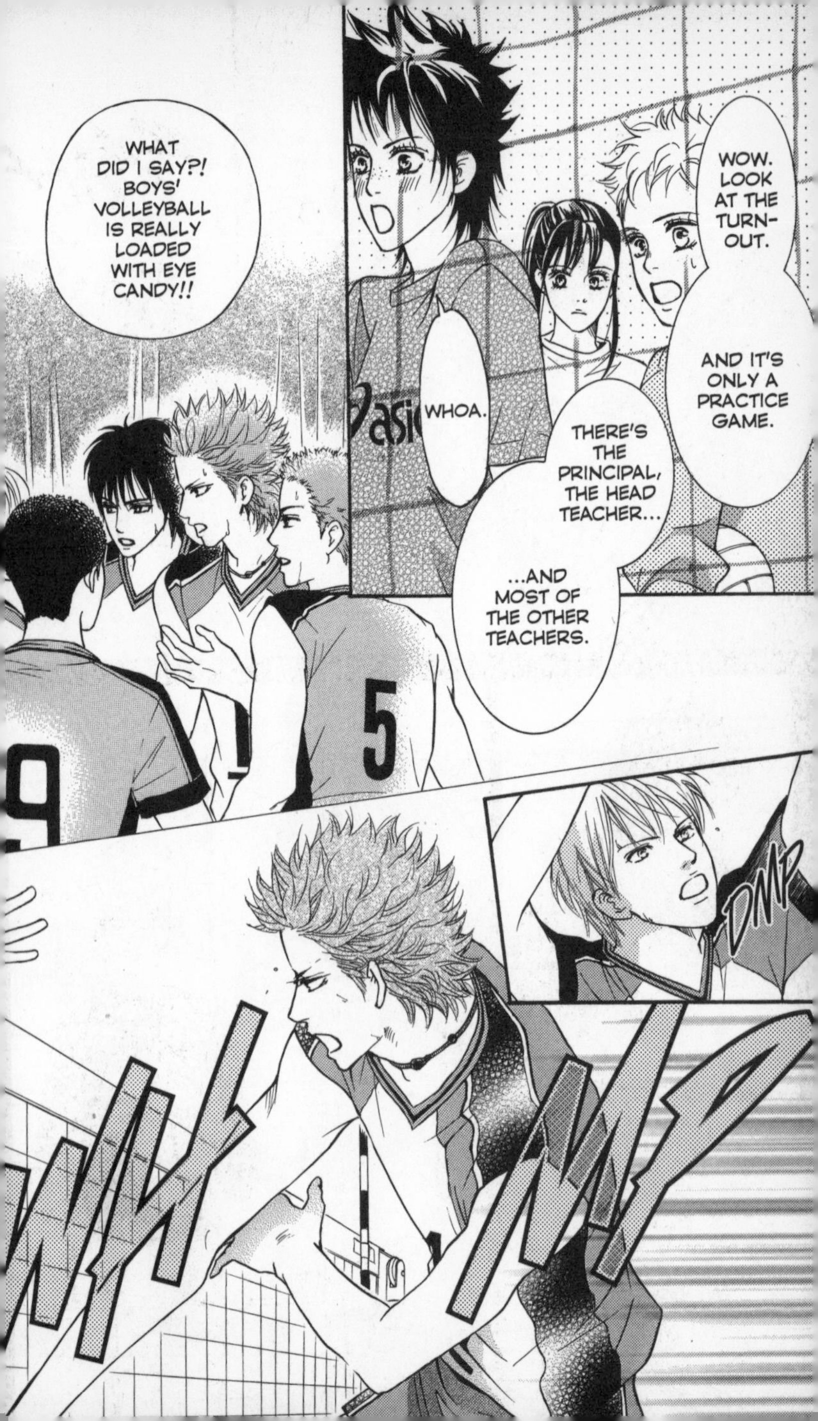
WOW. LOOK AT THE TURN-OUT.
AND IT'S ONLY A PRACTICE GAME.
WHOA.
THERE'S THE PRINCIPAL, THE HEAD TEACHER...
...AND MOST OF THE OTHER TEACHERS.
WHAT DID I SAY?! BOYS' VOLLEYBALL IS REALLY LOADED WITH EYE CANDY!!
DMP

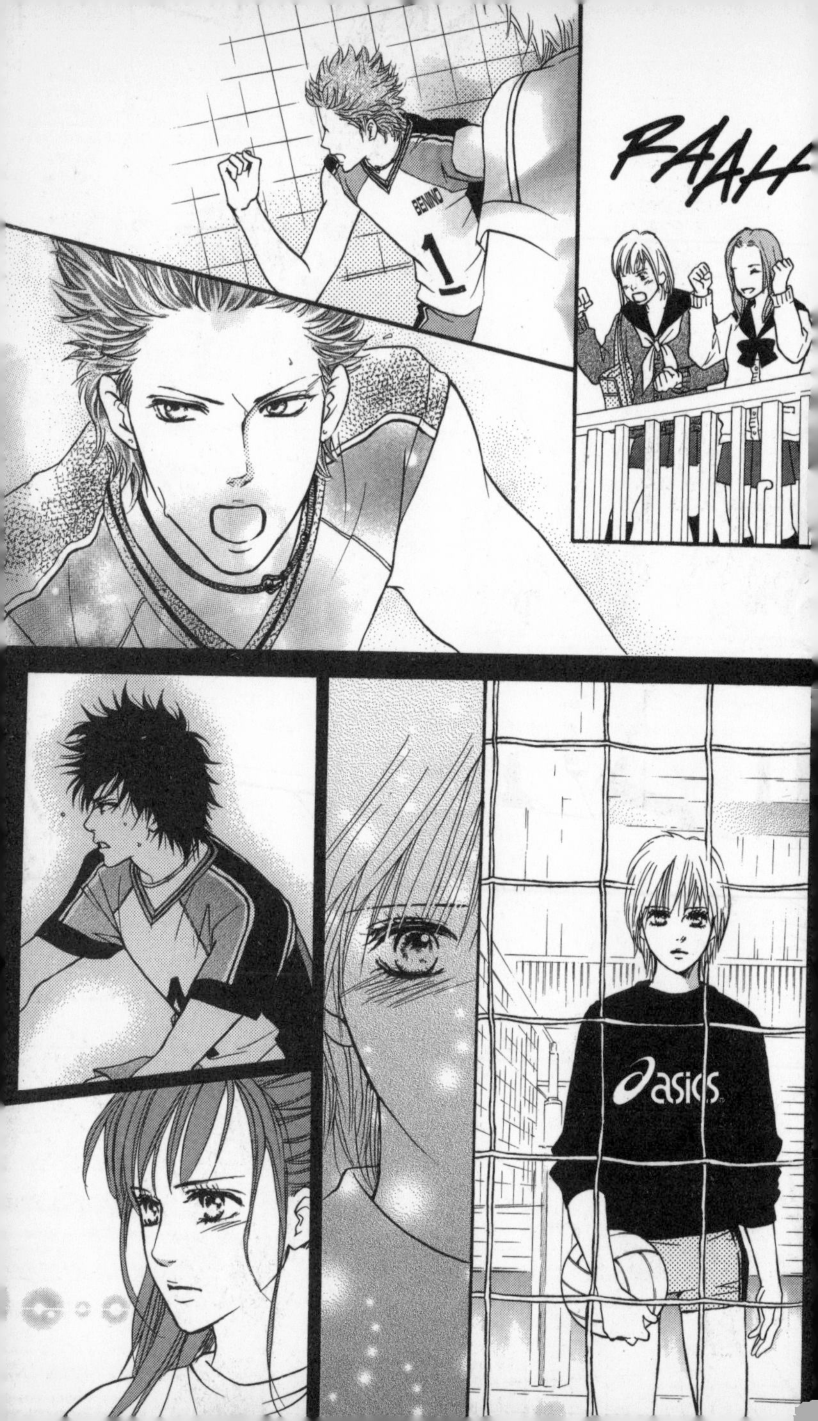
RAAH
BENINO
1
asics

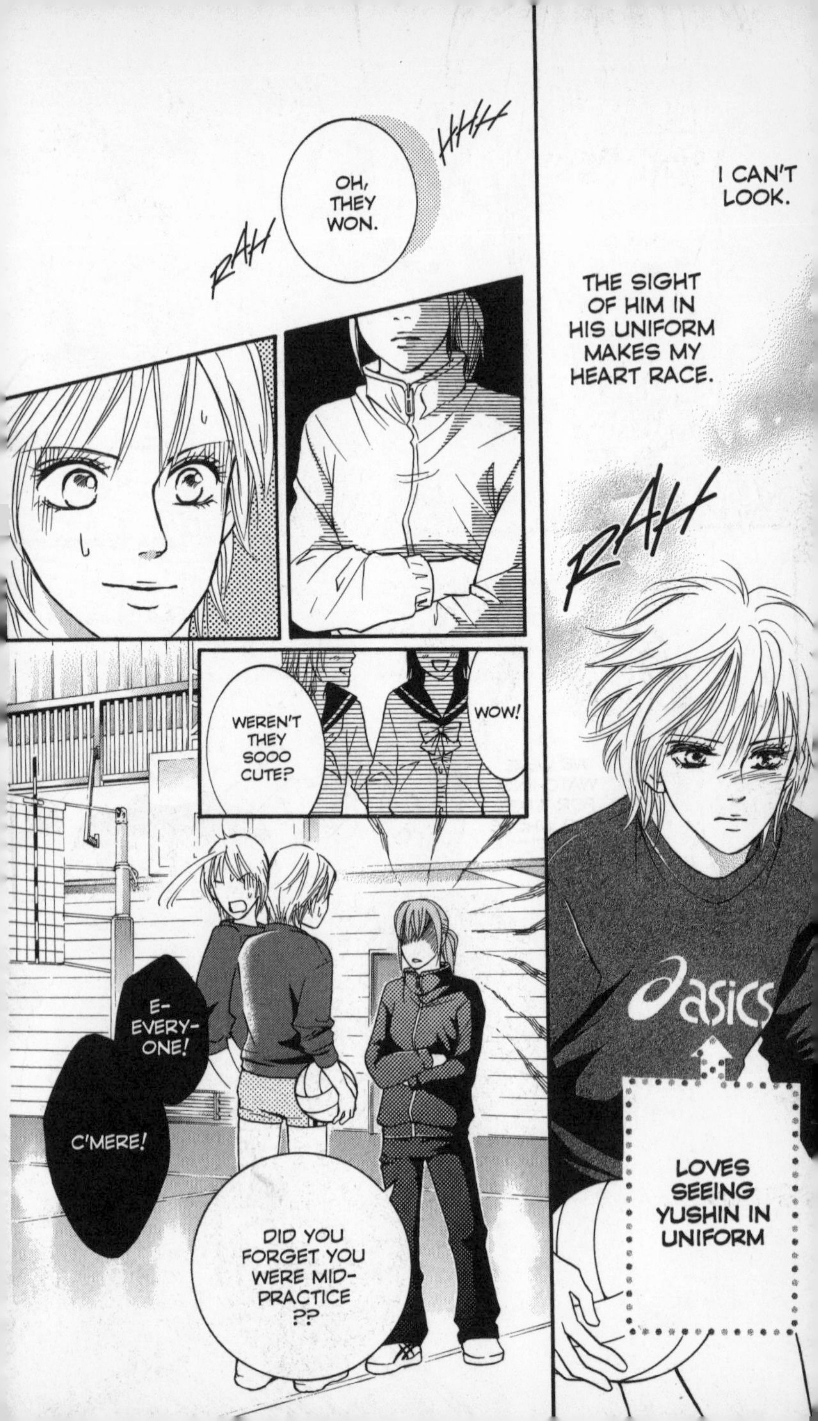
I CAN'T LOOK.
THE SIGHT OF HIM IN HIS UNIFORM MAKES MY HEART RACE.
RAH
LOVES SEEING YUSHIN IN UNIFORM
HHH
OH, THEY WON.
RAH
WOW!
WEREN'T THEY SOOO CUTE?
E-EVERY-ONE!
C'MERE!
DID YOU FORGET YOU WERE MID-PRACTICE??

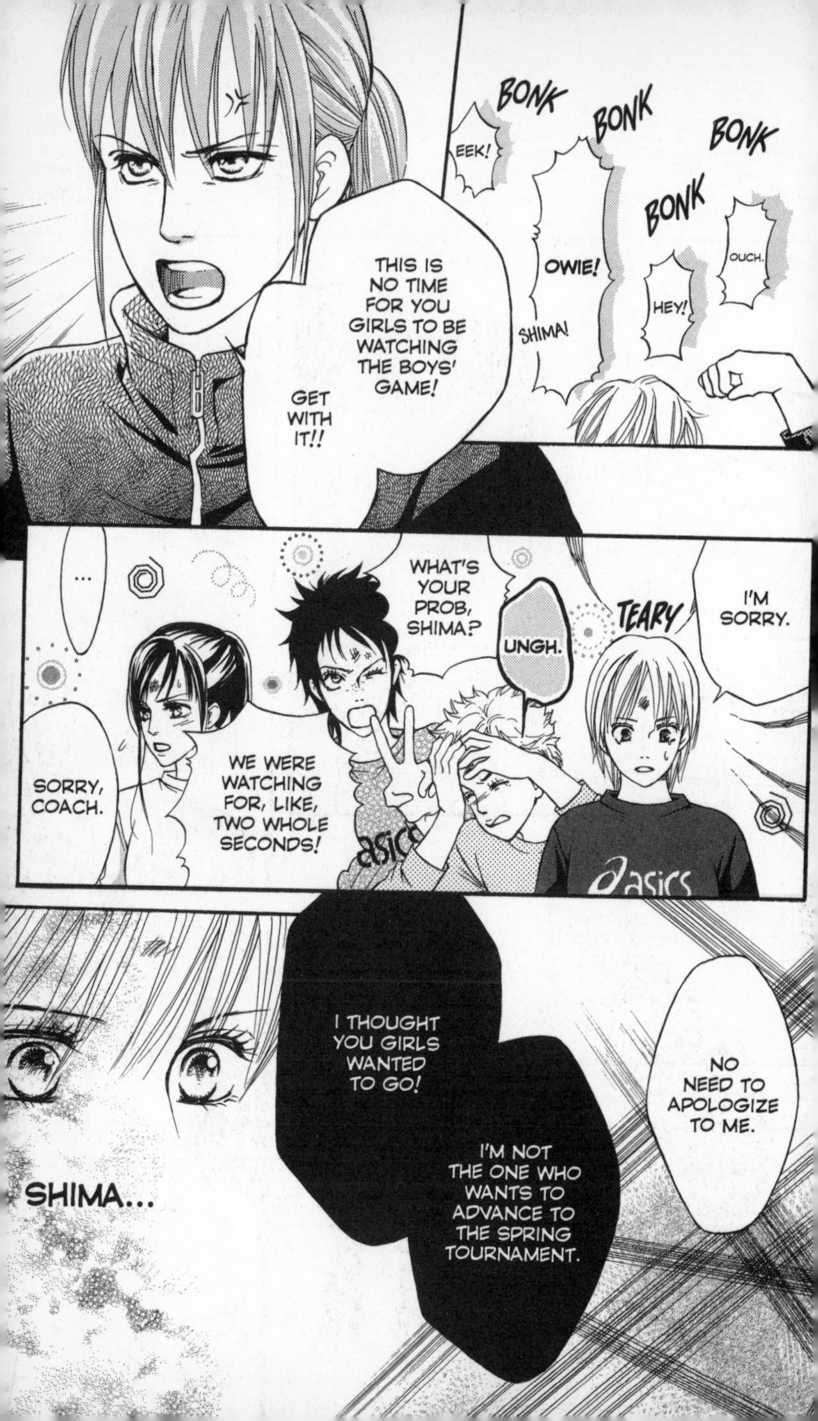
BONK
BONK
BONK
OUCH.
BONK
HEY!
OWIE!
SHIMA!
EEK!
THIS IS NO TIME FOR YOU GIRLS TO BE WATCHING THE BOYS' GAME!
GET WITH IT!!
I'M SORRY.
TEARY
UNGH.
WHAT'S YOUR PROB, SHIMA?
WE WERE WATCHING FOR, LIKE, TWO WHOLE SECONDS!
...
SORRY, COACH.
NO NEED TO APOLOGIZE TO ME.
I THOUGHT YOU GIRLS WANTED TO GO!
I'M NOT THE ONE WHO WANTS TO ADVANCE TO THE SPRING TOURNAMENT.
SHIMA...

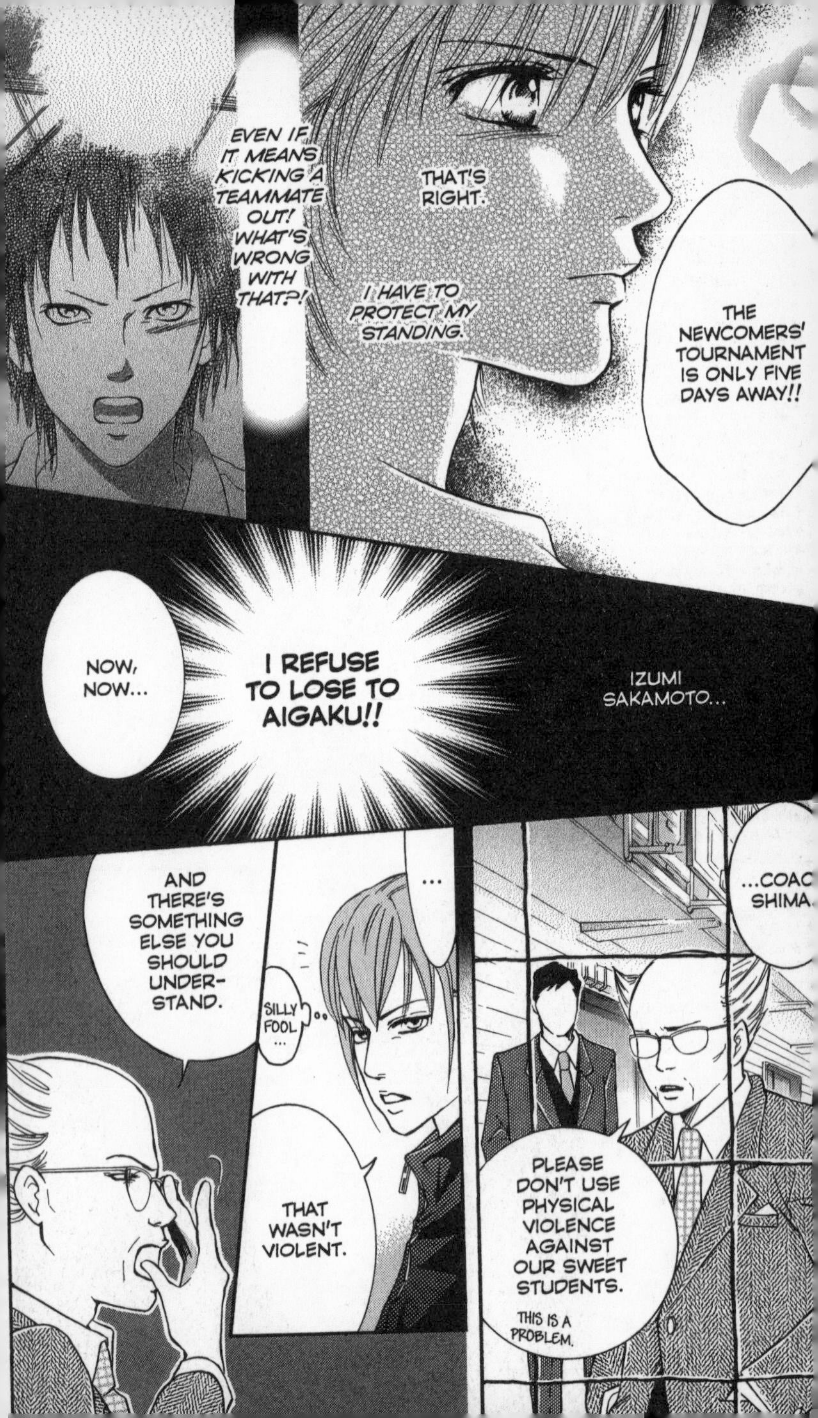
THE NEWCOMERS' TOURNAMENT IS ONLY FIVE DAYS AWAY!!
THAT'S RIGHT.
I HAVE TO PROTECT MY STANDING.
EVEN IF IT MEANS KICKING A TEAMMATE OUT! WHAT'S WRONG WITH THAT?!
IZUMI SAKAMOTO...
I REFUSE TO LOSE TO AIGAKU!!
NOW, NOW...
...COAC SHIMA.
PLEASE DON'T USE PHYSICAL VIOLENCE AGAINST OUR SWEET STUDENTS.
THIS IS A PROBLEM.
...
SILLY FOOL...
THAT WASN'T VIOLENT.
AND THERE'S SOMETHING ELSE YOU SHOULD UNDER-STAND.

MITSUBA CLUB

VoL. 3

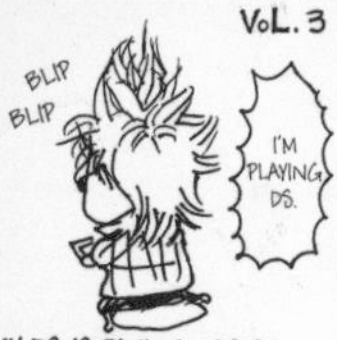
BLIP
BLIP
I'M PLAYING DS.

MY DS IS PINK. I WAS SO EXCITED WHEN I BOUGHT IT, BUT I HAVEN'T PLAYED ANYTHING BUT TETRIS ON IT. WHAT I REALLY WANT IS TO PLAY AN RPG BUT I DON'T HAVE THE CONFIDENCE THAT I WOULD RETURN, SO I'M RESTRAINING MYSELF. LAST YEAR I PLAYED A NEW FINAL FANTASY BUT PARTWAY THROUGH I GOT FRUSTRATED AND I ABANDONED IT. BESIDES THE MAIN STORY, THERE WERE TOO MANY SUBPLOTS AND I COULDN'T KEEP UP. I LIKE SIMPLE GAMES. IF I WIN A ONE-TO-ONE GAME, I'M AS HAPPY AND EXCITED AS A KID.

SPEAKING OF KIDS...I'VE HAD A FULL-ON VERBAL FIGHT WITH GRADE SCHOOL KIDS THREE TIMES. ALL AFTER I BECAME A GROWN-UP...WITH KIDS I DON'T EVEN KNOW. WHEN I WAS IN KYOTO, I LIVED NEAR A FAIRLY OLD HOUSE. SOME SCHOOLBOYS WERE KICKING THE CRUMBLING WALL OF THE HOUSE ON THEIR WAY HOME FROM THE STORE. AT FIRST I JUST SAID SOMETHING LIKE, "HEY, YOU SHOULDN'T DO THAT." BUT THEY RETORTED, "HUH? WHO ARE YOU? THIS YOUR PLACE?" AND THEN, "STUPID!" I FELT THE BLOOD RUSH TO MY HEAD AND I SHOUTED, "WHAT THE HECK DO THEY TEACH YOU KIDS IN SCHOOL?!" I SUNK TO THEIR LEVEL IN A SHOUTING MATCH AND I REMEMBER BEING REALLY PISSED OFF. SO UNADULT-LIKE. AND TO TOP IF OFF, I LOST THAT FIGHT...

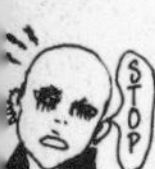
STOP

IF I WERE A REALLY TOUGH MIDDLE-AGED MAN, WOULD THE SCHOOLKIDS HAVE LISTENED TO ME?

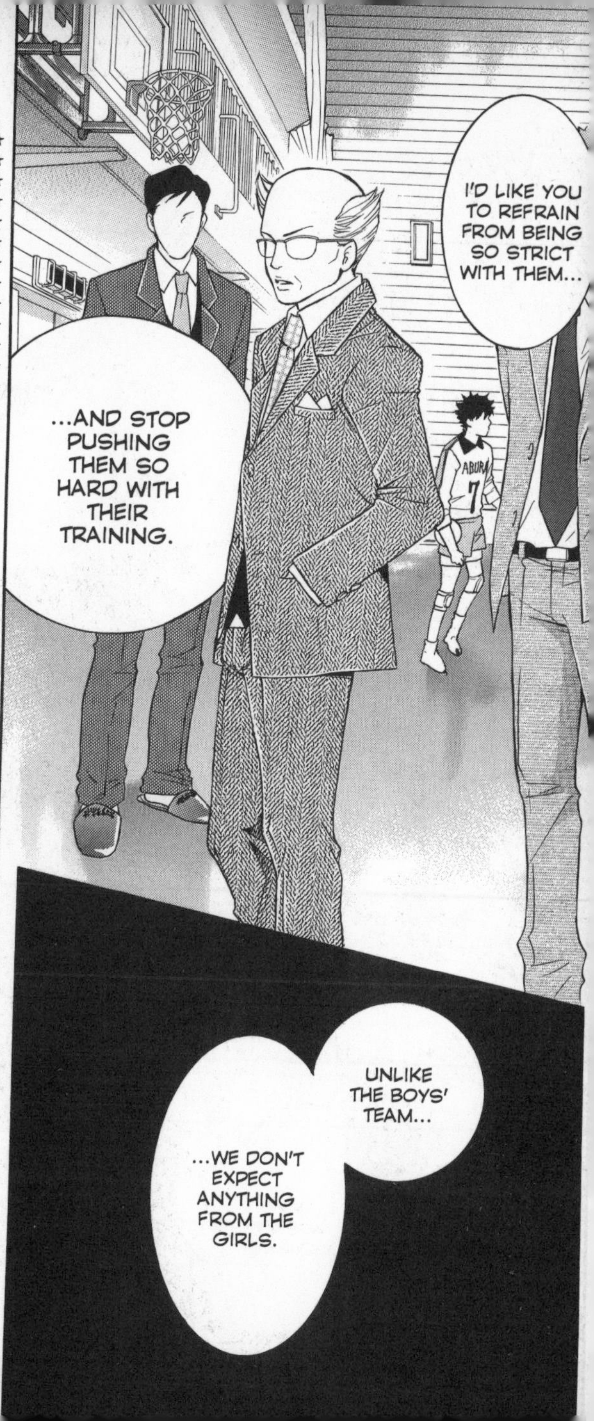
I'D LIKE YOU TO REFRAIN FROM BEING SO STRICT WITH THEM...
...AND STOP PUSHING THEM SO HARD WITH THEIR TRAINING.
UNLIKE THE BOYS' TEAM...
...WE DON'T EXPECT ANYTHING FROM THE GIRLS.

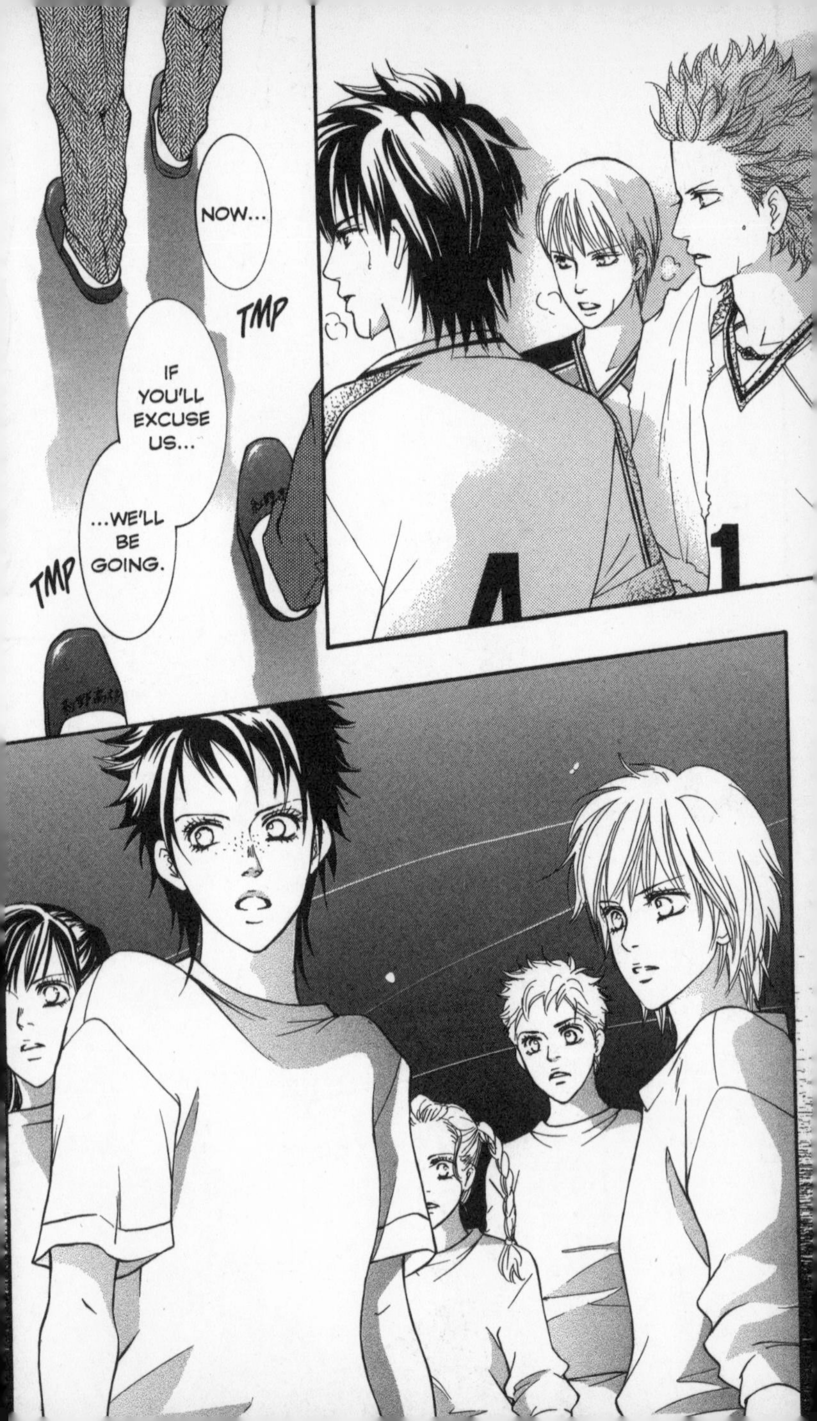
NOW...
TMP
IF YOU'LL EXCUSE US...
...WE'LL BE GOING.
TMP

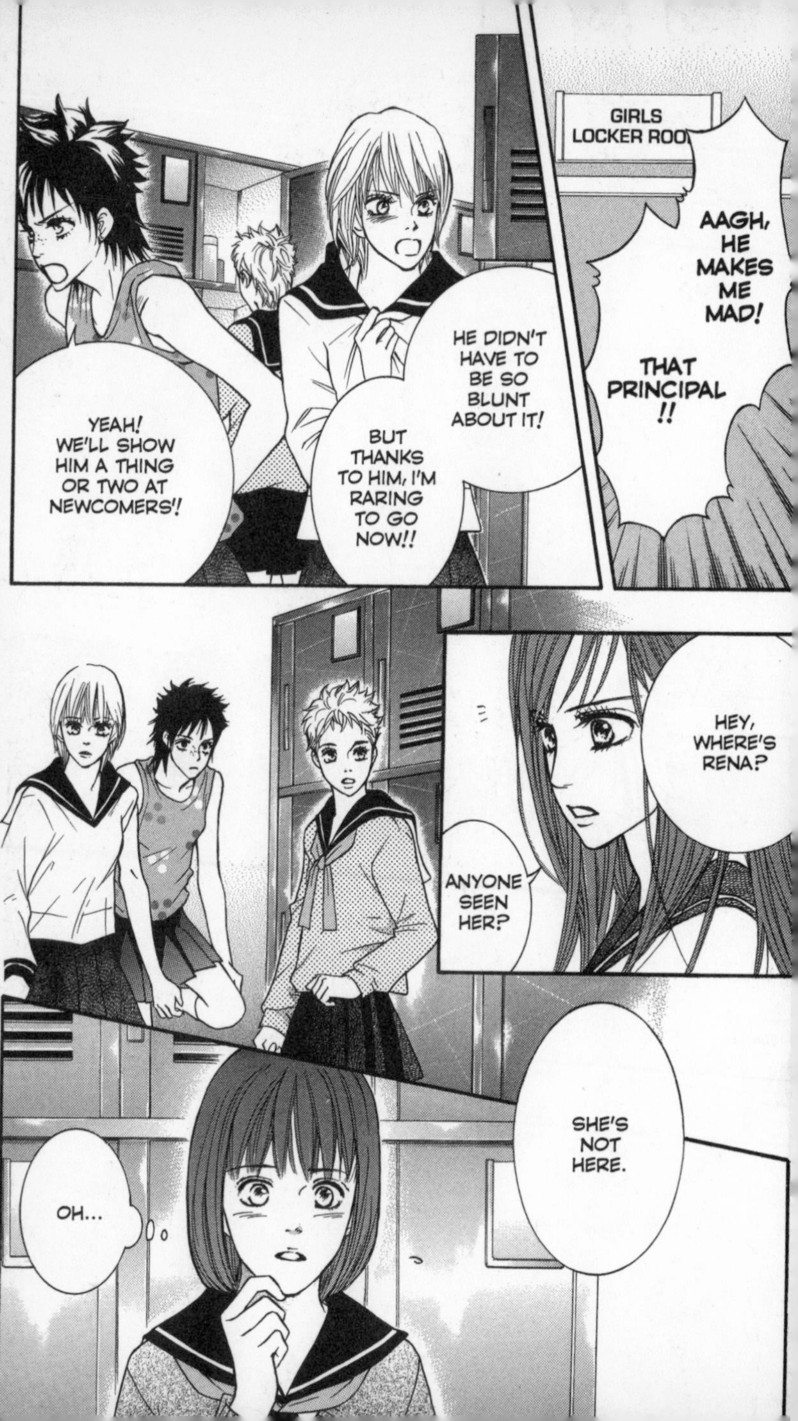
GIRLS LOCKER ROO
AAGH, HE MAKES ME MAD!
THAT PRINCIPAL!!
HE DIDN'T HAVE TO BE SO BLUNT ABOUT IT!
BUT THANKS TO HIM, I'M RARING TO GO NOW!!
YEAH! WE'LL SHOW HIM A THING OR TWO AT NEWCOMERS'!
HEY, WHERE'S RENA?
ANYONE SEEN HER?
SHE'S NOT HERE.
OH...

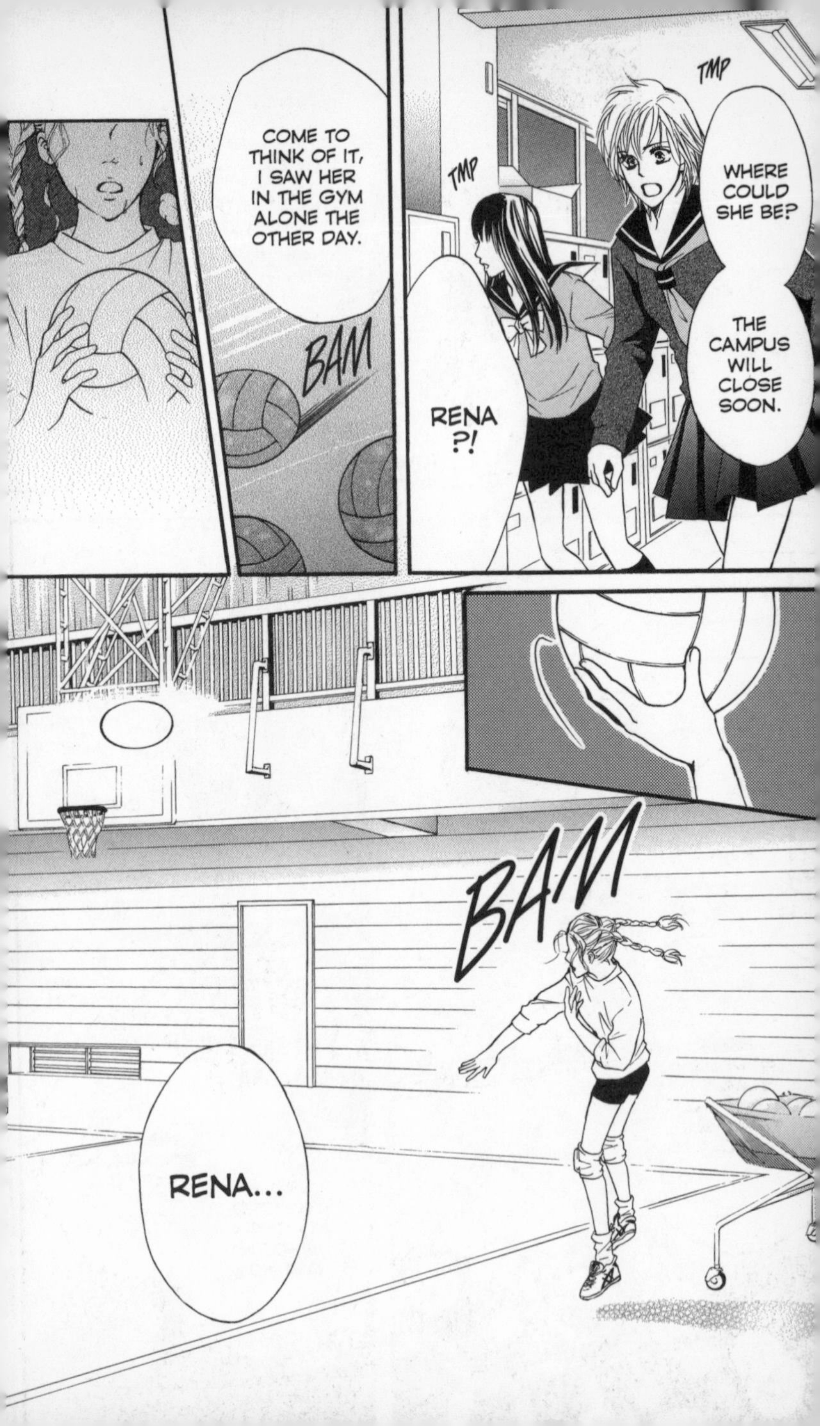
TMP
WHERE COULD SHE BE?
THE CAMPUS WILL CLOSE SOON.
TMP
RENA ?!
COME TO THINK OF IT, I SAW HER IN THE GYM ALONE THE OTHER DAY.
BAM
BAM
RENA...

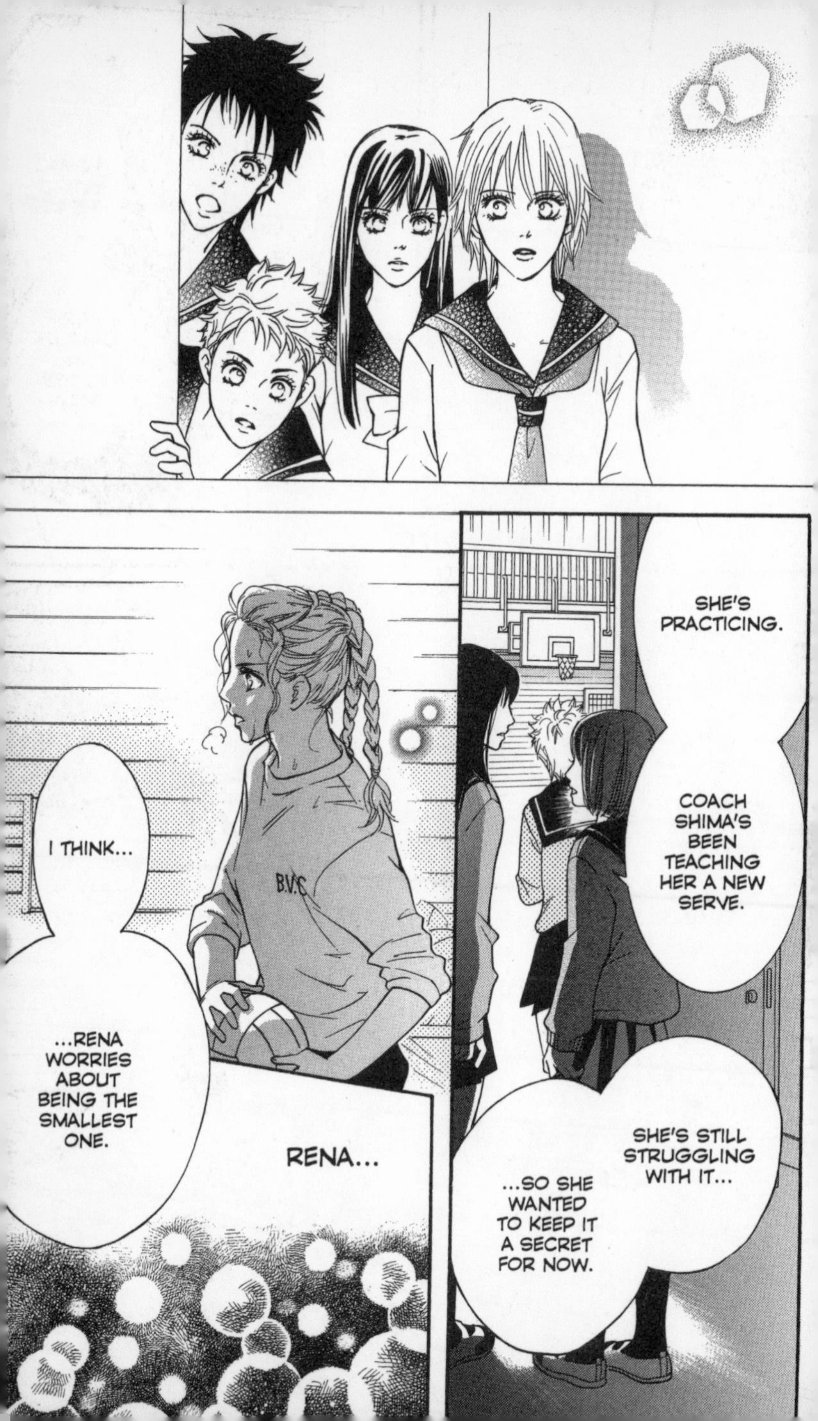
SHE'S PRACTICING.
COACH SHIMA'S BEEN TEACHING HER A NEW SERVE.
SHE'S STILL STRUGGLING WITH IT...
...SO SHE WANTED TO KEEP IT A SECRET FOR NOW.
I THINK...
...RENA WORRIES ABOUT BEING THE SMALLEST ONE.
RENA...
B.V.C

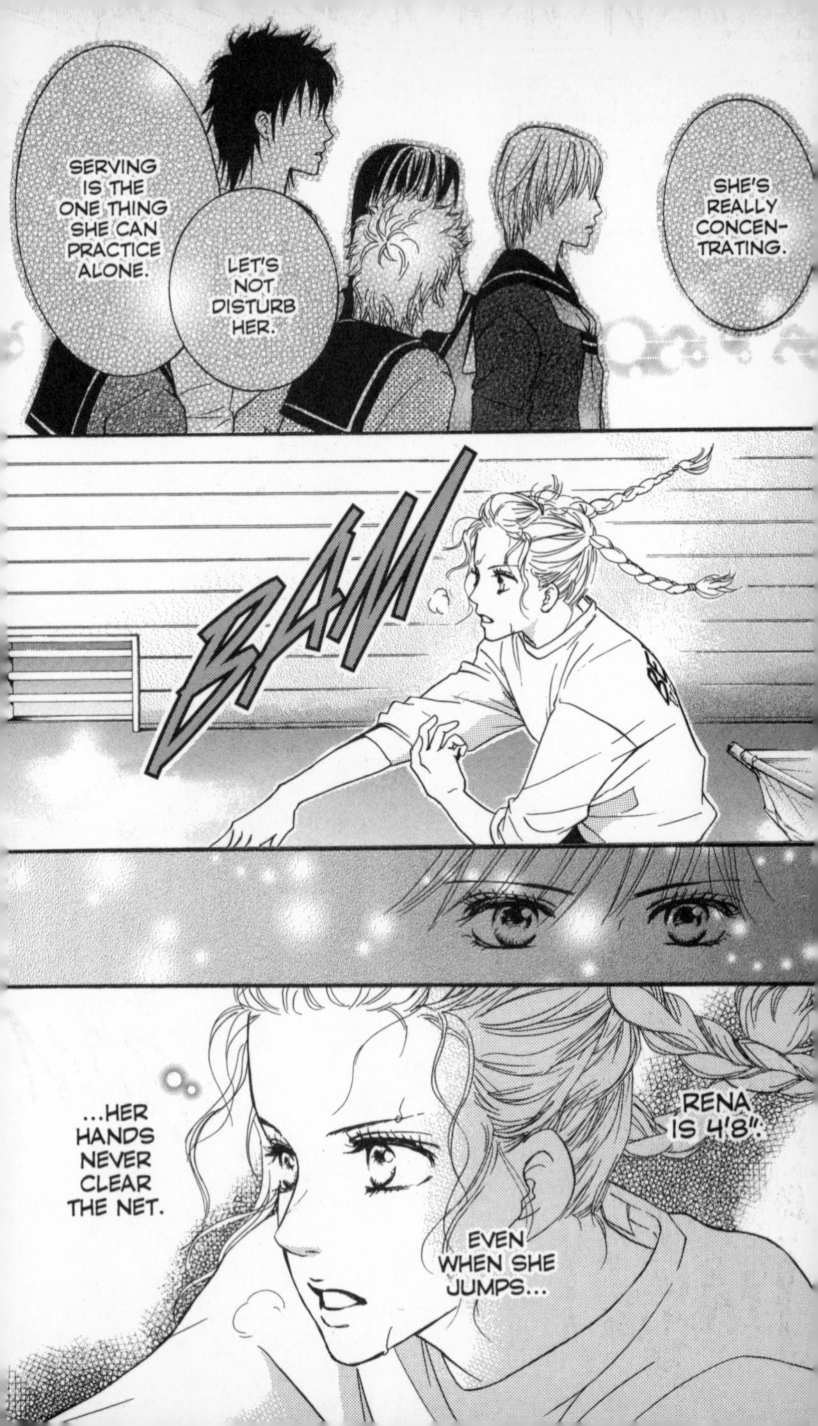
SHE'S REALLY CONCEN-TRATING.
LET'S NOT DISTURB HER.
SERVING IS THE ONE THING SHE CAN PRACTICE ALONE.
BAM
RENA IS 4'8".
EVEN WHEN SHE JUMPS...
...HER HANDS NEVER CLEAR THE NET.

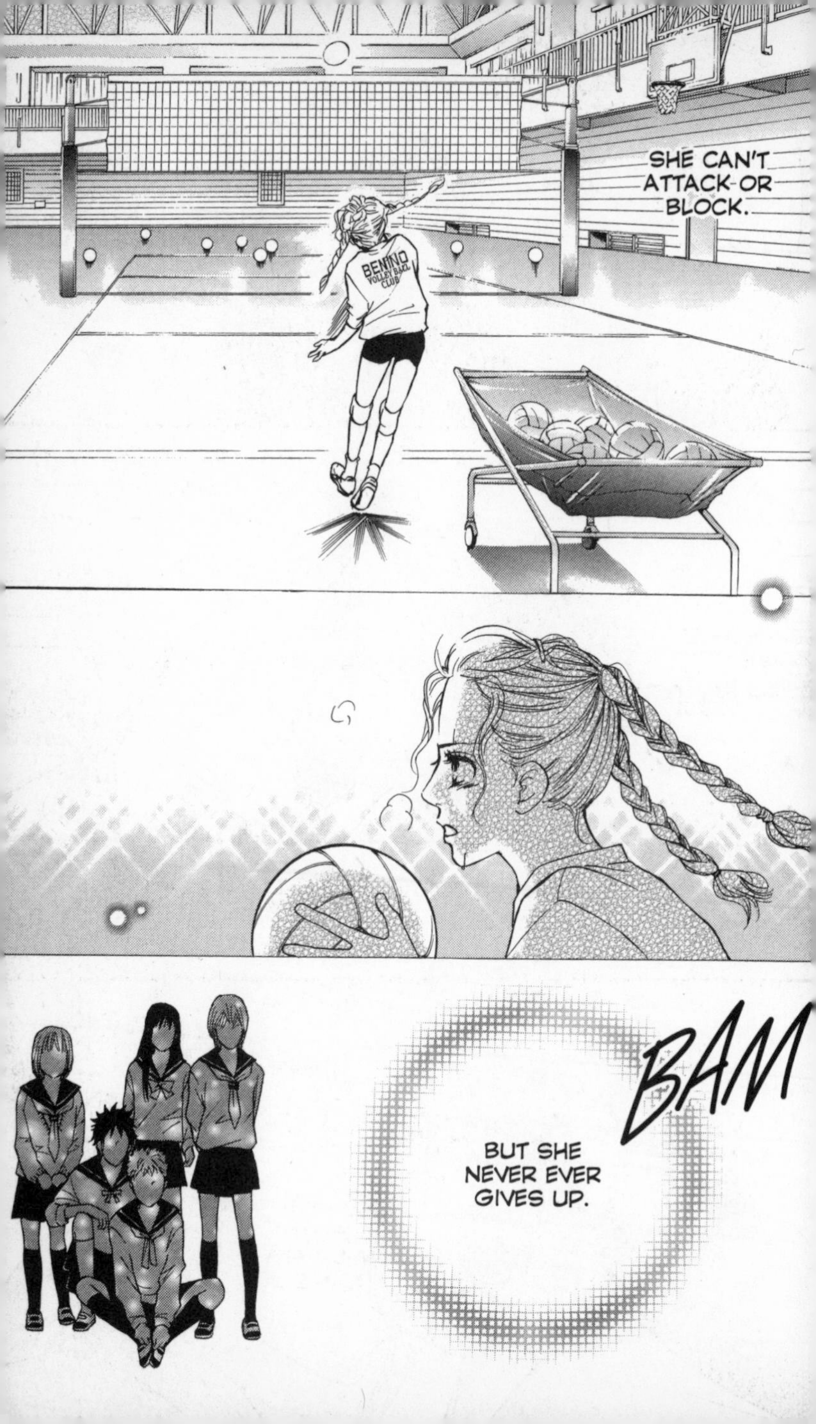
SHE CAN'T ATTACK OR BLOCK.
BENINO VOLLEYBALL CLUB
BAM
BUT SHE NEVER EVER GIVES UP.

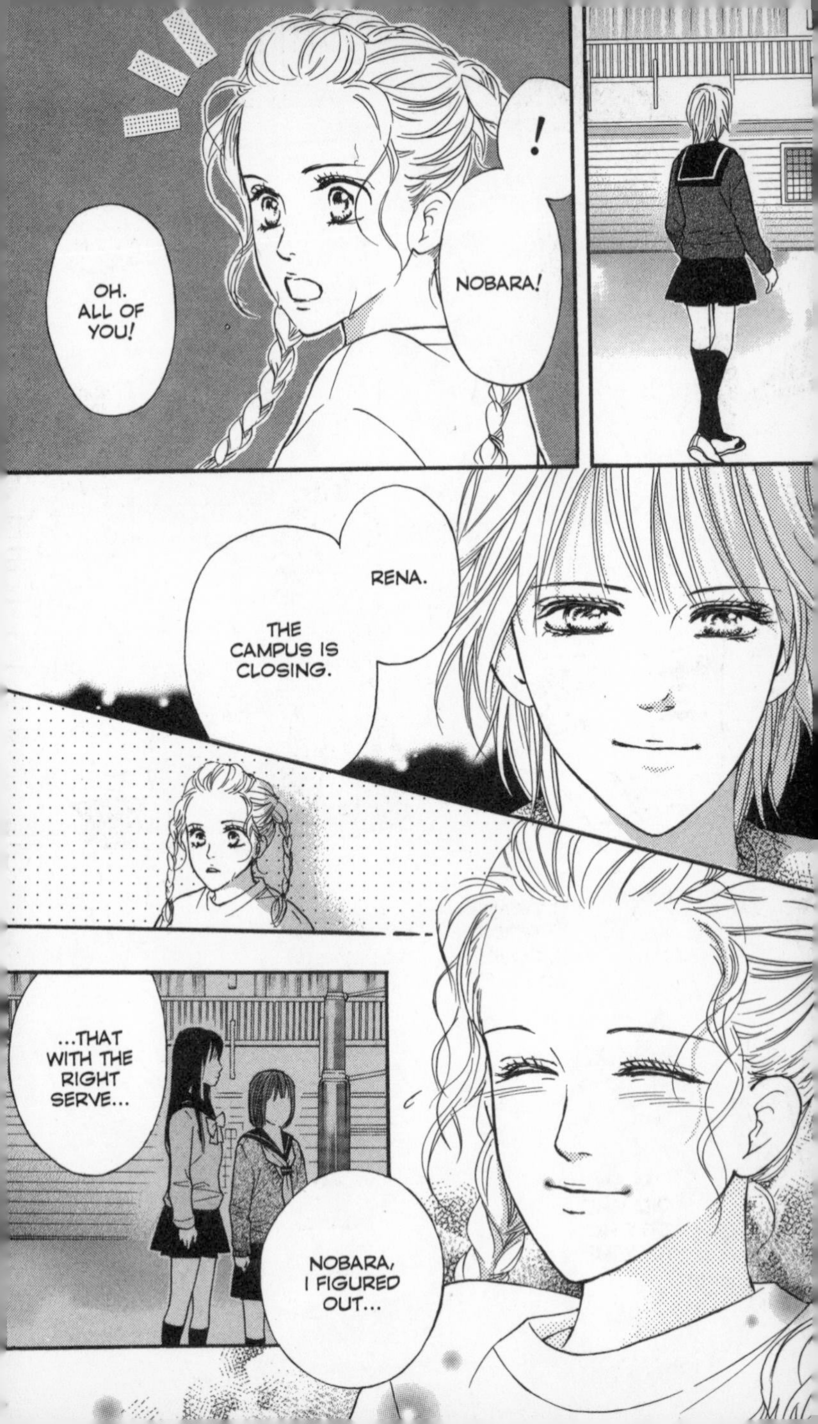
!
NOBARA!
OH. ALL OF YOU!
RENA.
THE CAMPUS IS CLOSING.
NOBARA, I FIGURED OUT...
...THAT WITH THE RIGHT SERVE...

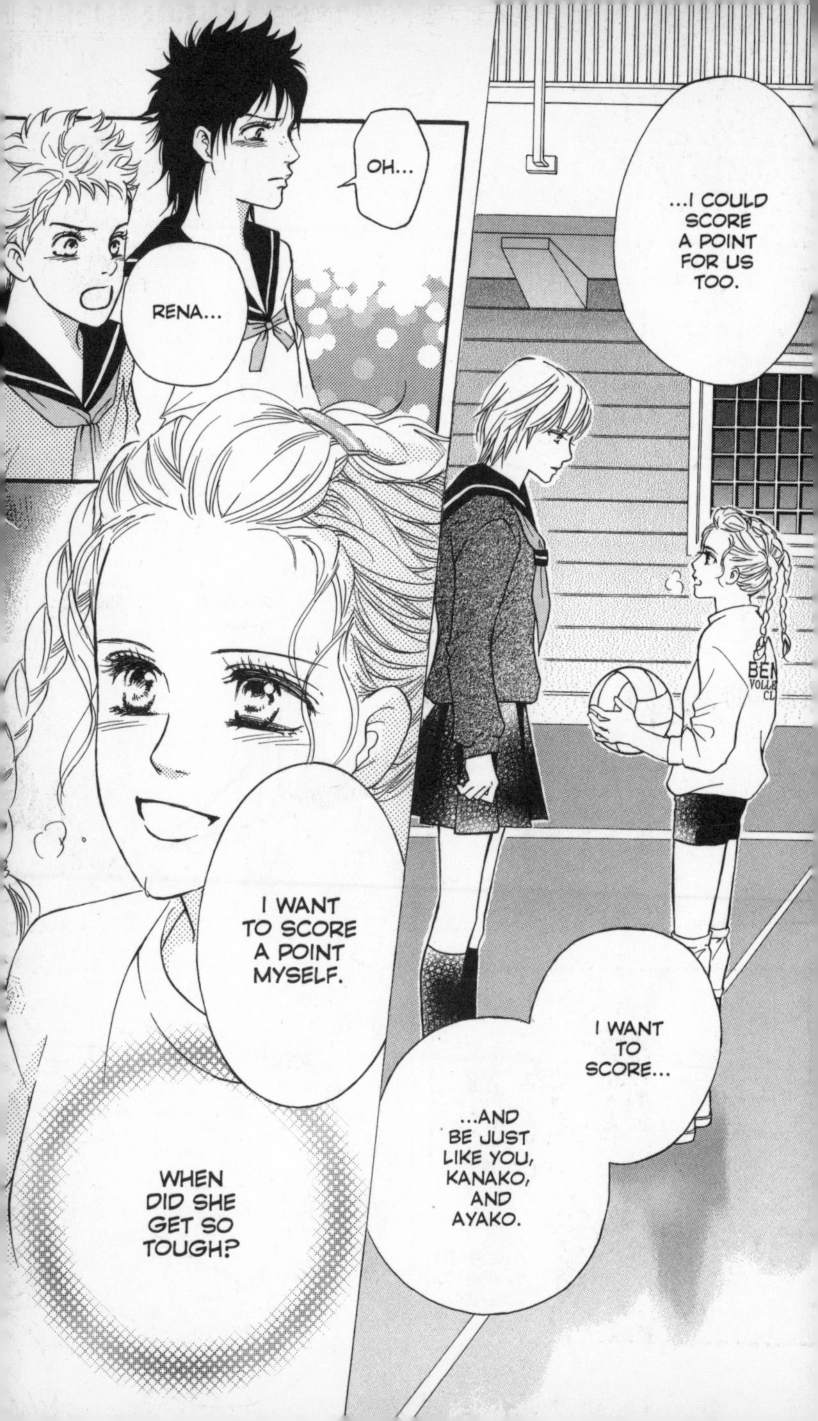
...I COULD SCORE A POINT FOR US TOO.
I WANT TO SCORE...
...AND BE JUST LIKE YOU, KANAKO, AND AYAKO.
OH...
RENA...
I WANT TO SCORE A POINT MYSELF.
WHEN DID SHE GET SO TOUGH?

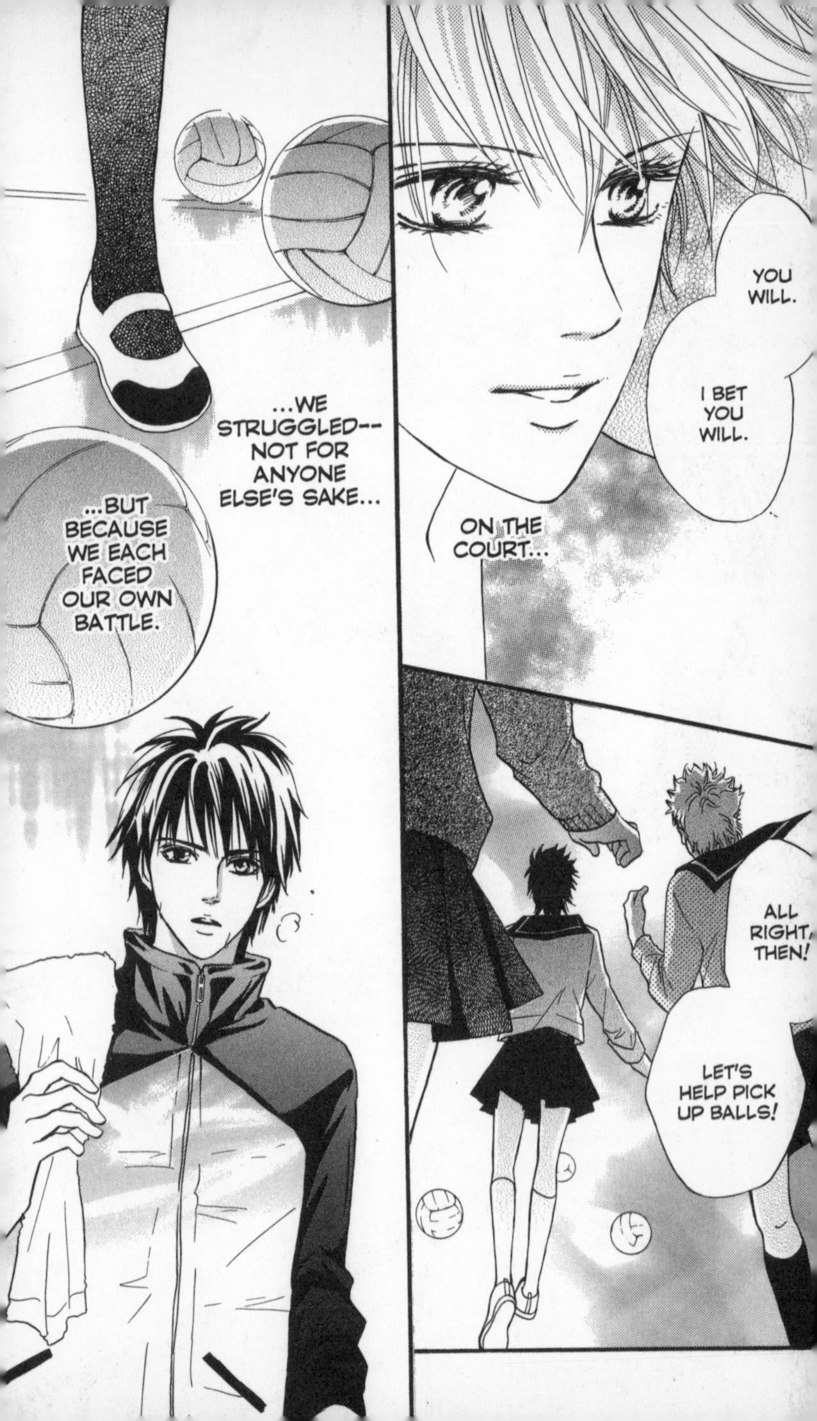
YOU WILL.
I BET YOU WILL.
ON THE COURT...
ALL RIGHT, THEN!
LET'S HELP PICK UP BALLS!
...WE STRUGGLED--NOT FOR ANYONE ELSE'S SAKE...
...BUT BECAUSE WE EACH FACED OUR OWN BATTLE.

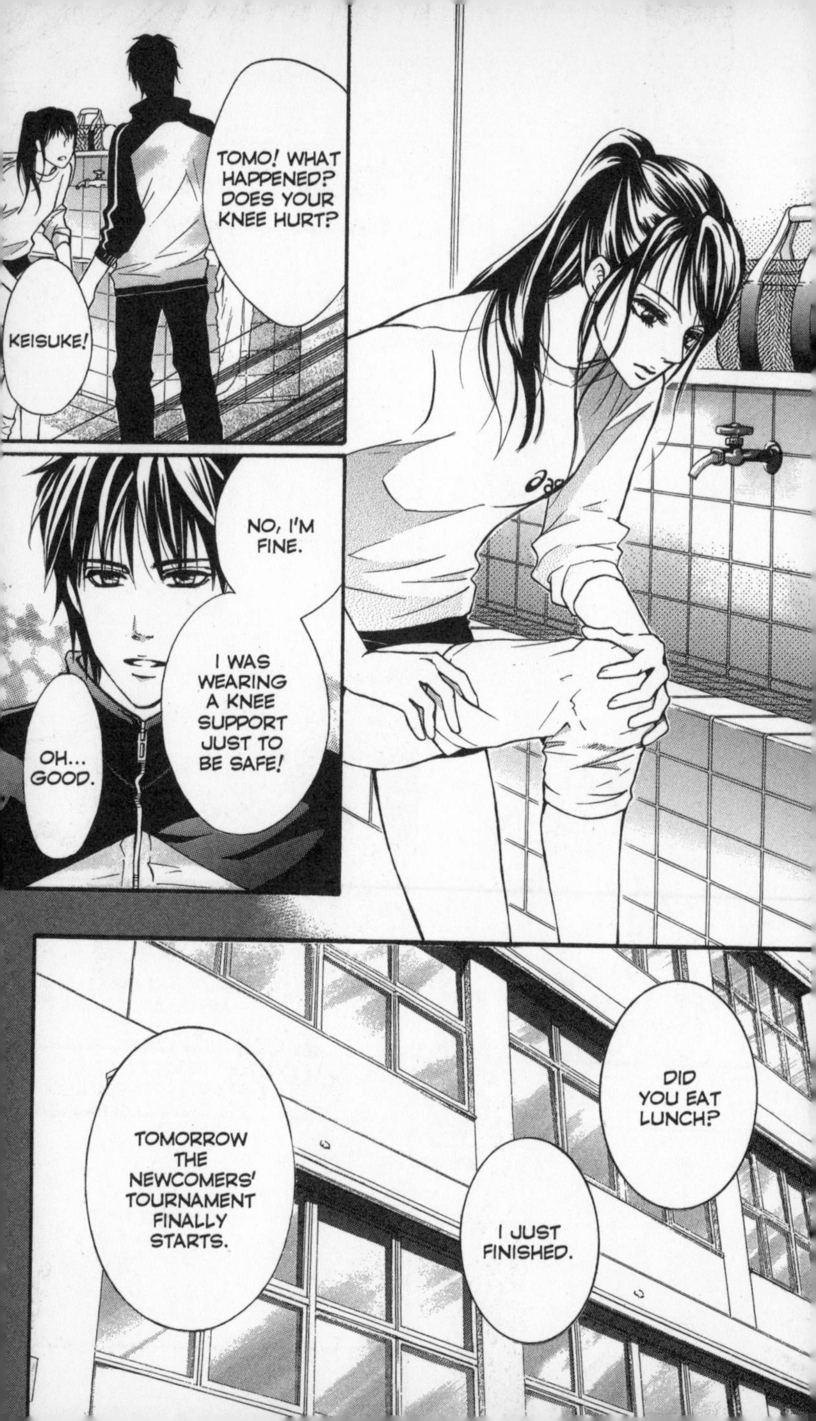
TOMO! WHAT HAPPENED? DOES YOUR KNEE HURT?
KEISUKE!
NO, I'M FINE.
I WAS WEARING A KNEE SUPPORT JUST TO BE SAFE!
OH... GOOD.
DID YOU EAT LUNCH?
I JUST FINISHED.
TOMORROW THE NEWCOMERS' TOURNAMENT FINALLY STARTS.

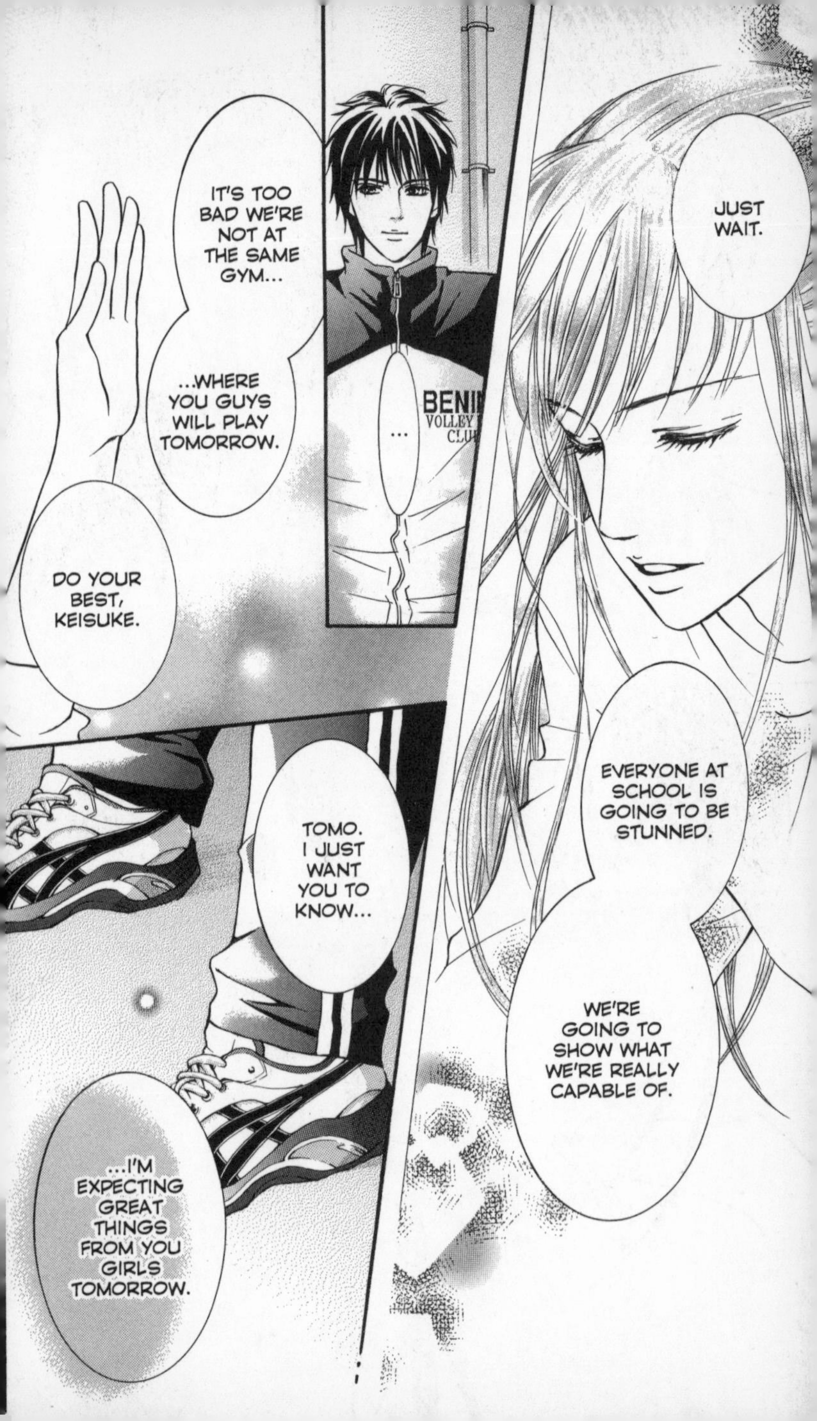
IT'S TOO BAD WE'RE NOT AT THE SAME GYM...
...WHERE YOU GUYS WILL PLAY TOMORROW.
...
BENI
VOLLEY
CLU
DO YOUR BEST, KEISUKE.
TOMO. I JUST WANT YOU TO KNOW...
...I'M EXPECTING GREAT THINGS FROM YOU GIRLS TOMORROW.
JUST WAIT.
EVERYONE AT SCHOOL IS GOING TO BE STUNNED.
WE'RE GOING TO SHOW WHAT WE'RE REALLY CAPABLE OF.

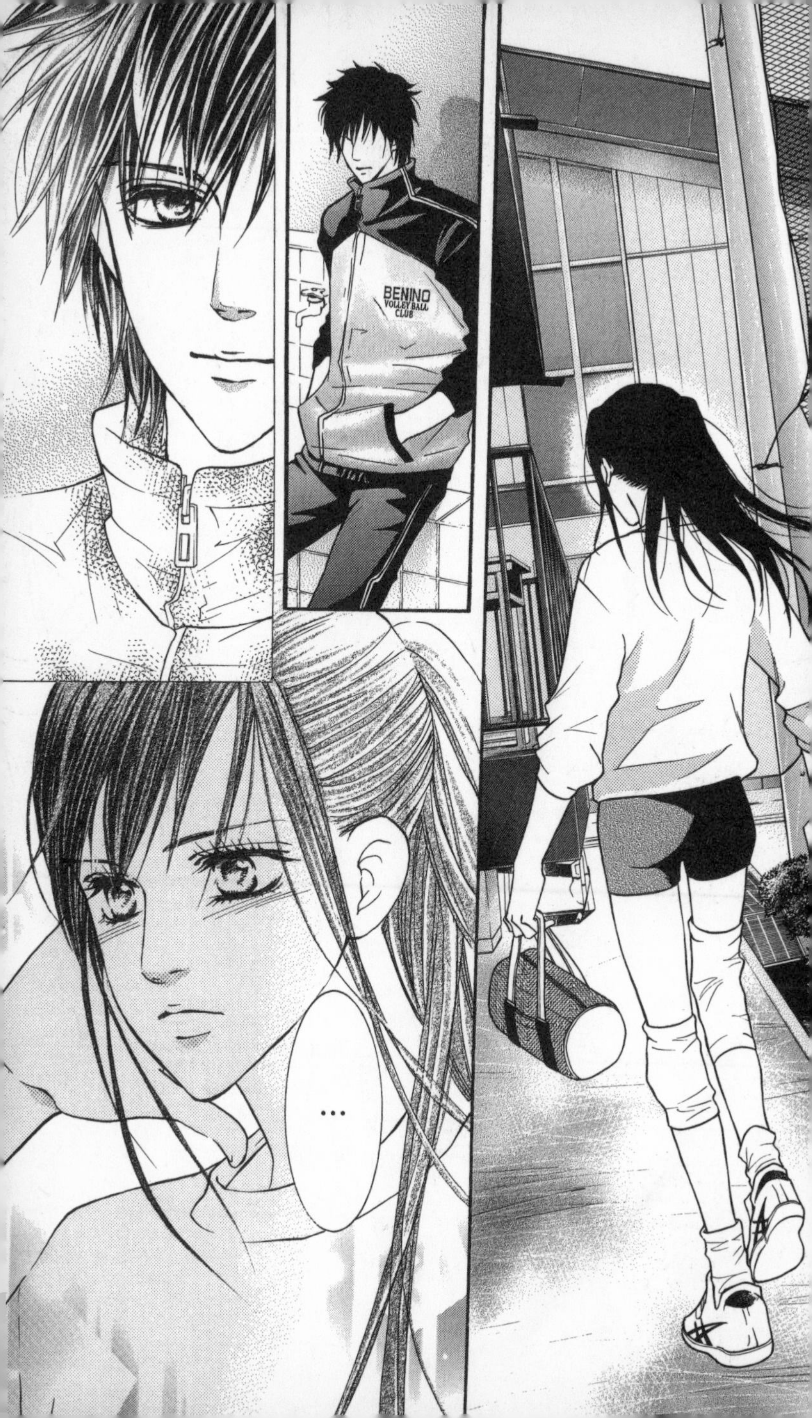
BENINO
VOLLEY BALL
CLUB
...

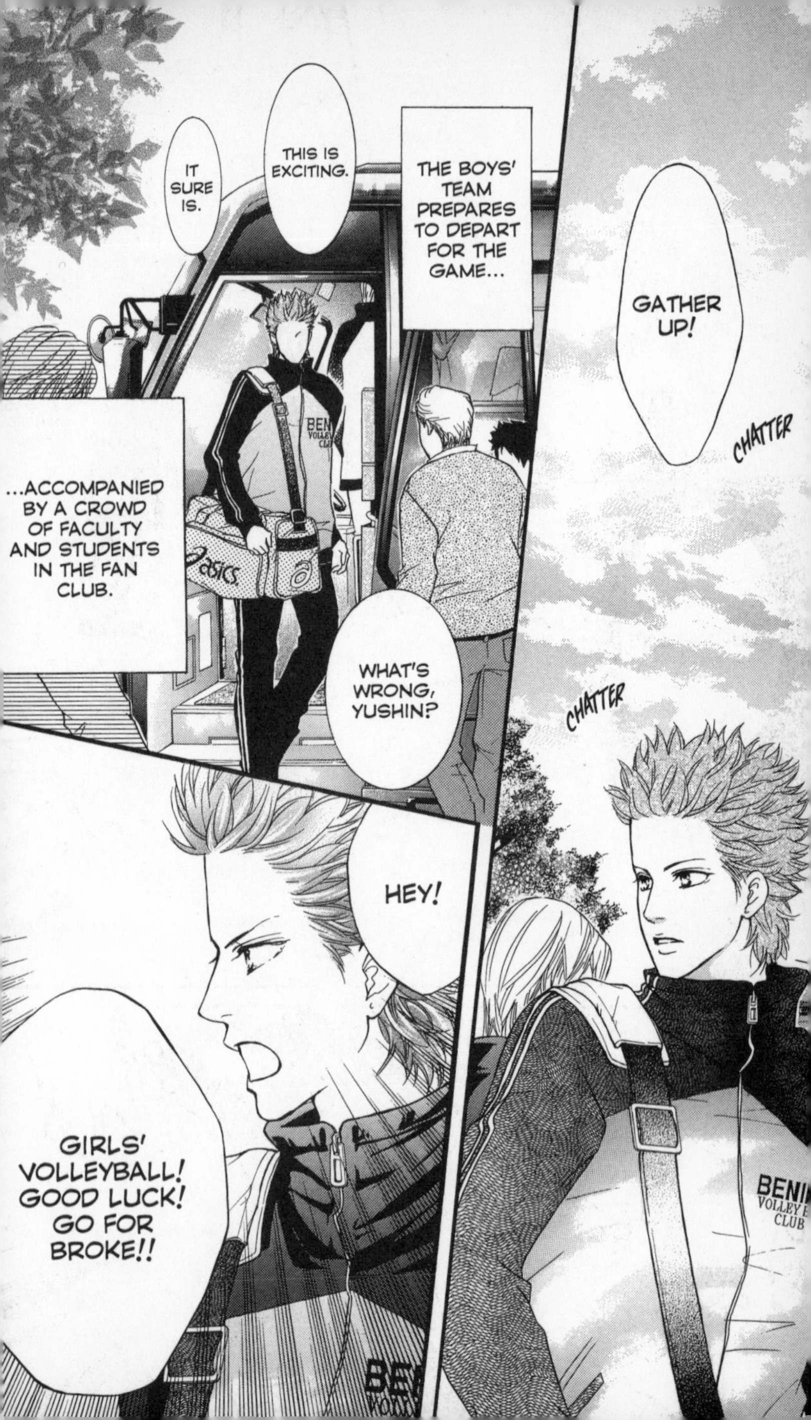
GATHER UP!
CHATTER
CHATTER
THE BOYS' TEAM PREPARES TO DEPART FOR THE GAME...
THIS IS EXCITING.
IT SURE IS.
...ACCOMPANIED BY A CROWD OF FACULTY AND STUDENTS IN THE FAN CLUB.
WHAT'S WRONG, YUSHIN?
HEY!
GIRLS' VOLLEYBALL! GOOD LUCK! GO FOR BROKE!!

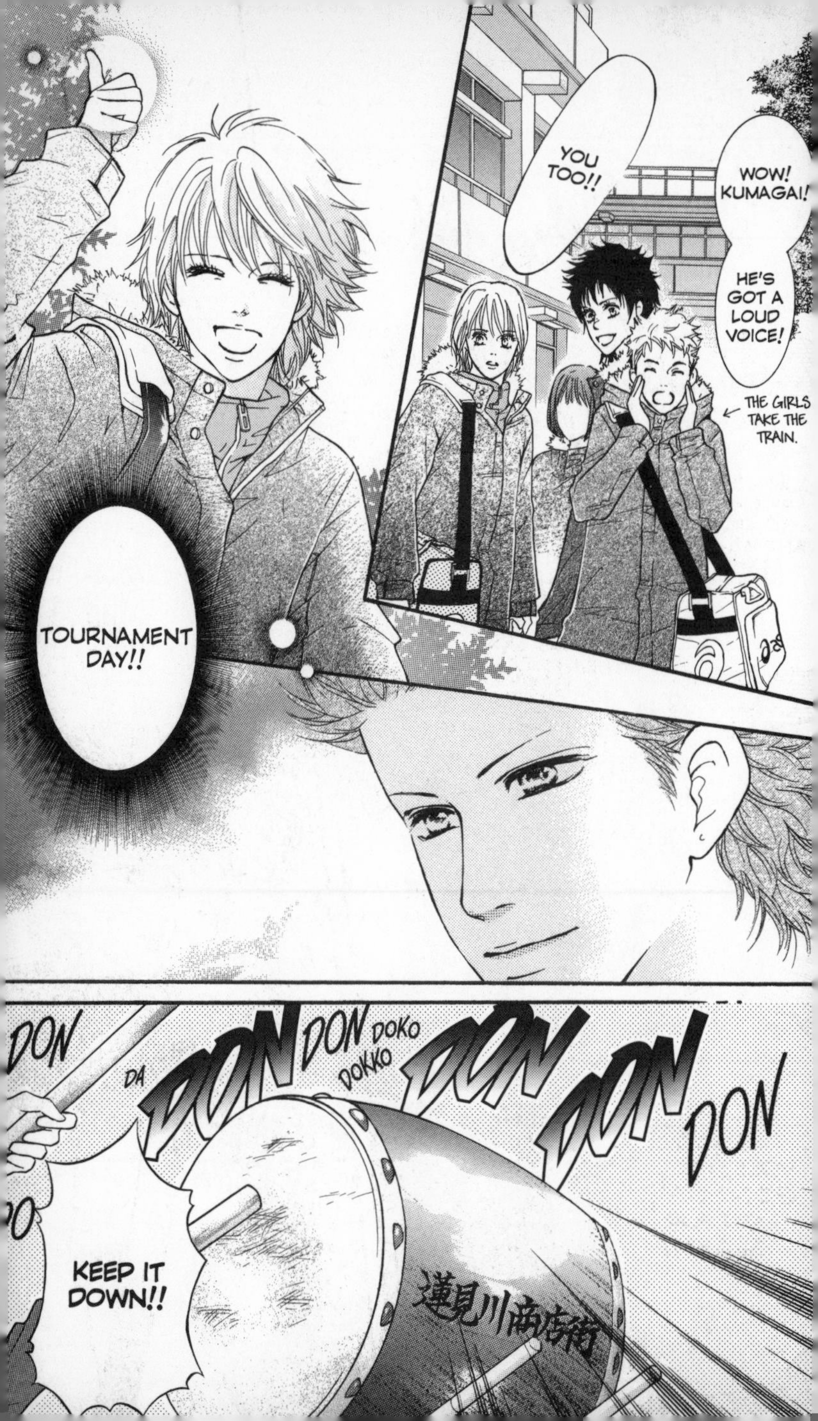
WOW! KUMAGAI!
HE'S GOT A LOUD VOICE!
THE GIRLS TAKE THE TRAIN.
YOU TOO!!
TOURNAMENT DAY!!
DON
DON
DON
DOKO DOKKO
DON
DON
DA
DON
KEEP IT DOWN!!
蓮見川商店街

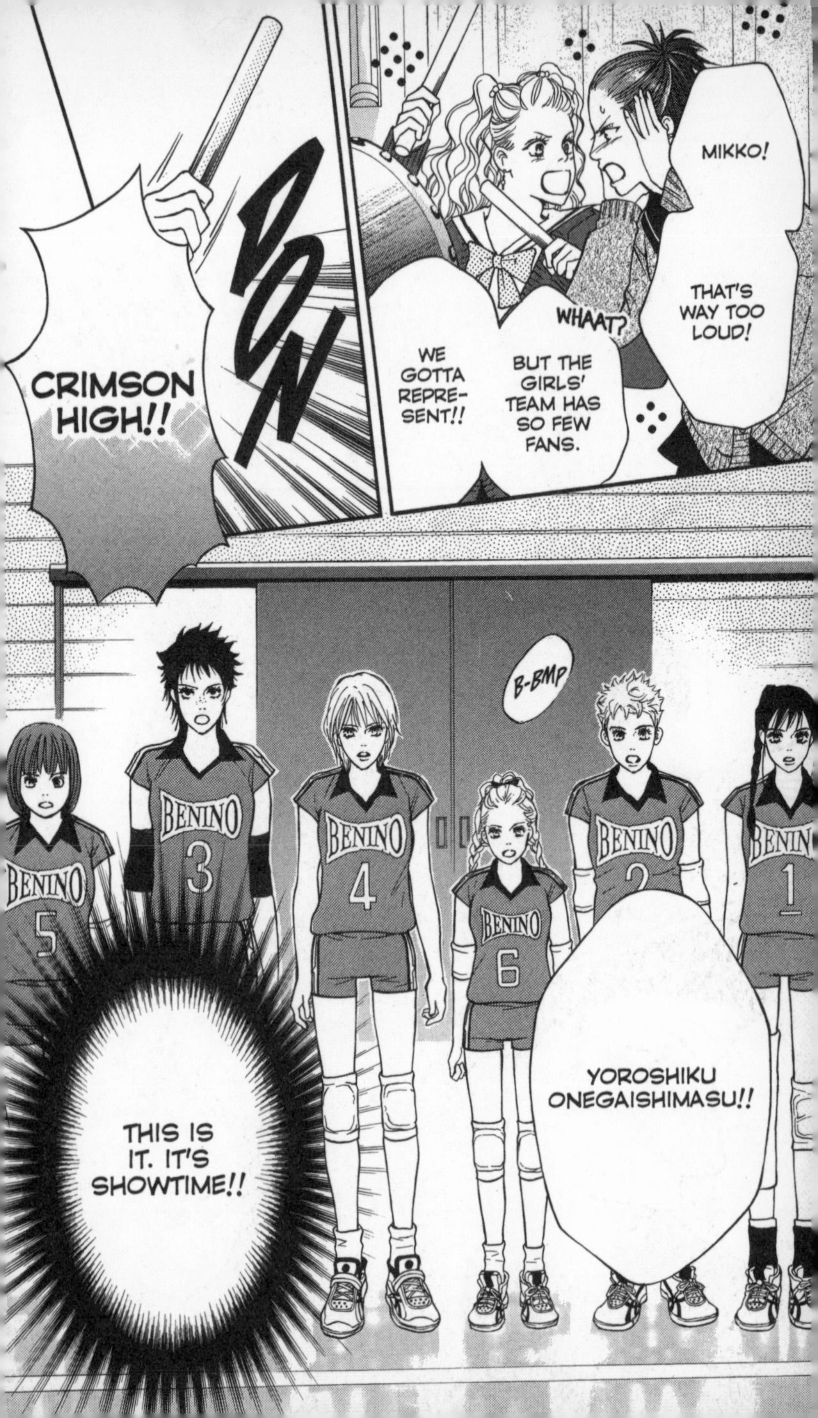
MIKKO!
THAT'S WAY TOO LOUD!
WHAAT?
BUT THE GIRLS' TEAM HAS SO FEW FANS.
WE GOTTA REPRESENT!!
DON
CRIMSON HIGH!!
B-BMP
YOROSHIKU ONEGAISHIMASU!!
THIS IS IT. IT'S SHOWTIME!!

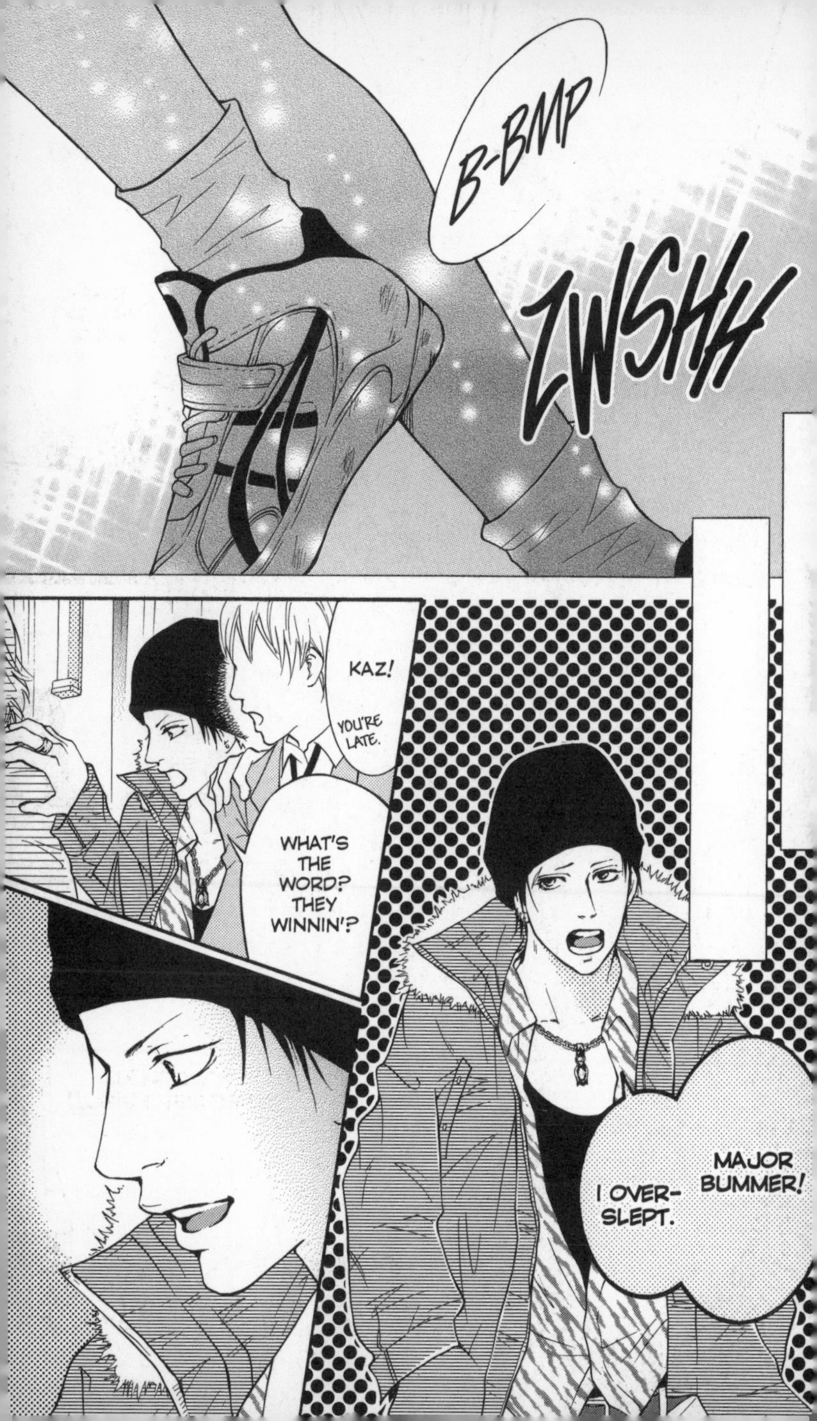
B-BMP
ZWSHH
MAJOR BUMMER!
I OVER-SLEPT.
KAZ!
YOU'RE LATE.
WHAT'S THE WORD? THEY WINNIN'?

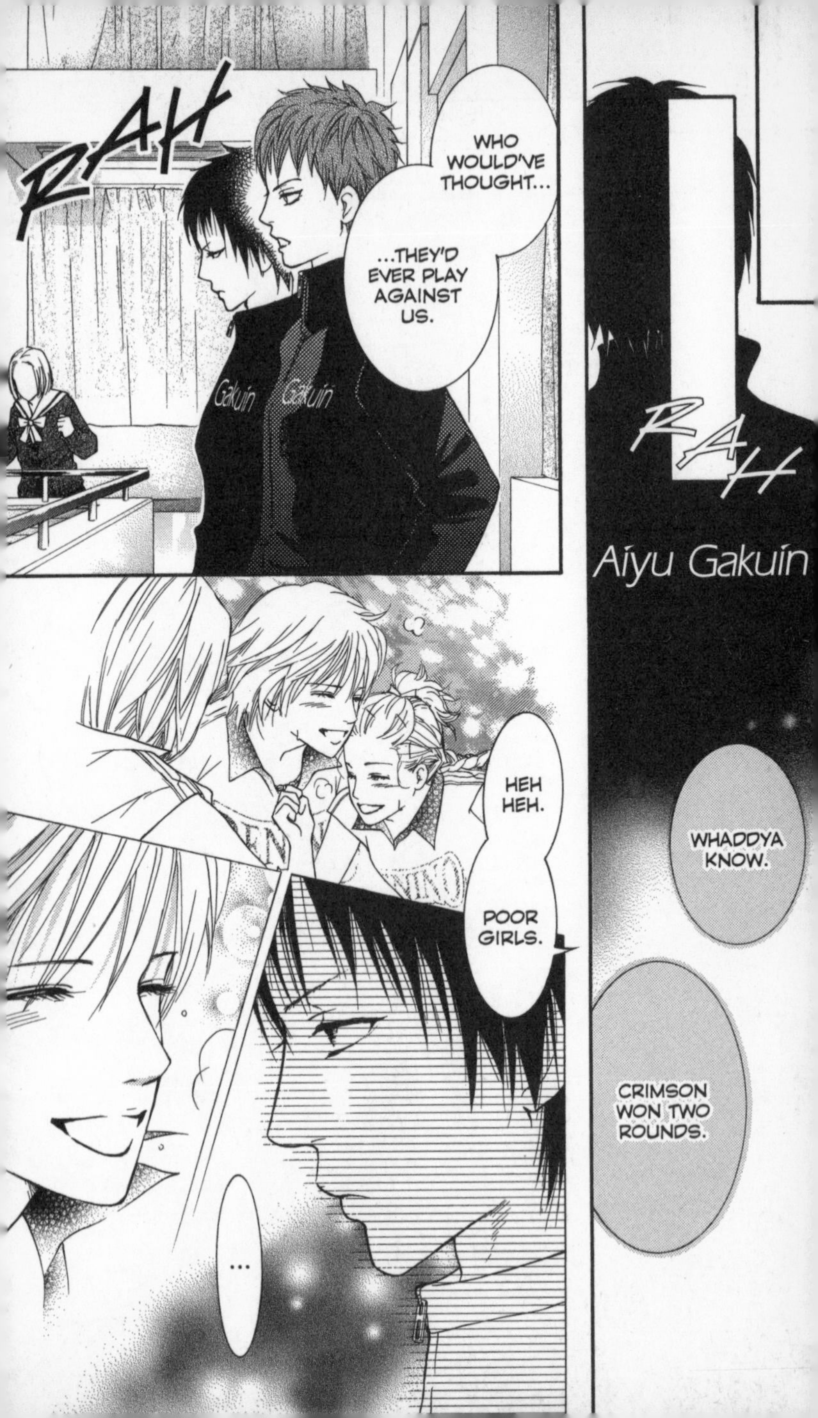
RAH
Aiyu Gakuin
WHADDYA KNOW.
CRIMSON WON TWO ROUNDS.
RAH
WHO WOULD'VE THOUGHT...
...THEY'D EVER PLAY AGAINST US.
HEH HEH.
POOR GIRLS.
...

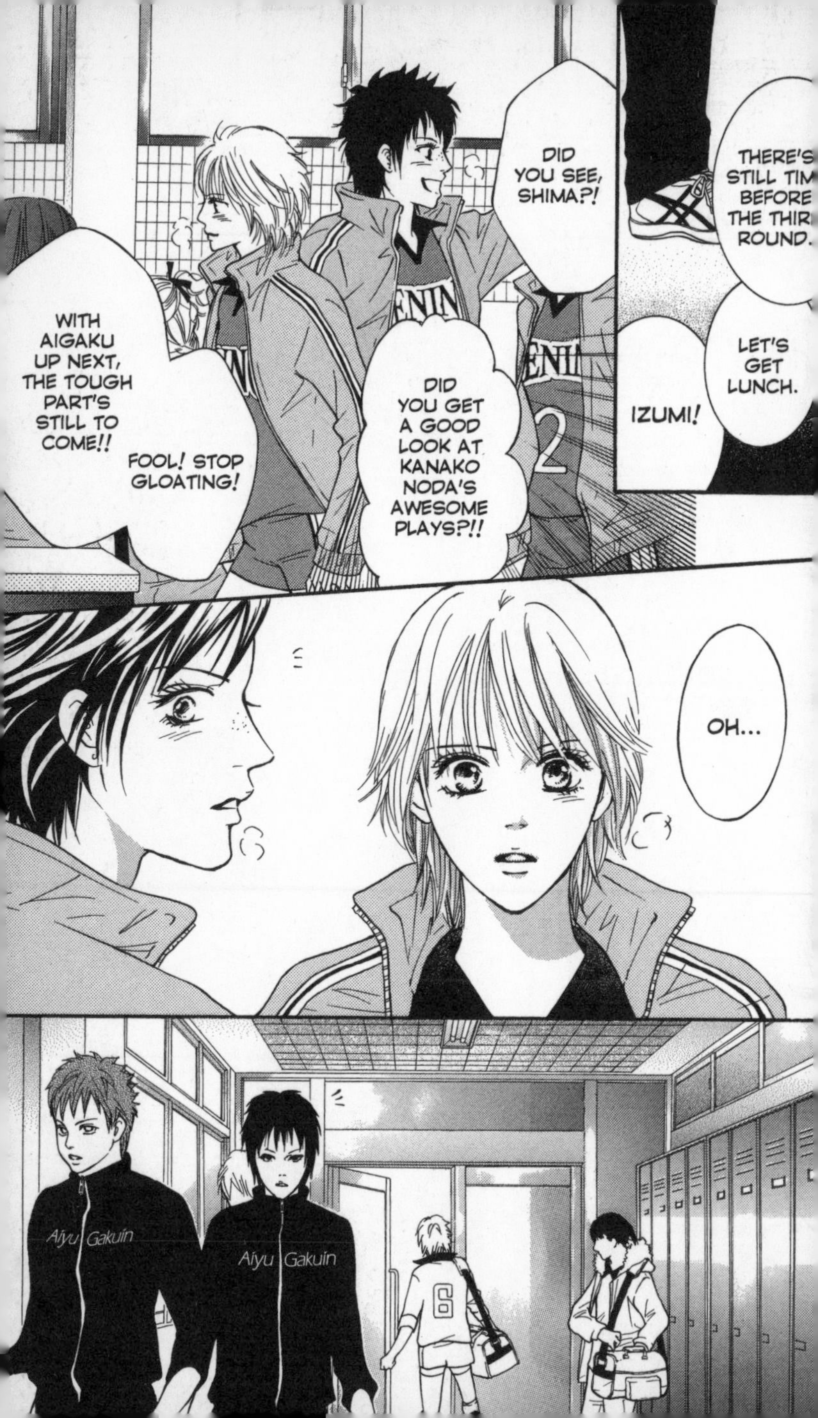
THERE'S STILL TIM BEFORE THE THIR ROUND.
LET'S GET LUNCH.
IZUMI!
DID YOU SEE, SHIMA?!
DID YOU GET A GOOD LOOK AT KANAKO NODA'S AWESOME PLAYS?!!
WITH AIGAKU UP NEXT, THE TOUGH PART'S STILL TO COME!!
FOOL! STOP GLOATING!
OH...
Aiyu Gakuin
Aiyu Gakuin

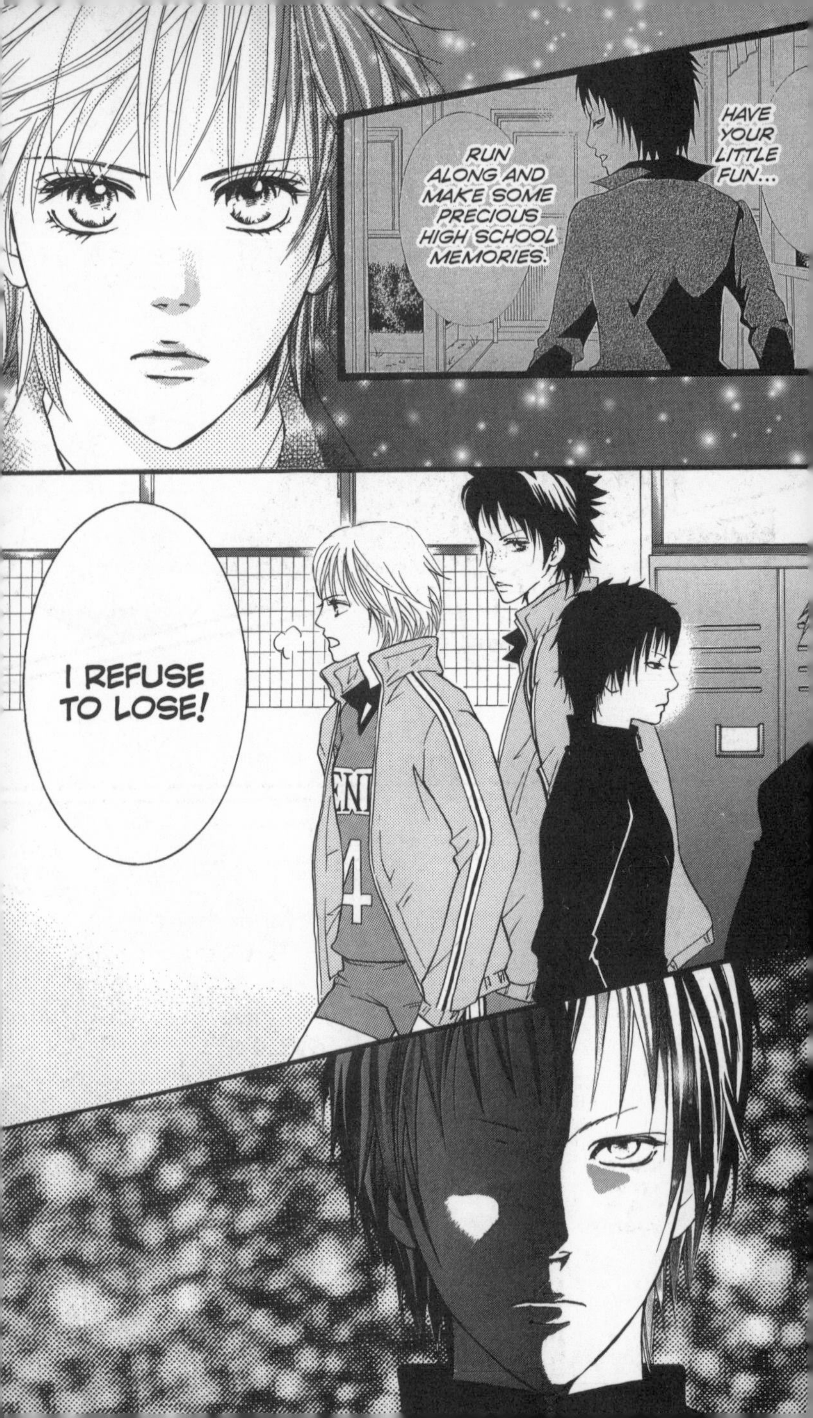
HAVE YOUR LITTLE FUN...
RUN ALONG AND MAKE SOME PRECIOUS HIGH SCHOOL MEMORIES.
I REFUSE TO LOSE!

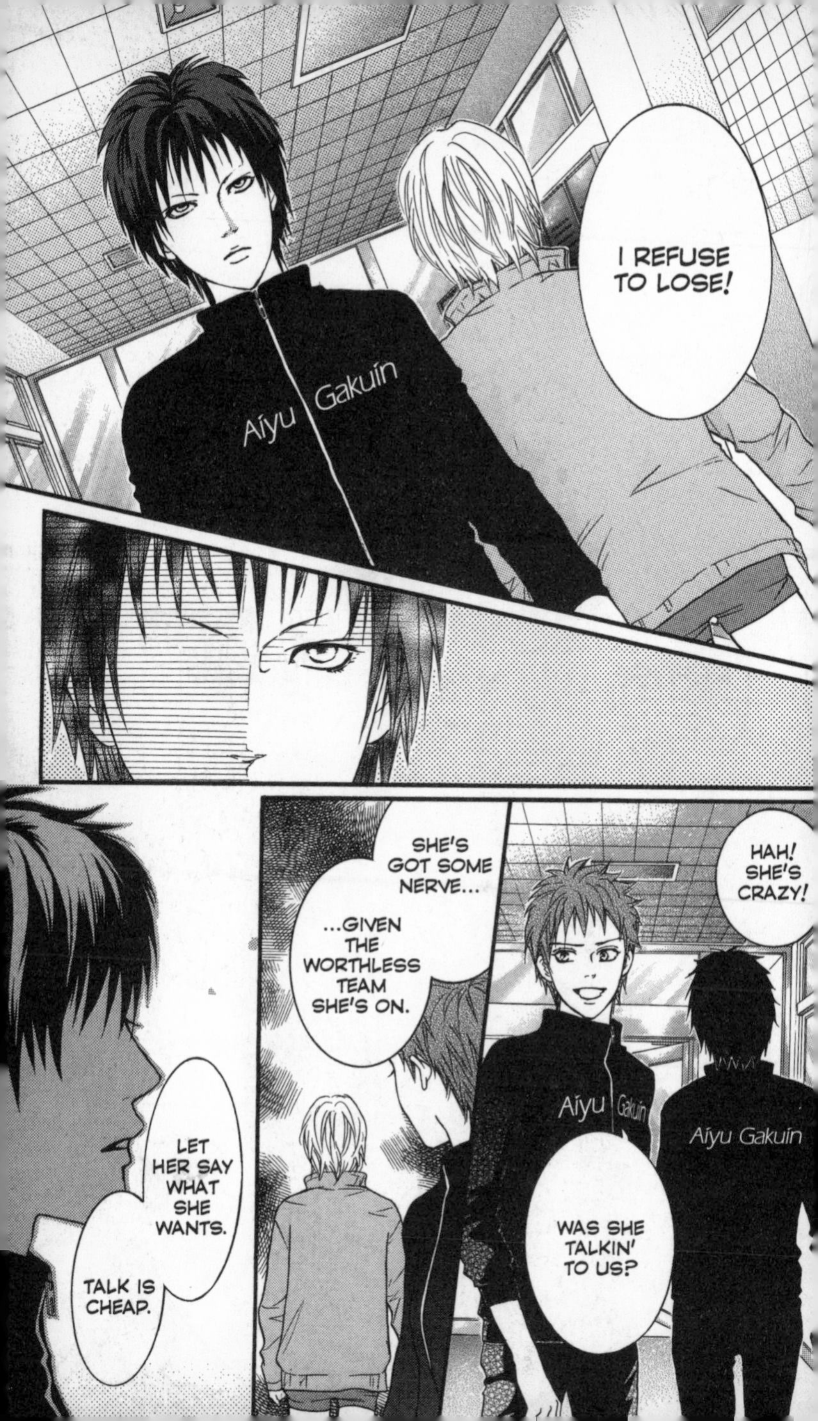
I REFUSE TO LOSE!
Aiyu Gakuin
HAH! SHE'S CRAZY!
SHE'S GOT SOME NERVE...
...GIVEN THE WORTHLESS TEAM SHE'S ON.
Aiyu Gakuin
Aiyu Gakuin
WAS SHE TALKIN' TO US?
LET HER SAY WHAT SHE WANTS.
TALK IS CHEAP.

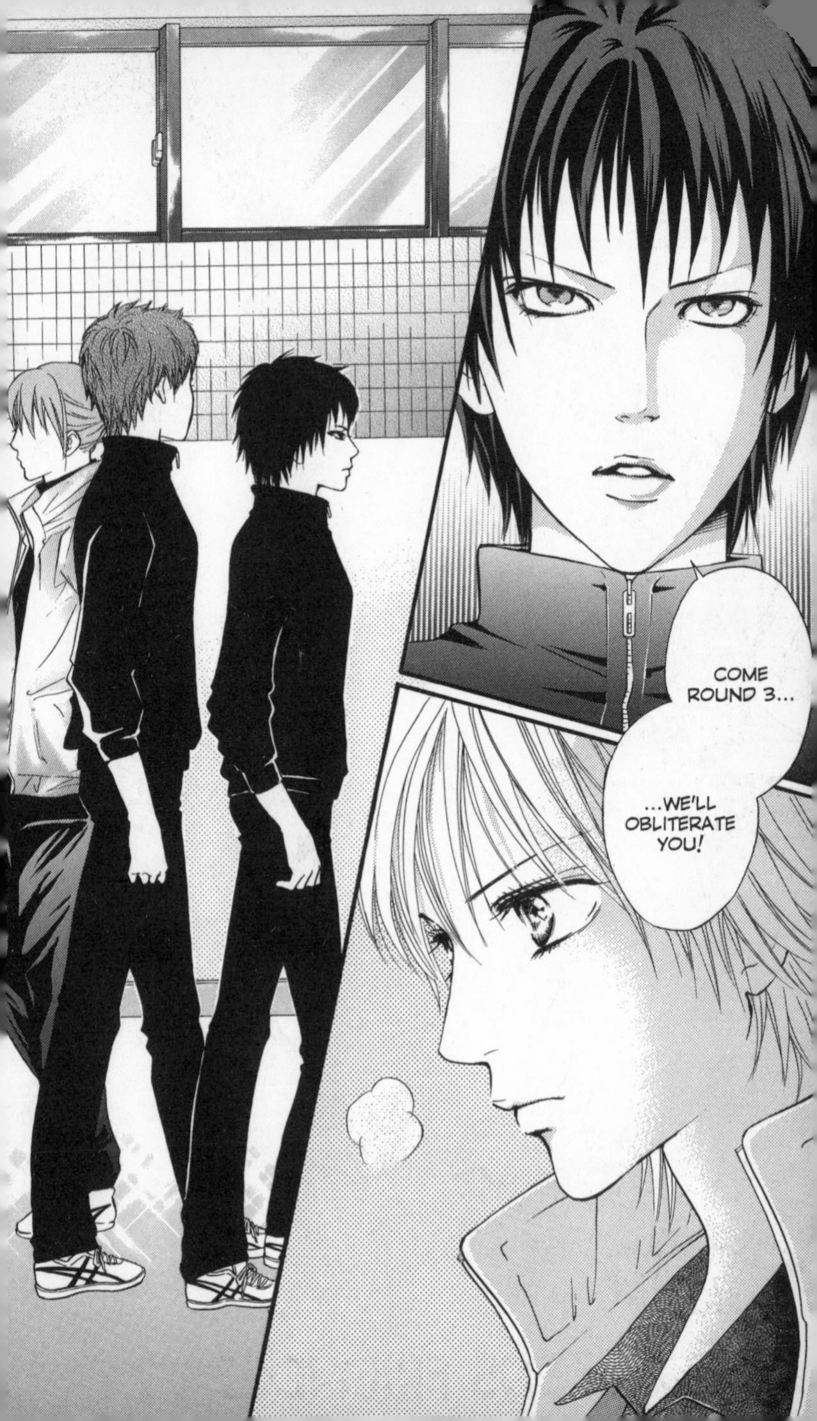
COME ROUND 3...
...WE'LL OBLITERATE YOU!

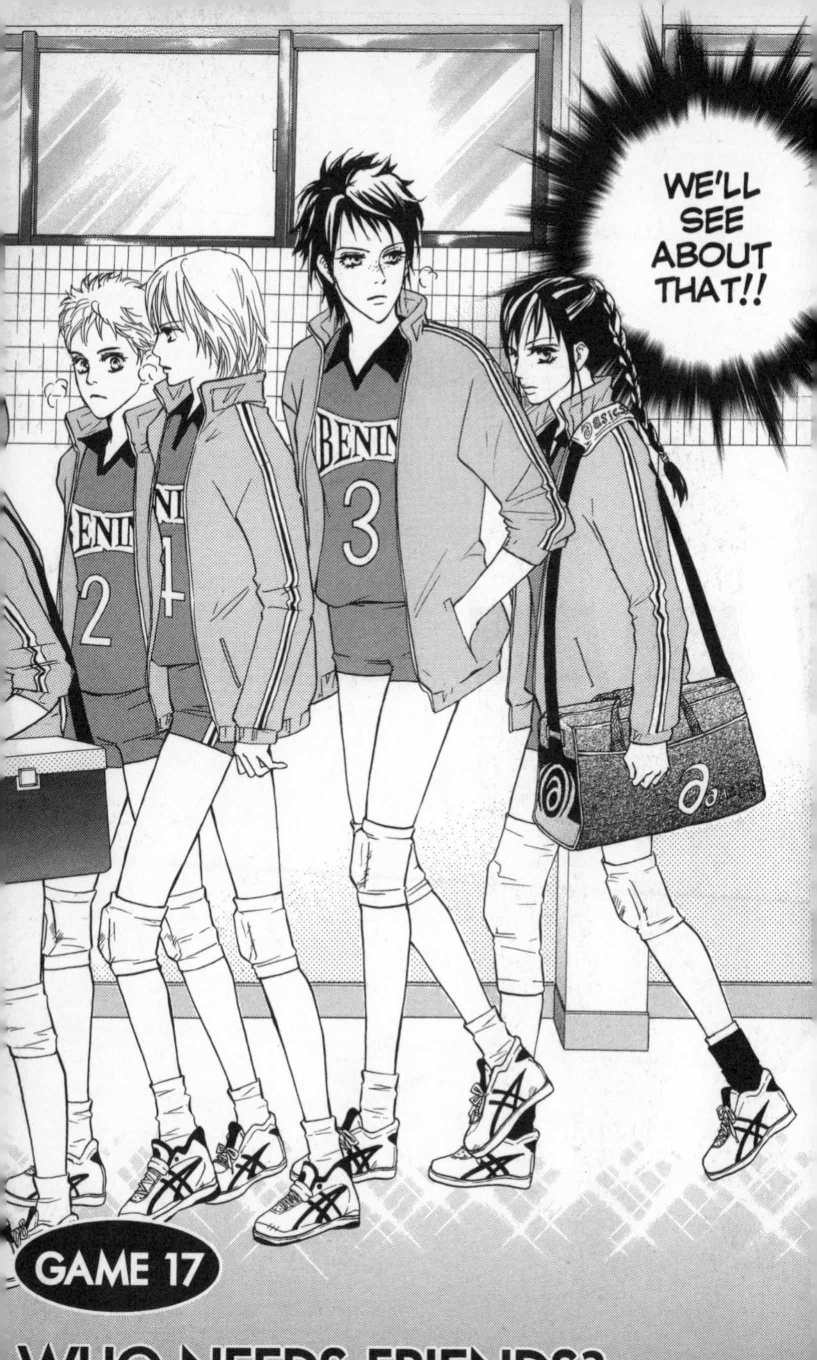
WE'LL SEE ABOUT THAT!!

GAME 17

WHO NEEDS FRIENDS?

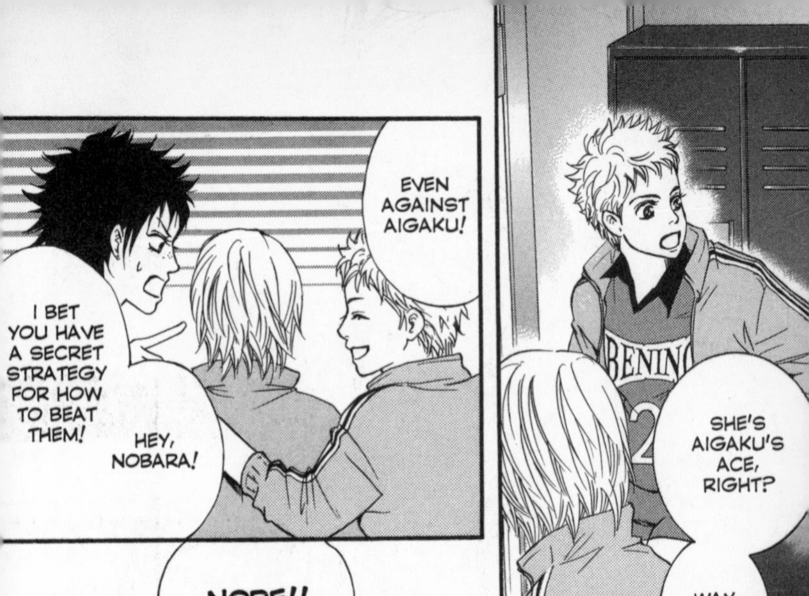
SHE'S AIGAKU'S ACE, RIGHT?
WAY TO GO, NOBARA!
YOU'RE FEARLESS!
EVEN AGAINST AIGAKU!
I BET YOU HAVE A SECRET STRATEGY FOR HOW TO BEAT THEM!
HEY, NOBARA!
NOPE!!
SLUMP

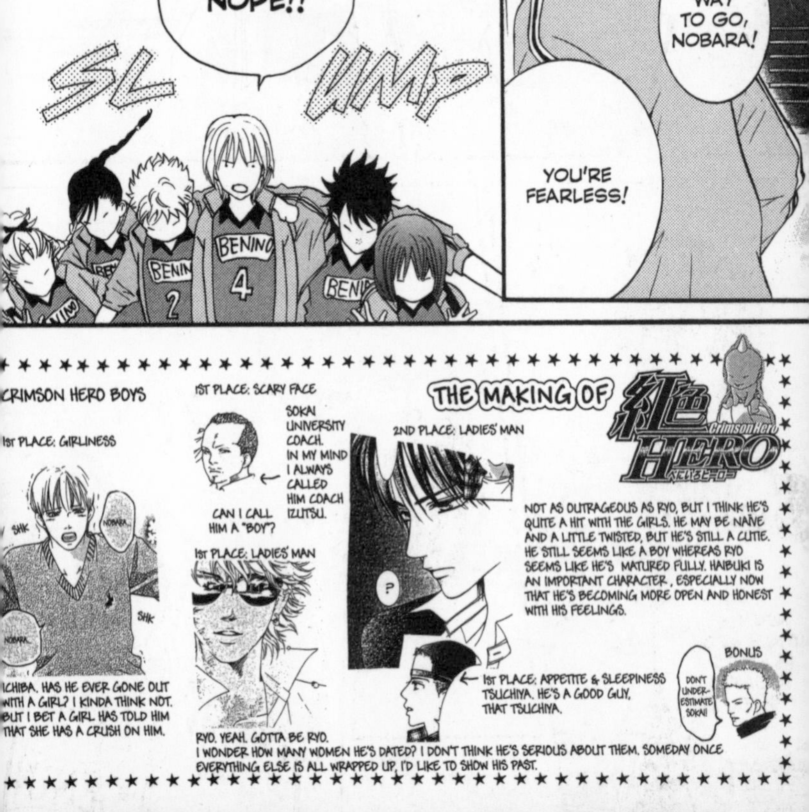
THE MAKING OF 紅色HERO Crimson Hero
CRIMSON HERO BOYS
1ST PLACE: GIRLINESS
SHK
NOBARA...
SHK
NOBARA...
ICHIBA. HAS HE EVER GONE OUT WITH A GIRL? I KINDA THINK NOT. BUT I BET A GIRL HAS TOLD HIM THAT SHE HAS A CRUSH ON HIM.
1ST PLACE: SCARY FACE
SOKAI UNIVERSITY COACH. IN MY MIND I ALWAYS CALLED HIM COACH IZUTSU.
CAN I CALL HIM A "BOY"?
1ST PLACE: LADIES' MAN
RYO. YEAH, GOTTA BE RYO. I WONDER HOW MANY WOMEN HE'S DATED? I DON'T THINK HE'S SERIOUS ABOUT THEM. SOMEDAY ONCE EVERYTHING ELSE IS ALL WRAPPED UP, I'D LIKE TO SHOW HIS PAST.
2ND PLACE: LADIES' MAN
?
NOT AS OUTRAGEOUS AS RYO, BUT I THINK HE'S QUITE A HIT WITH THE GIRLS. HE MAY BE NAÏVE AND A LITTLE TWISTED, BUT HE'S STILL A CUTIE. HE STILL SEEMS LIKE A BOY WHEREAS RYO SEEMS LIKE HE'S MATURED FULLY. HAIBUKI IS AN IMPORTANT CHARACTER, ESPECIALLY NOW THAT HE'S BECOMING MORE OPEN AND HONEST WITH HIS FEELINGS.
1ST PLACE: APPETITE & SLEEPINESS
TSUCHIYA. HE'S A GOOD GUY, THAT TSUCHIYA.
BONUS
DON'T UNDER-ESTIMATE SOKAI!

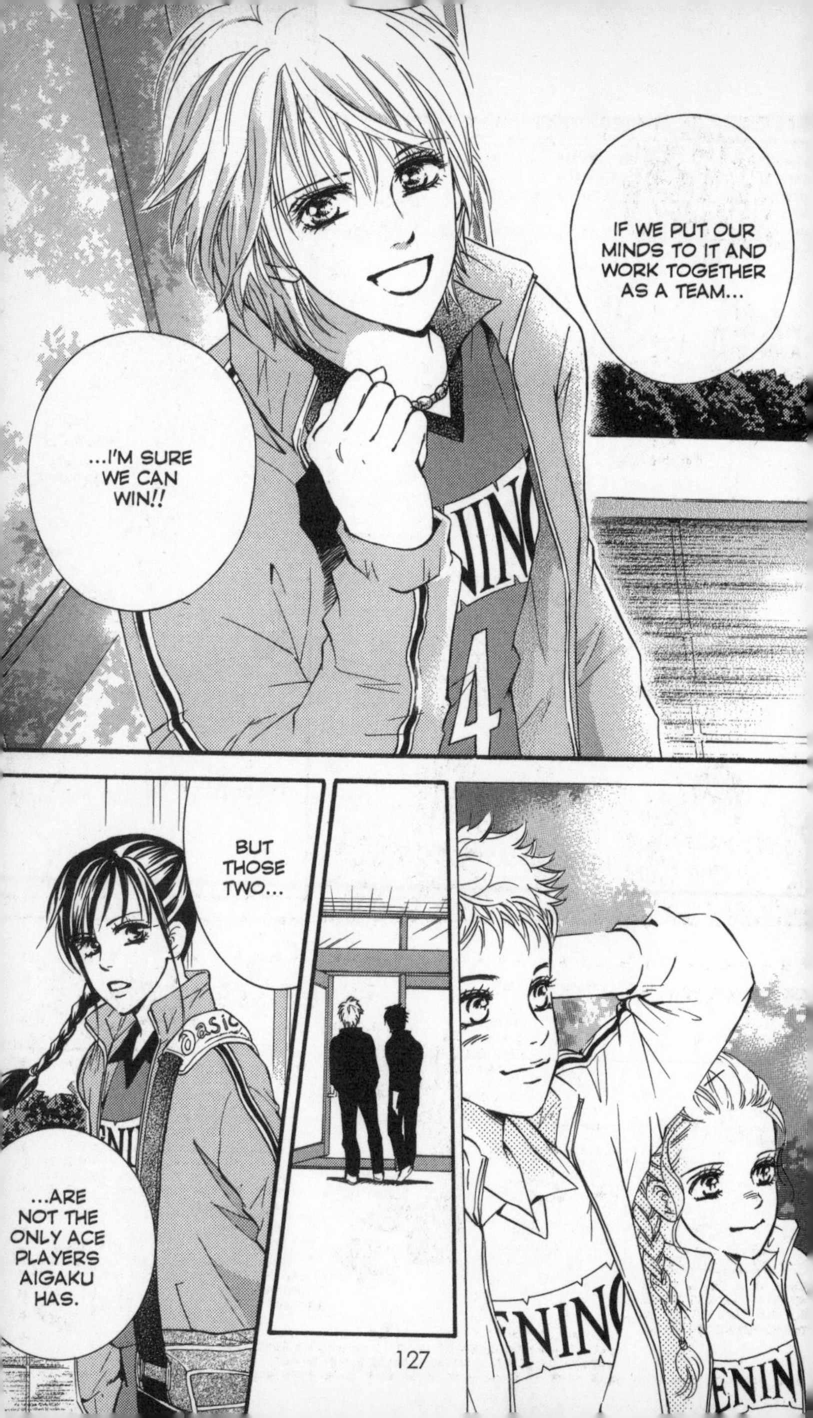
IF WE PUT OUR MINDS TO IT AND WORK TOGETHER AS A TEAM...
...I'M SURE WE CAN WIN!!
BUT THOSE TWO...
...ARE NOT THE ONLY ACE PLAYERS AIGAKU HAS.

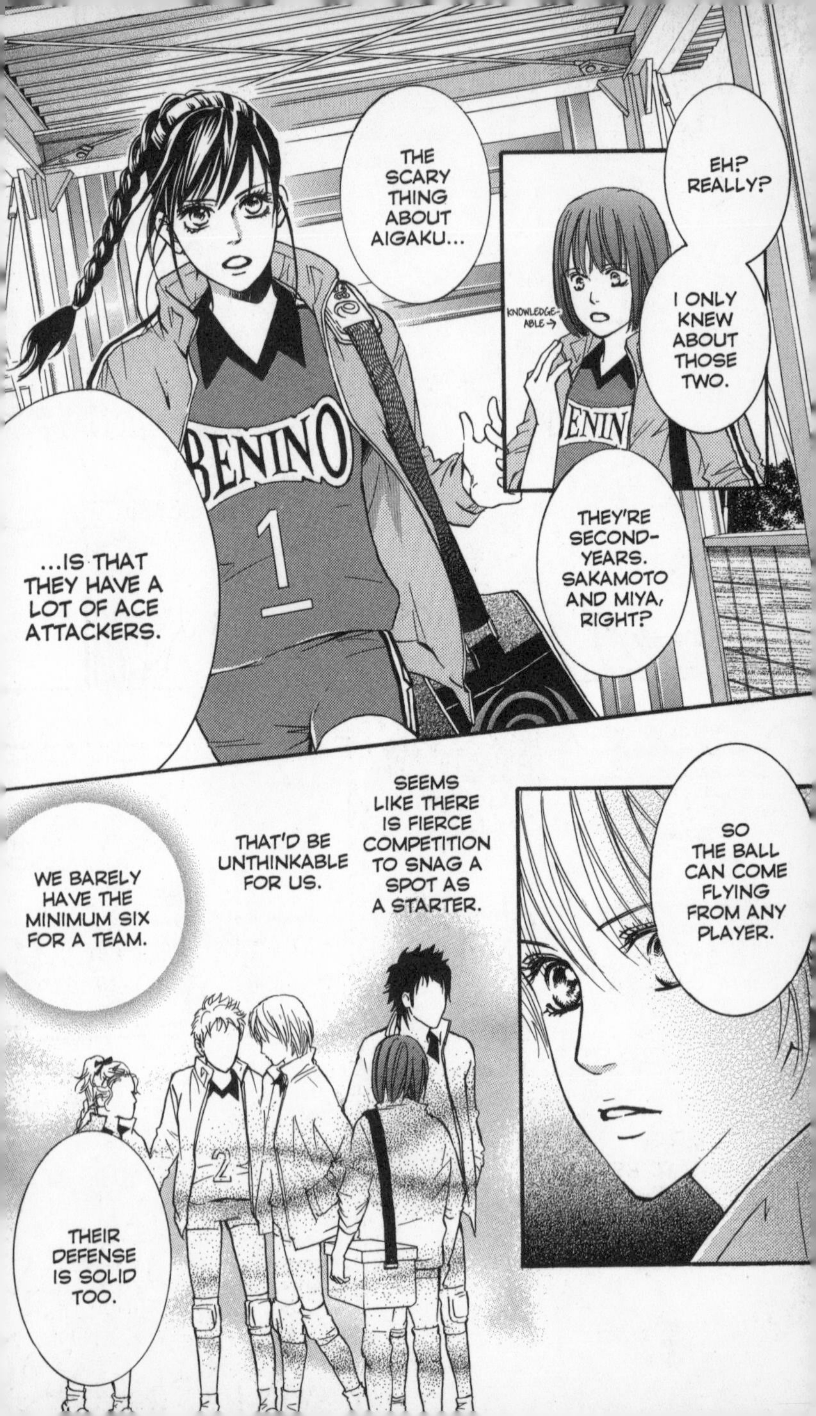
THE SCARY THING ABOUT AIGAKU...
...IS THAT THEY HAVE A LOT OF ACE ATTACKERS.
EH? REALLY?
I ONLY KNEW ABOUT THOSE TWO.
KNOWLEDGE-ABLE →
THEY'RE SECOND-YEARS. SAKAMOTO AND MIYA, RIGHT?
SO THE BALL CAN COME FLYING FROM ANY PLAYER.
SEEMS LIKE THERE IS FIERCE COMPETITION TO SNAG A SPOT AS A STARTER.
THAT'D BE UNTHINKABLE FOR US.
WE BARELY HAVE THE MINIMUM SIX FOR A TEAM.
THEIR DEFENSE IS SOLID TOO.

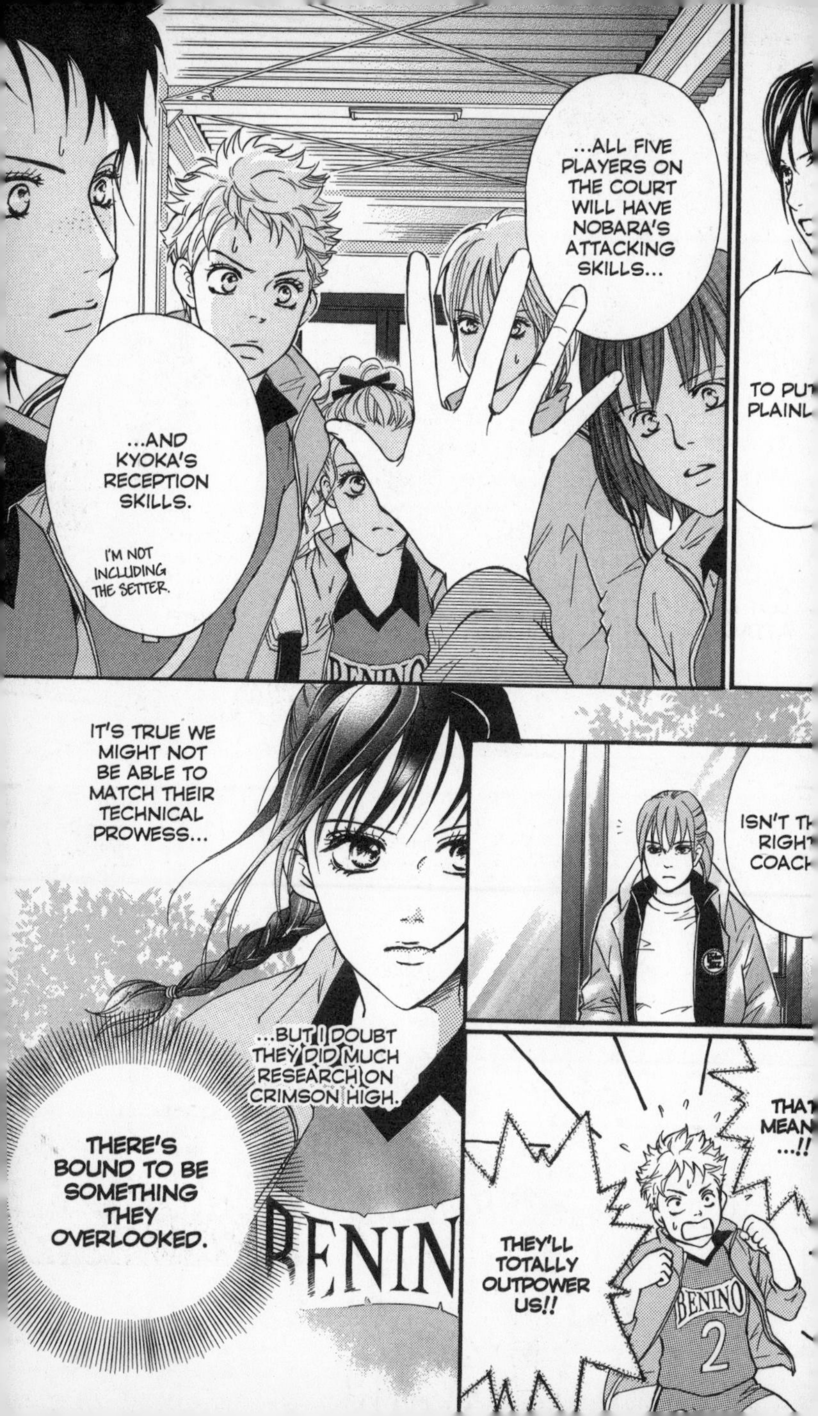
TO PUT PLAINL
...ALL FIVE PLAYERS ON THE COURT WILL HAVE NOBARA'S ATTACKING SKILLS...
...AND KYOKA'S RECEPTION SKILLS.
I'M NOT INCLUDING THE SETTER.
ISN'T TH RIGHT COACH
THAT MEAN ...!!
THEY'LL TOTALLY OUTPOWER US!!
IT'S TRUE WE MIGHT NOT BE ABLE TO MATCH THEIR TECHNICAL PROWESS...
...BUT I DOUBT THEY DID MUCH RESEARCH ON CRIMSON HIGH.
THERE'S BOUND TO BE SOMETHING THEY OVERLOOKED.

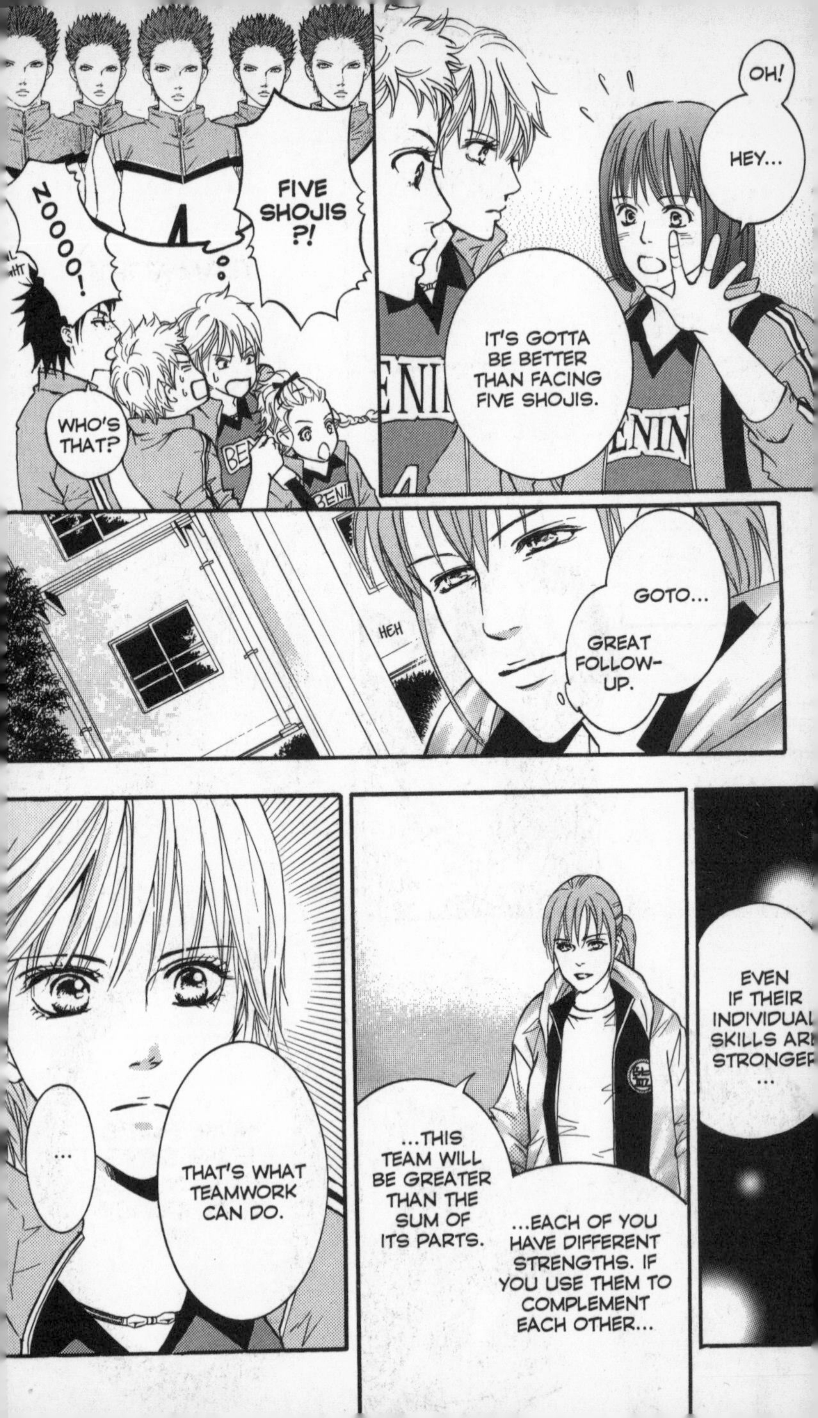
OH!
HEY...
IT'S GOTTA BE BETTER THAN FACING FIVE SHOJIS.
FIVE SHOJIS?!
ZOOOOO!
WHO'S THAT?
HEH
GOTO...
GREAT FOLLOW-UP.
EVEN IF THEIR INDIVIDUA SKILLS AR STRONGE ...
...EACH OF YOU HAVE DIFFERENT STRENGTHS. IF YOU USE THEM TO COMPLEMENT EACH OTHER...
...THIS TEAM WILL BE GREATER THAN THE SUM OF ITS PARTS.
THAT'S WHAT TEAMWORK CAN DO.
...

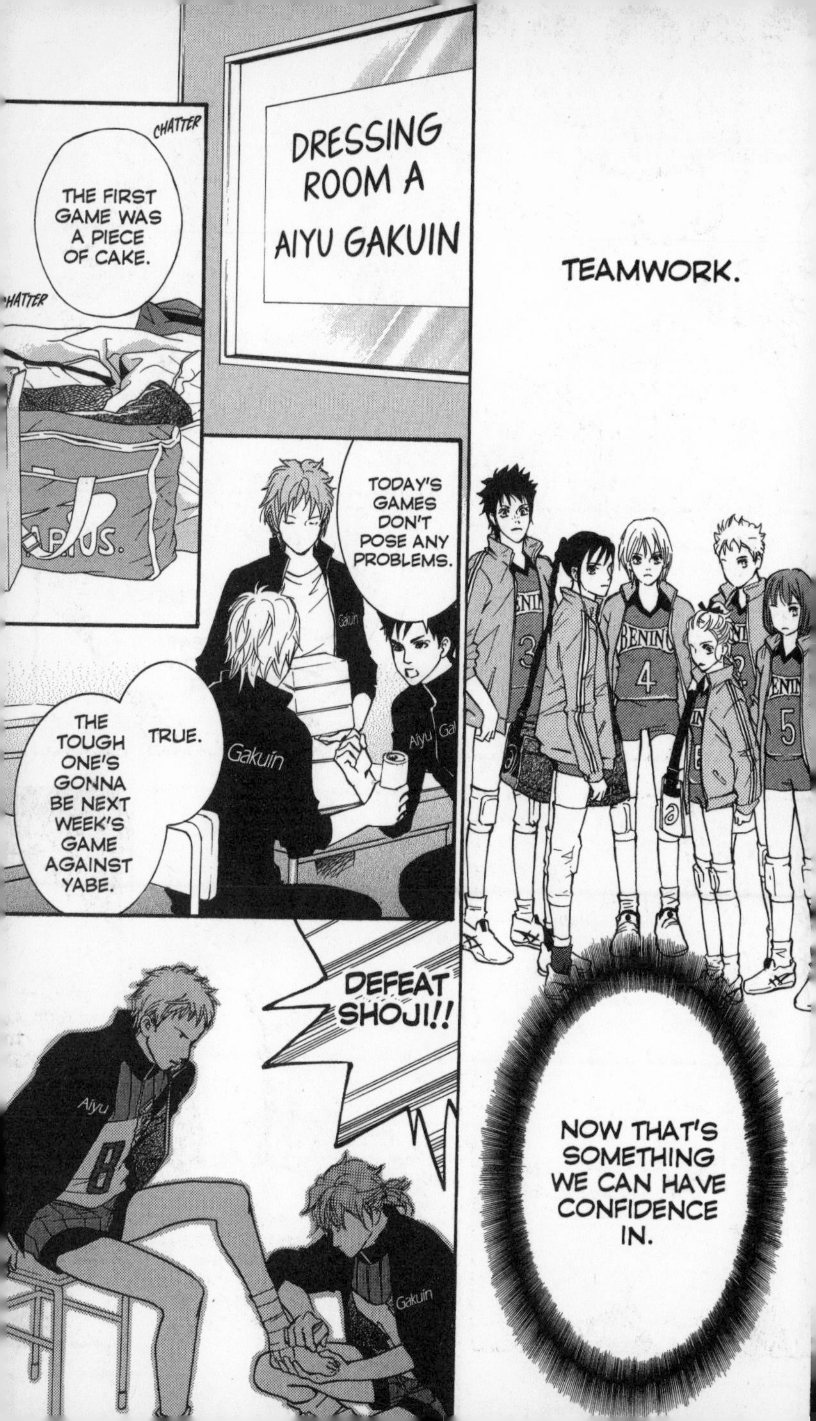
TEAMWORK.
NOW THAT'S SOMETHING WE CAN HAVE CONFIDENCE IN.
DRESSING ROOM A AIYU GAKUIN
CHATTER
THE FIRST GAME WAS A PIECE OF CAKE.
TODAY'S GAMES DON'T POSE ANY PROBLEMS.
TRUE.
THE TOUGH ONE'S GONNA BE NEXT WEEK'S GAME AGAINST YABE.
DEFEAT SHOJI!!

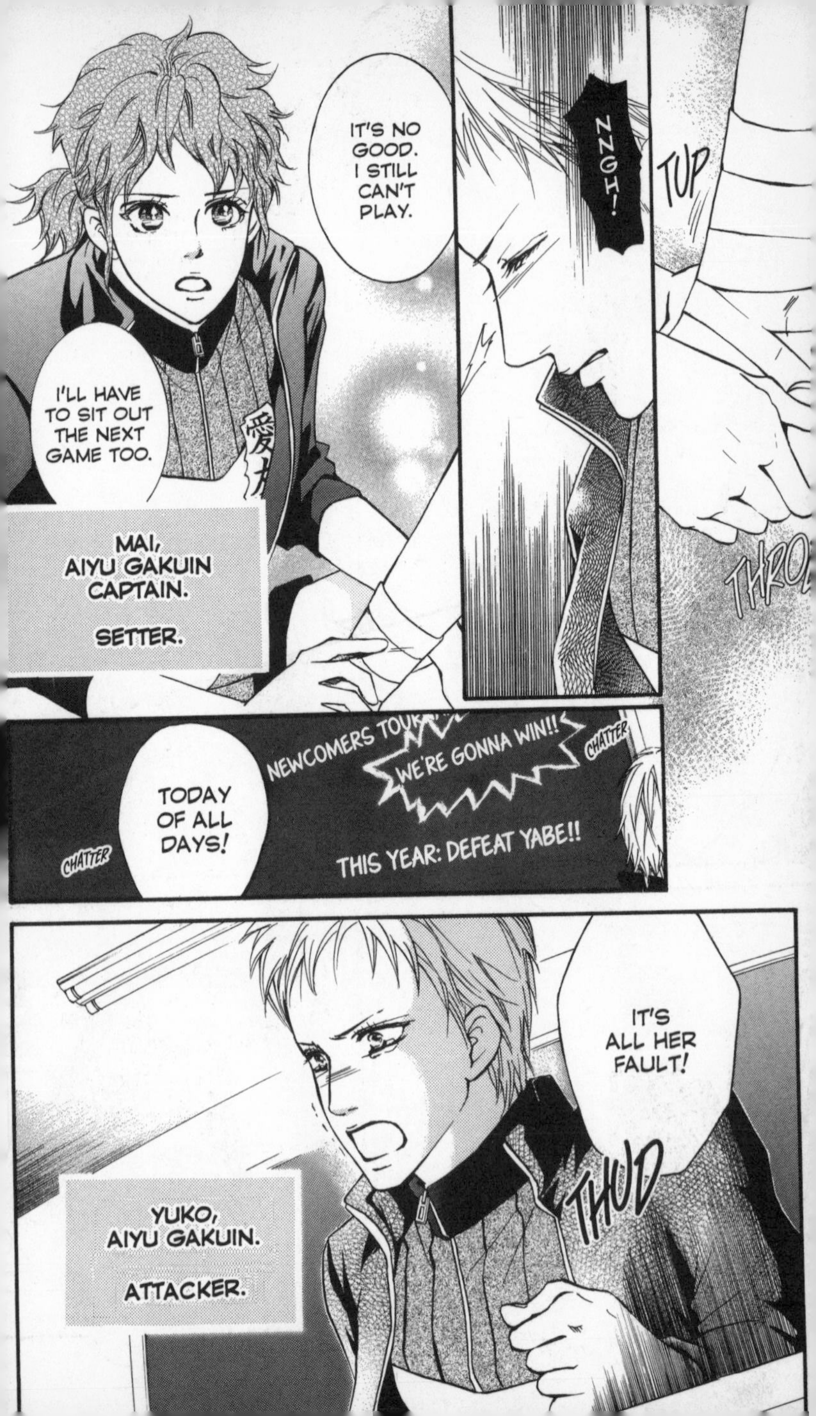
NNGH!
TUP
THRO
IT'S NO GOOD. I STILL CAN'T PLAY.
I'LL HAVE TO SIT OUT THE NEXT GAME TOO.
MAI, AIYU GAKUIN CAPTAIN.
SETTER.
CHATTER
WE'RE GONNA WIN!!
NEWCOMERS TOU
THIS YEAR: DEFEAT YABE!!
TODAY OF ALL DAYS!
CHATTER
IT'S ALL HER FAULT!
THUD
YUKO, AIYU GAKUIN.
ATTACKER.

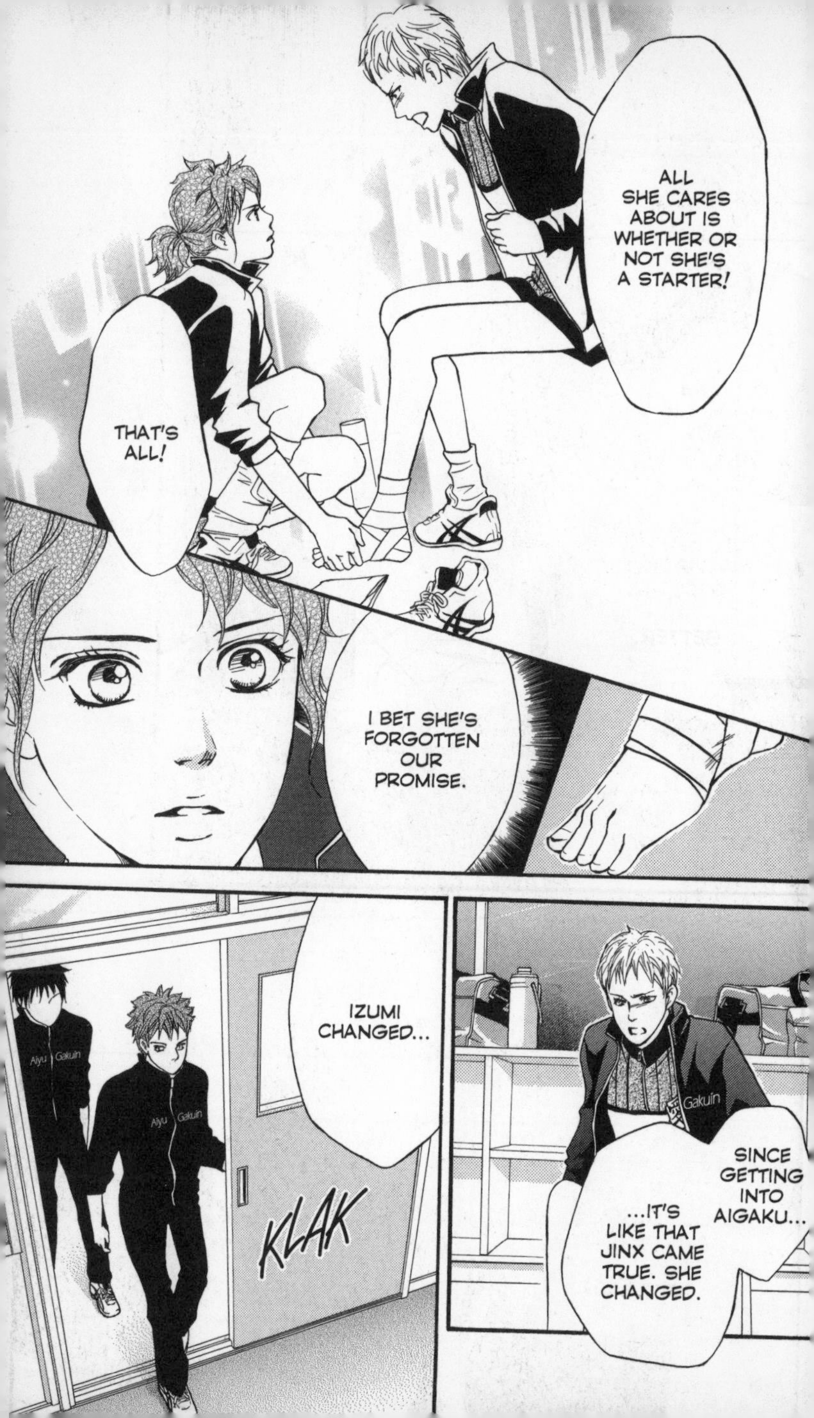
ALL SHE CARES ABOUT IS WHETHER OR NOT SHE'S A STARTER!
THAT'S ALL!
I BET SHE'S FORGOTTEN OUR PROMISE.
Gakuin
SINCE GETTING INTO AIGAKU...
...IT'S LIKE THAT JINX CAME TRUE. SHE CHANGED.
IZUMI CHANGED...
Aiyu Gakuin
Aiyu Gakuin
KLAK

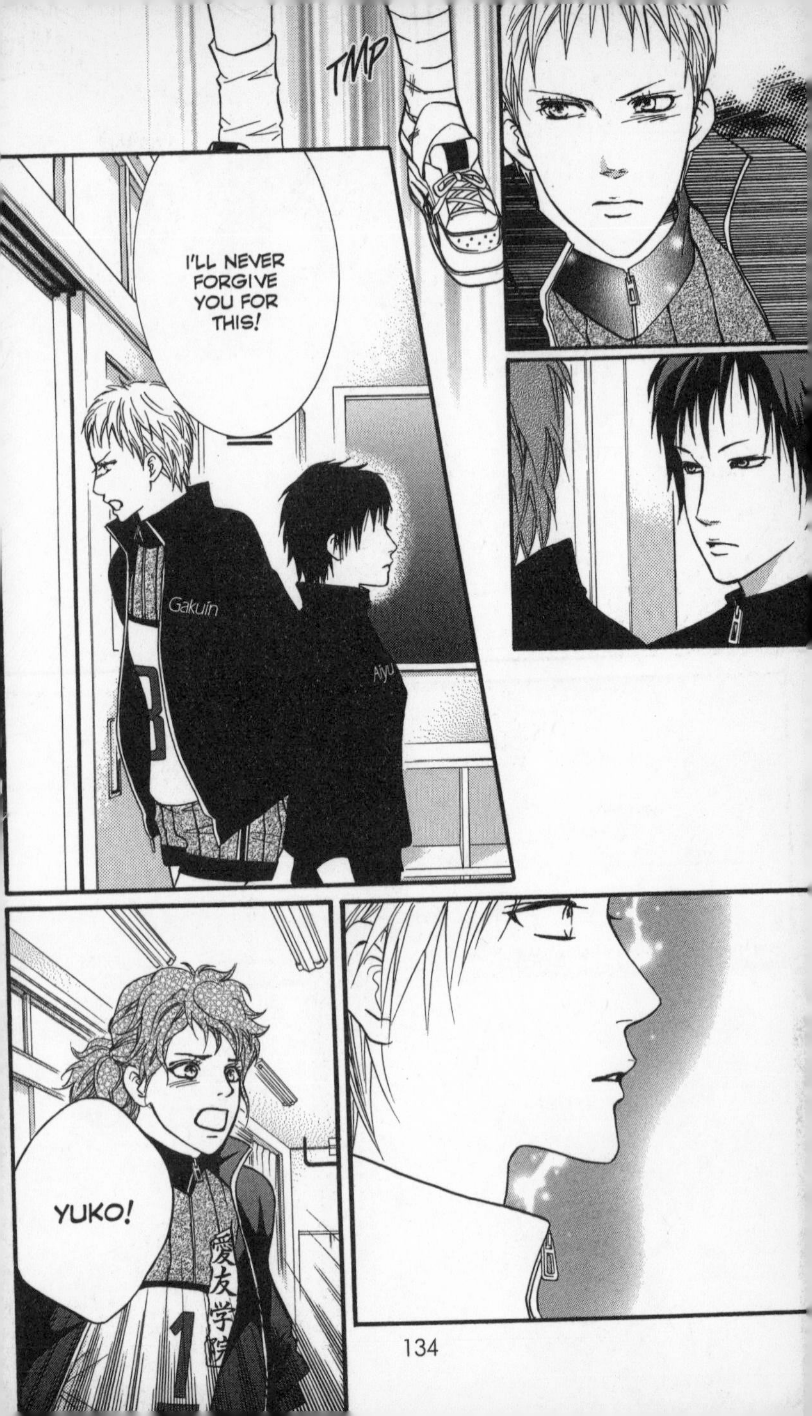
TMP
I'LL NEVER FORGIVE YOU FOR THIS!
YUKO!

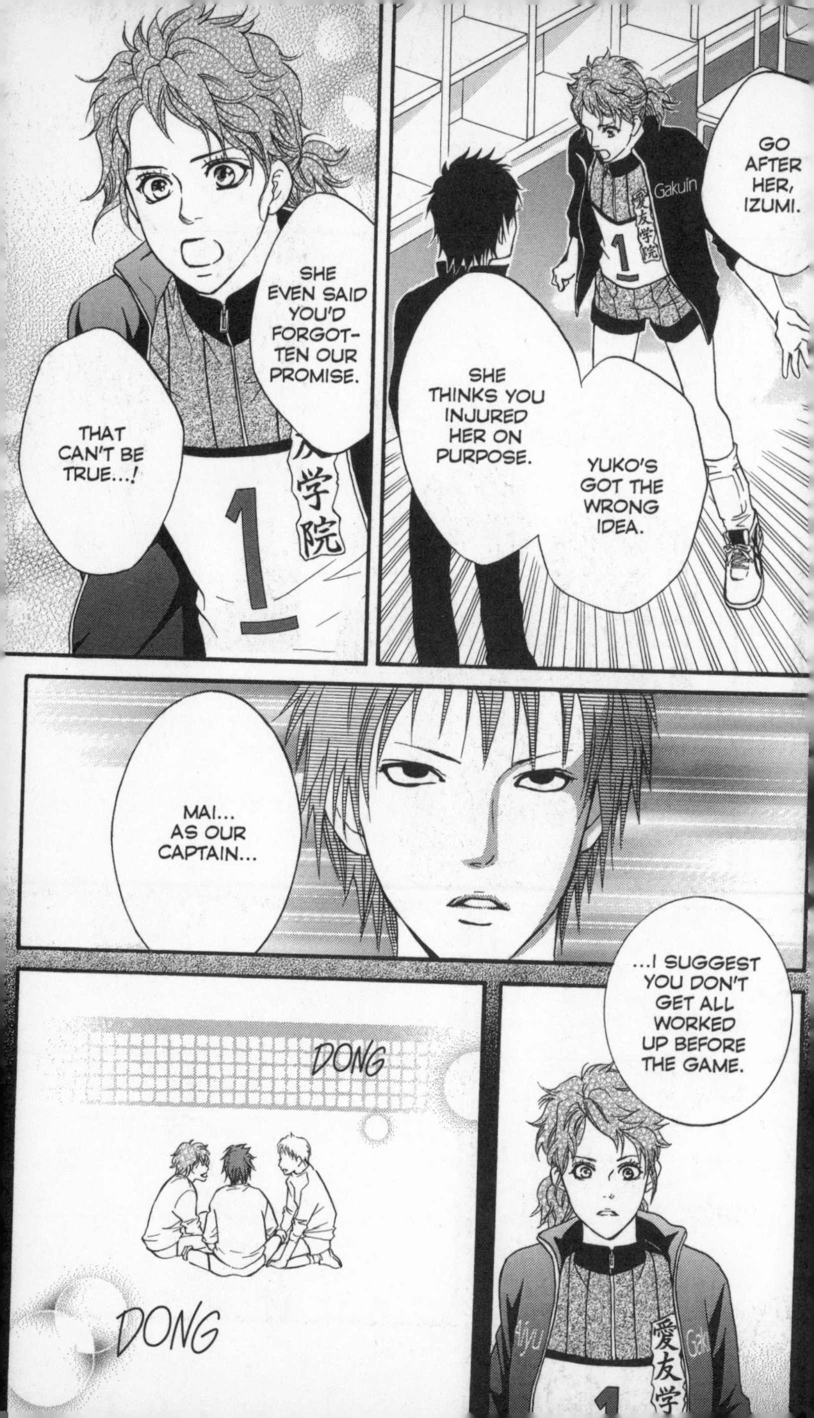
GO AFTER HER, IZUMI.
YUKO'S GOT THE WRONG IDEA.
SHE THINKS YOU INJURED HER ON PURPOSE.
SHE EVEN SAID YOU'D FORGOT-TEN OUR PROMISE.
THAT CAN'T BE TRUE...!
MAI... AS OUR CAPTAIN...
...I SUGGEST YOU DON'T GET ALL WORKED UP BEFORE THE GAME.
DONG
DONG

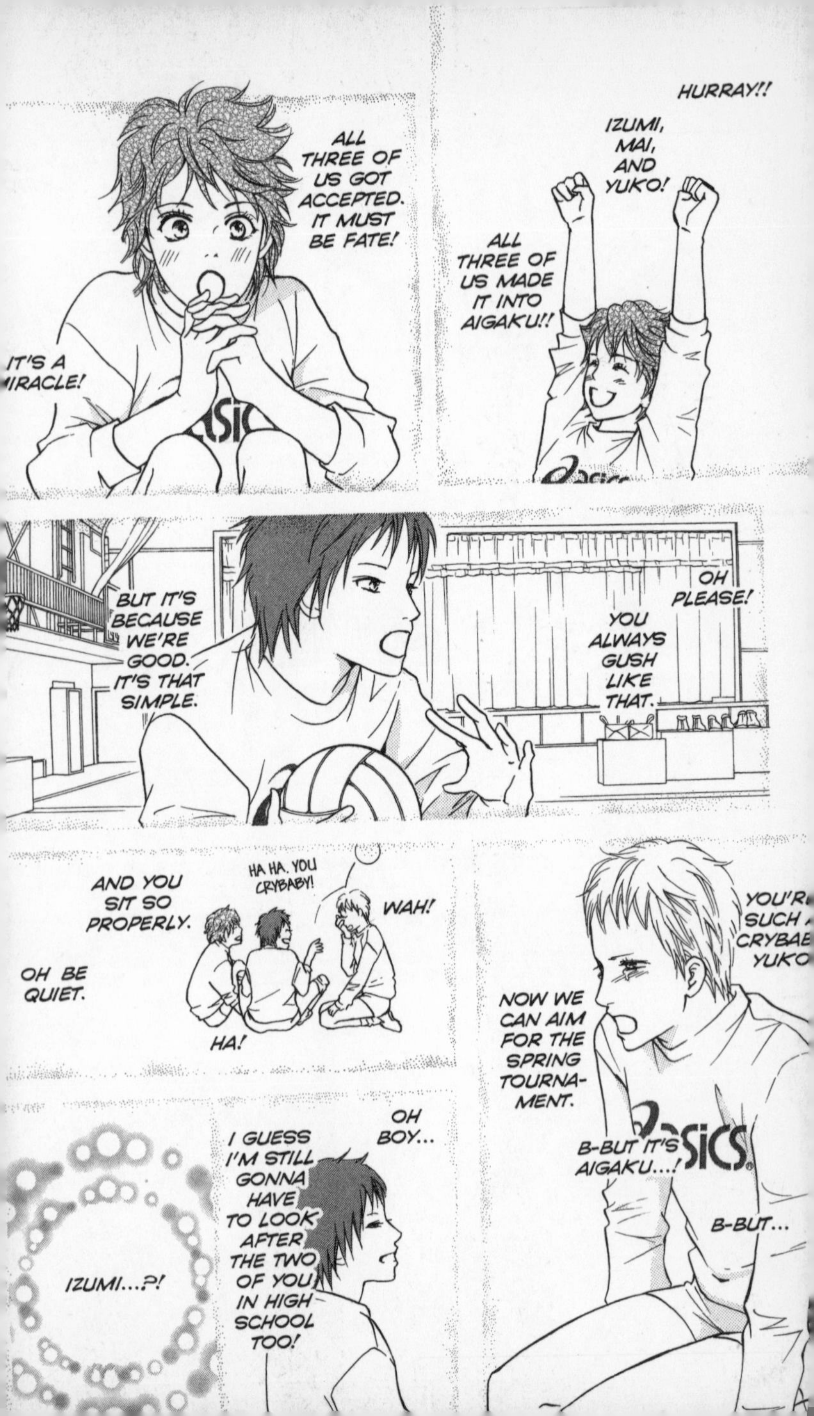
HURRAY!!
IZUMI, MAI, AND YUKO!
ALL THREE OF US MADE IT INTO AIGAKU!!
ALL THREE OF US GOT ACCEPTED. IT MUST BE FATE!
IT'S A IRACLE!
OH PLEASE!
YOU ALWAYS GUSH LIKE THAT.
BUT IT'S BECAUSE WE'RE GOOD. IT'S THAT SIMPLE.
YOU'R SUCH CRYBAE YUKO
NOW WE CAN AIM FOR THE SPRING TOURNAMENT.
B-BUT IT'S AIGAKU...!
B-BUT...
HA HA. YOU CRYBABY!
WAH!
AND YOU SIT SO PROPERLY.
OH BE QUIET.
HA!
OH BOY...
I GUESS I'M STILL GONNA HAVE TO LOOK AFTER THE TWO OF YOU IN HIGH SCHOOL TOO!
IZUMI...?!

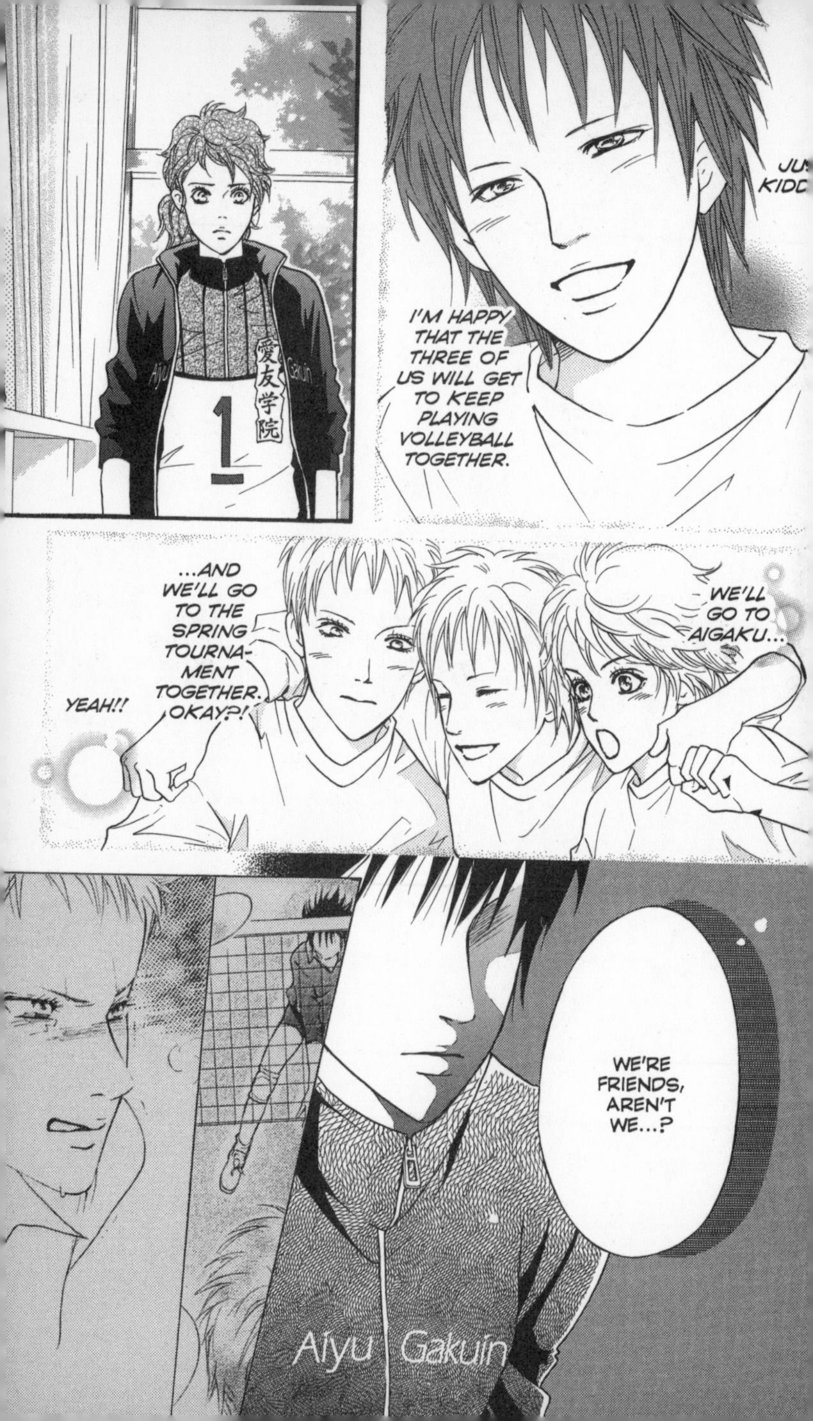
JU
KIDD
I'M HAPPY THAT THE THREE OF US WILL GET TO KEEP PLAYING VOLLEYBALL TOGETHER.
愛友学院
Aiyu Gakuin
1
WE'LL GO TO AIGAKU...
...AND WE'LL GO TO THE SPRING TOURNA-MENT TOGETHER. OKAY?!
YEAH!!
WE'RE FRIENDS, AREN'T WE...?
Aiyu Gakuin

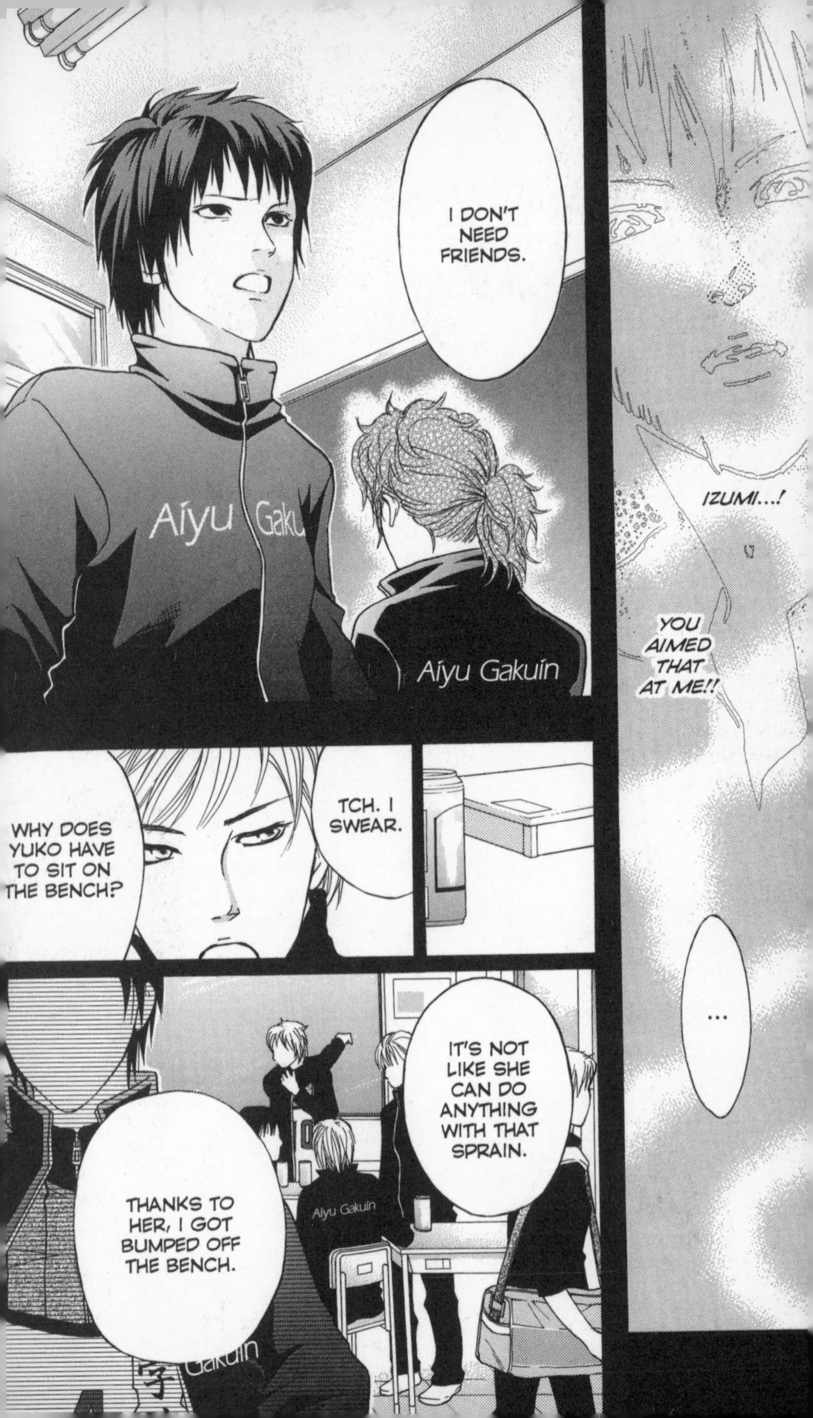
IZUMI...!
YOU AIMED THAT AT ME!!
...
I DON'T NEED FRIENDS.
TCH. I SWEAR.
WHY DOES YUKO HAVE TO SIT ON THE BENCH?
IT'S NOT LIKE SHE CAN DO ANYTHING WITH THAT SPRAIN.
THANKS TO HER, I GOT BUMPED OFF THE BENCH.

THAT WAS MIDDLE SCHOOL. THINGS ARE DIFFERENT NOW.

THE O
GEEZ
COA
DECID
IT.

WHAT ?!

STO
COMPL
ING

IT'S TIME! WHAT ARE YOU DOING?

FIRST-YEARS! HURRY UP AND HAUL OUR STUFF!

Y-YES!

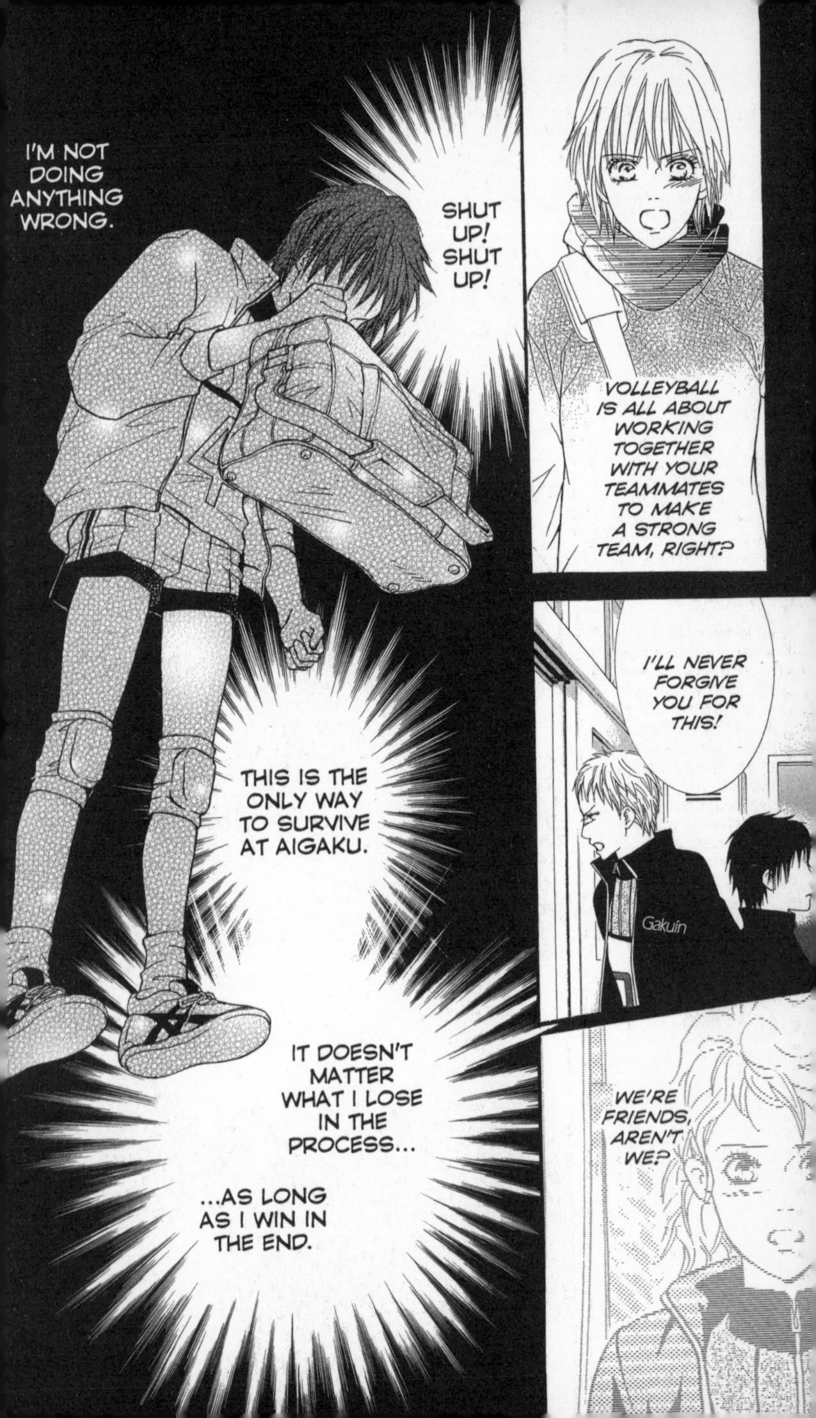
VOLLEYBALL IS ALL ABOUT WORKING TOGETHER WITH YOUR TEAMMATES TO MAKE A STRONG TEAM, RIGHT?
I'LL NEVER FORGIVE YOU FOR THIS!
Gakuin
WE'RE FRIENDS, AREN'T WE?
SHUT UP! SHUT UP!
I'M NOT DOING ANYTHING WRONG.
THIS IS THE ONLY WAY TO SURVIVE AT AIGAKU.
IT DOESN'T MATTER WHAT I LOSE IN THE PROCESS...
...AS LONG AS I WIN IN THE END.

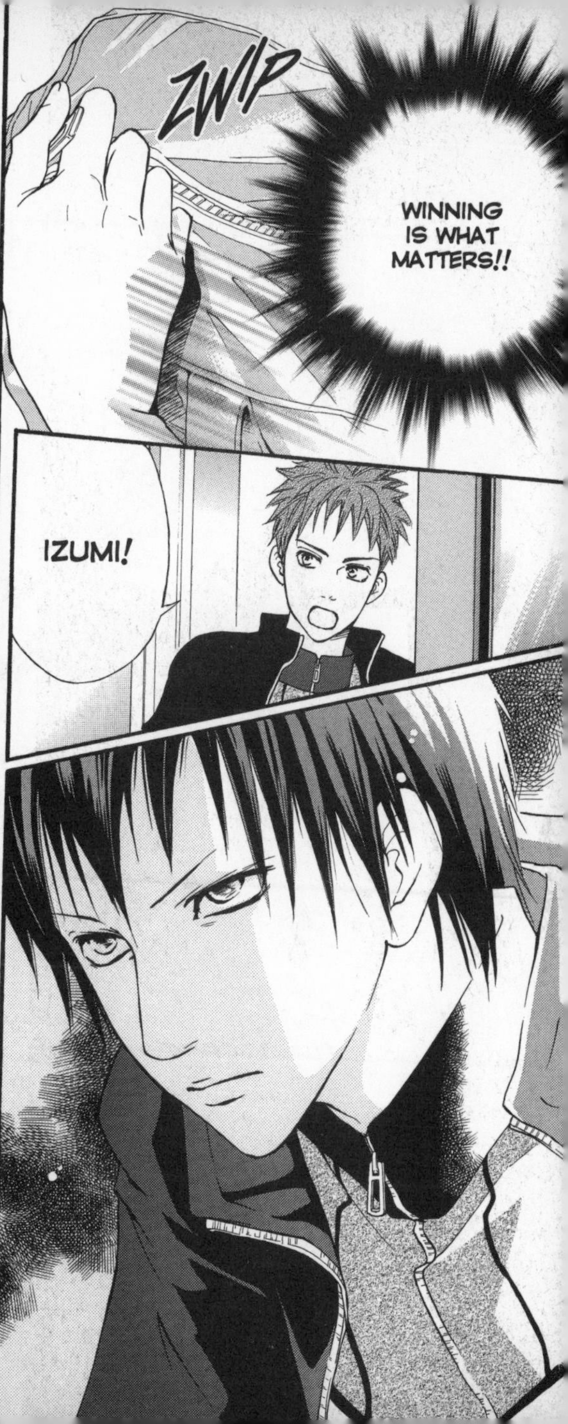
ZWIP
WINNING IS WHAT MATTERS!!
IZUMI!

MITSUBA CLUB
VoL.4

WELL, WE HAD A BIT OF THIS AND THAT, AND NOW IT'S ALREADY TIME FOR US TO PART AGAIN. I'M SORRY THERE WASN'T ANYTHING SUPER INTERESTING. MY DAILY LIFE IS EXTREMELY DULL. (SWEAT) OH YEAH, THE OTHER DAY I TOOK A PHOTO OF A PRAYING MANTIS. A CLOSE-UP. IT WAS ON MY BALCONY. A PREYING MANTIS!! IS THAT NO GOOD? AM I HOPELESS?

THANK YOU FOR YOUR LETTERS. I KEEP WANTING TO REPLY BUT HAVEN'T SO I APOLOGIZE FOR THAT. TO THE PERSON WHO SENT ME WINE FOR CHRISTMAS-- SORRY FOR THE BELATED THANK YOU. I REALLY ENJOYED IT. ♥♥♥

OH, AND IN GAME 14 WHERE TAKAHASHI APPEARS (NOBODY SEEMS TO HAVE NOTICED, BUT...), BEFORE HE HOISTS SUZUSHIRO UP, HE CHECKS THE FENCE. IT'S OLD AND HE WANTS TO MAKE SURE IT'S SAFE. TAKAHASHI...! YOU GO, TAKAHASHI! THIRD-YEARS TAKAHASHI AND SUZUSHIRO MAKE A NICE COUPLE, THOUGH AYAKO OFTEN GETS IN HIS WAY.

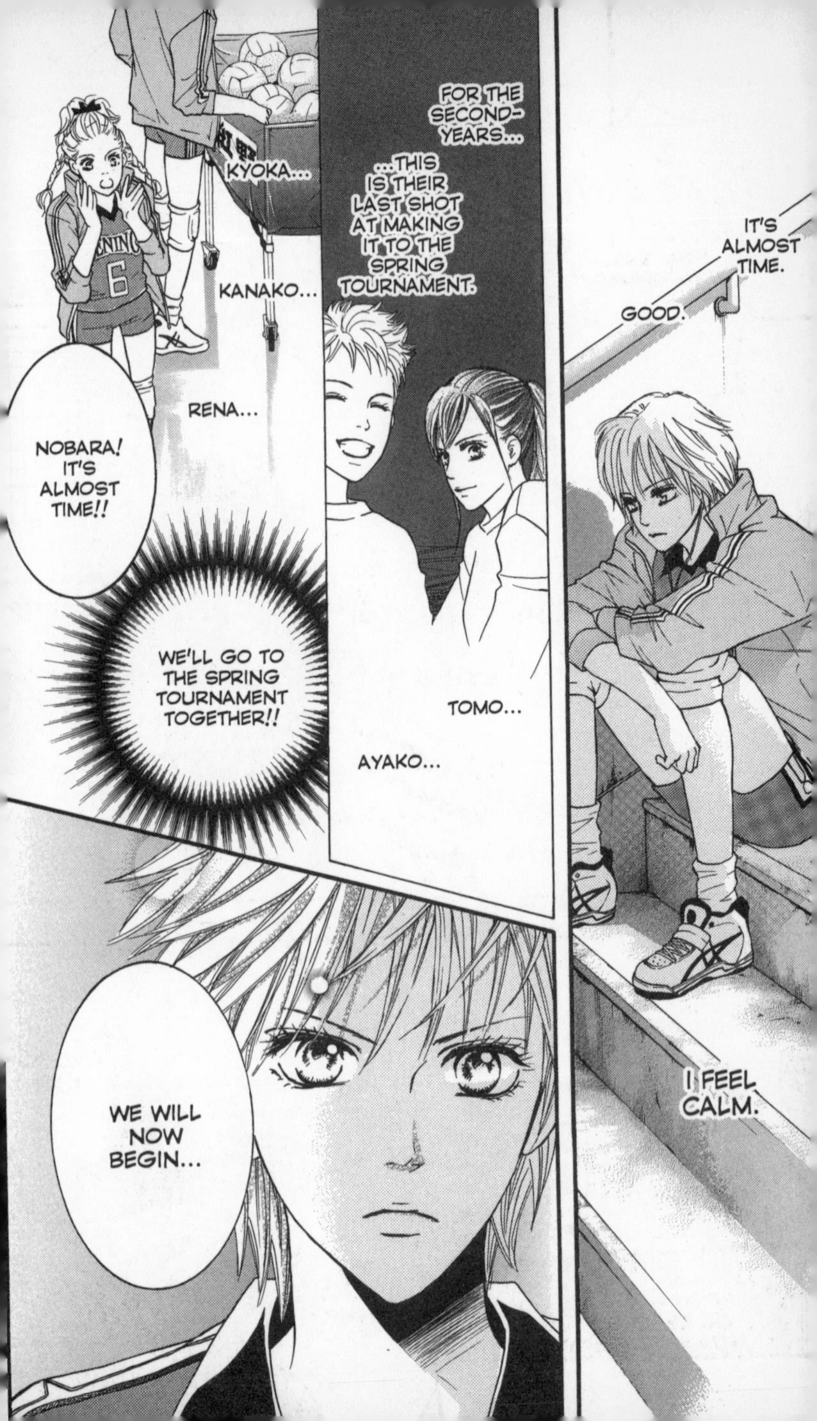
IT'S ALMOST TIME.
GOOD.
I FEEL CALM.
FOR THE SECOND-YEARS...
...THIS IS THEIR LAST SHOT AT MAKING IT TO THE SPRING TOURNAMENT.
TOMO...
AYAKO...
KYOKA...
KANAKO...
RENA...
NOBARA! IT'S ALMOST TIME!!
WE'LL GO TO THE SPRING TOURNAMENT TOGETHER!!
WE WILL NOW BEGIN...

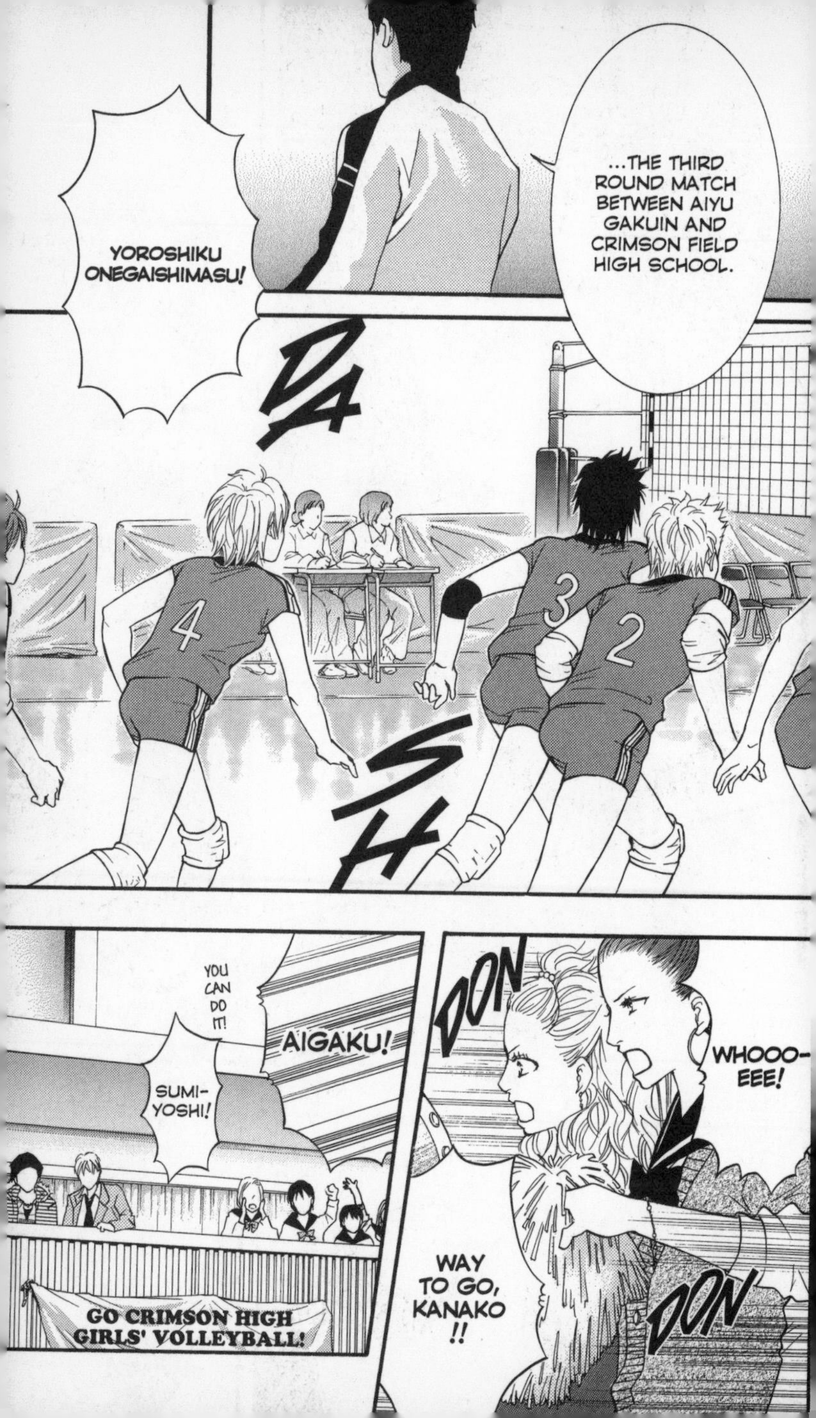
...THE THIRD ROUND MATCH BETWEEN AIYU GAKUIN AND CRIMSON FIELD HIGH SCHOOL.
YOROSHIKU ONEGAISHIMASU!
DASH
DON
WHOOOO-EEE!
WAY TO GO, KANAKO!!
DON
AIGAKU!
YOU CAN DO IT!
SUMI-YOSHI!
GO CRIMSON HIGH GIRLS' VOLLEYBALL!

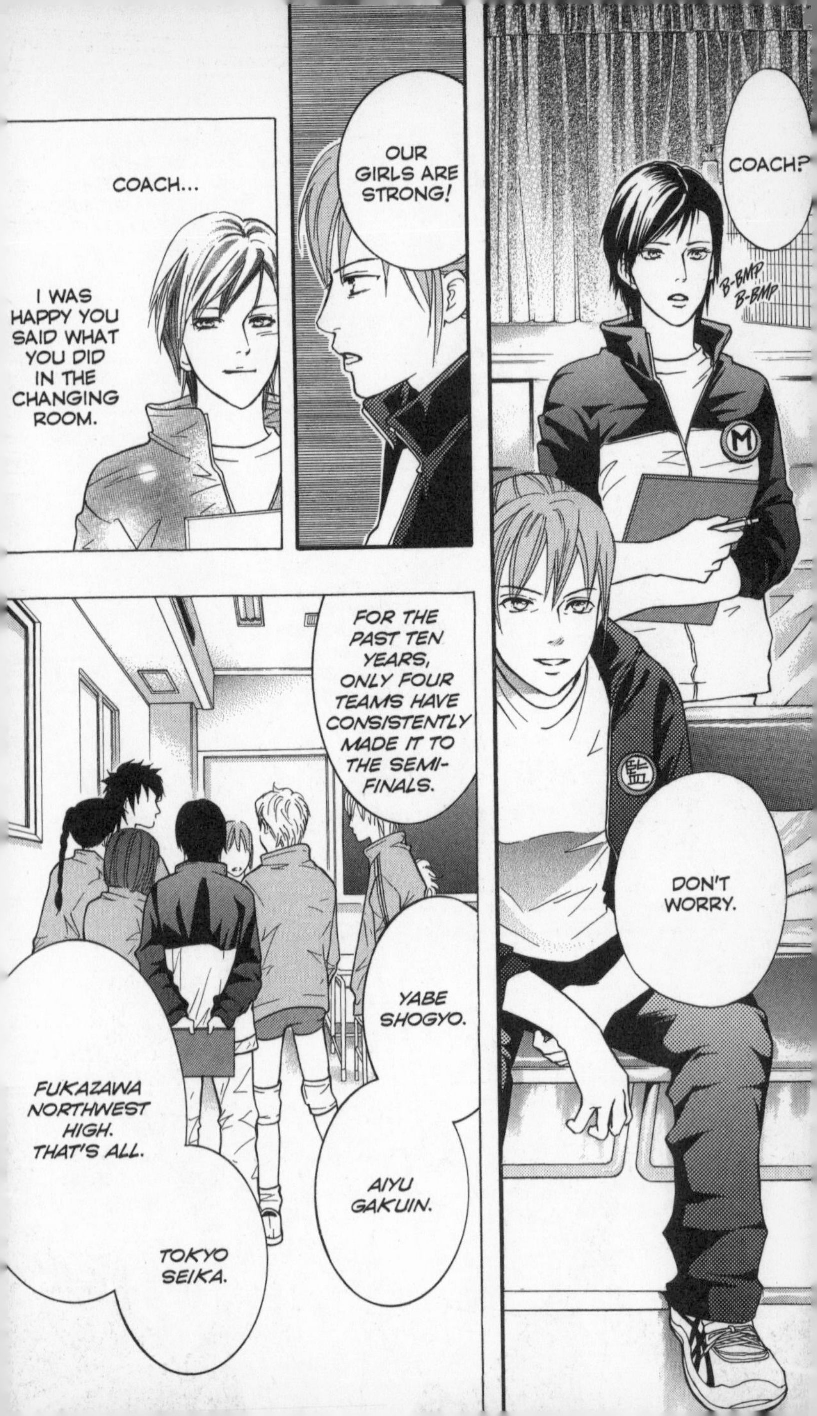
COACH?
B-BMP B-BMP
DON'T WORRY.
OUR GIRLS ARE STRONG!
COACH...
I WAS HAPPY YOU SAID WHAT YOU DID IN THE CHANGING ROOM.
FOR THE PAST TEN YEARS, ONLY FOUR TEAMS HAVE CONSISTENTLY MADE IT TO THE SEMI-FINALS.
YABE SHOGYO.
AIYU GAKUIN.
TOKYO SEIKA.
FUKAZAWA NORTHWEST HIGH. THAT'S ALL.

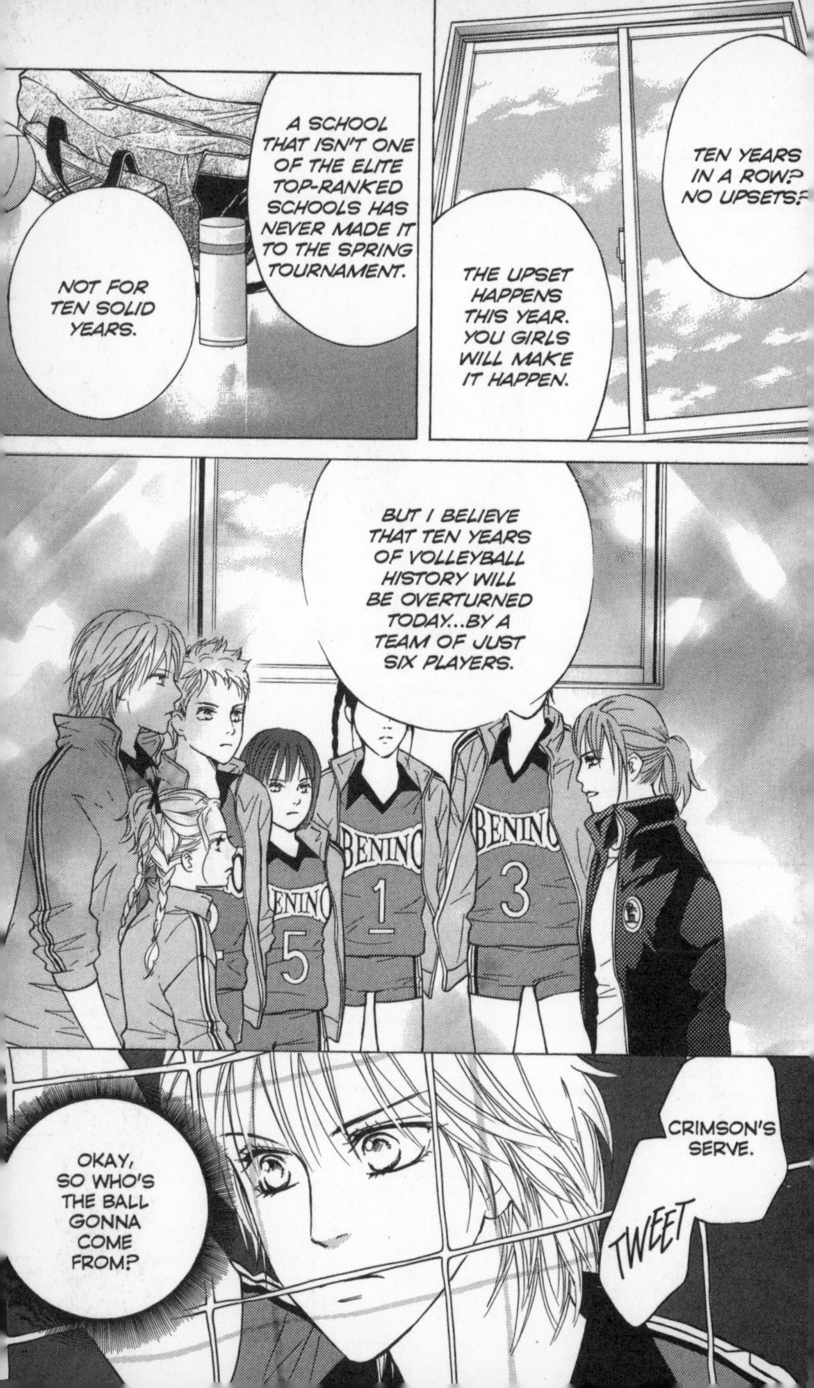
TEN YEARS IN A ROW? NO UPSETS?!
THE UPSET HAPPENS THIS YEAR. YOU GIRLS WILL MAKE IT HAPPEN.
A SCHOOL THAT ISN'T ONE OF THE ELITE TOP-RANKED SCHOOLS HAS NEVER MADE IT TO THE SPRING TOURNAMENT.
NOT FOR TEN SOLID YEARS.
BUT I BELIEVE THAT TEN YEARS OF VOLLEYBALL HISTORY WILL BE OVERTURNED TODAY...BY A TEAM OF JUST SIX PLAYERS.
BENINO
BENINO
BENINO
CRIMSON'S SERVE.
TWEET
OKAY, SO WHO'S THE BALL GONNA COME FROM?

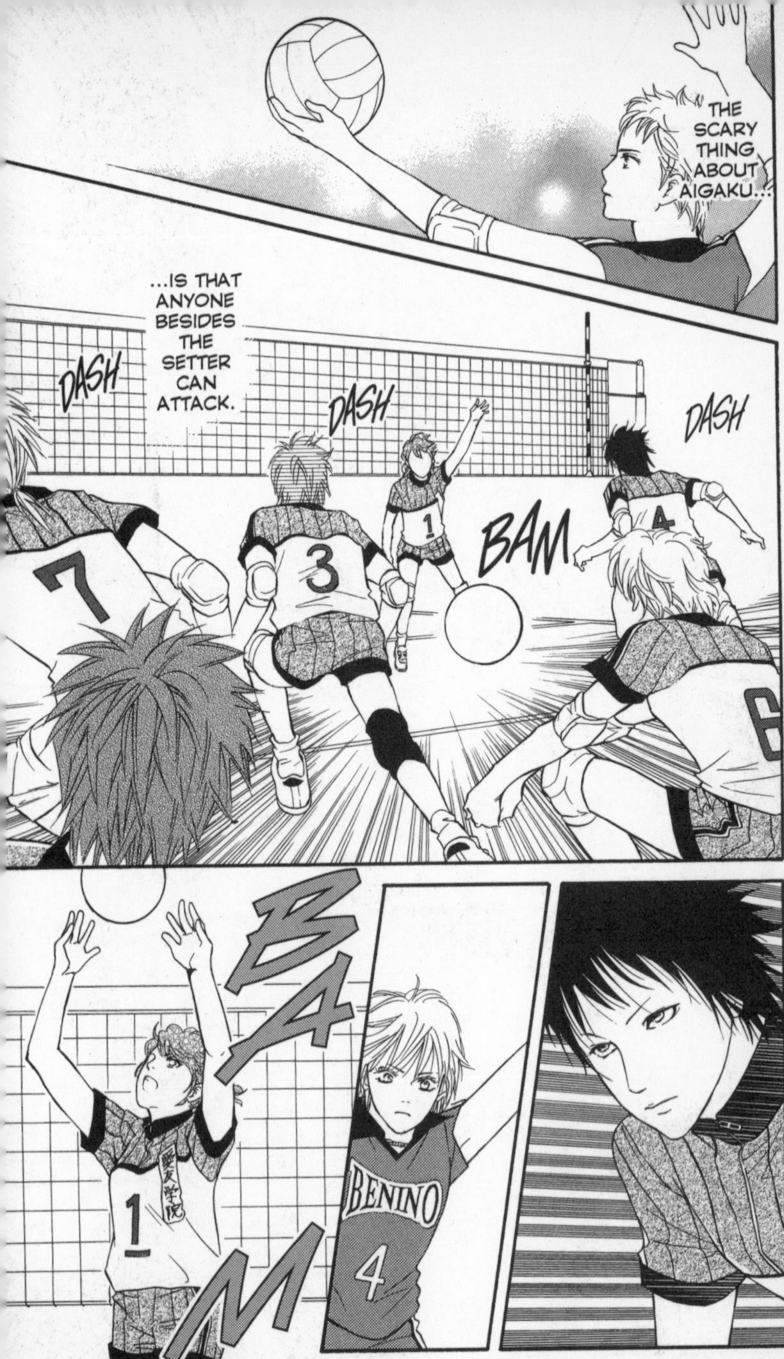
THE SCARY THING ABOUT AIGAKU...
...IS THAT ANYONE BESIDES THE SETTER CAN ATTACK.
DASH
BAM
DASH
DASH
BENINO
4
BAM
1

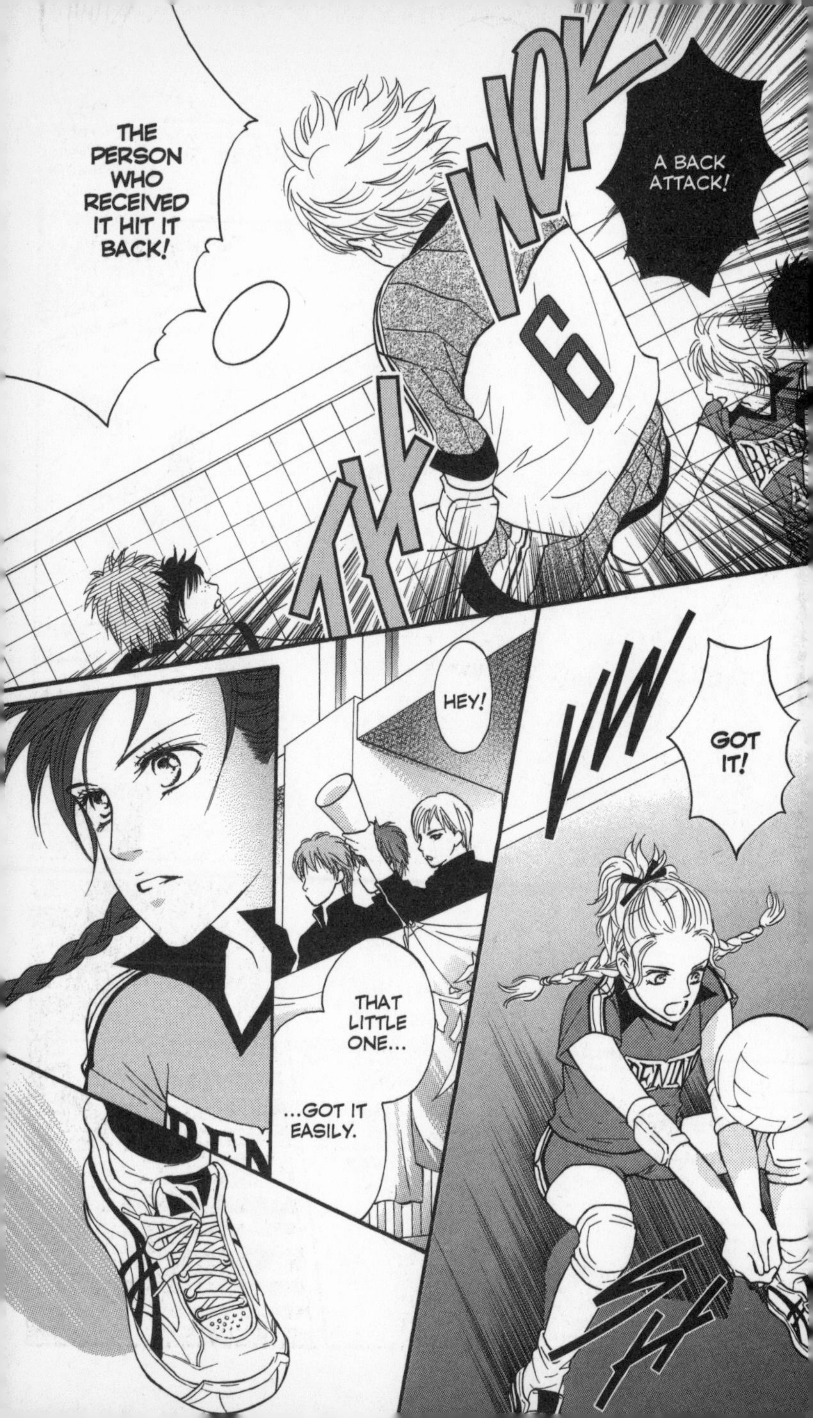
WOK
A BACK ATTACK!
THE PERSON WHO RECEIVED IT HIT IT BACK!
GOT IT!
HEY!
THAT LITTLE ONE...
...GOT IT EASILY.

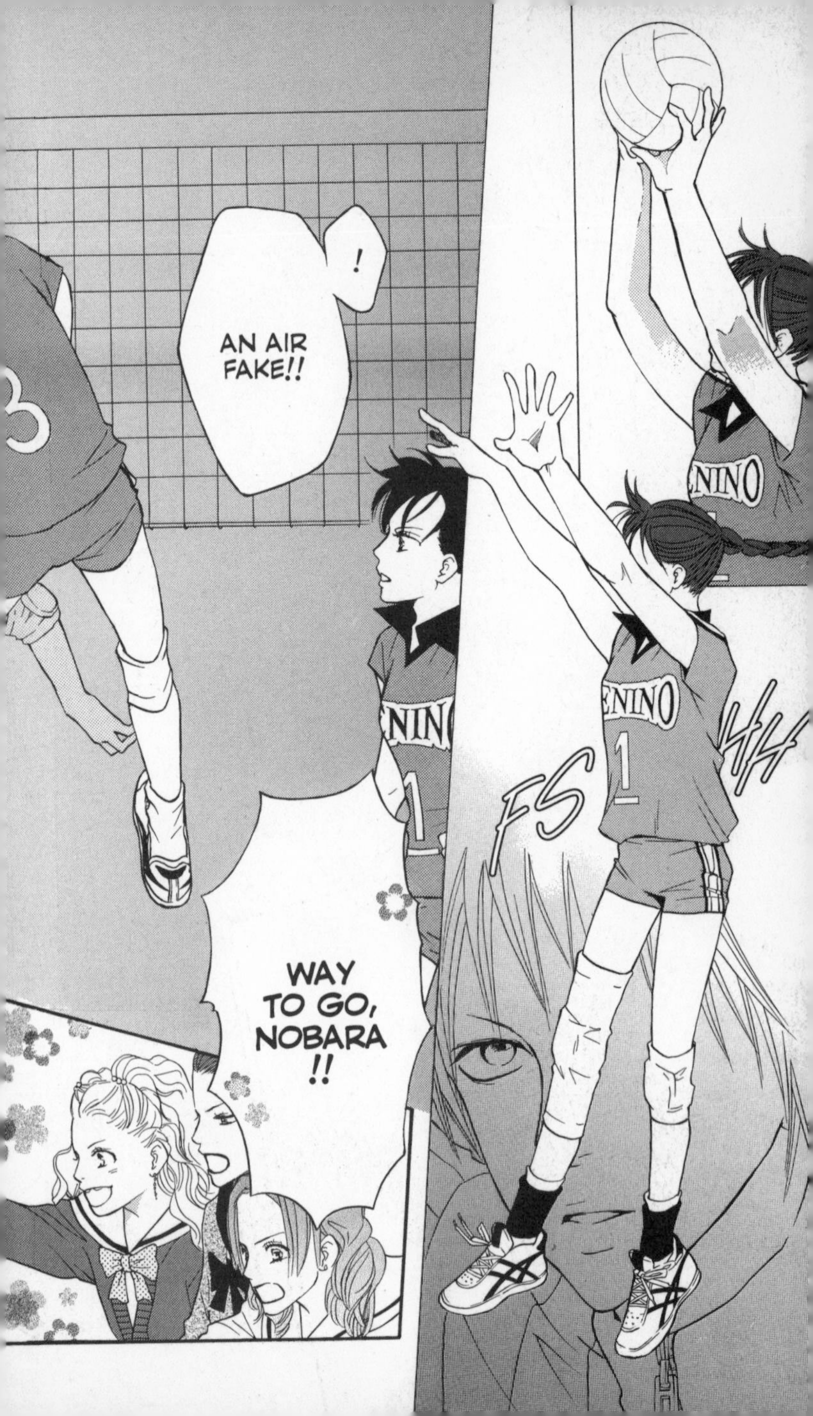
FSHH
!
AN AIR FAKE!!
WAY TO GO, NOBARA!!

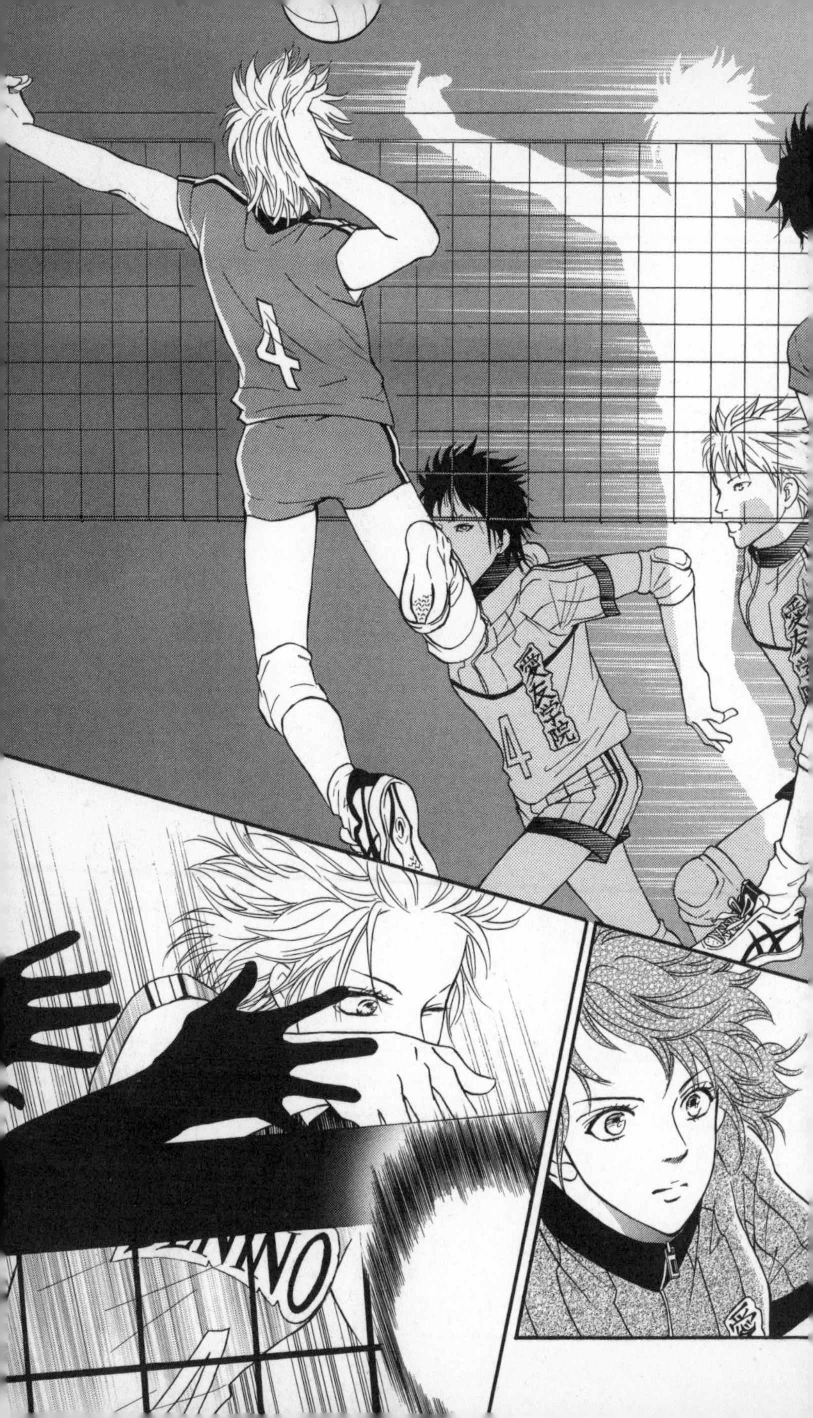
愛友学院

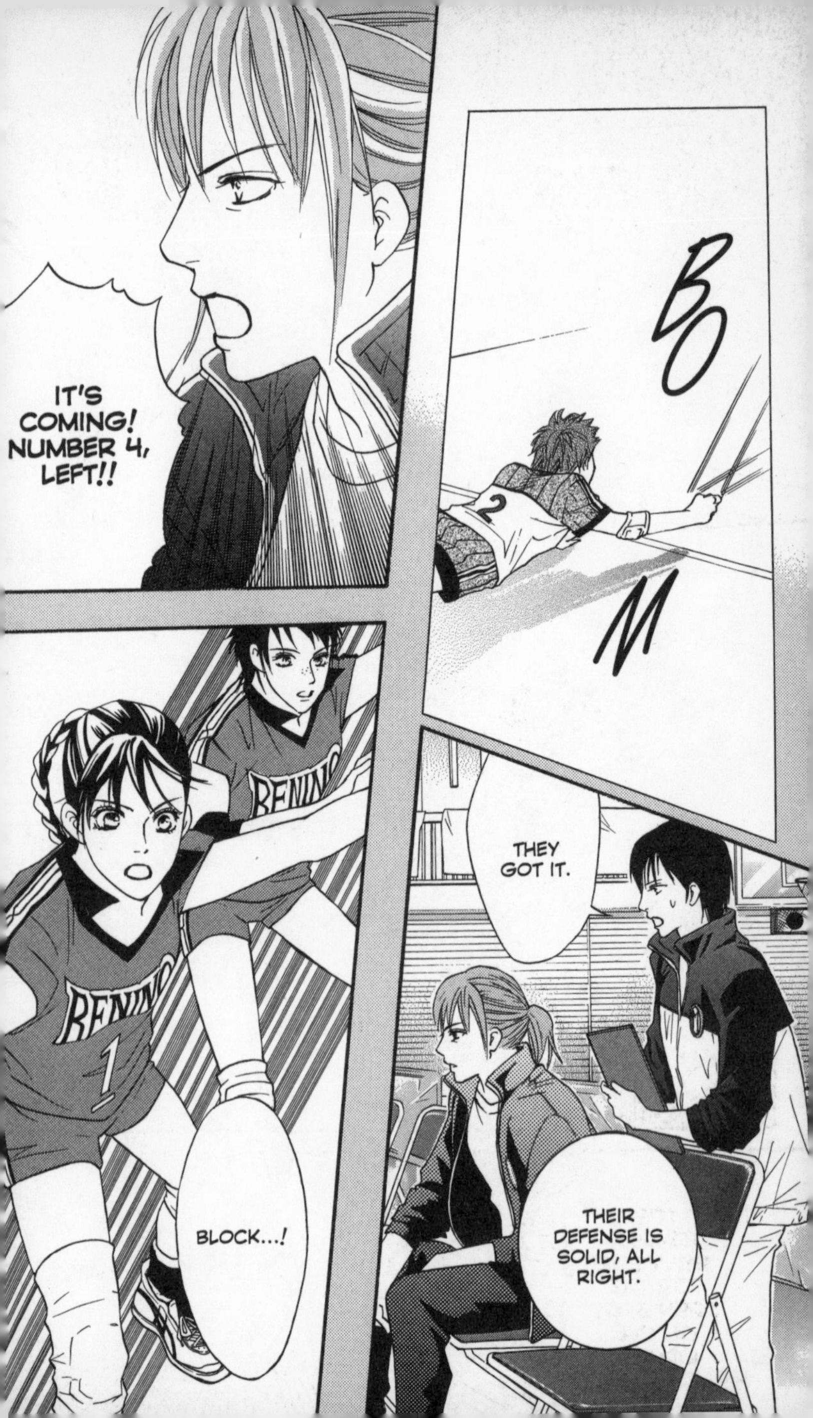
BOOM
IT'S COMING! NUMBER 4, LEFT!!
THEY GOT IT.
THEIR DEFENSE IS SOLID, ALL RIGHT.
BLOCK...!

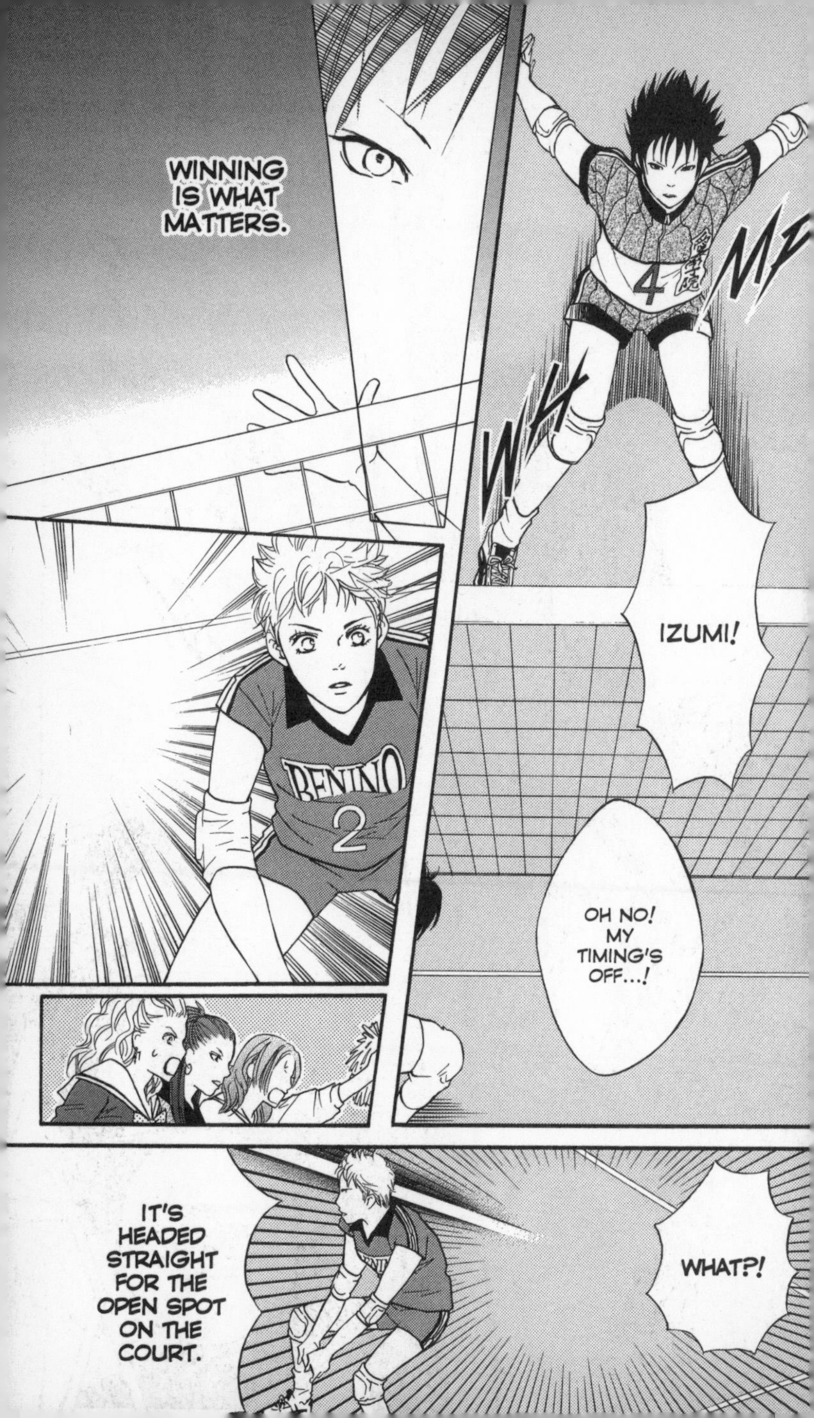
IZUMI!
OH NO! MY TIMING'S OFF...!
WINNING IS WHAT MATTERS.
WHAT?!
IT'S HEADED STRAIGHT FOR THE OPEN SPOT ON THE COURT.

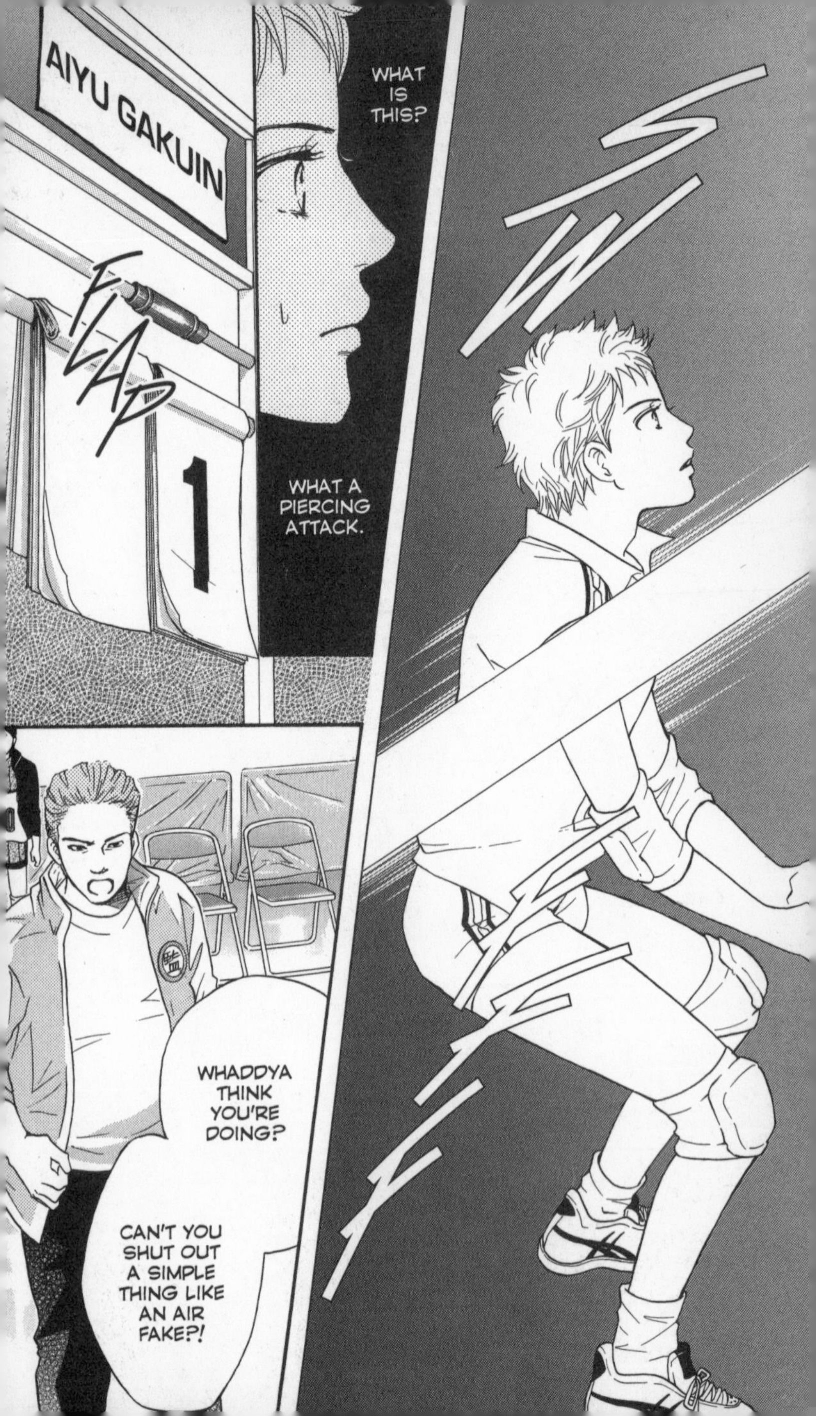
WHAT IS THIS?
AIYU GAKUIN
WHAT A PIERCING ATTACK.
FLAP
1
WHADDYA THINK YOU'RE DOING?
CAN'T YOU SHUT OUT A SIMPLE THING LIKE AN AIR FAKE?!

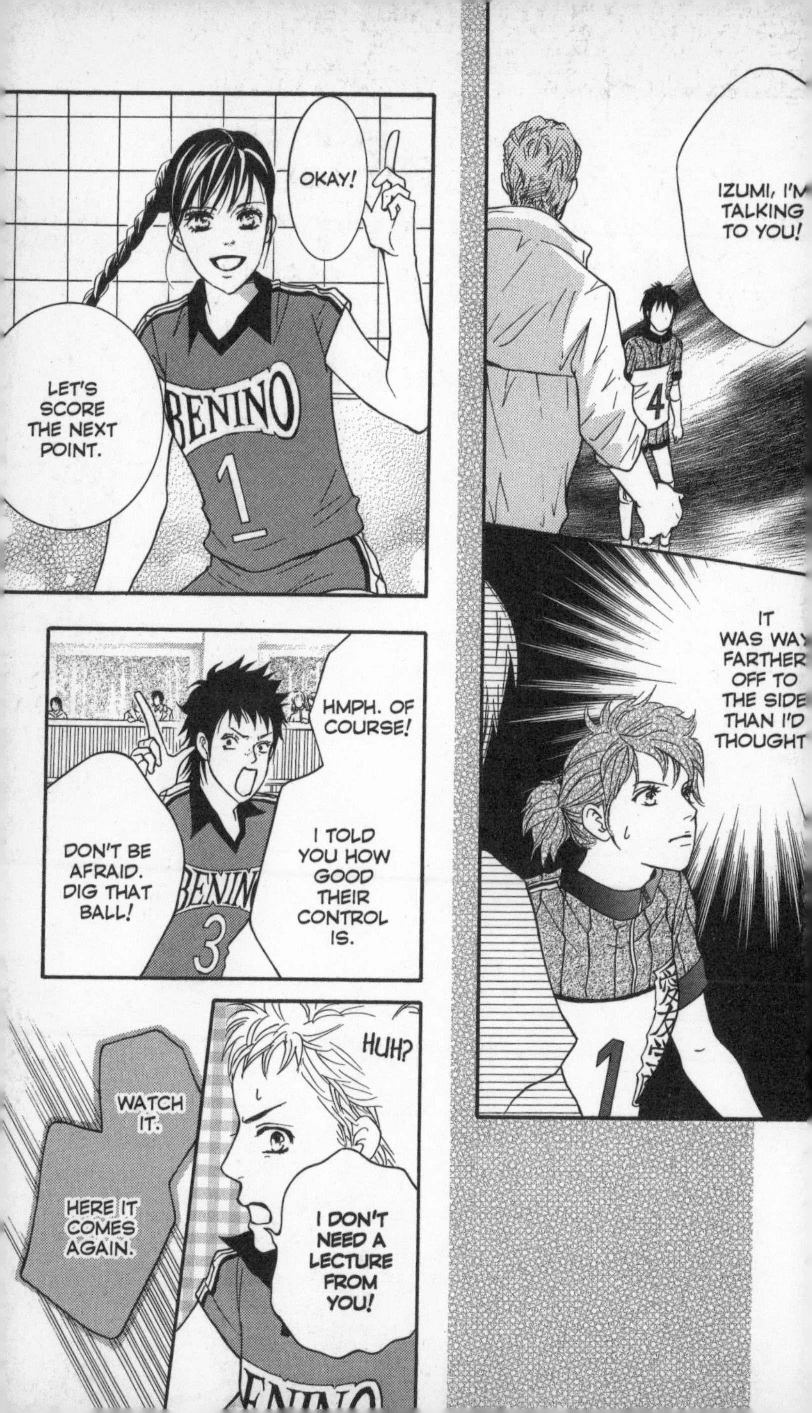
IZUMI, I'M TALKING TO YOU!
IT WAS WAY FARTHER OFF TO THE SIDE THAN I'D THOUGHT
OKAY!
LET'S SCORE THE NEXT POINT.
HMPH. OF COURSE!
I TOLD YOU HOW GOOD THEIR CONTROL IS.
DON'T BE AFRAID. DIG THAT BALL!
HUH?
I DON'T NEED A LECTURE FROM YOU!
WATCH IT.
HERE IT COMES AGAIN.

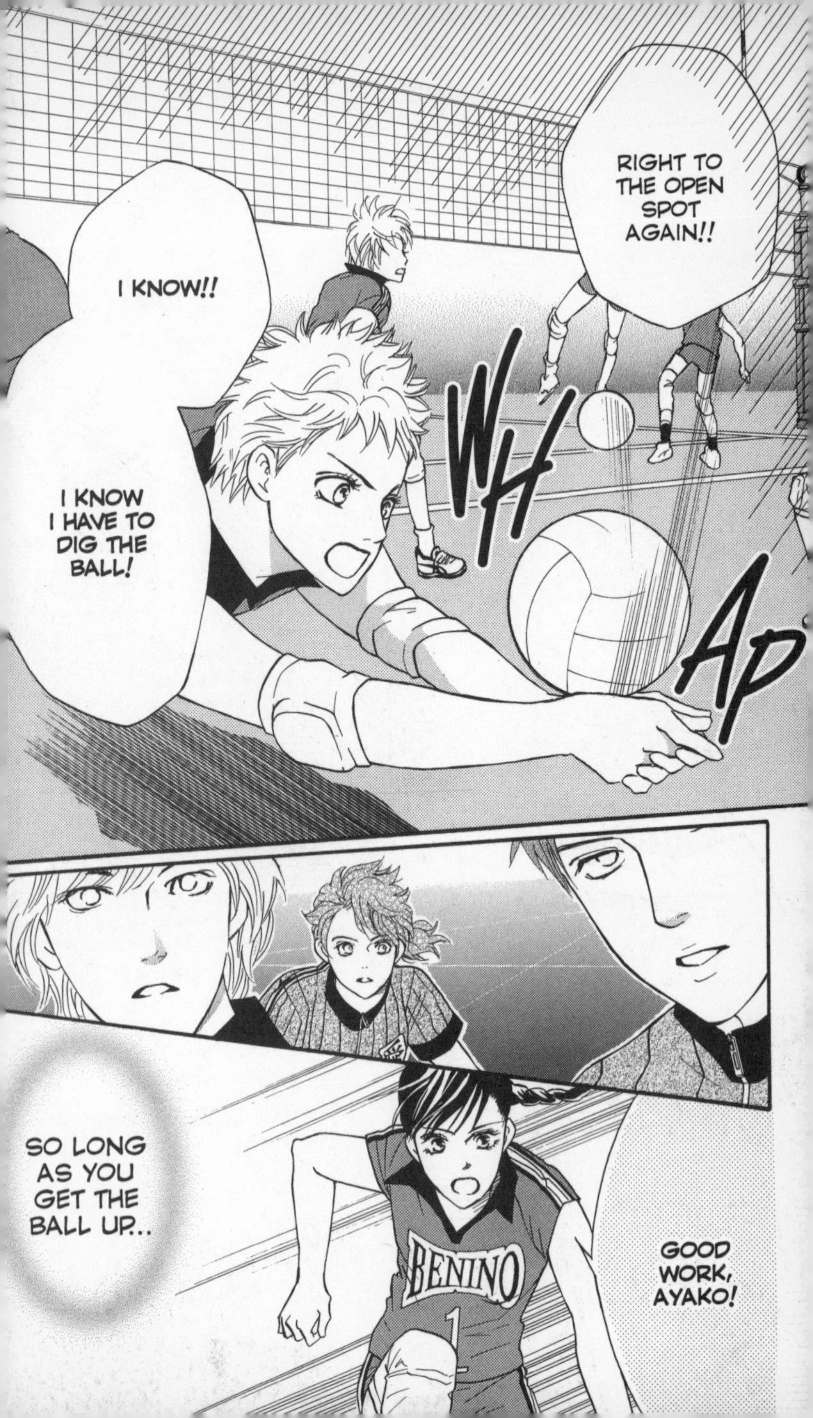
RIGHT TO THE OPEN SPOT AGAIN!!
I KNOW!!
WH
I KNOW I HAVE TO DIG THE BALL!
AP
GOOD WORK, AYAKO!
SO LONG AS YOU GET THE BALL UP...

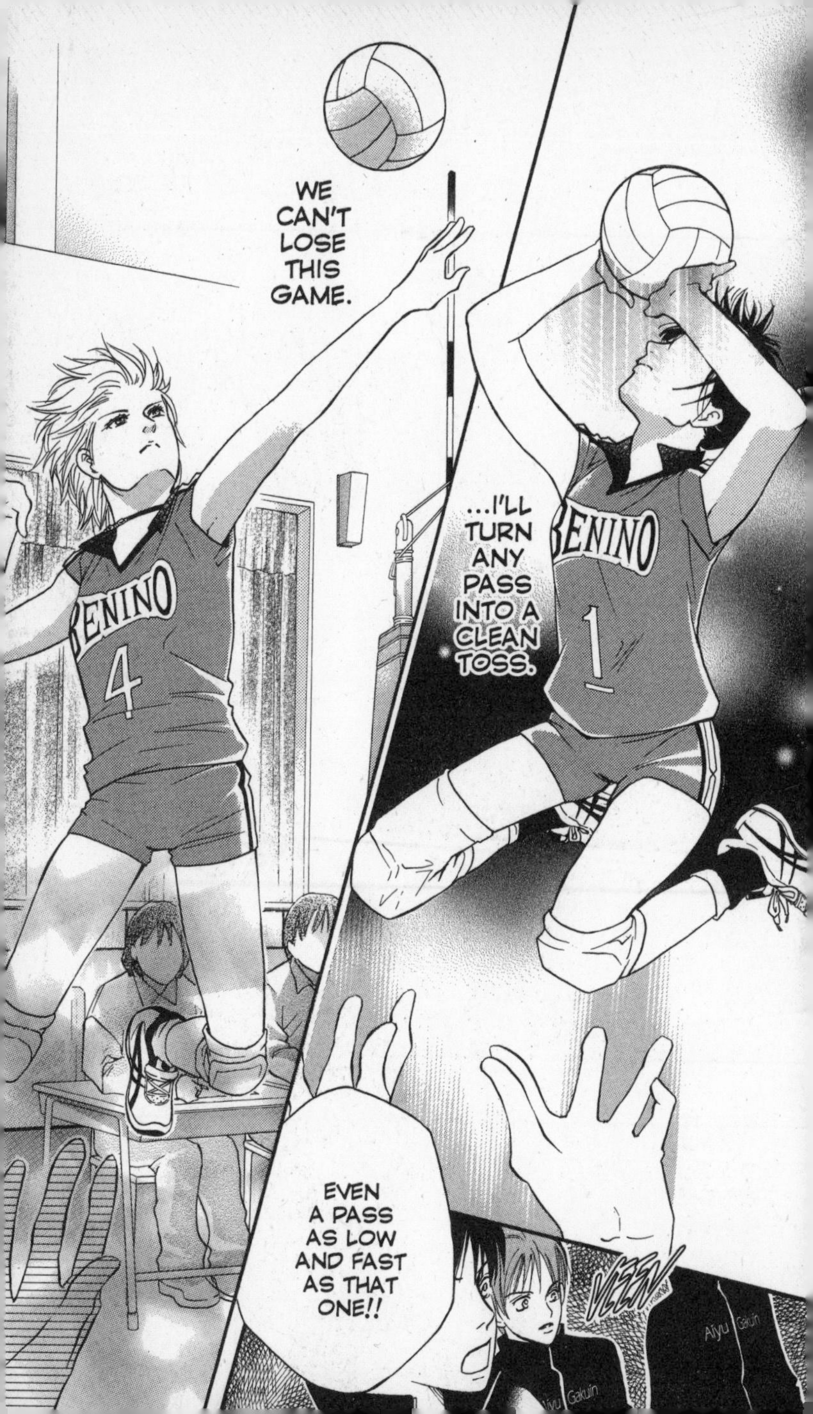
...I'LL TURN ANY PASS INTO A CLEAN TOSS.
EVEN A PASS AS LOW AND FAST AS THAT ONE!!
WE CAN'T LOSE THIS GAME.

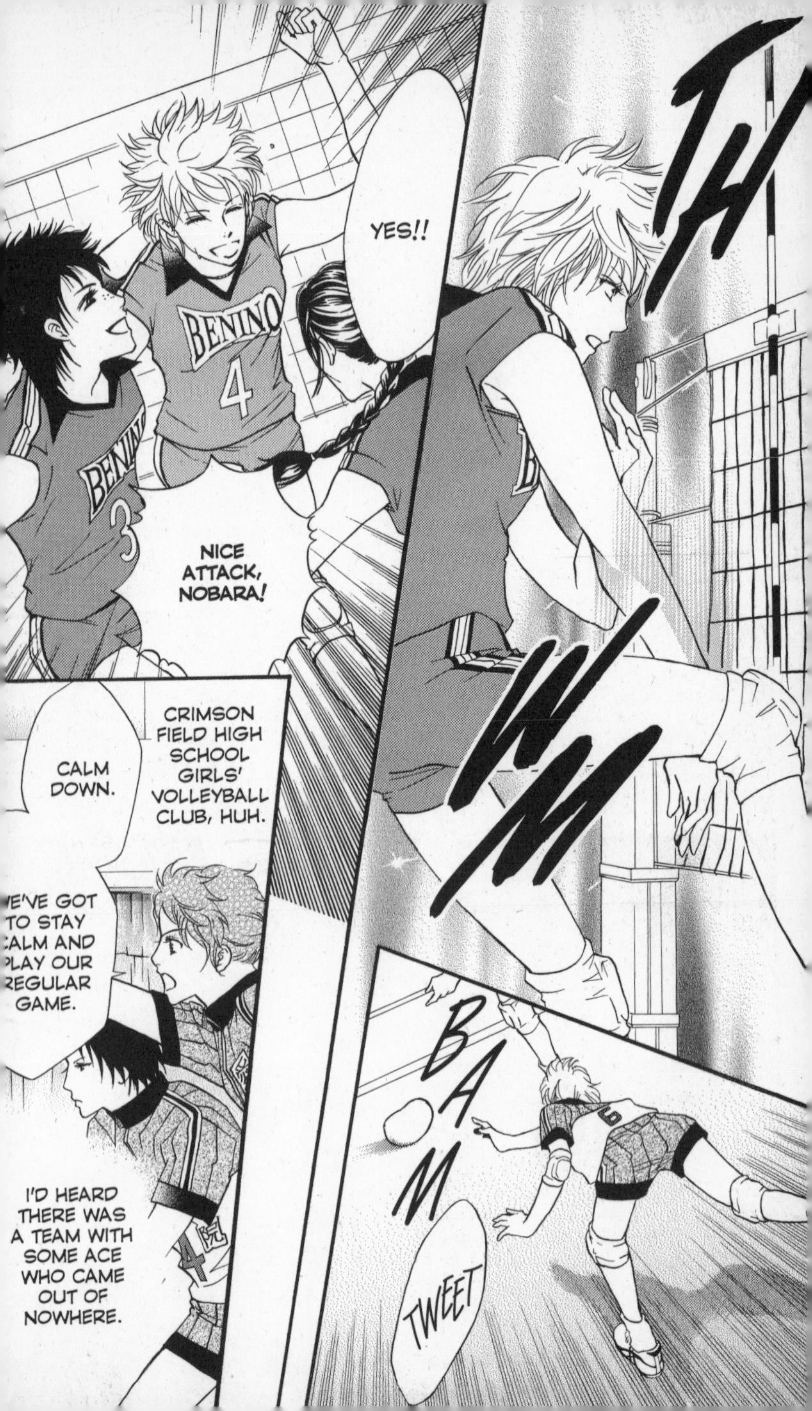
THWM
YES!!
NICE ATTACK, NOBARA!
BAM
TWEET
CRIMSON FIELD HIGH SCHOOL GIRLS' VOLLEYBALL CLUB, HUH.
CALM DOWN.
WE'VE GOT TO STAY CALM AND PLAY OUR REGULAR GAME.
I'D HEARD THERE WAS A TEAM WITH SOME ACE WHO CAME OUT OF NOWHERE.

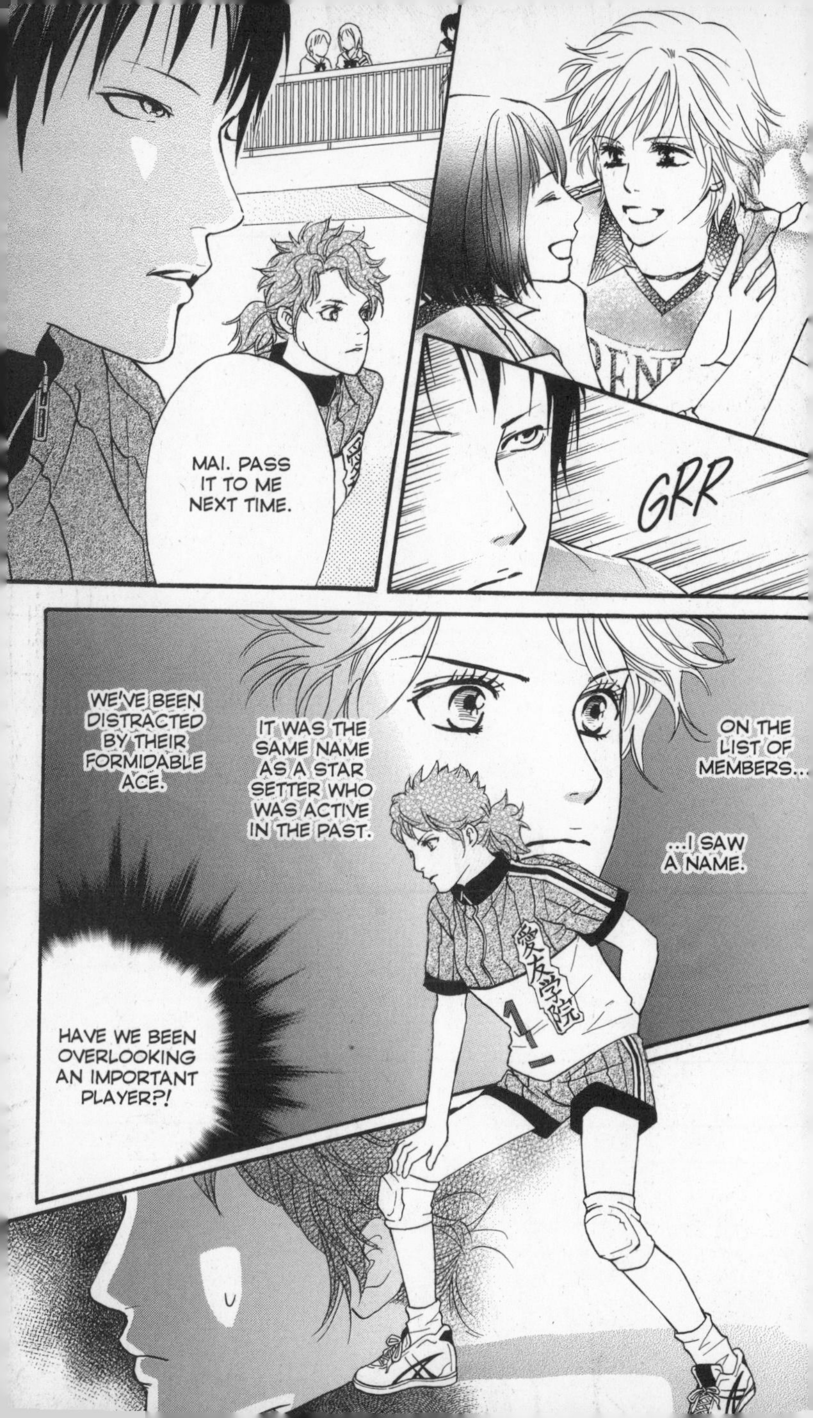
GRR
MAI. PASS IT TO ME NEXT TIME.
ON THE LIST OF MEMBERS...
...I SAW A NAME.
IT WAS THE SAME NAME AS A STAR SETTER WHO WAS ACTIVE IN THE PAST.
WE'VE BEEN DISTRACTED BY THEIR FORMIDABLE ACE.
HAVE WE BEEN OVERLOOKING AN IMPORTANT PLAYER?!
愛友学院
1

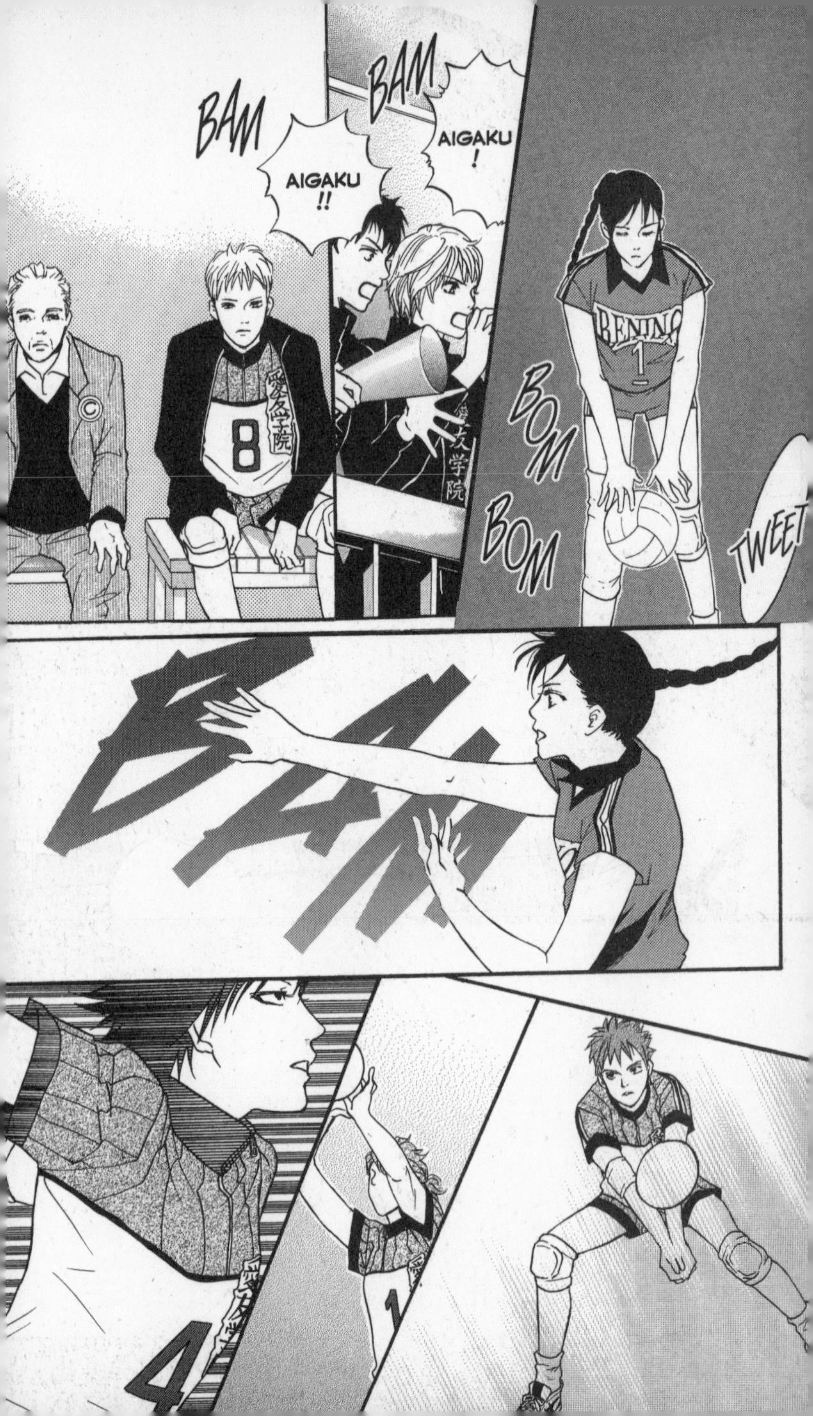
TWEET
BOM
BOM
BAM
AIGAKU !
BAM
AIGAKU !!
BAM

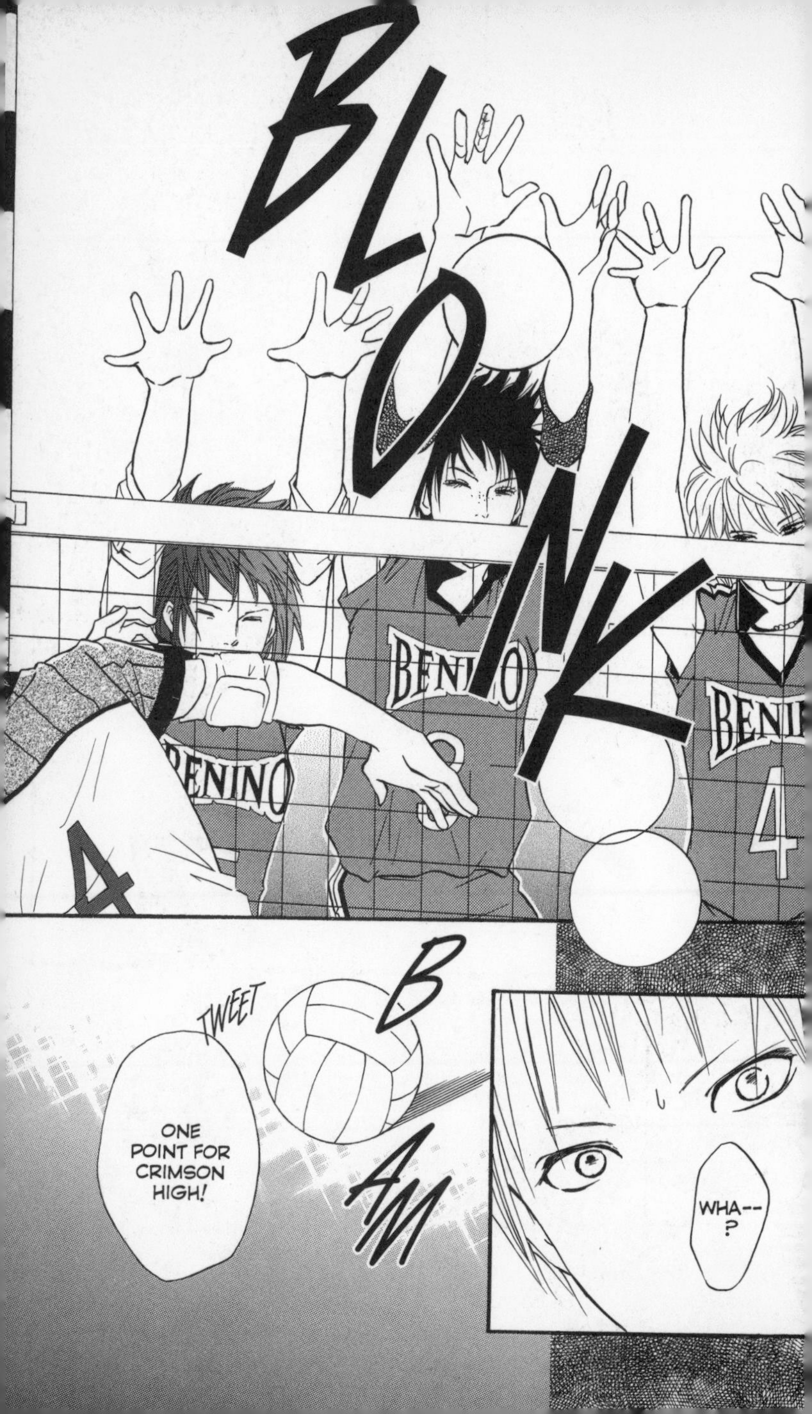
BLOONK
BENINO
WHA-- ?
TWEET
ONE POINT FOR CRIMSON HIGH!
BAM

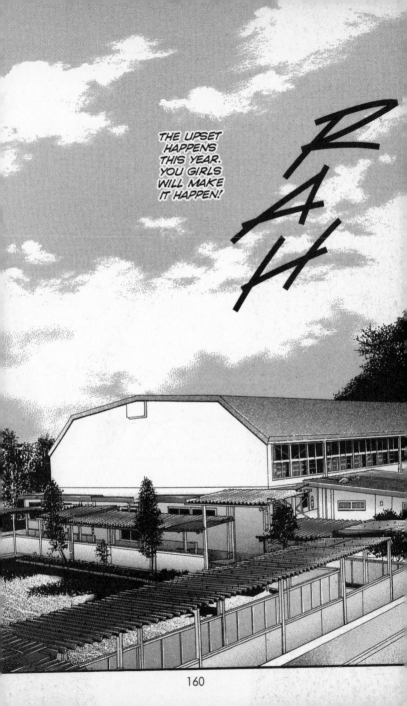

THE UPSET HAPPENS THIS YEAR. YOU GIRLS WILL MAKE IT HAPPEN!

RAH

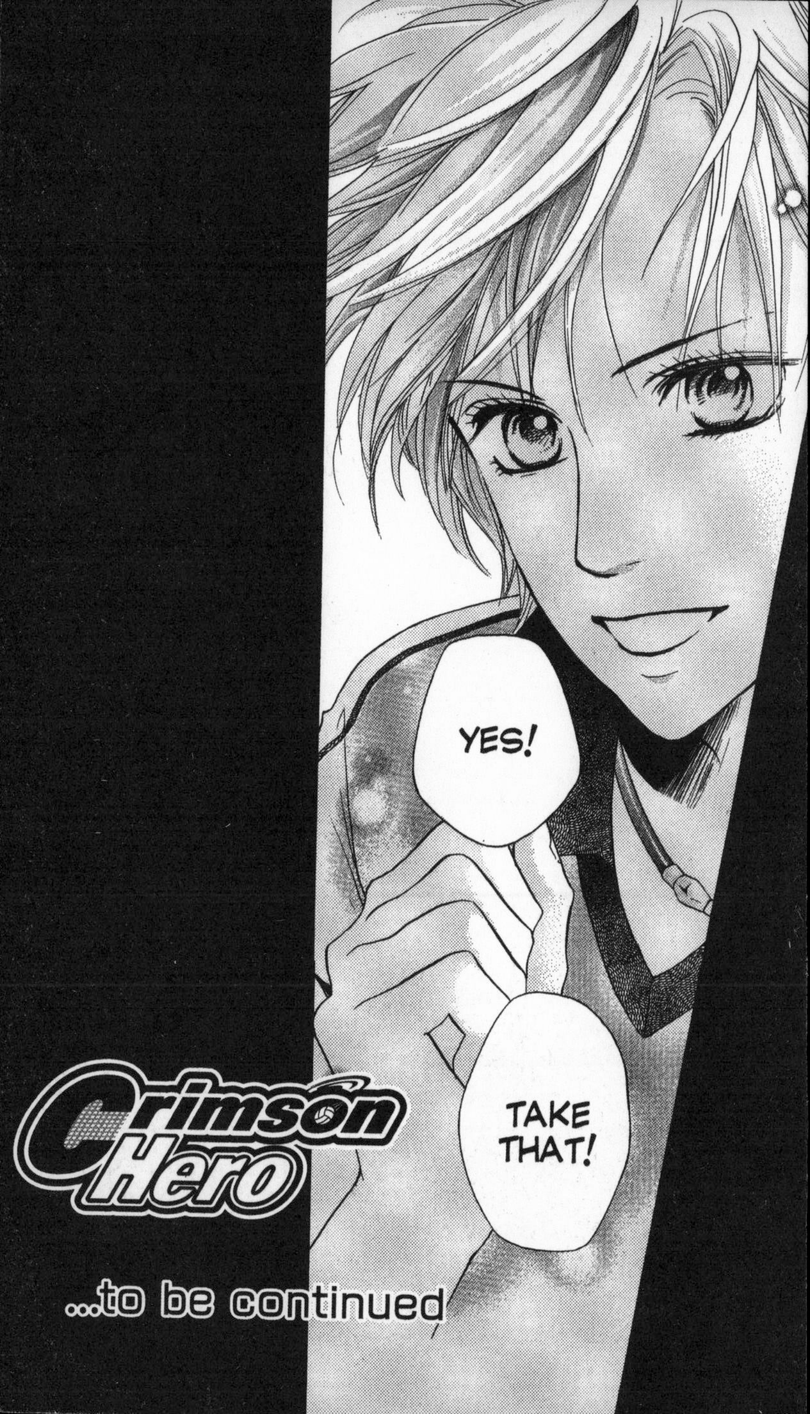
YES!
TAKE THAT!
Crimson Hero
...to be continued

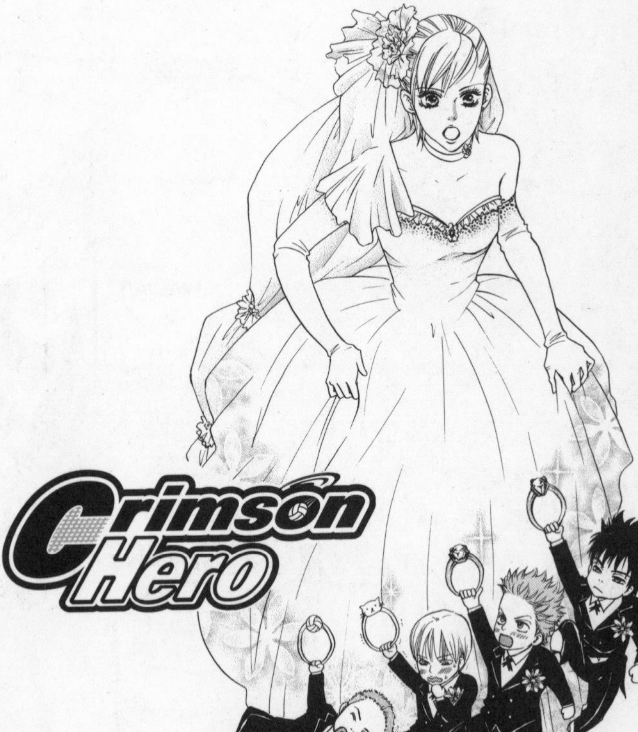
Crimson Hero

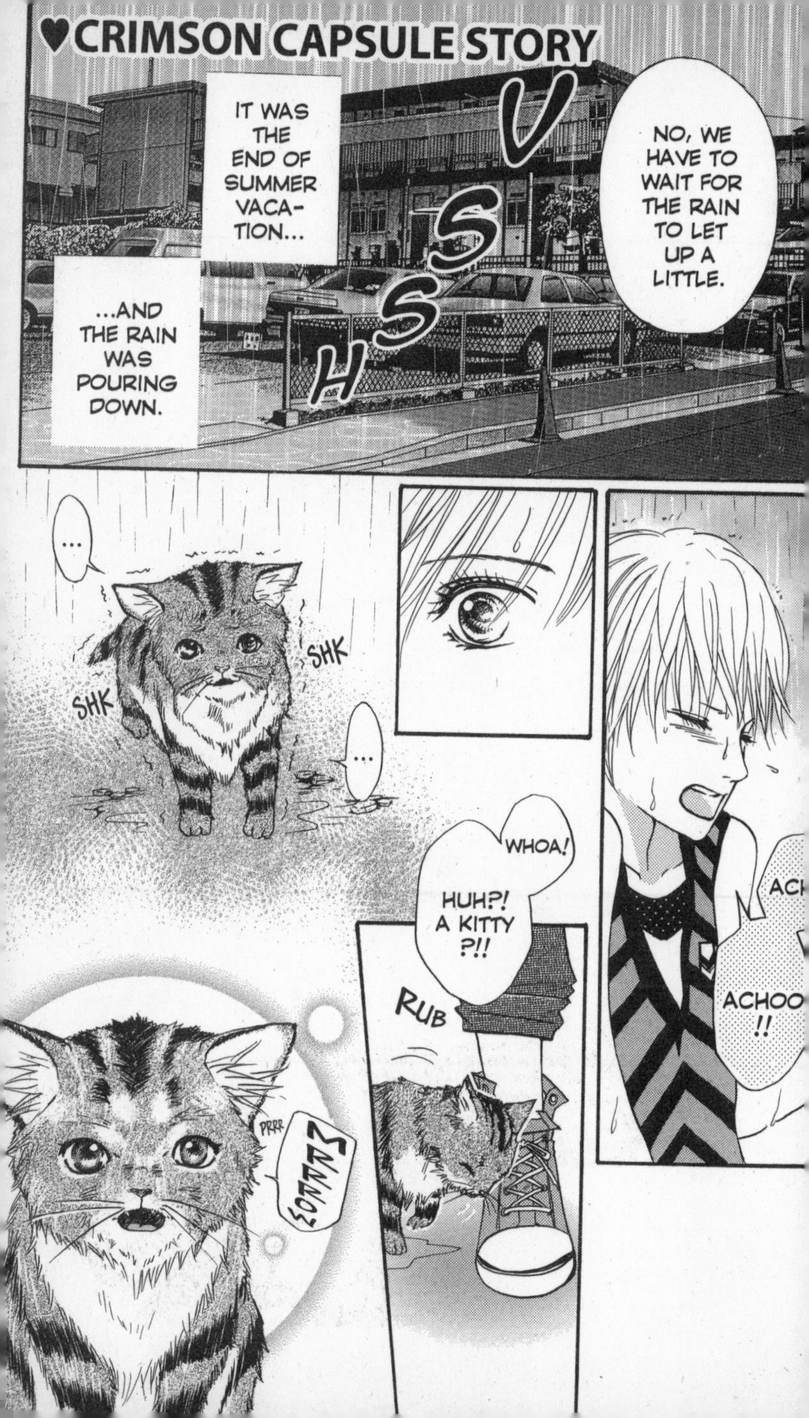
♥CRIMSON CAPSULE STORY
NO, WE HAVE TO WAIT FOR THE RAIN TO LET UP A LITTLE.
VSSH
IT WAS THE END OF SUMMER VACATION...
...AND THE RAIN WAS POURING DOWN.
ACH
ACHOO!!
...
SHK
SHK
...
WHOA!
HUH?! A KITTY?!!
RUB
PRRR
MRRROW?

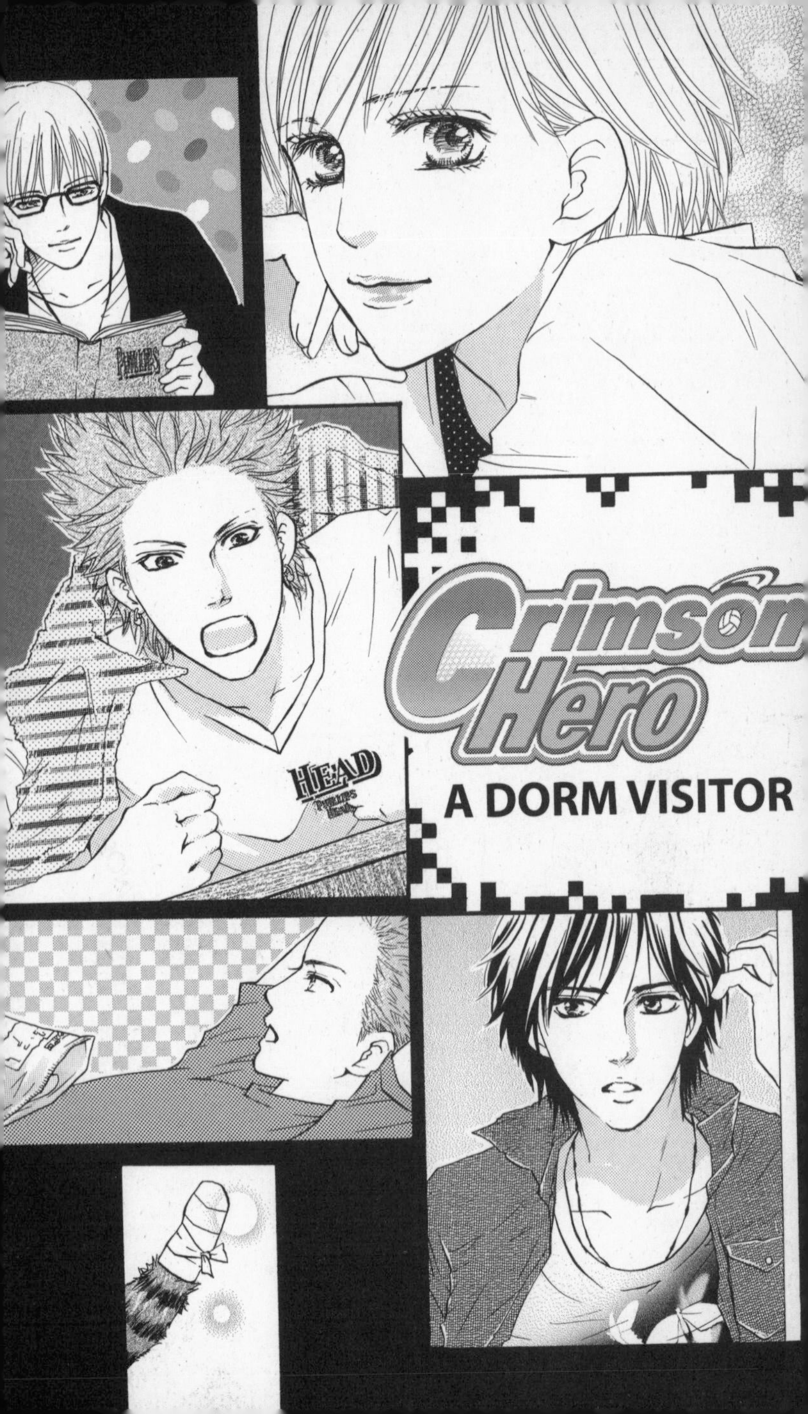
Crimson Hero
A DORM VISITOR

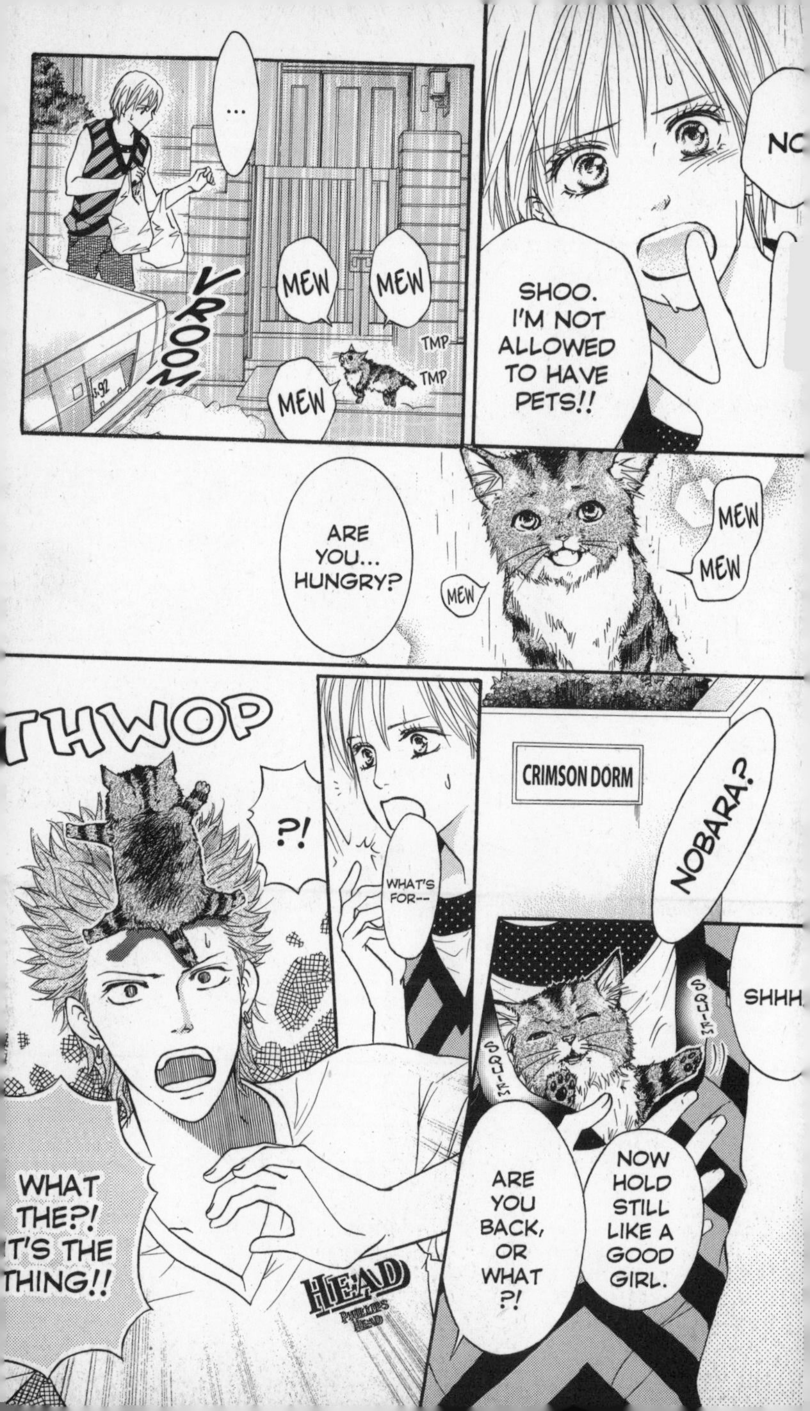
NO
SHOO. I'M NOT ALLOWED TO HAVE PETS!!
...
MEW
MEW
VROOM
TMP
TMP
MEW
MEW
MEW
MEW
ARE YOU... HUNGRY?
NOBARA?
CRIMSON DORM
SHHH
SQUIRM
SQUIRM
NOW HOLD STILL LIKE A GOOD GIRL.
ARE YOU BACK, OR WHAT?!
WHAT'S FOR--
THWOP
?!
WHAT THE?! T'S THE THING!!
HEAD
PHILLIPS HEAD

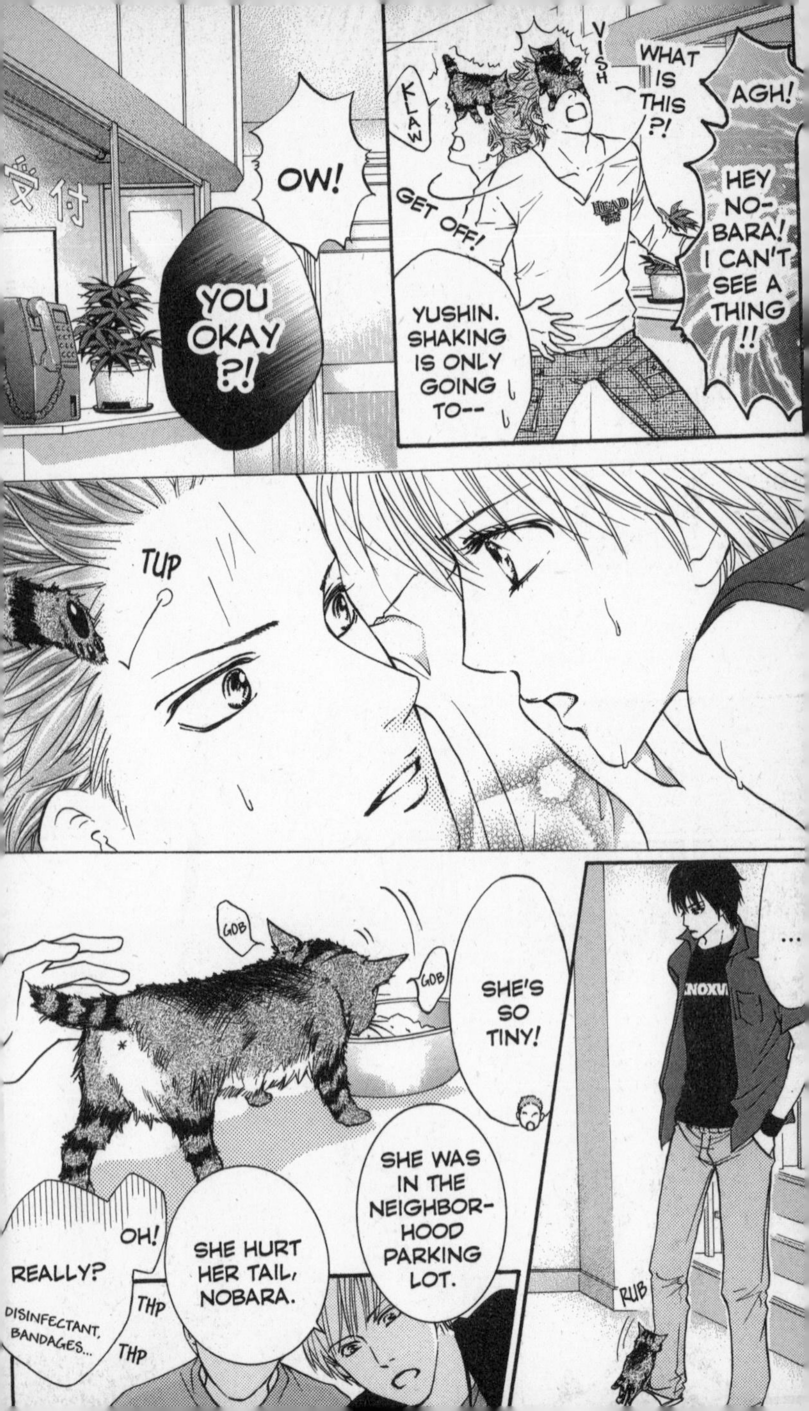AGH!
HEY NO-BARA! I CAN'T SEE A THING!!
WHAT IS THIS?!
VISH
KLAW
GET OFF!
YUSHIN. SHAKING IS ONLY GOING TO--
受付
OW!
YOU OKAY?!
TUP
...
RUB
SHE'S SO TINY!
GOB
GOB
SHE WAS IN THE NEIGHBOR-HOOD PARKING LOT.
SHE HURT HER TAIL, NOBARA.
OH!
REALLY?
THP
DISINFECTANT, BANDAGES...
THP

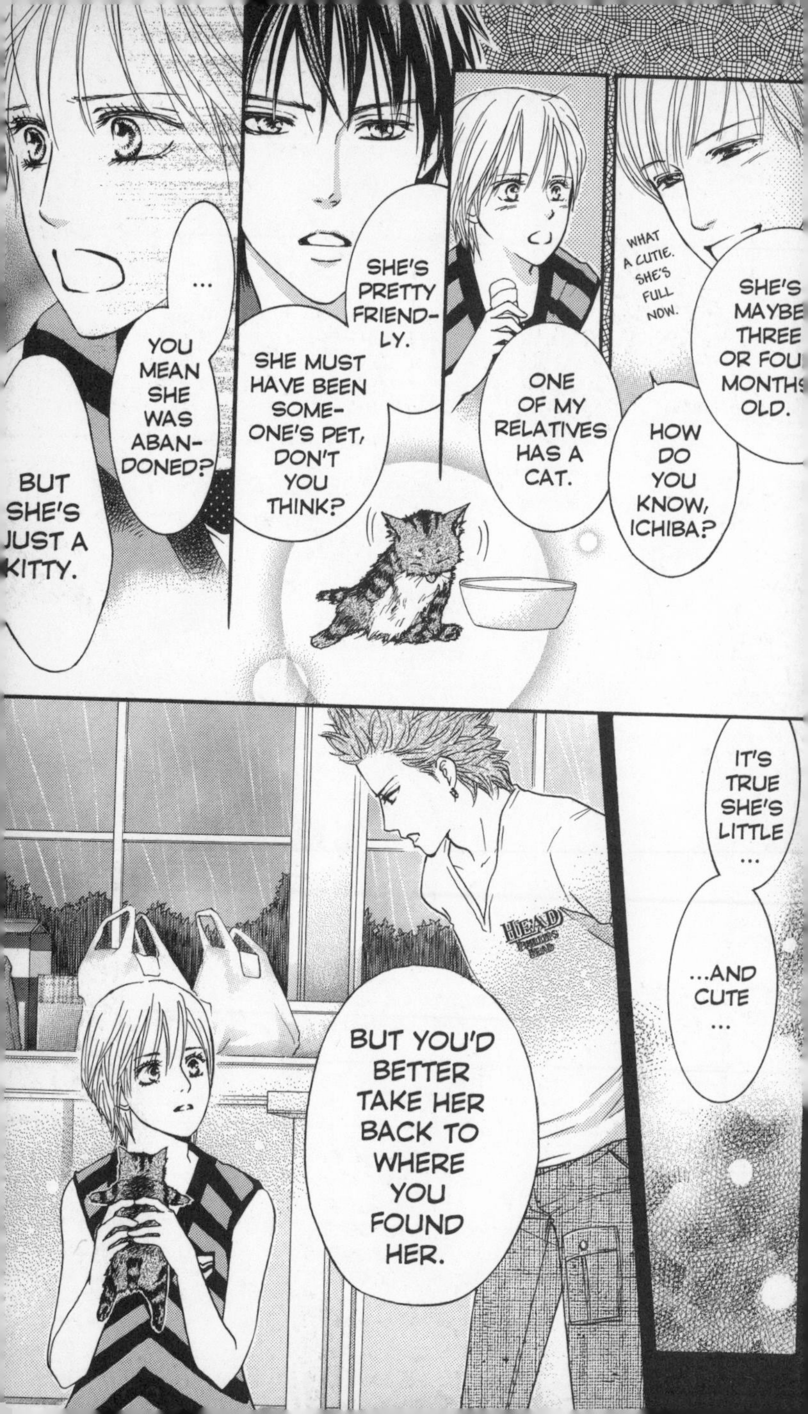
SHE'S MAYBE THREE OR FOU MONTHS OLD.
WHAT A CUTIE. SHE'S FULL NOW.
HOW DO YOU KNOW, ICHIBA?
ONE OF MY RELATIVES HAS A CAT.
SHE'S PRETTY FRIEND-LY.
SHE MUST HAVE BEEN SOME-ONE'S PET, DON'T YOU THINK?
...
YOU MEAN SHE WAS ABAN-DONED?
BUT SHE'S JUST A KITTY.
IT'S TRUE SHE'S LITTLE ...
...AND CUTE ...
BUT YOU'D BETTER TAKE HER BACK TO WHERE YOU FOUND HER.

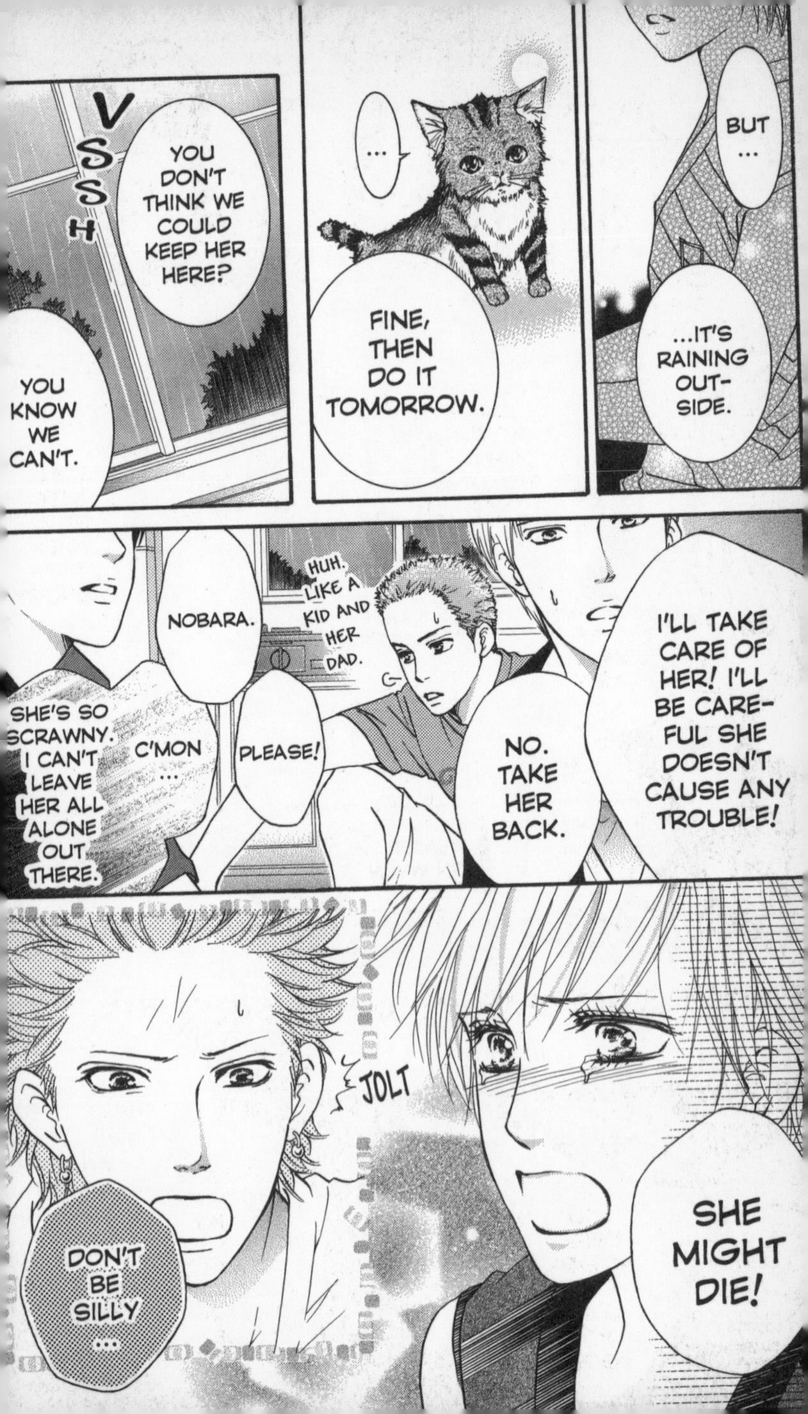
BUT ...
...IT'S RAINING OUT-SIDE.
...
FINE, THEN DO IT TOMORROW.
VSSH
YOU DON'T THINK WE COULD KEEP HER HERE?
YOU KNOW WE CAN'T.
I'LL TAKE CARE OF HER! I'LL BE CARE-FUL SHE DOESN'T CAUSE ANY TROUBLE!
NO. TAKE HER BACK.
HUH. LIKE A KID AND HER DAD.
NOBARA.
PLEASE!
C'MON ...
SHE'S SO SCRAWNY. I CAN'T LEAVE HER ALL ALONE OUT THERE.
SHE MIGHT DIE!
JOLT
DON'T BE SILLY ...

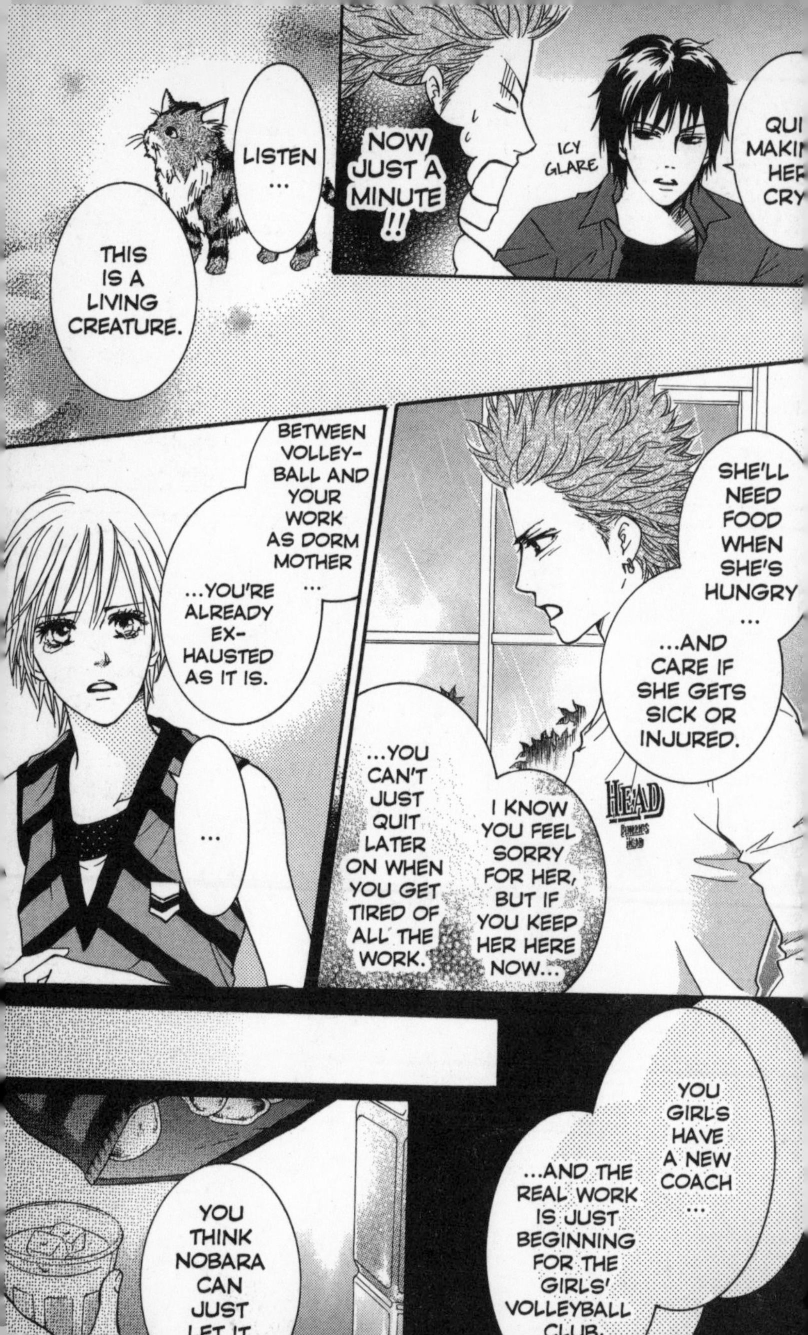
QUI MAKI HE CRY
ICY GLARE
NOW JUST A MINUTE !!
LISTEN ...
THIS IS A LIVING CREATURE.
SHE'LL NEED FOOD WHEN SHE'S HUNGRY ...
...AND CARE IF SHE GETS SICK OR INJURED.
HEAD
I KNOW YOU FEEL SORRY FOR HER, BUT IF YOU KEEP HER HERE NOW...
...YOU CAN'T JUST QUIT LATER ON WHEN YOU GET TIRED OF ALL THE WORK.
BETWEEN VOLLEY-BALL AND YOUR WORK AS DORM MOTHER ...
...YOU'RE ALREADY EX-HAUSTED AS IT IS.
...
YOU GIRLS HAVE A NEW COACH ...
...AND THE REAL WORK IS JUST BEGINNING FOR THE GIRLS' VOLLEYBALL CLUB,
YOU THINK NOBARA CAN JUST LET IT

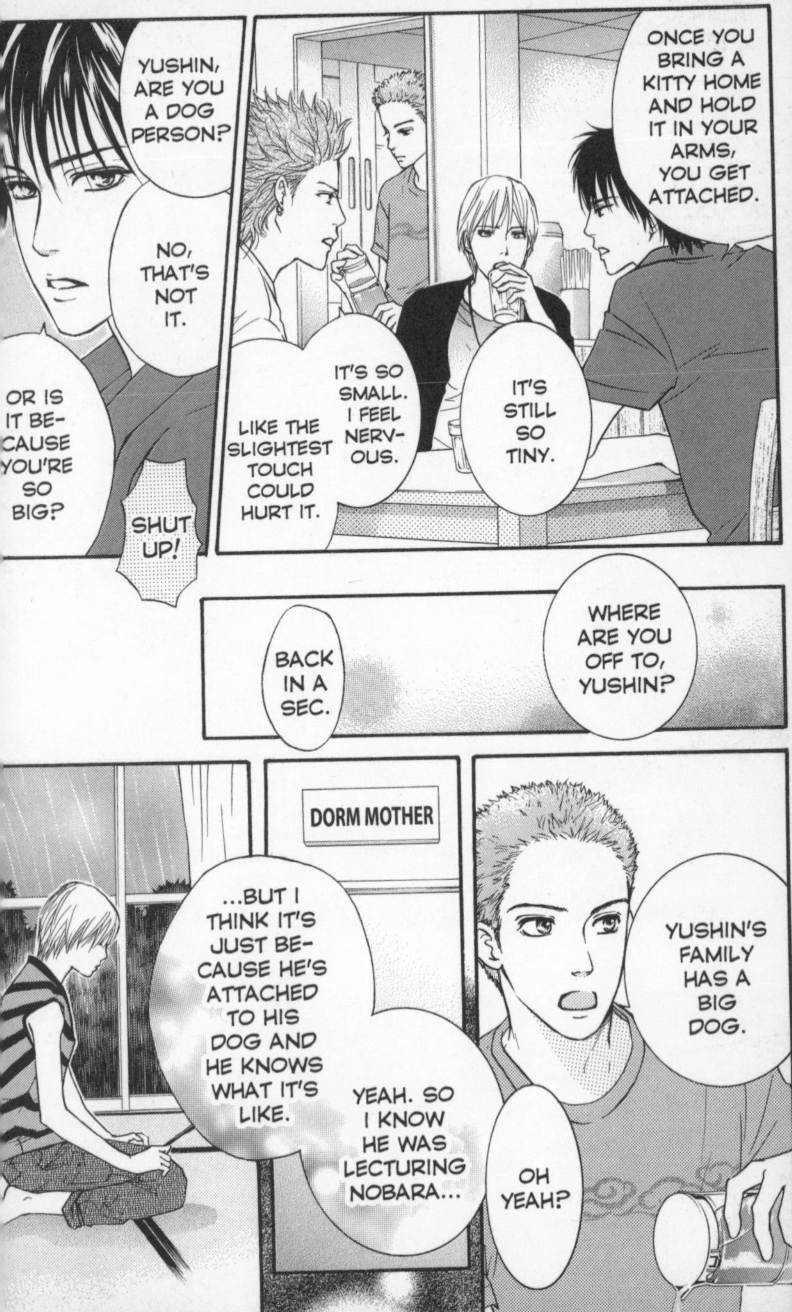
ONCE YOU BRING A KITTY HOME AND HOLD IT IN YOUR ARMS, YOU GET ATTACHED.
IT'S STILL SO TINY.
IT'S SO SMALL. I FEEL NERV-OUS.
LIKE THE SLIGHTEST TOUCH COULD HURT IT.
YUSHIN, ARE YOU A DOG PERSON?
NO, THAT'S NOT IT.
OR IS IT BE-CAUSE YOU'RE SO BIG?
SHUT UP!
WHERE ARE YOU OFF TO, YUSHIN?
BACK IN A SEC.
YUSHIN'S FAMILY HAS A BIG DOG.
OH YEAH?
YEAH. SO I KNOW HE WAS LECTURING NOBARA...
...BUT I THINK IT'S JUST BE-CAUSE HE'S ATTACHED TO HIS DOG AND HE KNOWS WHAT IT'S LIKE.
DORM MOTHER

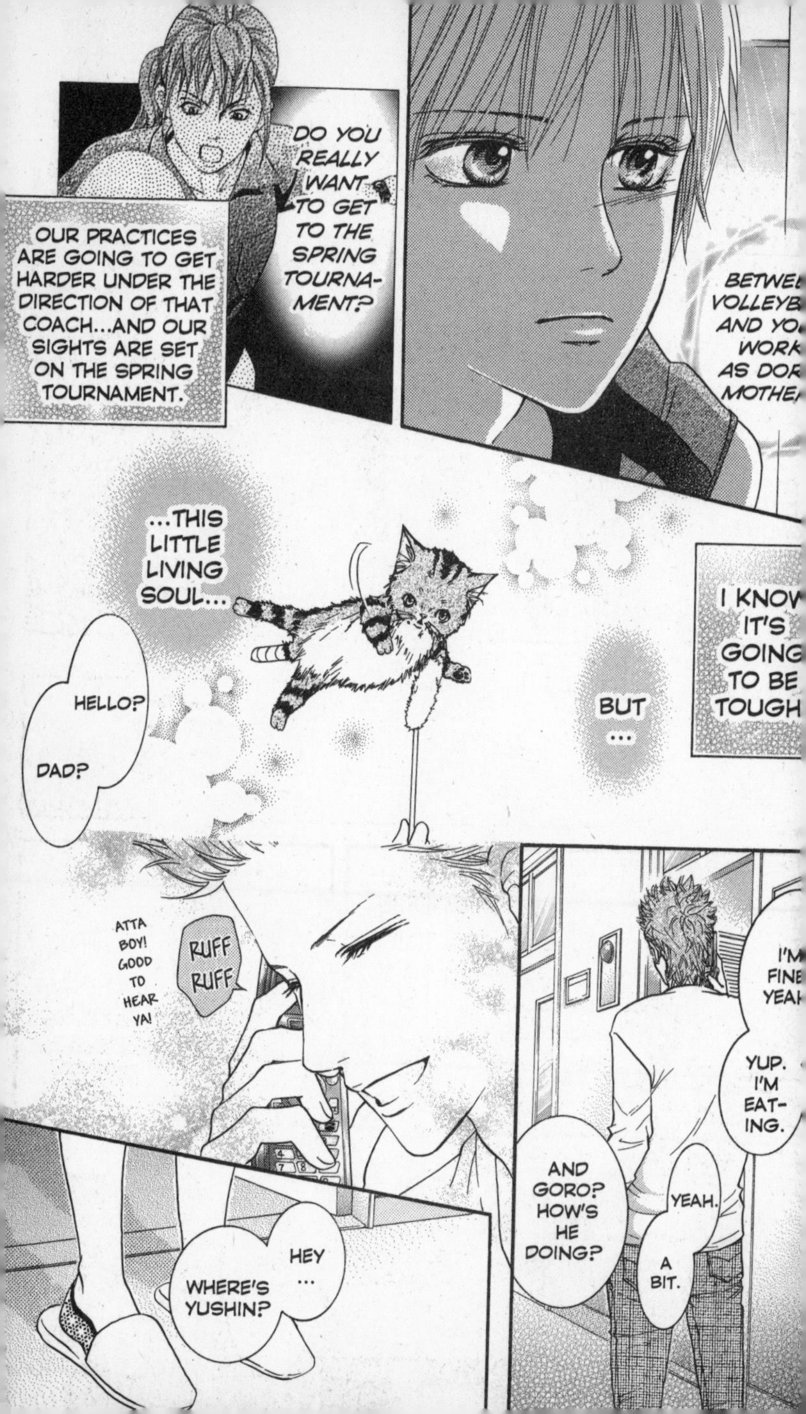
BETWE
VOLLEYB
AND YO
WORK
AS DOR
MOTHE
DO YOU REALLY WANT TO GET TO THE SPRING TOURNAMENT?
OUR PRACTICES ARE GOING TO GET HARDER UNDER THE DIRECTION OF THAT COACH...AND OUR SIGHTS ARE SET ON THE SPRING TOURNAMENT.
I KNOW IT'S GOING TO BE TOUGH
BUT ...
...THIS LITTLE LIVING SOUL...
HELLO?
DAD?
I'M FINE YEAH
YUP. I'M EATING.
YEAH.
AND GORO? HOW'S HE DOING?
A BIT.
RUFF RUFF
ATTA BOY! GOOD TO HEAR YA!
HEY ...
WHERE'S YUSHIN?

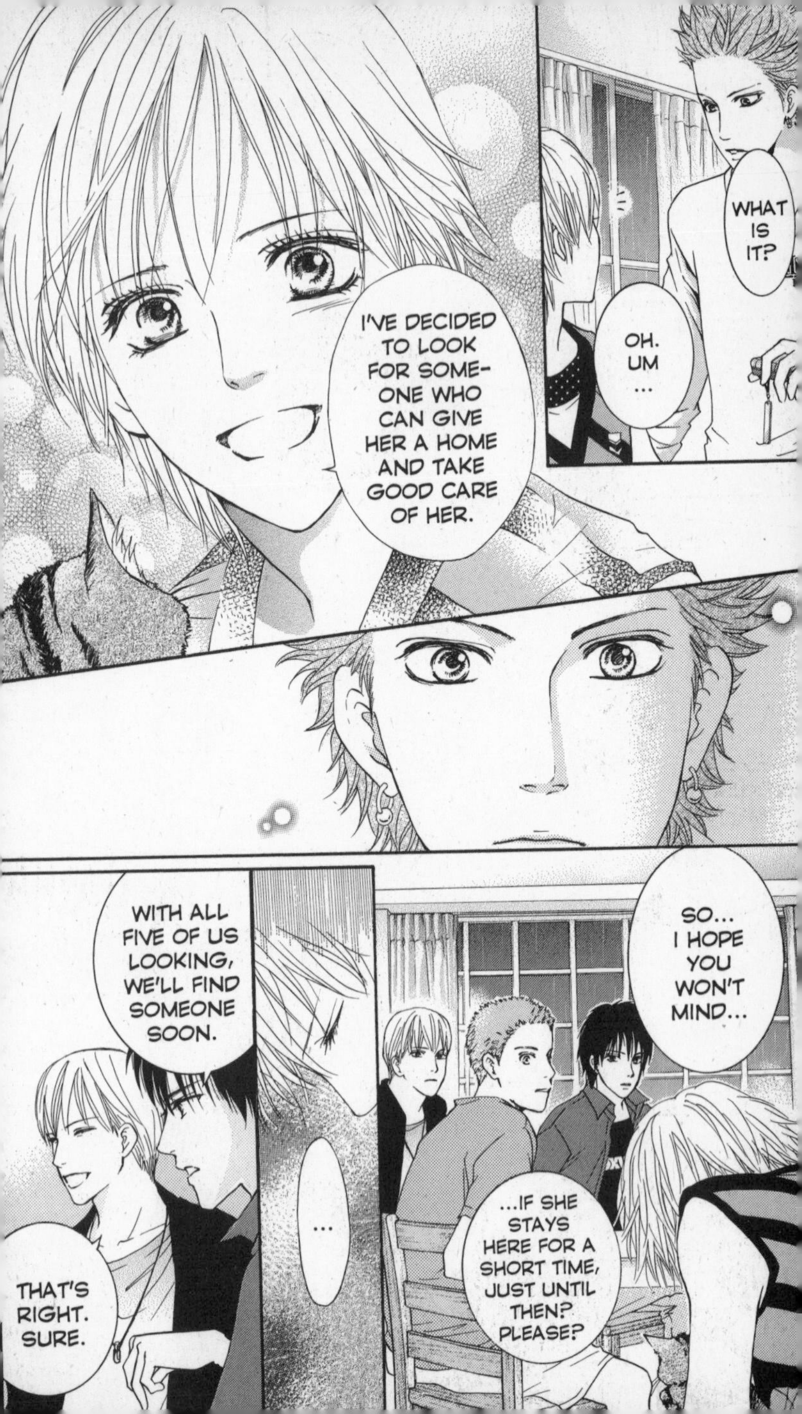
WHAT IS IT?
OH. UM ...
I'VE DECIDED TO LOOK FOR SOME-ONE WHO CAN GIVE HER A HOME AND TAKE GOOD CARE OF HER.
SO... I HOPE YOU WON'T MIND...
...IF SHE STAYS HERE FOR A SHORT TIME, JUST UNTIL THEN? PLEASE?
...
WITH ALL FIVE OF US LOOKING, WE'LL FIND SOMEONE SOON.
THAT'S RIGHT. SURE.

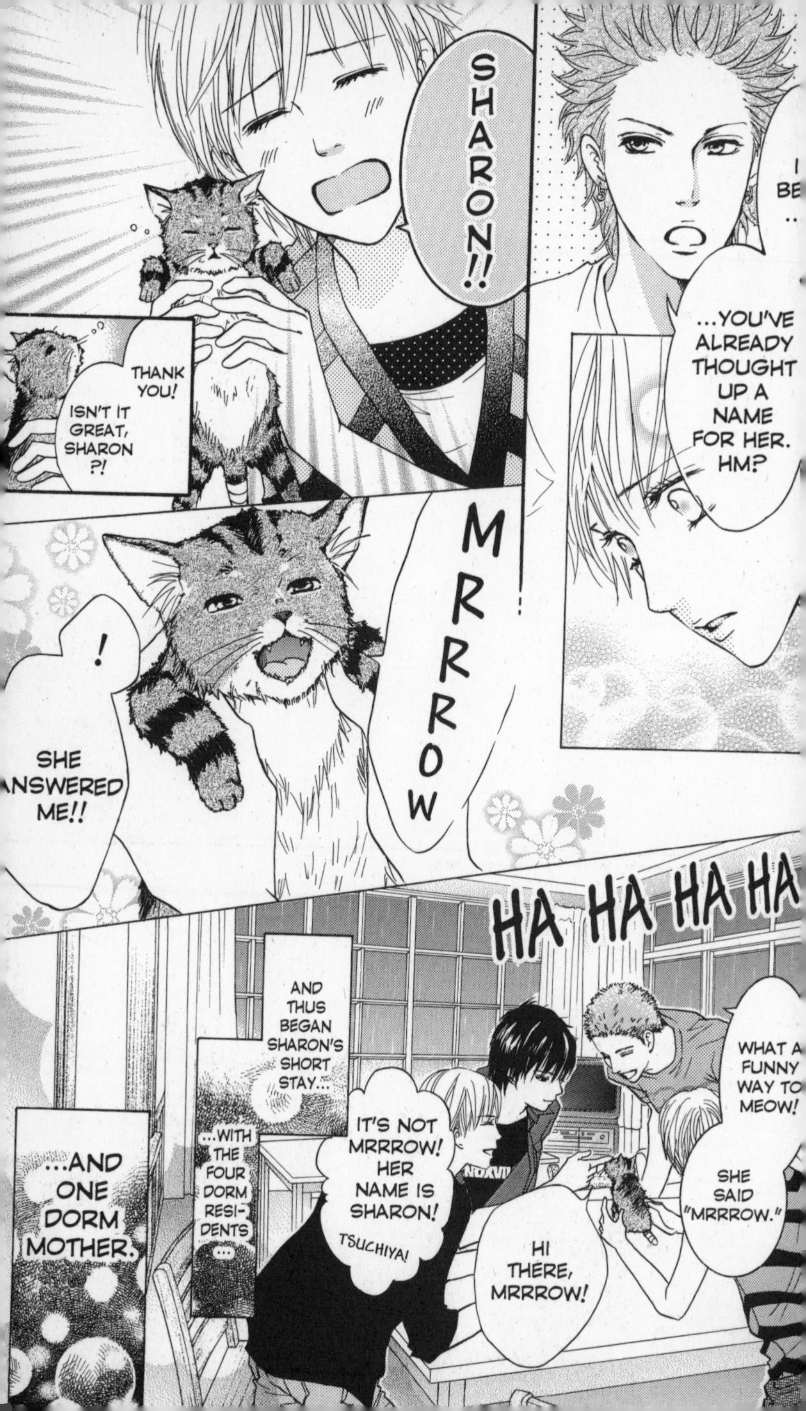
I BE...
...YOU'VE ALREADY THOUGHT UP A NAME FOR HER. HM?
SHARON!!
THANK YOU!
ISN'T IT GREAT, SHARON?!
MRRROW
!
SHE ANSWERED ME!!
HA HA HA HA
WHAT A FUNNY WAY TO MEOW!
SHE SAID "MRRROW."
HI THERE, MRRROW!
IT'S NOT MRRROW! HER NAME IS SHARON!
TSUCHIYA!
AND THUS BEGAN SHARON'S SHORT STAY...
...WITH THE FOUR DORM RESI-DENTS...
...AND ONE DORM MOTHER.

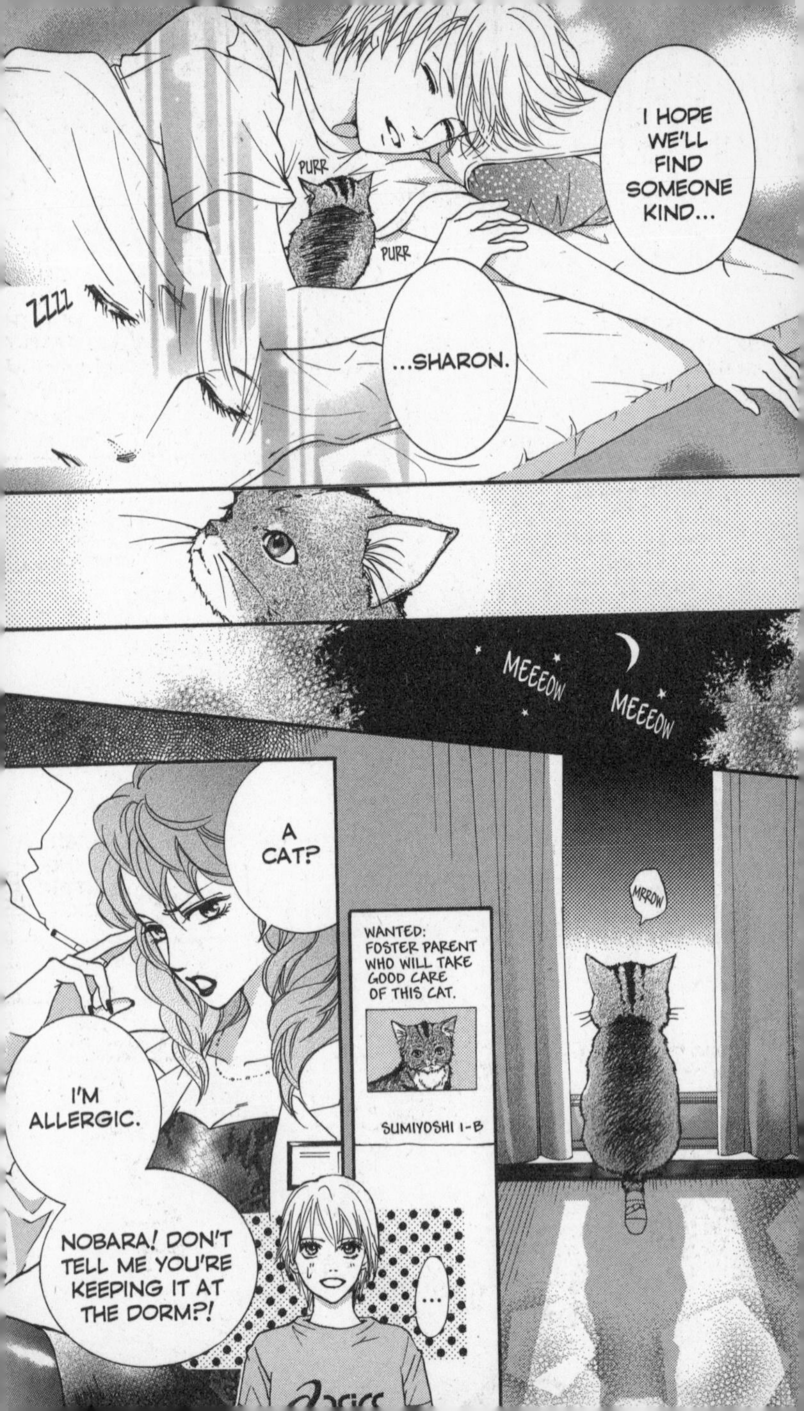
I HOPE WE'LL FIND SOMEONE KIND...
PURR
PURR
...SHARON.
ZZZZ
MEEEOW
MEEEOW
MRROW
WANTED: FOSTER PARENT WHO WILL TAKE GOOD CARE OF THIS CAT.
SUMIYOSHI 1-B
A CAT?
I'M ALLERGIC.
NOBARA! DON'T TELL ME YOU'RE KEEPING IT AT THE DORM?!
...

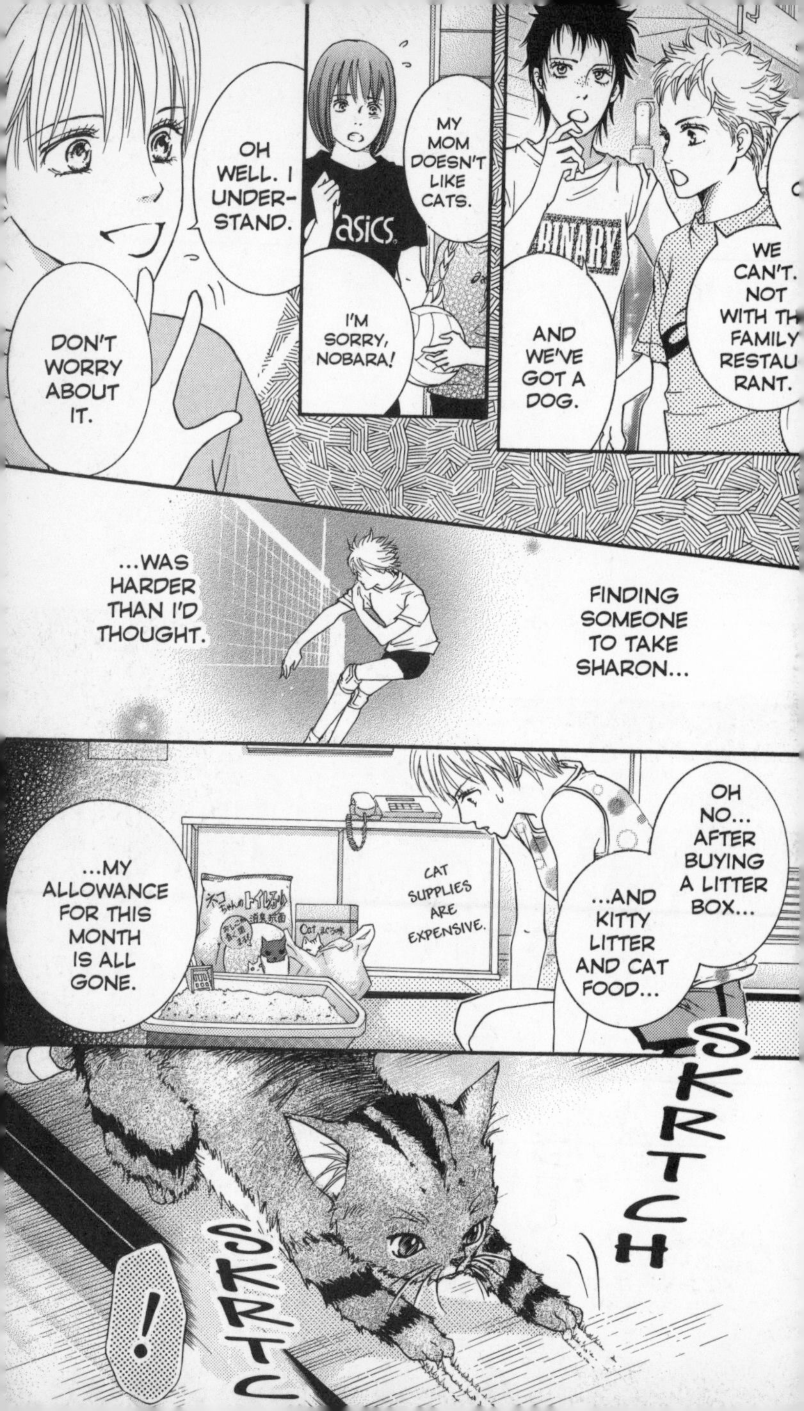
WE CAN'T. NOT WITH TH FAMILY RESTAU RANT.
AND WE'VE GOT A DOG.
MY MOM DOESN'T LIKE CATS.
I'M SORRY, NOBARA!
OH WELL. I UNDER-STAND.
DON'T WORRY ABOUT IT.
FINDING SOMEONE TO TAKE SHARON...
...WAS HARDER THAN I'D THOUGHT.
OH NO... AFTER BUYING A LITTER BOX...
...AND KITTY LITTER AND CAT FOOD...
CAT SUPPLIES ARE EXPENSIVE.
...MY ALLOWANCE FOR THIS MONTH IS ALL GONE.
SKRTCH
SKRTC
!

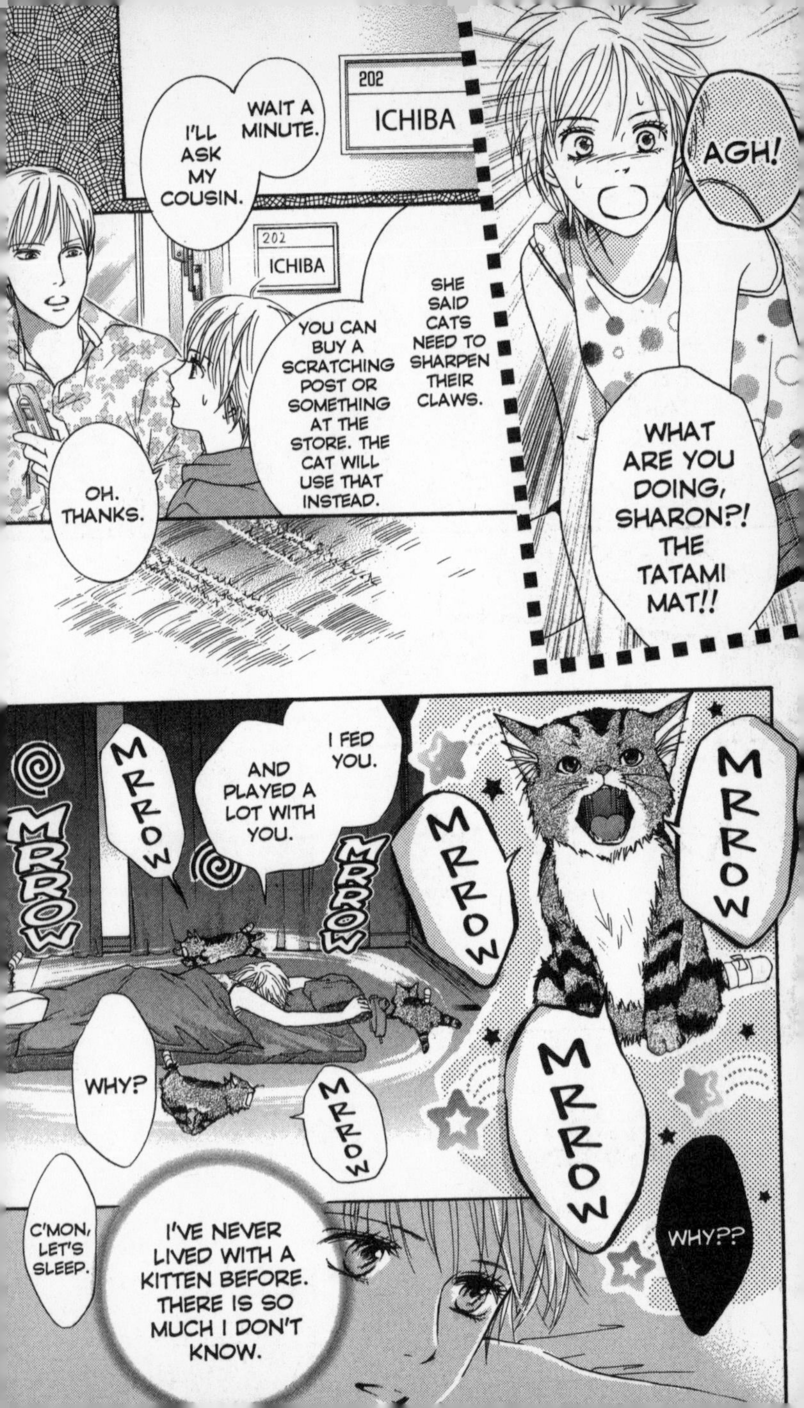
AGH!
WHAT ARE YOU DOING, SHARON?! THE TATAMI MAT!!
202
ICHIBA
WAIT A MINUTE.
I'LL ASK MY COUSIN.
202
ICHIBA
SHE SAID CATS NEED TO SHARPEN THEIR CLAWS.
YOU CAN BUY A SCRATCHING POST OR SOMETHING AT THE STORE. THE CAT WILL USE THAT INSTEAD.
OH. THANKS.
MRROW
MRROW
MRROW
I FED YOU.
AND PLAYED A LOT WITH YOU.
MRROW
MRROW
MRROW
WHY?
MRROW
WHY??
I'VE NEVER LIVED WITH A KITTEN BEFORE. THERE IS SO MUCH I DON'T KNOW.
C'MON, LET'S SLEEP.

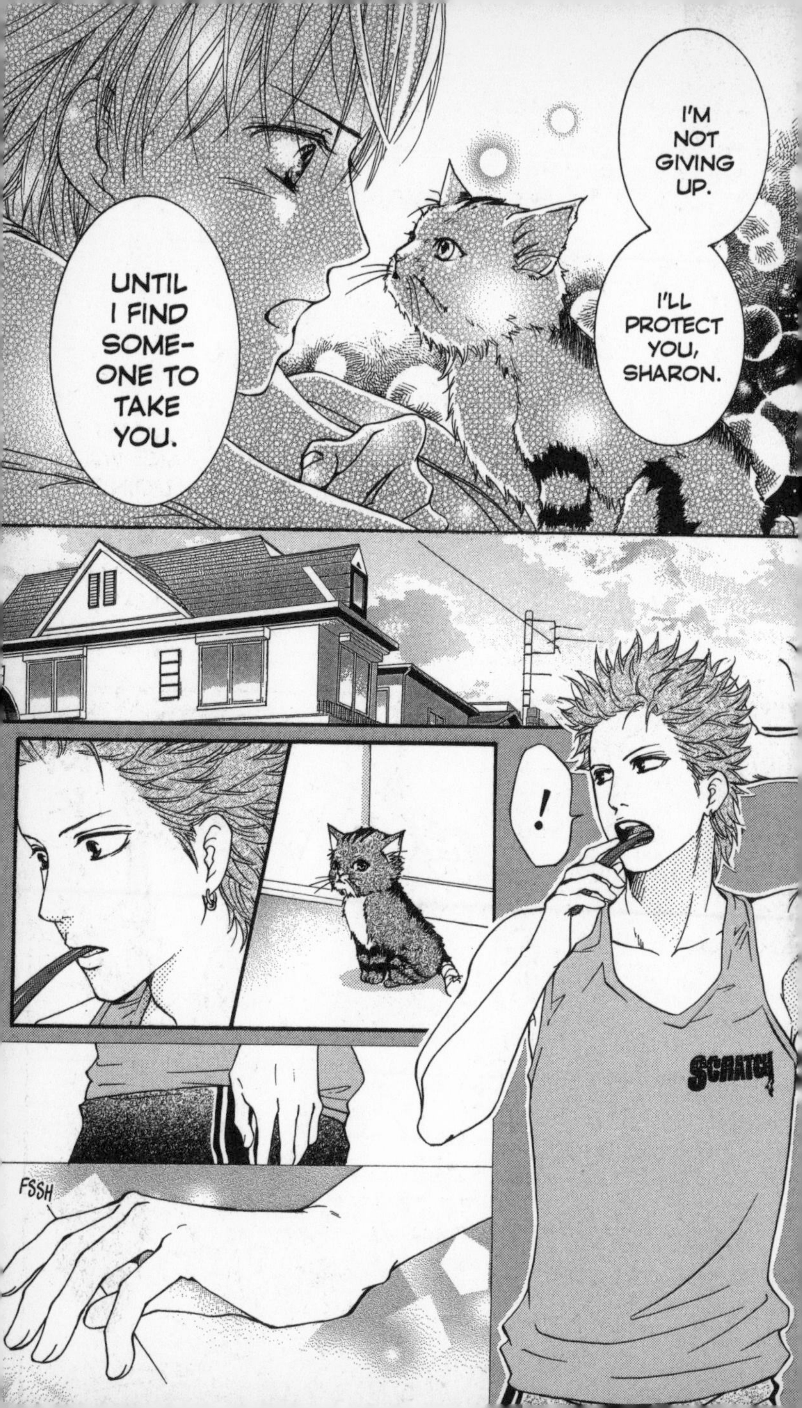
I'M NOT GIVING UP.
I'LL PROTECT YOU, SHARON.
UNTIL I FIND SOME-ONE TO TAKE YOU.
!
SCRATCH
FSSH

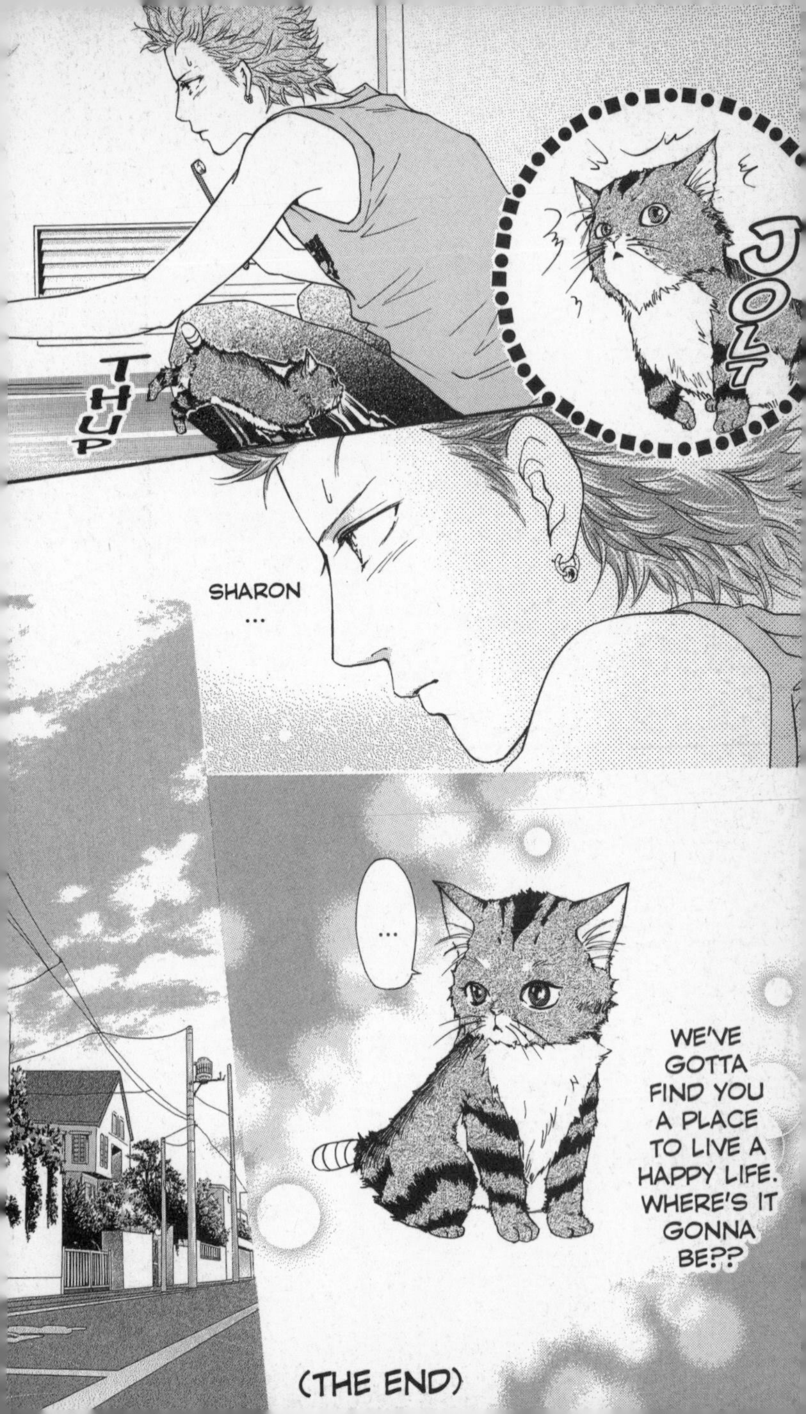
JOLT
THUP
SHARON ...
...
WE'VE GOTTA FIND YOU A PLACE TO LIVE A HAPPY LIFE. WHERE'S IT GONNA BE??
(THE END)

♥A whole year has zipped by in a flash. February was like the F1. Did it really happen? Did we have a February? Last year was a year when nothing went well. Maybe I just didn't have enough will power. This year I'll set out with a fresh burst of energy and I'll do my best.

—Mitsuba Takanashi, 2007

At age 17, Mitsuba Takanashi debuted her first short story, *Mou Koi Nante Shinai* (Never Fall in Love Again), in 1992 in *Bessatsu Margaret* magazine and now has several major titles under her belt.

Born in the Shimane Prefecture of Japan, Takanashi now lives in Tokyo, where she enjoys taking walks, watching videos, shopping, and going to the hair salon. Takanashi has a soft spot for the Japanese pop acts Yellow Monkey and Hide, and is good at playing ping-pong.

CRIMSON HERO

VOL. 10
The Shojo Beat Manga Edition

This volume contains material that was originally published in English in
Shojo Beat magazine, September–December 2008 issues. Artwork in the magazine may
have been slightly altered from that presented here.

STORY AND ART BY
MITSUBA TAKANASHI

Translation & English Adaptation/Naoko Amemiya
Touch-up Art & Lettering/Mark Griffin
Graphics & Cover Design/Courtney Utt & Julie Behn
Editor/Nancy Thistlethwaite

Editor in Chief, Books/Alvin Lu
Editor in Chief, Magazines/Marc Weidenbaum
VP, Publishing Licensing/Rika Inouye
VP, Sales & Product Marketing/Gonzalo Ferreyra
VP, Creative/Linda Espinosa
Publisher/Hyoe Narita

Printed in Canada

Published by VIZ Media, LLC
P.O. Box 77010
San Francisco, CA 94107

Shojo Beat Manga Edition
10 9 8 7 6 5 4 3 2 1
First printing, March 2009

YA
GN
Fic
Crimson Hero

www.viz.com   store.viz.com

High School DEBUT

By Kazune Kawahara

When Haruna Nagashima was in junior high, softball and comics were her life. Now that she's in high school, she's ready to find a boyfriend. But will hard work (and the right coach) be enough?

Find out in the *High School Debut* manga series—available now!

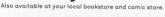

Tell us what you think about Shojo Beat Manga!

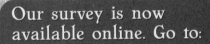

Our survey is now available online. Go to:

shojobeat.com/mangasurvey

Help us make our product offerings better!

Shojo Beat™

MANGA from the HEART

The Shojo Manga Authority

12 GIANT issues for ONLY $34.99*

The most **ADDICTIVE** shojo manga stories from Japan **PLUS** unique editorial coverage on the arts, music, culture, fashion, and much more!

That's 51% OFF the cover price!

Subscribe NOW and become a member of the Sub Club!

- **SAVE** 51% OFF the cover price
- **ALWAYS** get every issue
- **ACCESS** exclusive areas of www.shojobeat.com
- **FREE** members-only gifts several times a year

Strictly VIP!

3 EASY WAYS TO SUBSCRIBE!

1) Send in the subscription order form from this book
2) Log on to: www.shojobeat.com OR
3) Call 1-800-541-7876